MEASURING the IMMEASURABLE

MEASURING the IMMEASURABLE

THE SCIENTIFIC CASE *for* SPIRITUALITY

SOUNDS TRUE

BOULDER, COLORADO

Sounds True, Inc.
Boulder, CO 80306

Compilation copyright © 2008 by Sounds True

Contributing Authors: Daniel Goleman, Bruce H. Lipton, Candace Pert, Gary Small,
Jeanne Achterberg, Lynne McTaggart, Dan Siegel, Andrew Newberg, Peter Levine,
Larry Dossey, Gregg Braden, Robert Emmons, Peter Russell, James Austin, Marilyn
Schlitz, Dean Radin, Cassandra Vieten, Tina Amorok, William Tiller, Susanne C.
Segerstrom, Rick Hanson, Les Fehmi, Jim Robbins, Charles Tart, Owen Flanagan,
Dawson Church, Sandra Ingerman, Stanley Krippner, Garret Yount, Sara Warber,
Katherine N. Irvine, Joan H. Hageman, Ian Wickramasekera

Book design by Rachael Tomich

Printed in Canada

Library of Congress Cataloging-in-Publication Data
    Goleman, Daniel.
    Measuring the immeasurable : the scientific case for spirituality / Daniel Goleman
    ... [et al.].
        p. cm.
    Includes bibliographical references and index.
    ISBN 978-1-59179-654-1 (hardcover)
    1. Religion and science. 2. Spirituality. I. Title.
    BL240.3.G65 2008
    201'.65--dc22

                            2008016112

10 9 8 7 6 5 4 3 2

Contents

PART 2 Biology, Psychology, the Brain, and Quantum Physics
Neuroscience, Epigenetics, Energy Psychology, Quantum Physics, Eudaimonics, Buddhism, and the Brain

PART 3 Investigating the Science of Spiritual Practices

Meditation, Prayer, Distant Healing, Qigong, Reiki, and Other Practices

Introduction

TAMI SIMON

I am not a person who needs science or research to convince me of the benefits of spiritual practice or of the power of living in a heart-centered way. As a long-time meditator, it has become clear to me that spiritual discoveries—direct experiences of the interconnectedness and sacredness of all life—are self-authenticating. When I meditate on a regular basis, I feel more fulfilled and more in love with life. I have also found that when I meditate regularly, the people around me enjoy being with me more and find me more available for connection. The feedback I've gotten about the benefits of spiritual practice—both from my internal experience and from the world around me—has been consistent and clear. Additionally, the guiding principles of a spiritual life—for example, living with compassion, gratitude, and generosity—are values that live in my heart and are perfectly self-evident to me.

Why, then, is Sounds True publishing *Measuring the Immeasurable: The Scientific Case for Spirituality*? Why do we need to measure the benefits of spirituality, if they are so clear to those who seek the truth through direct experience? There are, as it turns out, several important reasons.

As a society, we value what we can count. Without qualitative proof that a system or practice offers benefits, it's an uphill battle toward social acceptance. We need scientific evidence of the results of spiritual practice so that experts in such fields as education, healthcare and medicine, psychology and psychiatry, can seriously consider the inclusion and integration of spiritual approaches in their work. If we are able to measure, for example, how slow, calm breathing lowers cortisol levels in the blood and therefore reduces stress and anxiety, then slow, calm breathing can become a medical prescription—not simply a practice marginalized to the world of yogis and meditators.

Additionally, many people already on a spiritual path may draw strength and validation from having their subjective experiences confirmed by the objective tools of science. For some people, the language of science is the language of the prevailing authority of our time. If there are scientific studies that confirm and validate the experiential realizations of mystics, saints, sages, and intentional healers, this may provide important support and encouragement to some spiritual practitioners.

Moreover, what if research—and specifically the emerging field of neuroscience—can help spiritual practitioners refine and hone the way we approach traditional contemplative practices? It's only in the last century, with the invention of the electroencephalographic (EEG) machine, that scientists have had an objective way to measure brain activity; it's more recent still that researchers have begun to take an active interest in exploring the correlations between contemplative practice and brain structure and function. From the use of biofeedback in meditation practice to the manipulation of our brainwave patterns through auditory stimulation, the possibilities for scientific discovery are endless. If research findings and "new spiritual technologies" can help accelerate our access to expanded states of consciousness, I am interested and want to know more.

In gathering the essays for this anthology, we heard from some experts in the field that they felt such a volume of essays was "premature"—that further studies needed to be completed before scientific claims about the benefits of spirituality could be made. This is indeed a fledgling field, but one that, in my opinion, calls for the active, creative engagement of the general public *right now*. We need to understand the research that currently exists so that we can encourage and fund additional research in the directions that are most meaningful to us and will yield results with practical applications for our troubled world. *Measuring the Immeasurable: The Scientific Case for Spirituality* introduces the reader to this new field of inquiry through the writings of forty-three different scientific researchers, journalists, healers, and visionaries. Our hope is that it furthers the dialogue in this important new area of inquiry, utilizing the best of our scientific measuring tools to deepen our understanding of what matters most—our moment-to-moment connection with each other and the wholeness of life.

PART 1

The Science of Intention, Enhancing Quality of Life, Health, Emotional Well-Being, and Consciousness

Gratitude, Compassion, Emotional Awareness, Consciousness, and Transformation

Providing an enlightening snapshot of the historical relationship between science and spirituality, Peter Russell, author of *From Science to God: A Physicist's Journey into the Mystery of Consciousness*, leads us through such questions as: Is there a "God Spot" in the brain that is responsible for enlightened experiences? Will new scientific developments ultimately allow us to understand how to become liberated mentally and spiritually? Can science facilitate spiritual states of consciousness? Looking to the future, Russell asks us to consider science and spirituality working together hand in hand, leading us toward new possibilities.

Exploring Deep Mind

PETER RUSSELL

Science and spirituality have never made easy bedfellows. Their views on the nature of the cosmos have often clashed, and the more our scientific understanding of the world has grown, the deeper that clash has become.

Yet it has not always been this way. For centuries, the principal arbiter of truth was the Church; there was no separate science as we know it. The split began some 350 years ago with René Descartes. He divided the cosmos into two realms: the realm of things that could be physically measured—the world of time, space, and matter—and the realm of thought, the world of consciousness and spirit. Descartes wanted to avoid incurring the wrath of the Vatican—he had seen Galileo brought before the Inquisition for supporting Copernicus, and

Giordano Bruno burnt at the stake for similar heresies—so he declared that his "natural philosophy" would focus its attention on the world of matter. The world of the spirit he would leave to the Church.

And so it has been for 350 years. Western science has largely ignored the world of conscious experience—and with apparently good reasons. First, mind cannot be weighed, measured, or otherwise pinned down in the way that matter can. Second, scientists have sought to arrive at universal, objective truths, independent of an observer's viewpoint or state of mind. To this end they have deliberately avoided subjective considerations. And third, there was no need to explore mind; the workings of the universe could be explained without having to consider the troublesome subject of consciousness.

So successful has this materialist science been, it appears to have triumphed over religion. Astronomers have looked out into deep space, to the edges of the known universe; cosmologists have looked back into "deep time," to the beginning of creation; and physicists have looked down into the "deep structure" of matter, to the fundamental constituents of the cosmos. From quarks to quasars, they find no evidence of God. Nor do they find any need for God. The universe seems to work perfectly well without any divine assistance.

A SCIENCE OF MIND

In doing away with the notion of some almighty supernatural being, Western science would appear to have done away with religion, and hence with spirituality. Yet the real concern of spirituality is not with the realms of deep space, time, or matter, but with "deep mind," the one realm that science has chosen not to investigate. Those who have investigated this realm are the mystics, yogis, rishis, roshis, lamas, shamans, and other spiritual adepts who have explored consciousness firsthand—which, it could be argued, is the only way to explore consciousness. They have delved beneath the surface levels of the mind, observed the arising and passing of thought, and looked beyond, to the source of their experience and the essence of their own consciousness.

Such a subjective approach is not usually considered to be very scientific. It is hard to quantify or validate the knowledge so gained. Moreover, the worldviews this exploration engenders often appear to contradict the prevailing scientific worldview. Nevertheless, in terms of the underlying scientific process, this approach is not as unscientific as it might first appear.

The word "science" stems from the Latin *scire*, "to know." In its most general sense science may be defined as a path to gaining reliable knowledge through careful observation and testing. To achieve this, a "scientific method" has emerged. A relevant example of this process in practice is the investigation into the electrical activity of the human brain during meditation. First you would seek to isolate the subject of study. So, you might put the person in an electromagnetically shielded room to reduce electrical noise ("noise" in the technical sense of unwanted information). Then, in order to get as much useful information as possible, you would ensure that the electrodes made good electrical contact with the scalp. You would then take measurements while the person was meditating, and also when they were not, in order to ensure that the data gathered were the effects of meditation. You might also record data from a "control" group who were just relaxing. Having performed your experiments, you would gather the results, draw conclusions, and publish them, not just to secure tenure, but so that others can study them and see if they agree. If the general consensus concurred with your findings, you could say you had established some reliable knowledge about brain activity during meditation.

Similar principles can be applied to the direct exploration of your own mind. First, you might seek to remove yourself from as much external noise as possible by choosing a quiet place where you are unlikely to be disturbed. Since you want to observe the mind clearly, you would probably adopt a posture that encouraged an alert wakefulness. Then, in order not to be distracted by external events, you could close your eyes.

As you turn your attention within and begin to observe your mind, one of the first things you notice is the almost incessant flow of thoughts and inner dialogue. You might be worrying about things you have not done, planning a future action, solving a problem, or going over a conversation. This internal noise continually distracts the attention from the subject of investigation—the mind itself. To reduce this internal chatter, you might employ some meditation practice—you could think of it as an experimental technique to quiet the mind. Then, as subtler aspects of the mind came into focus, you might gain new insights into the nature of consciousness.

This is essentially the process undertaken by countless people throughout human history as they have delved into the mysteries of the mind. And they, too, have published their conclusions—not in peer-reviewed academic journals, but in spiritual and mystical texts: *The Upanishads, The Tao Te Ching, The Tibetan Book of the Great Liberation, The Cloud of Unknowing.* Studying them, we find that beneath their different languages and cultures lies a remarkable consistency—what Aldous Huxley called the *Perennial Philosophy*, the wisdom that reappears time and again across the world. It would seem that the subjective approach does indeed lead to a consensus on the nature of mind.

BEYOND THOUGHT

What have these "inner scientists" discovered? One finding is obvious. As the self-talk that normally occupies much of our awareness subsides, there comes a growing sense of peace.

Reducing mental activity further leads to a state where all verbal thinking ceases. At this level of consciousness, people discover a much deeper, all-pervasive peace. Some call it bliss, others joy or serenity; but all agree that the pleasures of everyday life pale in comparison to this profound sense of inner well-being.

Another quality that is found in this inner quiet is love. This is not the love we know in our daily lives, a love that is usually focused on a particular person or circumstance. It is unconditional love, love that does not depend for its arising on any external conditions.

Some also report a profound shift in their sense of self. When all the thoughts, feelings, and memories by which we usually define ourselves have fallen away, the sense of a separate self dissolves. Instead there is an identity with the essence of being. What we hitherto called "I" turns out to be nothing but awareness itself.

In some cultures, this transcendent quality has been interpreted in terms of the Divine, and for seemingly good reason. Most of the qualities encountered at the core of one's being—peace, love, omnipresence, truth, forgiveness, compassion, light—are qualities traditionally ascribed to God. If you believe in such a being, then these mystical states may well be experienced as contact, or even unity, with God.

Other cultures have different interpretations. In Buddhism, for example, which has no concept of God, these qualities are seen as part of one's true nature. They are inherent qualities of the unconditioned mind—awareness that is unsullied by the agitation of everyday thoughts and concerns. This in no way diminishes the experience; it is just as magnificent, ineffable, and humbling—and equally transforming.

Western science may have done away with the idea of some almighty being presiding over the affairs of the universe, but it has, until now, had nothing to say about the realm of deep mind.

From this perspective, the apparent clash between science and spirituality dissolves. They are complementary views on reality, each exploring a different realm. Only when we mistakenly assume them to be referring to the same realm does a conflict arise.

ENTER PSYCHOLOGY

Over the last century, a new scientific discipline has emerged that begins to bridge these two realms. This is psychology, the study of the *psyche*, or mind. Like any science, it has branched into several disciplines, ranging from psychotherapy and psychiatry to social and experimental psychology. The latter, wishing to remain an objective science, has generally relied upon observations in the physical world, focusing its studies on brain or behavior.

In the fifties and sixties, experimental psychology made some early forays into the study of spiritual experiences when researchers in Asia and the United States investigated yogis and Zen monks during meditation. They looked mainly at metabolic changes and general shifts in electrical activity of the brain. What they found did indeed indicate a relaxed state of mind.

The field was given a boost in the late sixties and early seventies, when large numbers of people began taking an interest in Eastern teachings and meditation. One practice in particular—Transcendental Meditation, the technique taught by Maharishi Mahesh Yogi—gathered a lot of interest (aided by The Beatles' own interest in the subject). The benefits that TM meditators were claiming caught the attention of a number of researchers, and within a few years several dozen papers had been published on the subject. As before, they supported the claim that practitioners were experiencing a state of deep rest, both physically and mentally. Some of the TM studies broke new ground, showing an increased coherence between the activity of the left and right sides of the brain. Others found various metabolic changes that suggested meditation was producing the opposite reaction to the stress response, leading one scientist to dub it "the relaxation response." Such findings, particularly those showing the benefits to personal health, were undoubtedly a primary factor behind the rapid growth in popularity of TM during the seventies.

Over the years, the work has continued, and the interest grown. Many more people have been studied, and from a variety of traditions. Looking deeper into the physiological and neurological changes, researchers have employed more sensitive equipment and new technologies such as MRI and radioactive isotopes. Others have chosen to study more experienced practitioners—Buddhist monks and Christian nuns with many years of dedicated practice behind them. And it is here that some of the most interesting discoveries are being made.[1]

GOD IN THE BRAIN?

Some of this research caught the popular imagination when researchers claimed to have discovered a "God spot" in the brain. Stimulation of this region, they said, could account for ecstatic experiences and the belief in God. But further research showed that things were not quite that simple, other regions of the brain being intimately involved in these states as well. Moreover, in years to come, as we gain more knowledge about the brain and its functioning, we shall undoubtedly find the situation to be much more complex than it appears today.

The conclusion that many draw from such studies is that spiritual experiences can now be explained in terms of brain function. Science would once again appear to have triumphed

---

1   *Editor's note:* Later chapters of this book discuss this work in detail, documenting the changes in particular areas of the brain associated with deep meditation or spiritual ecstasy.

over religion. But there is really nothing very surprising about these findings. It is a fundamental assumption of the neurosciences that there is a close correlation between brain activity and conscious experience. We should expect, therefore, that changes in consciousness as distinctive as the cessation of verbal thought, the dissolution of a separate sense of self, and a feeling of deep serenity would show corresponding changes in the brain. And it is fascinating to begin to discover what these changes might be. But this does not mean that these experiences can simply be reduced to brain activity—any more than love can. Falling in love can be a life-transforming experience, but few who are struck by love would dismiss it, relegating their feelings to neuronal activity in the limbic system, or an increase in the hormone oxytocin. When the rubber hits the road of life, it is our experience that moves us.

Mystical experiences can be equally profound and moving. For some it is the sense of liberation that comes from opening to one's true nature. For others, it may be the profound relief and ease in truly letting go. Or it can even be a falling in love: falling into the essence of love, or being in love with the whole of creation. Whatever form it takes, these states are sufficiently powerful to transform lives, turning sinners into saints, peasants into prophets. They have inspired great poetry, music, and painting, spawned new philosophies, and given birth to many of the world's spiritual teachings. Knowing there is an accompanying brain state does not diminish their value. It does not lower our appreciation of Wordsworth or Beethoven, or lessen the practical wisdom in the writings of Plato or the teachings of the Buddha.

The most significant aspect of the current scientific studies of meditation and spiritual experience is not that they can explain these experiences in terms of brain function, but that they are corroborating the claims of many spiritual teachings.

No longer can skeptics sit back and say it is all just wishful thinking, self-delusion, or an over-vivid imagination. These advanced practitioners are experiencing some profound shifts in consciousness. We may not yet fully appreciate the nature or significance of such shifts, but nevertheless, the changes seem mostly to be for the good.

SELF-LIBERATION

In most studies, the researchers themselves have not had the same depth of experience as the spiritual adepts they are studying, and this can lead to misleading interpretations. For example, to equate the dissolution of the self with a decrease in the brain processes that govern our orientation in space, hypothesizing that this leads to a corresponding loss of boundaries between the self and the rest of the world, misses the real nature of this state.

For experienced meditators, the dissolution of the self is something far more fundamental and significant than a loss of spatial boundaries. In these deep states, there is no longer a subject-object relationship to experience, no longer a separate "I" observing experience or thinking thoughts. Experience happens, just as before. Thoughts may still arise in the mind. But, paradoxical as it may sound, there is no one thinking them. The individual sense of self that is so familiar, a seeming part of every experience, is seen to be but a construct in consciousness, another experience arising in the mind.

To many people this sounds like a pretty weird state, and difficult to comprehend. Philosophers have argued at length as to whether it is even possible for there to be an experience without a separate observing self. However, when a person first drops into the state, there is often a sense of obviousness about it. There comes the realization that it has been this way all along; it was just not recognized before.

If this were as far as it went, the dissolution of the self would remain an intriguing curiosity. However, as just about everyone who has stepped out of the normal self-centered mode of consciousness can testify, it results in a profound shift in attitude toward others and the world. From the moment we are born we are conditioned to believe that we are a unique individual self. We derive a sense of identity from what we have or do in the world, our history and our circumstances, our education, job, social status, and beliefs. Any such derived identity is a conditional one—conditional upon events and circumstance. As such it is forever vulnerable. If our sense of who we are is threatened, we may find ourselves defending, reasserting, or otherwise bolstering our threatened sense of self.

When this sense of self is seen for what it is—awareness itself—the need to affirm the conditioned self disappears. In its place comes a profound liberation. The background mental tension that results from holding on to an identity dissolves—as when a muscle that you did not know was tense relaxes, resulting in unexpected and profound relief. There is more room for compassion, humility, wisdom, and the capacity to respond to a situation in terms of what the situation needs, rather than what the ever-vulnerable, artificial sense of self needs. (This is a much more profound and valuable shift in consciousness than simply losing one's spatial boundaries.)

TRANSPERSONAL PSYCHOLOGY

Another school of psychology, which has studied the benefits of spiritual experiences from a different angle, is humanistic psychology. Founded in the 1950s by pioneers such as Abraham Maslow, Carl Rogers, and Rollo May, humanistic psychology sought to understand what it means to be fully human. They were interested not so much in mental illness, but in what made for exceptional mental health.

One factor that Maslow himself became fascinated by was what he called "peak experiences." These he described as especially joyous moments, involving feelings of intense well-being, wonder, and awe, and sometimes a transcendence of self. Clearly he is describing spiritual experiences, if in somewhat neutral language. Maslow describes how the experience can leave a permanent mark on the person, changing them for the better. They may discover greater enthusiasm and creativity, a deeper meaning in life and renewed sense of purpose. Such people also tend to become more empathetic and compassionate.

These are values that the world today badly needs. It is becoming increasingly apparent that humanity is in crisis. When we look for the underlying causes we find, time and again, the human factor—human decisions based on human desires, needs, and priorities, often driven by human fear, greed, and self-centeredness. It is clear that the crisis is, at its root, a crisis of consciousness.

If we are to navigate our way safely through these challenging times, we need to make some significant shifts in attitudes and values. We need to recognize that inner peace does not depend on what we own, our social status, the roles we play, or how wealthy we are. We need to be free from the dictates of a conditioned sense of self that is at the mercy of external circumstances, needing continual defense and affirmation. We need to develop a love and compassion that reaches beyond our immediate circle of family and friends, a care that embraces strangers and people of different races and backgrounds—and also the many other species with whom we share this planet. We need to know in our hearts that their well-being is our well-being.

SPIRITUAL TECHNOLOGIES

What is the most effective way of promoting such shifts in consciousness? The evidence points to spiritual experience. Rather than distracting us from the course of scientific progress, spirituality could be our saving grace.

Our burgeoning scientific knowledge has led to a plethora of technologies that have enabled us to control and manipulate our world. The underlying goal has been to free ourselves from unnecessary suffering and increase our well-being. Successful as it has been in many ways, this material approach has not achieved all that was hoped for. Despite our abundant luxuries and freedoms, there is little evidence that people today are any happier than they were fifty years ago. Moreover, our incessant chasing of worldly satisfactions has brought us to the brink of global catastrophe.

Spiritual teachings have likewise sought to liberate people from suffering and promote well-being, but their path has been inward. They have sought to understand how our minds become trapped in dysfunctional patterns and have developed various techniques and practices—we might call them spiritual technologies—that free us from the inner causes of suffering and bring the deep relief and ease we all long for.

Thus the most important question to come from the growing research into spirituality is: Can science help facilitate these states of consciousness? This does not mean, as some would suggest, that if we give people the right sort of stimulation in the right area of the brain, we could trigger a spiritual experience. A sense of well-being, yes. The feeling of awe or joy, perhaps. But the realization that we are not who we thought we were, but something far more magnificent? I doubt it. We are a long way from that.

Nevertheless, synergies may be possible. Just about every spiritual tradition in the world has made recommendations as to lifestyles, diets, attitudes, and practices that would promote one's spiritual awakening. The more we come to understand these states, the more we may discover new ways to facilitate them.

Just what these might be we can only guess. The very nature of discovery and innovation makes the future unpredictable—and to some degree unimaginable. What is important is that we recover our respect for spirituality, acknowledge its critical value for the world today, and seek as full an understanding of deep mind as we now have of deep space, time, and matter.

How do our bodies manufacture emotion? How are our emotions connected to our thoughts? How is our brain connected to our mind, our body, and ultimately, our consciousness? These are some of the questions that Dr. Candace B. Pert, author of *Everything You Need to Know to Feel Go(o)d*, tackles in the following excerpt from her book and a lecture she gave in Tucson, Arizona. Building on her acclaimed research about the "the molecules of emotion," she explains how thoughts and feelings can influence the physiology of pain, and how the mind and emotions can influence experience. She also points us toward an understanding of why we are capable of creating reality.

The Science of Emotions and Consciousness

CANDACE PERT, PH.D., WITH NANCY MARRIOTT

I looked out at my audience, said a silent prayer, introduced myself, and then brought up my first slide. On the screen was a gorgeous, sexy woman, dressed in black and reclining in ecstatic abandonment. A hush fell over the audience as they took it in—a magazine ad for the perfume Opium—and I continued speaking, launching into the information they'd come to hear. . . . This essay is the substance of my lecture.

THE LECTURE AT TUCSON

Bliss! That's what I know a lot about; that's what I studied as a graduate student at the Johns Hopkins School of Medicine in 1973. It was there, along with my mentor, Dr. Sol Snyder, that I discovered the opiate receptor, the key to the body's mechanism for pleasure. The breakthrough caused a revolution in brain science and sent reverberations throughout all of the biological disciplines.

For years, scientists had theorized that drugs acted in the body by attaching to receptors to exert their effects. But no one had ever done simple experiments that demonstrated how this worked. No one had proved that receptors even existed at all until I developed a test-tube method in our lab at Hopkins to measure the opiate receptor and earned my PhD. As an Associated Press news release flew around the world, I found myself at the center of the scientific community's attention. This was the first receptor to be measured by a method that would later be used to measure many more newly discovered receptors.

But the burning question that everyone wanted answered was: Why was there a natural mechanism, the opiate receptor, that allowed drugs like morphine and heroin to act in the body? What followed was a mad dash on both sides of the Atlantic for the discovery of the body's own morphine. A British laboratory won the prize, identifying a tiny protein chain of amino acids called endorphin as the opiate receptor's key. Endorphin, a peptide bound to the opiate receptor, produces a natural high that drug companies everywhere hoped to capitalize on as a natural, nonaddictive analgesic, but it wasn't to be.

In retrospect, the opiate receptor discovery was important not because it led to identifying the body's own morphine, but because it opened a new avenue of exploration for the invention of drug therapies for disease. The fact that we could now demonstrate that there are receptors on the cells where the body's own chemicals attach—and even measure them—meant that we could make new external chemicals in the lab, commonly known as drugs, to access the cell in the same way. This avenue eventually led to Peptide T, the AIDS therapeutic that I'm currently developing with my husband, Michael.

A BODYWIDE, PSYCHOSOMATIC NETWORK

Over the decade following the discovery of these newly identified substances, my lab and others around the world rushed to map them, finding endorphin and opiate receptors in parts of the brain known to be associated with the emotions. The amygdala and hypothalamus, two structures within the limbic (or old emotional) brain, were found to be loaded with what I came to call the molecules of emotion. But we were surprised to also find insulin receptors in the brain, along with ones for virtually every other peptide in the body. Insulin is a large peptide secreted by the pancreas to regulate the level of sugar in the blood. What was it doing in the brain? For years, neuroscientists had claimed the brain as the seat of emotions, pointing to the fact that when brain structures in or near the limbic system were stimulated during neurosurgery, intense emotional expression of early memories occurred. But we found that these molecules of emotion aren't just in the limbic system, but throughout the body, linked to form a comprehensive system of communication including the endocrine, digestive, and reproductive systems—literally, every system in the organism.

We eventually were able to show a network of intercellular communication humming along under the coordinated efforts of these informational molecules of emotion, which we called the "psychosomatic network." The brain, we proposed, is just one nodal point of entry into this psychosomatic network that has many nodal points, including the spinal cord and the sensory organs. The system could be accessed from different places, depending on a person's focus of attention. For example, if you know any teenage boys, you know that their gonads will tend to override any other information entering this system and drive the organism in a predictable behavior.

The old paradigm held that the brain is the seat of consciousness, and the mind is the brain's by-product. But we can no longer say that brain is to mind as kidney is to urine; the mind is not the product of any organ, not even the brain. Awareness is the property of the whole organism; and in the psychosomatic network, we see the conscious and the unconscious mind infusing every aspect of the physical body. This is why I can say: The body *is* the subconscious mind.

CURRENTS OF EMOTION

Besides receiving and processing information to unify a single bodymind, the peptides and receptors are clumped to form ion channels to pump ions in and out of the cell. This rhythmic, pulsating movement creates an electrical current that meanders through the body, influencing the state of excitability or relaxation of the entire organism.

One of the most studied receptors is the GABA receptor, which is where the drugs Valium and alcohol bind. (GABA is the name for the corresponding endogenous, or internal, substance.) When those two drugs bind simultaneously at the GABA receptor, because someone has just popped a Valium and then poured a drink, the chloride ion leaks into the cell through the receptor-modulated ion channel. The effect of this flow is to create deep relaxation, as the threshold for neuronal firing gets very high. This is why the combination of alcohol and Valium can kill, which we now understand is what happened back in the sixties when famed columnist Dorothy Kilgallen unintentionally overdosed and died.

The set points of brain-cell excitability vary from place to place and from individual to individual, depending on which receptors are occupied by which neurotransmitters, other informational substances, or drugs. The differences in these thresholds can be the cause of much mischief, especially for marital relationships. The high-strung, excitable, talkative wife and the near-comatose husband with his nose in the newspaper are in an electrochemically incompatible mode that, if not modulated, could easily lead to trouble!

THE MATTER OF CONSCIOUSNESS

I propose that the matter of consciousness—the measurable, material substance—is the vibrating, moving, breathing, pumping molecular complexes of receptors and their ligands, as they bind to every cell of your body. The activity of these molecules creates an electrical charge and continually generates a current throughout your bodymind to keep you awake, alert, and conscious.

This is why I can say that the molecules of emotion are those of consciousness. Emotions span the material and the immaterial realm; they're the bridge linking the two. Just like the simultaneous particle and wave properties of light, the molecules of emotion go both ways. They're physical substances that you can see and weigh on a gel in the laboratory, ones that vibrate with an electrical charge in the living animal; and at the same time they're a kind of wave between people that conveys information. They're both physical and psychological, linking brain to body in one vast network of communication, to coordinate the entire bodymind.

In the Eastern view, consciousness comes first, and molecules are simply a metaphor, an afterthought, to explain consciousness. I'm amazed by how, over the years, I've come to understand and finally embrace this concept. Even more astonishing is that the science I've done supports the closure of the East/West gap, whether we focus on molecules or consciousness, matter or spirit. The two seeming opposites are simply flip sides of the same coin, or end points in a wide spectrum that's completely traversed by emotion.

NEW MIND, NEW THOUGHTS

Some very astounding data has come out of the National Institutes of Health laboratory of Dr. Eva Mezey that makes all of this easier to understand. Dr. Mezey recently proved irrefutably that mind and body are one by showing that stem cells migrate from the bone marrow into the brain and become neurons. Equally astounding is that her paradigm-jolting work was allowed to surface, given that the initial reaction to her data resulted in her lab nearly being closed.

Stem cells—cells that are undifferentiated and have yet to become organ cells—are made in the bone marrow, which we already knew. We also knew that stem cells move through the blood to other systems and organs. But the news that they move out of the bone marrow, eventually becoming neurons in the nervous system, was shocking.

Dr. Mezey found this migration happening not only in response to illness, as when stem cells grew into immune cells, but as a matter of course. And even more shocking was that these stem cells weren't just showing up in the spinal cord (which I consider an extension of the brain), but also in the highest part of the brain, a structure known as the "frontal cortex."

The first experiments were done by injecting bone marrow from a male mouse into a female mouse, but were repeated in a clever way with humans. Dr. Mezey used female subjects—some were children, some were older women—who had leukemia and had been treated with bone marrow transplanted from males. None lived more than a few years, and of the eighteen cases she was able to study, every one of the females upon autopsy had plenty of neurons with the male Y chromosomes in them. In other words, male stem cells were in the females' brains, irrefutable evidence that brain cells travel from the bone marrow into the brain.

The bones are giving rise to the brain! Ancient Chinese medicine says that *chi*, loosely translated as "the life force," originates in the bone. Now we are showing in our Western model that cells start as baby stem cells born in the bone marrow, become immune-like cells as they pass through the body, and then arrive in the brain as brain cells. This migration, our lab had shown in the eighties, was directed by the molecules of emotion in a process known as chemotaxis. We used to think that by the age of five, you had all the brain cells you were going to get. Then neuroscientists discovered that your brain keeps growing when you're a teen, and your frontal cortex doesn't stop developing until you're twenty-five. But the new research shows that the growth of brain cells never stops— this replenishment, the influx of new brain cells, is going on throughout your entire life! Neurogenesis, the birth of new cells appearing, moving, and becoming neurons in the brain, used to be controversial; it now is one of the hottest areas of research in biomedical science today. So what does this all mean? Well, it means that you can learn and change and grow, because you're literally making a new brain every day. Since you sat down in your seat here tonight, you've made thousands of new neurons! You're literally being given the opportunity to think new thoughts, to change your mind, to create the reality you experience from moment to moment. It's no longer just a truism that thinking positively is a good idea—thank you, Dr. Norman Vincent Peale! If you have uplifting thoughts, you're building a very different brain than if you have negative ones.

EMOTION AND MEMORY

Classically, the hippocampus is the structure in the brain associated with memory, because when you remove it surgically, a person will have deficits in memory. But contrary to what many neuroscientists believe, this doesn't necessarily prove that the hippocampus is the seat of memory.

In fact, recent findings support the theory that recall is stored throughout the body, not in the brain alone. Dr. Eric R. Kandel, a neurobiologist at Columbia University College of Physicians and Surgeons, received a Nobel Prize for Medicine in 2000 for showing that memory resides at the level of the receptor. The activity of cellular binding throughout the body can impact neuronal circuitry, influencing memory and thinking.

When a receptor is flooded with a peptide or other ligand, the cell membrane is changed in such a way that the probability of an electrical impulse traveling across the membrane is affected. Remember, wherever there's a receptor, there's also a vibrating electrode or diode where circuits can change. This, in turn, affects the choice of neuronal circuitry that will be used, impacting brain activity. These recent discoveries are important for appreciating how memories are stored not only in the brain but in the body as well, where a psychosomatic network extends throughout all systems of the organism. A major storage area is in the receptors distributed near the spinal cord, between nerve and ganglia, and all the way out to the internal organs and the surface of the skin. This means that your memories are in your spinal cord, as well as all throughout your bodymind.

Whether your memories are conscious or not is mediated by the molecules of emotion. They decide what becomes a thought rising to the surface, and what remains buried deeply in your body. What this means is that much of memory is emotion driven, not conscious, although it can sometimes be made conscious by intention. The emotions that you're able to experience can bring a recollection to the surface; if your feelings are suppressed, however, they can bury that same memory far below your awareness, where it can affect your perceptions, decisions, behavior, and even health, all unconsciously.

Buried, painful emotions from the past make up what some psychologists and healers call a person's "core emotional trauma." The point of therapy—including bodywork, some kinds of chiropractic, and energy medicine—is to gently bring that wound to gradual awareness so it can be reexperienced and understood. Only then is choice—a faculty of your frontal cortex—possible, allowing you to reintegrate any disowned parts of yourself, let go of old traumatic patterns, and become healed, or whole.

Very clear studies done by Dr. Donald Overton show that there are *dissociated* (not connected) *states* of learning and memory. His data demonstrates that what you learn in one drug-induced state, you can't retrieve from your memory at a later time unless you're in the same condition. If you're smoking cigarettes and drinking coffee to prepare for an exam, you won't be able to remember enough information to pass unless you're doing those things when you take the test. This is because various substances (such as alcohol, nicotine, and caffeine) create altered states of consciousness with different emotions and memories, and therefore, different modes in which to learn.

In other words, you acquire knowledge with your entire bodymind, not just with your brain. Also, learning is an emotional event, impacted by how you're feeling. There are tons of data showing that you can't grasp new information in a state of fear. I've lectured to educators about how punishment and threats actually inhibit the learning process.

DRUGS AND THE BODYMIND
Emotions are like drugs, all of which—Valium, alcohol, methamphetamine, the opiates, and marijuana—work because they

use the same receptors as the internal ligands. Drugs, just like the peptides in the body, find their way to the exact keyhole on a cell's surface in order to bind. For marijuana, the chemical cannabinoid fits into the marijuana receptor. And our own internal version, endocannabinoid, is the only substance made in the body that can fit that receptor, too.

External drugs and internal juices: both of these hum in one giant, emotionally vibratory field as they bind to receptors and make things happen. Your emotions follow the same pathways as your peptides and their receptors, and the same routes as the drugs that you're prescribed or take illegally. All three—drugs, natural ligands such as peptides, and emotions—operate through the same mechanism, which is binding at the site of the receptor.

This is important, because how you think and feel—your emotional state at any given moment—can actually impact the movement, the division, and every other activity of your cells in much the same way as your internal juices and pharmaceutical drugs do. This is a central idea of my theory of emotions—that there's a physical substrate for your feelings, just as there is for the action of drugs and their effects in your body.

Scientists have identified many types of receptors on our cells that fit internal juices that have known equivalent external drugs, but not all of the scores of known receptors have known external matches. For example, if a plant growing in a rain forest in Brazil made people angry when they ingested it, no one would try to smuggle it into the country and sell it for recreational use. The plants that get cultivated are the ones that make us feel good.

BODYMIND IDENTITY
Just as drugs do, emotions trigger altered states of consciousness, each with different memories, behaviors, postures, and

even physical processes. We can learn a lot from looking at so-called multiple personality disorder (MPD), a condition that exists when a person exhibits many personalities, each with its own identity and often physiology.

MPD is usually considered a pathological condition, but I believe that normal people like you and me have many subpersonalities, with one more dominant than the others depending on which stimuli are influencing us. A CEO is a very different person in the boardroom than she is when she's at home playing with her toddler. But is it just the behavior that's different? It may appear so, but in the new paradigm of physiology, we see that much more is actually going on.

Psychologists and authors Drs. Hal and Sidra Stone have utilized this concept in their approach to consciousness and transformation, which they call Voice Dialogue, used to access hidden or deep parts of the personality and integrate all of them into the whole. If you've ever had the experience of speaking to your spouse or child one morning and the next day feeling as if you're dealing with someone who seems to be a completely different person, then you know what I'm talking about.

But my point is that the accessing of different personalities is a natural expression of how the molecules of emotion are constantly coordinating our memories at the level of our physiology. To expect everyone to be the same all the time is to buy in to the myth that emotions don't matter and don't play a powerful role in who we are, affecting our very identity from moment to moment.

One way to understand how we're all multiple personalities (and that this is normal) is to think of "white" light, which is the sum of all of its visible frequencies. Light may appear white or colorless, but if you filter it through a prism, you see a rainbow of different colors. People are like that, too: we may appear to be a solid, single identity, but we're actually made up of many different states and personalities, each one coordinated by our molecules of emotion. These chemicals in our body are continually orchestrating the movement within us of different states of consciousness, moods, and memories—and even physical conditions and alterations.

PAIN AND AROUSAL

We've seen how our molecules of emotion impact memory, learning, and identity. Now let's look at how they impact our perception of pain and the state of arousal or alertness we experience. There's a structure in your brain that sets your threshold of pain—that is, how much you can tolerate a harmful stimulus—called the peri-aqueductal gray (PAG). This is loaded with endorphins, opiate receptors, and many other informational substances that are emotion modulated. Your perception of whether something hurts a lot or a little passes through this gateway and is strongly informed by your emotions.

The PAG isn't near your frontal cortex, but there are neurons in your frontal cortex that project down into the PAG, making it possible to have conscious control over the degree of pain or alertness that you experience. This means that you can choose how to interpret the stimuli around you. You're doing this unconsciously all the time, but you can train yourself to interpret stimuli consciously at the threshold that you choose. One way to do so is with repeated affirmations that can help you reframe certain sensations in your body and promote healing.

For example, if I worry about a little buzzing sensation in my knee, and I think, *Oh no, there's that bum knee again. It's going to give out on me someday!*, then I'm projecting a negative belief on that experience. I become emotionally involved in a story about my knee, which then influences my molecules to follow my message.

On the other hand, I can respond with interest rather than fear, choosing to feel the buzzing in my knee as a sign that something is obviously moving around in there—opening, closing, and changing—and my knee wants me to stay tuned! That will send an entirely different message to my physiology through the many emotional informational substances that are communicating with my knee and connected to pain centers in my brain.

Remember, the bodymind is a vast network of communicating molecules, involving every cell, organ, and system of the organism. Pain in the knee is determined by emotions impacting molecules in your brain. In fact, any pain is really felt in the brain, which is the final common pathway.

This is useful, because if you know that your thoughts and feelings can influence your physiology for pain, you realize it is possible to decrease chronic-pain conditions, such as fibromyalgia, without drugs, by using various methods that access your conscious and subconscious input. Similarly, natural-childbirth training, which can be mastered by just about any woman, transforms pain and fear into pride of accomplishment and satisfaction.

Once again, not only do different emotional states have varied capacities for learning and memory, but they also have different set points of pain and arousal, whether triggered by drugs or by our internal informational substances. The ways that you can change your pain threshold resemble the memory or learning variations that I described earlier, in that your state of mind can affect your experience of reality. Your state of healing and well-being (that is, living pain free), as well as the ability to stay asleep or be alert, will change depending on your emotional state. "Change your mind and change your pain" would be a more helpful aphorism to have in the vernacular than "No pain, no gain."

All of this demonstrates again how emotions are the key to consciousness, determining from minute to minute what you experience, what you feel, and even who you are.

YOU CREATE YOUR OWN REALITY

Back in the seventies and eighties, whenever our laboratory at the NIMH mapped endorphin receptors, we always found them rich in areas that process incoming sensory information, such as sight, sound, smell, taste, or touch. We saw this clearly in the so-called dorsal horn on the back of the spinal cord, where "touchy-feely" kinds of information enter the nervous system from the body. Receptors for endorphins and other neuropeptides (such as bombesin, VIP, insulin, and others) are all confined to a stunning narrow stripe on visualization.

These neuropeptide receptors are never found in the ventral horn, which is the motor part of the spinal cord that directs movement. This is the same in other sensory pathways to the brain, not just for the sense of touch carried in the cord. Wherever the nerves first enter the brain, carrying sensory information about sight, sound, and the like, there are sites that are always heavily encrusted with the receptor molecules of emotion.

Different senses have pathways with varying degrees of filtering of information. Vision is very highly refined; it travels six synapses from the time light first strikes your retina, travels to the occipital lobe at back of your brain, and then hits four more way stations before reaching consciousness in the frontal cortex. In contrast, smell only takes one synapse before it hits deep within your amygdala, and then is relayed to your higher brain.

Remember, those molecules along the sensory stopping points are storage sites for memory—but of what? Well, they're recollections of every perception that you've ever had, from your earliest consciousness of bliss at your mother's breast to the emotional upset you had after a fight with your boss the other day. They're all stored at the site of the receptors, which are most densely populated where information is coming in, not going out.

In other words, your experience of so-called reality is filtered through your memories, giving your experience a spin, adding meaning, and even making part of each situation go or stay unconscious if the event is too painful to remember, as in the case of a core emotional trauma.

We're constantly resonating with what we already know to be true. Everything that you feel is filtered along a gradient of past experience and memory that's stored in your receptors— there isn't any absolute or external reality! What you experience as reality is your story of what happened.

This has huge implications for healing traumas from the past. Even if you had a perfect childhood, I'm pretty sure that if you went to junior high school, you endured emotional pain. We tend to underestimate and even deny that we're all damaged in some way, just as we refuse to acknowledge that we all have multiple personalities. But experiences in childhood and even adolescence leave scars that affect every aspect of our lives. It's interesting that the word trauma refers to both psychic and physical damage. When this anguish is fully processed, constant bliss is a possibility.

FRONTAL CORTEX AND BLISS

Your frontal cortex is the part of your brain that's key in understanding how reality is created. This structure is behind the forehead, and it's what makes us distinct from the apes. Our DNA is 99.4 percent the same as that of chimpanzees, our closest relatives, but chimps barely have a frontal cortex. That 0.6 percent difference must have a lot to do with frontal-cortex development, and it's this part of the brain that makes us human.

What does the frontal cortex do? Think of it as the "executive level" of consciousness, where you plan for the future and also where you can choose to direct your attention. Just how important these two capacities are is shown by the results of hundreds of neuropsychology experiments conducted on brain-damaged subjects who were asked to sort cards. A normal person can easily change the criteria by which they sort, due to a capacity for *selective attention*, an ability to consciously shift focus to something else at any given moment. But if you have damage in your frontal cortex, you can't pay attention selectively, and you can't truly choose.

I want to revisit those sensory way stations for a moment and show you another aspect of the frontal cortex: how incoming sensory information is filtered along synapses loaded with opiate receptors. In 1981, I published a paper in *Science* with Mort Mishkin and Agu Pert (my husband at the time) entitled "Opiate Receptor Gradients in Monkey Cerebral Cortex: Correspondence with Sensory Processing Hierarchies." In this paper, we reported how more opiate receptors are found in the frontal cortex than in any other part of the brain or body, and how we found an increasing gradient along the sensory way stations in the cerebral cortex of monkeys. The experiments were done in monkeys who'd already been well studied to determine the information-processing going on at each synapse. In the animals, we were able to carefully map the opiate-receptor density.

Our data showed that as you travel up from the back of the brain (where the occipital cortex first receives sight) to the frontal cortex, you find, as you progress forward and upward, that there are more and more opiate receptors—exponentially more as you move up to the frontal cortex. As I've mentioned, the frontal cortex is the place in the brain where we make choices and plan for the future, and what we saw in the lab was that those pathways are increasingly mediated by the molecules of bliss—the endorphins and their opiate receptors.

This increasing gradient of pleasure and bliss was apparent whether we were looking at hearing or vision. Both sensory pathways increased in opiate receptors as information moved toward the front of the brain. I interpret this finding to mean that pleasure and bliss increasingly influence our criteria of choice as incoming information climbs higher and higher up the sensory way stations. In other words, we make moment-to-moment choices about what to pay attention to and what to plan for in the future based on the pleasure that we get from our choices. No pleasure? Well, then we aren't very likely to choose it. Without a frontal cortex, we'd be like simpler animals, who have no capacity to choose other than to react to or avoid potential pain and death.

But because we have a frontal cortex—that very important 0.6 percent of DNA difference from the chimps—and it's loaded with opiate receptors and endorphins, we can experience the higher-consciousness states of bliss and love, what the mystics call "union with the divine." Our biology actually makes this possible!

Unity: this is our spiritual/biological heritage as humans. Animals don't have a seventh chakra, no mystical third eye or crown connecting them to something beyond—at least my chocolate Labrador retriever, Tory, hasn't indicated that to me yet! Humans do, and the potential for higher consciousness is built right into our anatomy. Beyond just feeling good, we can feel God, and from that state of bliss and union, we have the capacity to create a future for ourselves . . . and for our planet.

MANIFESTATION OF YOUR DESIRES
Attention is important for creating reality, especially when combined with intention. In fact, manifestation, the skill of

imagining what you want and making your dreams come true, can be learned. I've understood from mystics and the teachings of Eastern sages that such things are possible, and in fact, I've learned to meditate with the intention of removing obstacles to the further manifestation of Peptide T in the world. By focusing attention on a mantra or on breathing, a state of quiet and calm alertness can be achieved. Interestingly, the frontal cortex receives input from neuronal fibers sprouting from a tiny cluster of cells at the base of the brain that make norepinephrine, the brain's own amphetamine. I've theorized for some time that the frontal cortex strengthens and even enlarges from frequent meditation, just as a muscle in the body gets pumped up from weight training. This has been proven to be true in experiments showing a resulting thickened layer of cells in this part of the brain, performed by Dr. Richard Davidson, director of the Laboratory for Affective Neuroscience at the University of Wisconsin, in collaboration with the Dalai Lama!

THE FUTURE

If we're so powerful, I also wonder, what do we want to create for this human existence, this planet of six billion people hurtling through space? It really is the next question to ponder, so I want to conclude my remarks with some speculation about what the future holds, especially the future of medicine. I think that there will be more and more emphasis on wellness rather than disease. The health that I'm predicting we'll see more of is psychosomatic well-being, involving not just the physical body, but the mental, emotional, and spiritual self as expressed in the corporeal. We can't afford to keep leaving out these aspects of the human experience in treating illness. Energy medicine and psychology, along with forms of chiropractic that treat emotional as well as physical release and alignment, will become more and more popular as the science explaining the mechanisms of these approaches comes to light. I'm confident that the medicine of the future will include the whole picture: body, mind, and spirit, with a special emphasis on alleviating stress, which is often the result of emotional overload.

As science explores the brain ever more deeply, new information is coming to light about how our lifestyle affects brain function. How does the brain react to relaxation and mental exercise? Can we heighten cognition and brain function to achieve the most heightened awareness and consciousness? In the following essay, Dr. Gary Small, director of the UCLA Memory and Aging Research Center and author of several books, most recently *The Longevity Bible: Eight Essential Strategies for Keeping Your Mind Sharp and Your Body Young*, reviews a study conducted to determine the effects of a healthy longevity lifestyle program on cognition and cerebral metabolism in people with age-related complaints. Our ability to pursue spiritual practice is inextricably linked to our brain's ability to function and achieve full awareness; as this study concludes, a healthier lifestyle may be a big step toward maintaining and even improving brain function.

Effects of a Fourteen-Day Healthy Longevity Lifestyle Program on Cognition and Brain Function

GARY SMALL, M.D.

Many elements contribute to a better quality of life, a heightened awareness, and a more fulfilling day-to-day experience. Expanding the scientific frontier of cognition and brain metabolism in an effort to improve memory and brain function is a valuable step in the journey toward achieving long-term health, happiness, and even spirituality as it is defined: "the quality or state of being." In the following article are the findings of a longevity lifestyle program in relation to brain function that reveals how our lifestyle may, within a relatively short time period, have an impact on both our brain function and memory ability. Through studies like these, it is possible for us to improve our memories, and ultimately our long-term quality of life.

As people age, their risk for cognitive decline increases. An estimated 40 percent of people sixty-five years and older have age-associated memory impairment characterized by self-perception of memory loss and a standardized memory test score demonstrating lower objective memory performance compared with young adults.[1, 2] Such mild age-related memory changes are often relatively stable over time. In contrast, patients with mild cognitive impairment, characterized by greater cognitive decline without impairment in the activities of daily living, are at risk for progressing to Alzheimer disease at a rate approximating 15 percent each year.[3] The MacArthur study of successful aging[4] found that certain lifestyle habits are associated with health and vitality as people age and, for the average individual, such nongenetic influences can account for a higher proportion of cognitive and physical health than genetic factors. Epidemiologic, laboratory, and clinical evidence point to several lifestyle behaviors that may maintain brain health and lower the risk for dementia, including mental and physical activity, diet, and response to stressful stimuli.[5-7] These and other lifestyle habits are not only associated with better health status, but also to increased longevity.[4, 8]

Studies of rodents in enriched environments have found more neurons in their hippocampal memory centers than in rodents living in ordinary laboratory cages.[9] Research in humans has shown that the risk for developing Alzheimer disease is lower in people who have been mentally active.[10] People with advanced educational and professional accomplishments tend to have greater density of neuronal connections in brain areas involved in complex reasoning.[11] Other studies of specific memory techniques, including visualization, elaboration, and association, have been shown to improve objective memory performance scores.[12] These discoveries support the conclusion that mental stimulation and cognitive training may not only improve memory performance, but also stave off future cognitive decline.

When laboratory animals exercise regularly, they develop new neurons in the hippocampus, whereas inactive animals do not.[13] The physical exercise may increase cerebral blood flow, which in turn promotes neural growth. Studies of physically active people show that they have a lower risk for Alzheimer disease compared with inactive individuals.[14] A study of healthy older adults found that mental tasks involving executive control improved in a group that was prescribed a cardiovascular conditioning program but not in a control group that was prescribed only stretching and toning.[15] Excess body fat increases an individual's risk for such illnesses as diabetes and hypertension, which can increase the risk for dementia, cerebrovascular disease, and cognitive decline.[16]

Epidemiologic studies have found lower rates of dementia in geographic areas where populations eat diets low in animal fats.[17] Diets high in omega-3 fats from olive oil or fish,[18] as well as those rich in antioxidant fruits and vegetables,[19] are associated with less age-related cognitive decline. In addition, diets that avoid processed and refined foods and emphasize low glycemic index carbohydrates may reduce the risk for type 2 diabetes, stroke, and vascular dementia.[20, 21] Studies of laboratory animals show that prolonged exposure to stress hormones has an adverse effect on the hippocampus, a brain region involved in memory and learning.[22] Human investigations[23] indicate that several days of exposure to high levels of the stress hormone cortisol can impair memory. Proneness to psychologic distress also is associated with an increased risk for Alzheimer disease.[24]

Data from controlled clinical trials on the short-term benefits of many of these lifestyle strategies are limited. Moreover, cognitive and brain function effects of combining several strategies together are not known. To this end, we studied a fourteen-day program that combined healthy lifestyle behaviors associated with a lower risk for dementia—mental and physical exercises, healthy diet, and stress reduction techniques—on cognitive ability and brain function.

METHODS

Subjects and Clinical Assessments: We studied seventeen right-handed white adults who were selected from a pool of 344 potential volunteers recruited through advertisements, media coverage, and referrals from physicians and families. After telephone screening, forty-nine individuals were seen for clinical evaluation. We excluded volunteers who had major medical or neuropsychiatric illnesses that could affect cognitive status as well as those who were unwilling to make a commitment to undergo the study procedures as described. To be included in the study, volunteers needed to have objective cognitive performance scores that were normal for their age group. All subjects had mild age-related memory complaints, which is present in nearly half of individuals age 50 and older.[2] All subjects had neurologic and psychiatric evaluations, routine screening laboratory tests, and magnetic resonance imaging scans to rule out reversible causes of cognitive impairment,[25] and volunteers meeting diagnostic criteria for dementia[26] or mild cognitive impairment[3] were excluded. All subjects were given a Mini-Mental State Examination[27] and Hamilton Rating Scale for Depression.[28] Volunteers were excluded if they were taking drugs that could influence cognition (e.g., cholinesterase inhibitors, sedative-hypnotics) or supplements (e.g., phosphatidyl serine, ginkgo biloba) that could have such effects. Volunteers with a history of excessive alcohol, caffeine, or tobacco use were also excluded from participation.

At baseline and follow up (within one week after completing the fourteen-day program), subjects received objective cognitive assessments, including a multitrial verbal learning and memory test[29] and a word-generation (letter-fluency) test.[30] Subjects also completed a standardized measure of self-awareness of memory ability, the Memory Functioning Questionnaire (MFQ).[31] The MFQ is a sixty-four-item instrument that provides four-unit weight factor scores measuring frequency of forgetting, seriousness of forgetting, retrospective functioning (changes in current memory ability relative to earlier life), and mnemonics use. Higher scores indicate higher levels of perceived memory functioning (e.g., fewer forgetting incidents, less frequent mnemonic use). For a sample of 639 adults aged 16 to 89 years, Cronbach alpha internal consistency alphas ranged from 0.82 to 0.93 for different scales on the MFQ, and test-retest reliabilities, over a three-year period, ranged from 0.22 to 0.64.[32]

All scanning procedures were performed within two weeks of clinical assessments. Informed consent was obtained in accordance with the recommendations and requirements of the Radiation Safety Committee and the Institutional Review Board of the University of California, Los Angeles, Healthy Lifestyle Program. After baseline assessments and scanning procedures were completed, each subject in the intervention group received a notebook with the fourteen-day healthy longevity lifestyle program, which is detailed elsewhere.[33] This program provides simple instructions so that subjects were able to readily follow several healthy lifestyle strategies—memory training, physical conditioning, relaxation techniques, and diet—that are associated with a lower risk for dementia.[7–10, 12, 14–21, 23, 24] The conceptual basis of the program involved developing a usable guide to initiating lifestyle and behavior strategies associated with improved cognitive abilities and a lower risk for cognitive decline. The exercises build gradually over a fourteen-day period so they are readily learned and integrated into the volunteer's daily schedule. In addition to brain teasers and mental puzzles, the program provides daily exercises that teach memory techniques to help focus attention and improve visualization and association skills for better retention and recall.

These memory techniques begin at a basic level and increase in complexity over the two-week period. For example, the first day, subjects are given an exercise to focus attention to improve learning and concentration (e.g., subjects are instructed to concentrate on two random details of the clothing or accessories on a family member). After attention skills improve the first few days, exercises are introduced to improve visualization and association skills for better mnemonic techniques. Cardiovascular conditioning exercises such as brisk walks are recommended each day. Daily brief relaxation exercises are designed to lower stress and help subjects to focus their attention. Suggested shopping lists and menus guide subjects to follow a healthy diet plan, including five daily meals emphasizing antioxidant fruits and vegetables, omega-3 fats, and low glycemic index carbohydrates. The brief fourteen-day period was chosen so that volunteers would not be daunted by a requirement for an extensive commitment. Moreover, it was predicted that the time period would be adequate for participants to adapt to and feel comfortable with the lifestyle changes so they would continue them beyond the initial two-week period. Exercises and suggested menus were described in simple terms and the amount of time needed to follow the exercises totals from 30 to 45 minutes each day. Before initiating the program, a research nurse reviewed the daily instructions with each subject. The research nurse monitored self-reports of compliance through participants' daily notes and post-treatment interviews to ensure that volunteers were able to follow the recommended program exercises and diet. The volunteers in the control group were instructed to continue their usual lifestyle habits during the two-week period between clinical and brain imaging procedures.

RESULTS

Subjects were on average middle-aged (overall mean age: fifty-three years; standard deviation: 10; range: 35 to 69 years) and college-educated, and did not have evidence of cognitive impairment or depression. The intervention and control groups did not differ significantly in mean age or years of educational achievement, proportion of females, or in mean baseline scores on the Mini-Mental State Examination and Hamilton Rating Scale for Depression.

Mean baseline subjective and objective cognitive measures did not differ significantly between the intervention and control groups. Changes in cognitive measures were not significantly different between the intervention and control groups. However, for the objective measures, the intervention group improved significantly in verbal fluency, whereas the control group did not. Subjects in the intervention group showed a 5 percent decrease in left dorsolateral prefrontal activity compared with baseline (Z 3.30, p control group showed no significant change in brain metabolism, and direct statistical comparison of the two therapy arms demonstrated that the decline in this region, involving a stretch of prefrontal cortex in the vicinity of Brodmann's areas 8, 9, and 10, was significantly greater in the intervention group than in the control group.

DISCUSSION

To our knowledge, this is the first study to show that combining several healthy lifestyle strategies will change measures of cognitive and brain function in a relatively brief time period.

The results suggest that a program combining mental and physical exercise, stress reduction, and healthy diet can have significant short-term effects on brain metabolism and cognitive performance.

The Statistical Parametric Mapping (SPM) analysis identified a change in cerebral activity in the intervention group in a brain region that modulates several mental functions relevant to the lifestyle intervention. Previous studies have demonstrated that working memory, the ability to retain information for brief periods, requires an intact dorsolateral prefrontal cortex.[34] A study using functional MRI found that semantic organizational strategies engage this same region.[35] The dorsolateral prefrontal cortex also mediates anxiety symptoms, and this regional metabolic reduction may in part have resulted from the intervention's relaxation exercises.[36] The significant change observed in the left hemisphere is also consistent with the verbal emphasis in the program's memory training exercises.

Moreover, the observations that the intervention group experienced both improved objective verbal fluency and significant change in left dorsolateral prefrontal metabolism are consistent with previous work showing that verbal fluency is associated with activation in this same brain region.[37] Future studies will determine specific effects of individual components of the program and whether a combination of healthy lifestyle strategies produces a greater effect than individual strategies.

The finding that the intervention reduced regional cerebral metabolic rates could correspond to subjects developing greater cognitive efficiency during mental rest, and previous studies are consistent with this hypothesis. PET scans of volunteers playing a computer game for the first time show high cerebral glucose metabolic rates, but after several months of practice, when the volunteers become proficient at the game, their scans display significantly lower rates of glucose metabolism.[38] This lower brain activity with improved mental performance suggests that with time, practice, and familiarity, our brains can essentially adapt themselves to achieve comparable performance levels with less work. The present study suggests that such an improvement in brain efficiency may occur over relatively brief periods of intervention.

In a previous functional MRI study,[39] our group found that middle-aged and older adults with a genetic risk for Alzheimer disease had greater MR signal activity in the dorsolateral prefrontal cortex during a memory task compared with those without such a genetic risk. Moreover, higher MR signals at baseline correlated with lower verbal memory scores two years later. Future studies may determine whether such apparent neural compensatory responses to genetic risk would change after a lifestyle intervention such as the one used in the present study.

We did not find significant changes in subjective cognitive measures in the intervention group, which could reflect the small sample size as well as the insensitivity of the MFQ to measure short-term changes in memory self-awareness (several items in the questionnaire focus on longer-term memory abilities). Self-awareness of cognitive improvement is helpful in encouraging individuals to continue a healthy life style beyond a two-week period. By contrast, worry and concern about memory performance has been associated with worse objective memory performance scores.[40] The current study combined several different lifestyle approaches. Previous research indicates that combining different kinds of interventions can augment the overall effect on age-related health outcomes. For example, investigators have combined a healthy diet with regular physical exercise to reduce the risk for developing type 2 diabetes.[41] A strategy combining stress reduction with physical activity has been found to lower the risk for ischemic chest pain in cardiac patients, compared with exercise alone.[42]

Several methodological issues deserve comment. The small sample size and relatively brief intervention period limits how much any conclusions from these results can be generalized. Because volunteers were living in the community and not strictly monitored on how closely they followed the healthy lifestyle program, compliance would be expected to be lower than in a closely monitored, residential intervention program. Moreover, without objective measures of physical activity, dietary intake, or degree of compliance with memory and relaxation exercises, the actual lifestyle behavior changes in the intervention group are not known. The research nurse monitored activity self-reports, but recall bias could have influenced these reports. Thus, the observed changes in outcome measures may have reflected nonspecific or placebo effects of being given a program that participants were only claiming to have followed.

The nature of the cerebral metabolic results, however, would argue against such a possibility, because the brain region showing highly significant results was not a random region, but rather one that controls brain functions that were specific targets of the program (e.g., working memory, verbal fluency). Although we recruited a convenience sample of volunteers who may have already been following a healthy lifestyle regimen, such a convenience sample would be expected to reduce any differences between groups rather than exaggerate them. Our significant findings, despite such methodological limitations, suggest that people may be able to enjoy the benefits of healthy lifestyle programs when they follow them on their own without the assistance of a professional staff.

In summary, a fourteen-day healthy lifestyle program improved measures of verbal fluency and reduced left dorsolateral prefrontal cortical metabolism, suggesting that such a program may result in greater cognitive efficiency of a brain region involved in working memory functions. Future longitudinal studies will determine the long-term effects of such combined interventions and whether they eventually lower the risk for developing dementia.

This study was supported by the Department of Energy (DOE contract DE-FC03-87-ER60615), General Clinical Research Centers Program M01-RR00865, the Fran and Ray Stark Foundation Fund for Alzheimer's Disease Research, and the Judith Olenick Elgart Fund for Research on Brain Aging. Presented in part at the International Conference on Alzheimer's Disease and Related Disorders (July 2004) and the Annual Meeting of the American College of Neuropsychopharmacology (December 2005).

The author thanks Ms. Andrea Kaplan, Ms. Debbie Dorsey, Ms. Gwendolyn Byrd, and Ms. Teresann Crowe-Lear for help in subject recruitment, data management, and study coordination.

In many religious and secular value systems, compassion and empathy are considered essential to a healthy emotional and spiritual life. The question remains: is it possible to prove that compassion and empathy can actually *heal?* Compassion is essential to many types of prayer and good will, but is it an active ingredient for change? In what follows, Dr. Larry Dossey, bestselling author of *Healing Words: The Power of Prayer and the Practice of Medicine* and, most recently, *The Extraordinary Healing Power of Ordinary Things*, guides readers through studies that test these questions in prayer and in doctor-patient relationships.

Compassion and Healing

LARRY DOSSEY, M.D.

Compassion: to suffer with another; sympathy for the suffering of others, often including a desire to help
Empathy: the ability to identify with and understand another person's feelings or difficulties

The most profound healing event I personally remember was being touched by a nurse when I was recovering from anesthesia following an appendectomy. The surgery was a rushed-up affair that took place in the Student Health Center at the University of Texas at Austin, when I was a senior student preparing to enter medical school. I never met the surgeon beforehand; he thought a meeting was unnecessary. Neither did I meet the anesthesiologist in advance; he was too busy. When I awakened I was anxious, alone, and in pain. I still did not know who my physician was, or what he had found during surgery. The nurse simply held my hand. Her lingering touch conveyed to me—silently, powerfully, unequivocally—that everything was going to be all right. It was; the pain vanished, along with the anxiety and sense of isolation. This simple act is seared into my memory as a profound example of the power of compassion.

Heck, I became so enthusiastic about nurses I married one— Barbara—nine years later, thirty-five years ago.

COMPASSION, WISDOM TRADITIONS, AND GOLDEN RULES

An emphasis on compassion and empathy lies at the heart of the major religious traditions that have sustained and nourished humanity for over two millennia. As theologian Karen Armstrong says, most of these traditions came into being at roughly the same time, during the so-called Axial Age, about 900 to 200 BCE. "Why should we go back to these ancient faiths?" Armstrong asks. "Because they were the experts. In this period of history people worked as hard to find a cure for the spiritual ills of humanity as we do today trying to find a cure for cancer."[1]

We often forget that these great teachings had nothing to do with religion and religiosity. As Armstrong explains, "What has intrigued me is that none of them was interested in doctrines or metaphysical beliefs. . . . [At that time] a religion was not about accepting certain metaphysical propositions: it was about behaving in a way that changed you. . . . What the Axial sages put forward was that compassion was the key. Compassion doesn't mean feeling sorry or pity for people but feeling with the other, learning to dethrone yourself from the centre of your world and put another there. Not only would this be the test for any religiosity but it would also be the means of entering into enlightenment." Compassion, therefore, now as then, involves radical surgery on the notions of I, me, and mine.

Golden Rules are endorsements of compassion and empathy, and because compassion runs through all the great Axial traditions, it is not surprising that some version of the Golden Rule is found in all of them. Confucius was the first to propound such a recommendation: "Do not do to others as you would not have done to you." As Armstrong says, "[Confucius] was the person who equated religion with compassion—it was compassion: it wasn't about theology, it wasn't about going to heaven, it wasn't about defining what you meant by the divine or the sacred, it wasn't about being right. It was about 'human-heartedness,' the exercise of compassion." The Confucian sage Mencius agreed, saying, "One should not behave towards others in a way which is disagreeable to oneself."

Rabbi Hillel, the older contemporary of Jesus, once told a pagan who had asked him to define the whole of Judaism, "That which is hateful to you do not do to your neighbor. That's the Torah. The rest is commentary; go and learn it." As all Christians know, Jesus propounded a similar version: "And as ye would that men should do to you, do ye also to them likewise" (Luke 6:31, KJV).

In Taoism, we find, "Regard your neighbor's gain as your own gain, and your neighbor's loss as your own loss." Within Islam, we read, "Not one of you truly believes until you wish for others what you wish for yourself." Similar views permeate traditions outside the Axial traditions. For example, the Roman pagan religion contained this exhortation: "The law imprinted on the hearts of all men is to love the members of society as themselves." And as Black Elk (1863–1950), a Sioux medicine man, said of Native American spirituality, "All things are our relatives; what we do to everything, we do to ourselves. All is really One." And from the Pima tradition,

"Do not wrong or hate your neighbor. For it is not he whom you wrong, but yourself."[2]

Compassion, of course, is not limited to the religious. The contemporary philosophy of secular humanism, which many religious fundamentalists love to hate, also affirms compassion and empathy. In the *Humanist Manifesto II*, we find, ". . . critical intelligence, infused by a sense of human caring, is the best method that humanity has for resolving problems. Reason should be balanced with compassion and empathy and the whole person fulfilled."[3]

A TREASURE HIDDEN IN PLAIN SIGHT

At first glance, there seems to be nothing new about valuing compassion; it's an idea that has been around for thousands of years in both the religious and secular worlds. But perhaps it is the universality of compassion that has lulled us into undervaluing its importance. Compassion has largely become a treasure hidden in plain sight, a phenomenon toward which we are selectively blind.

Of course, everyone *says* compassion is important, and compassion and empathy are widely acknowledged by health care professionals to be characteristics of humane care. However, when serious illness strikes, they are often regarded as less important than physical interventions such as drugs and surgical procedures. But as we shall see, a variety of evidence suggests that compassion and empathy are correlated with positive health outcomes, and they can evoke measurable physiological effects in sick persons, even when the individual is unaware that these factors are being extended to them. As a consequence, compassion and empathy should not be regarded as optional niceties in medical care, but as fundamental factors promoting recovery from any illness.

EVIDENCE OF A COMPASSION EFFECT

Mind-body researcher Jeanne Achterberg is a veteran explorer of indigenous healing methods and the role of imagery and visualization in health care. These interests led her to the island of Hawaii, where she spent two years observing the culture and healing methods of indigenous healers, many of whom took her into their confidence and freely shared with her their methods.

Achterberg was interested in exploring whether healers can exert a positive influence on a distant individual with whom they have no sensory contact, as healers universally claim. She and her colleagues at North Hawaii Community Hospital in Waimea recruited eleven indigenous healers to participate in a healing experiment.[4] The healers were not casually interested in healing; they had pursued their healing tradition for an average of twenty-three years. Each of them was asked to select a person they knew, with whom they had previously worked professionally, and with whom they felt an empathic, compassionate, bonded connection, to serve as the recipient of their healing intentions. Although the researchers referred to the healing endeavors as distant intentionality (DI), the healers themselves described what they did in various ways— prayer, sending energy, good intentions, or wishing for the highest good.

Each recipient was isolated from all forms of sensory contact with the healer and placed in an fMRI scanner. The healers then sent their various forms of DI to their subjects at random, two-minute intervals that could not have been anticipated by the recipient.

When the fMRI brain scans of the subjects were analyzed, significant differences in brain function were found between the experimental (send) and control (no-send) conditions. There was less than approximately one chance in ten thousand that these differences could be explained by chance ($p = 0.000127$). The brain areas that were activated during the healing or send periods were the anterior and middle cingulate, precuneus, and frontal regions.

When the experiment was repeated, using subjects with whom the healers felt no empathic bonding, no significant fMRI changes were found in the recipients during either the send or no-send conditions.

This study suggests that compassionate, empathic healing intentions can exert measurable physical effects on a recipient, even when the recipient is not aware when the attempt is being made. This study appears to shred the perennial complaint of skeptics that these are placebo effects, due only to suggestion, expectation, and positive thinking on the part of the recipient.

Achterberg's study does not stand alone. Several prior experiments have examined correlations in brain function between empathic individuals who are widely separated and who have no sensory contact with each other.[5-8]

Achterberg's experiment was a proof-of-concept study designed to test whether a nonlocal, compassion-mediated, physiological effect exists. It did not explore whether or not such an effect could alter the course of an illness. But prior studies have done just that.

In 1998, researcher Elisabeth Targ and her colleagues at the University of California-San Francisco School of Medicine/California Pacific Medical Center studied the effect of distant healing intentions on patients with advanced AIDS.[9] In a double-blind pilot study, they found that AIDS patients who were extended healing intentions from veteran, seasoned healers fared better than those who were not: 40 percent of those not sent healing intentions died, compared to none of those who were extended healing intentions. The study was expanded and repeated. By this time, multidrug, antiretroviral therapy had come into widespread use, and all the subjects in both the intervention and control groups were treated with such. Probably as a consequence, there were no deaths in either group in the expanded study. However, the intervention group who received distant healing intentions had a statistically lower incidence of AIDS-associated illnesses, a lower rate of hospitalization, shorter hospital stays, fewer physician visits, and better psychological profiles during the course of their illness, when compared with the control group that was treated with only antiretroviral medications.

The healers in this study, as in the Achterberg experiment that would come later, were not casually interested in healing; healing was a serious pursuit for them and they had spent many years practicing their calling.

Nearly all gifted healers recognize the importance of deep caring and love toward the individual in need. Their depth of compassion may set them apart from less-experienced healers, and may account for why some healing studies achieve positive results while others do not.

This is a touchy point. Many people insist that healing is a purely democratic pursuit that can be practiced with equal facility by anyone. This is a noble thought, but is probably an exaggeration. We recognize different levels of excellence in all pursuits. Prodigies exist in music, literature, athletics, mathematics, cooking, art, and so on. Why should healing be different? And the difference may be due largely to the degree of compassion, empathy, and sense of oneness the healer is able to summon during the actual healing effort.

SUPPORTIVE EVIDENCE

Studies exploring nonlocal healing effects are numerous. In a 2003 analysis of this field, Jonas and Crawford found over 2,200 published reports, including 122 controlled laboratory studies and 80 randomized controlled trials.[10] How good are the controlled clinical and laboratory studies? Using strict Consolidated Standards of Reporting Trials (CONSORT criteria) to assess the quality of the studies, Jonas and Crawford gave an "A," the highest possible grade, to laboratory studies involving the effects of intentions on inanimate objects such as sophisticated random number generators. They gave a respectable "B" to the nonlocal healing studies involving humans, cells, tissues, plants, and animals.

The depth and breadth of this research remains little known among health care professionals. Consequently, the occasional critiques of this area are almost never comprehensive, and they often rely on philosophical and theological propositions about whether remote healing *can* or *should* work, and whether experiments involving healing intentions and prayer are heretical or blasphemous.[11, 12] Dossey and Hufford have examined the twenty most common criticisms of this field and found most of them unconvincing.[13]

On balance, these studies, of which approximately one-half show statistical significance, attest to the fundamental importance of compassion and empathy in healing. Although researchers have no "compassion meters," the healers themselves generally insist that an emotional bond is crucial in eliciting the healing effect, a contention that, as mentioned, was affirmed in the Achterberg and Targ experiments.

HYPOTHESES

An obstacle to a serious consideration of this evidence is the lack of an accepted explanation of how these studies *could* be true. However, many hypotheses recently have been advanced by a variety of scholars, including Nobelists, in fields such as neurobiology, mathematics, and physics.[14] Several invoke concepts based on recent discoveries in quantum physics. Researcher Dean Radin, in his recent book *Entangled Minds*, suggests quantum entanglement as a hypothesis for nonlocal, paranormal or psi-type events, including distant healing effects. In the following passage, one may substitute "nonlocal healing effects" for "psi":

If physics prohibits information from transcending the ordinary boundaries of space and time, then from a scientific point of view psi is simply impossible. But here's where things become interesting. . . . [T]he old prohibitions are no longer true. Over the past century, most of the fundamental assumptions . . . have been revised. . . . This is why I propose that psi is the human experience of the [quantum-]entangled universe. . . . [T]he ontological parallels implied by [quantum] entanglement and psi are so compelling that I believe they'd be foolish to ignore.[15]

Quantum physics does not validate nonlocal, compassion-based healing or any other consciousness-mediated event, but it does provide potent metaphors that may prove helpful in understanding these phenomena.

In any case, the lack of an explanatory theory does not invalidate data. Often in the history of medicine we have known *that* something works before we have understood *how* it works, as our use of aspirin, colchicine, penicillin, general anesthetics, and many other therapies attests.

COMPASSION AND TEARS

A revealing study of patients with rheumatoid arthritis (RA) suggests that we cry as a way of relieving chronic pain and inflammation.[16] Japanese researchers at Tokyo's Nippon Medical School exposed RA patients to deeply emotional visual stimuli, and correlated various neuroendocrine and immune responses (NEIRs) in their bodies with how easily they were brought to tears. These responses included blood levels of the stress hormone cortisol, the immune protein interleukin-6, and CD4, CD8, and natural killer immune cells. They found that patients who were easily moved to tears generally did better clinically over the course of a year than those who did not cry, with less pain, swelling, and need for pain medications. The researchers concluded that shedding tears suppresses the influence of stress on their NEIRs, making their RA easier to control.

Shedding tears in this study demonstrated an ability to experience compassion, empathy, and a sense of connectedness with the evocative situation or the person in need. This experiment suggests that compassion is good for the individual experiencing it, as well as for the person to whom it is directed. This is consistent with the adage that healing efforts benefit the healer as well as the healee.

This study goes against the grain of the grin-and-bear-it school, which says that pain and illness should be endured without complaint or whimper.

BREAKING THE BOND

People commonly say that they pray for their loved ones when they are sick. This implies that they know the individual in need, that an emotional bond exists between them, and that they are willing to pray for them unconditionally and without reservation.

In contrast, many healing studies involve strangers praying for strangers. Moreover, the double-blind nature of these experiments means that healing is not unconditional, because the patients are told that they may or may not be prayed for; they are in a cloud of uncertainty. As a result of these conditions, in these experiments the rich personal connection, emotional bonding, and unconditional support between loved ones is severely reduced or eliminated. These are surely reasons why these studies frequently show marginal, neutral, or even negative results.

An example is the well-known 2006 prayer study from Harvard Medical School involving 1,802 post-coronary artery bypass surgery patients at six U.S. hospitals.[17] Of these patients, 604 were told they might or might not be prayed for, and were; 597 were told they might or might not be prayed for, and were not; 601 were told they would be prayed for, and were. Prayers were offered by two Catholic groups and one Protestant. The intercessors were provided brief written prayers they were required to recite, but were otherwise free to use their own. They were provided with the first name and the initial of the last name of the prayer recipients. Prayers were initiated on the eve or day of surgery and continued for two weeks.

Among the group told that they might or might not be prayed for and were, 52 percent had post-surgical complications. Among those patients told they might or might not be prayed for, and were not, 51 percent had postsurgical complications. Among the group told they would be prayed for and were, 59 percent had postsurgical complications. There is no agreement among analysts why prayer did not demonstrate a healing effect, and why those who knew with certainty that they would be prayed for fared the worst of all.

Perhaps the reasons underlying these results are straightforward. Nowhere on earth is prayer used the way it was employed in the Harvard experiment (except in other prayer experiments). In real life, prayer is employed lovingly, compassionately, and empathically between loved ones, and it is offered unconditionally, not as a "maybe" or a "perhaps."

The media had a field day with the Harvard study. "Don't pray for me! Please!" trumpeted a *Newsweek* report.[18]

Wrenching healing from a real-life context and artificializing it to suit the whims of researchers is a recipe for experimental disaster. Only by honoring the crucial role of compassion, empathy, and unconditional love—admirably demonstrated in the Achterberg study—can researchers hope to reveal some of the mysteries of healing.

A perennial criticism by busy health care practitioners is that time is limited and resources are few; therapists don't have the time required to deliver adequate physical care, let alone create a compassionate, empathic bond with a patient.

The difficulties of conveying compassion may be overrated. Oncologist Linda A. Fogarty, of Johns Hopkins University School of Hygiene and Public Health, and colleagues demonstrated that conveying compassion and empathy need not be time intensive. They found that a physician's being perceived as compassionate and empathic could be achieved by showing patients a compassion-oriented video whose duration was only forty seconds.[19]

Another objection against rendering compassionate care is that it makes patients excessively dependent on their physicians, thereby increasing greater consumption of health care resources. In other words, if patients *like* the doctor-patient encounter, they'll want more of it. Researcher D. A. Redelmeier of the University of Toronto and his colleagues showed that this is not necessarily the case. In a randomized, controlled study involving homeless adults who rely on emergency rooms for care, they tested whether compassionate care, by improving patient satisfaction, can alter subsequent use of emergency services. They found that compassionate care of homeless adults *decreases* repeat visits to the emergency department, compared to care delivered in an emotionally neutral way.[20]

Medical educators may be waking up to the value of compassion in healing. In 2006, medical schools in Israel altered their admission procedures to require the presence of compassion and empathy in every entering medical student. High grades and intellectual skills continued to be important, but were judged insufficient to qualify one for admission. "It bothered us," said Professor Moshe Mittelman, head of the admissions committee at Tel Aviv University, "that here and there you meet a doctor about whom you say, 'He may know medicine, but he is not a decent human being.' We are a school that educates people to work in the medical profession, which is not only science but also humanism and dealing with people."[21]

The majority of healing studies suggest that a healing effect is real and that it is mediated by compassion and empathy. Evidence further suggests that an empathic, compassionate bond between physicians and patients can be established quickly, and that compassionate care does not result in an increased demand for health care services.

Why does this matter? Compassion and empathy are humanitarian gestures that not only make needy patients feel better, but are also correlated with measurable physiological effects and improved clinical outcomes. For these reasons, they are important elements in the decent care of any illness.

Objections to compassion and empathy as integral components in disease treatment often conceal a mind-body duality in which emotional, psychological, and spiritual factors are considered less real than physical ones. But as the above evidence suggests, mind-body separation is not fundamental. As researcher Emily Mumford and colleagues suggested over two decades ago, "It is often argued that the medical care system cannot afford to take on the emotional status of the patient as its responsibility. Time is short and costs are high. However, it may be that medicine cannot afford to ignore the patient's emotional status assuming that it will take care of itself."[22]

It is a measure of our physicalistic age that we require "hard" evidence for the value of compassion in caring for the sick. Historians may look back with amazement at how we agonized over the role of compassion in healing, when for nearly all of human history its importance was self-evident.

Yet the vision remains. The value of compassion has been obvious to some of the truly great scientists of our age. No better example exists than Albert Einstein, whose ringing endorsement of compassion deserves to be a mantra for our time, because it is a remedy for the myriad hatreds that separate us from one another and from our endangered natural world:

> *A human being is part of a whole, called by us Universe, a part limited in time and space. He experiences himself, his thoughts and feelings, as something separated from the rest—a kind of optical delusion of his consciousness. This delusion is a kind of prison for us, restricting us to our personal desires and to affection for a few persons nearest us. Our task must be to free ourselves from this prison by widening our circles of compassion to embrace all living creatures and the whole of nature in its beauty.*[23]

In his research, Dr. Dan Siegel, author of *The Mindful Brain: Reflection and Attunement in the Cultivation of Well-Being*, journeys deep into the concept of mindfulness and attunement and explores how it relates to the quality of our lives, relationships with others, and neurological brain function capacities—including a thickening of the prefrontal lobes. In the following adapted excerpt, he addresses questions such as: How does being mindful affect our daily lives and our brain? How do attunement and mindfulness change the way we live our lives?

Reflections on The Mindful Brain

DAN SIEGEL, M.D.

Welcome to a journey into the heart of our lives. Being mindfully aware, attending to the richness of our experiences, creates scientifically recognized enhancements in our physiology, our mental functions, and our interpersonal relationships. Being fully present in our awareness opens our lives to new possibilities of well-being.

Almost all cultures have a form of practice to help develop awareness of the moment. The major religions of the world utilize some form of focusing one's attention, from meditation to prayer, yoga to Tai chi. Each of these traditions may have its own particular approach, but they share in common the power of intentionally focusing awareness in a way that transforms people's lives.

Why is this mindful awareness so universal an ideal goal across our human family? Can we find a common thread that links these practices that might help us understand the power of this way of being to enhance health, relationships, and well-being?

MINDFULNESS AS AN ATTUNED RELATIONSHIP WITH ONESELF
In my own field of studying interpersonal relationships within families, we use the concept of "attunement" to examine how one person, a parent for example, focuses attention on the internal world of another, such as a child or a spouse. This focus on the mind of another person harnesses neural circuitry that enables two people to "feel felt" by each other. This state is crucial for people in relationships to feel vibrant and alive, to feel understood, and to feel at peace. Research has shown that such attuned relationships promote resilience and longevity.

We'll explore how the process of attunement may lead the brain to grow in ways that promote balanced self-regulation and a process called neural integration that enables flexibility and self-understanding. This way of feeling felt, of feeling connected in the world, may help us understand how becoming attuned to oneself may promote these physical and psychological dimensions of well-being with mindful awareness.

Turning to the brain can help us see the commonality of mechanisms between these two forms of internal and interpersonal attunement. By examining the neural dimension of functioning and its possible correlation with mindful awareness, we may be able to expand our understanding of why and how mindfulness creates the documented improvements in immune function, inner sense of well-being, and our capacity for rewarding interpersonal relationships.

We will be using this integrative approach to bring together various ways of knowing to understand mindfulness in perhaps a broader way than any single perspective might permit. At the foundation we will try to combine first-person knowing with scientific points of view. Turning to the brain and attachment studies is not meant to favor these two fields over any other: this will be a starting point in our journey. As you'll see, a variety of fields will come into play as we examine the research on memory, narrative, wisdom, emotion, perception, attention, and learning along with explorations that go deeply into internal subjective experience.

DEFINING THE MIND

Before we explore the various ways of thinking about mindfulness and focusing the mind in the moment, we might want to ask the basic question: what is the mind?

I have found a useful definition of the mind, supported by a range of scientists from various disciplines, to be "a process that regulates the flow of energy and information."

Our human mind is both embodied and relational. Embodied means that the mind involves a flow of energy and information that occurs within the body, including the distributed nervous system we'll refer to by using the simple term, "brain." Relational signifies that dimension of the mind involving the flow of energy and information that occurs between people. Right now this flow from me as I type these words to you as you read them is shaping our minds—yours and mine. Even as I am imagining who you might be and what your response is, I am changing the flow of energy and information in my brain and body as a whole. As you absorb these words your mind is embodying this flow of energy and information as well.

SOME BENEFITS

Studies have shown that specific applications of mindful awareness improve the capacity to regulate emotion, to combat emotional dysfunction, to improve patterns of thinking, and to reduce negative mind-sets. Mindfulness can even treat and prevent depression, changing the imbalance of circuits in the brain.

Research on some dimensions of mindful awareness practices reveals that the body's functioning is greatly enhanced: healing, immune response, stress reactivity, and a general sense of physical well-being are improved with mindfulness (Davidson et al., 2003). Our relationships with others are also improved, as we see that the ability to perceive the nonverbal emotional signals from others is enhanced and our ability to sense the internal worlds of others is augmented (Ekman, 2006). In these ways we come to compassionately feel the feelings of others and to empathize, to understand another's points of view.

We can see the power of mindful awareness to achieve these many and diverse beneficial changes in our lives when we consider that this form of awareness may directly shape the activity and growth of parts of the brain responsible for our relationships, our emotional life, and our physiological response to stress.

MINDFUL AWARENESS

Direct experiencing in the present moment has been described as a fundamental part of Buddhist, Christian, Hindu, Islamic, Jewish, and Taoist teaching for centuries (Goleman, 1988; Armstrong, 1993). In these religious traditions, from mystical Christianity with centering prayer (Keating, 2005; Fitzpatrick-Hopler, 2006) to Buddhist mindfulness meditation (Kornfield, 1993, 2008; Thich Nhat Hahn, 1991; Wallace, 2006), one sees the use of the idea of being aware of the present moment in a different light from the cognitive aspect of mindfulness.

Many forms of prayer in different traditions require that the individual pause and participate in an intentional process of connecting with a state of mind or entity outside the day-to-day way of being. Prayer and religious affiliation in general have been demonstrated to be associated with increased longevity and well-being (Pargament, 1997). The common overlap of group belonging and prayer makes it hard to tease apart the internal from the interpersonal process, but in fact we may find that this is just the point: pausing to become mindful may indeed involve an internal sense of belonging.

In recent research, the clinical application of the practice of mindfulness meditation derived from the Buddhist tradition has served as a focus of intensive study on the possible neural correlates of mindful awareness. Here we see the use of the term "mindfulness" in a way that numerous investigators have been trying to clearly define (Bishop et al., 2004; Baer et al., 2006). These studies across a range of clinical situations, from the medically ill with chronic pain to psychiatric populations with disturbances of mood or anxiety, have shown the effective application of secular mindfulness meditation skills taught outside of any particular religious practice or group membership. These studies have demonstrated positive effects on mind, body, and relationships.

In many ways, scholars see the nearly 2,500-year-old practice of Buddhism as a form of study of the nature of mind (Lutz, Dunne, and Davidson, 2006) rather than a theistic tradition. It is possible to practice Buddhist-derived meditation, and ascribe to aspects of the psychological view of the mind from this perspective, for example, and maintain one's beliefs and membership in other religious traditions. In contemplative mindful practice, one focuses the mind in specific ways to develop a more rigorous form of present-moment awareness that can directly alleviate suffering in one's life.

Jon Kabat-Zinn has devoted his professional life to bringing mindfulness into the mainstream of modern medicine. In Kabat-Zinn's view, "An operational working definition of mindfulness is: the awareness that emerges through paying attention on purpose, in the present moment, and nonjudgmentally to the unfolding of experience moment by moment." (Kabat-Zinn, 2003, 145–146). This "nonjudgmental" view in many ways can be interpreted to mean something like "not grasping on to judgments," as the mind seems to continually come up with reactions that assess and react. Being able to note those judgments and disengage from them may be what "nonjudgmental" feels like in practice. "On purpose" implies that this state is created with intention to focus on the present moment. As the Inner Kids program for young children to learn basic mindfulness skills states, mindfulness is "Being aware of what's happening as it's happening" (Kaiser-Greenland, 2006).

Kabat-Zinn goes on to note that the Buddhist origins of this view of mindfulness and the natural laws of the mind reveal

> *a coherent phenomenological description of the nature of the mind, emotion, and suffering and its potential release, based on highly refined practices aimed at systematically training and cultivating various aspects of mind and heart via the faculty of mindful attention (the words for mind and heart are the same in Asian languages; thus "mindfulness" includes an affectionate, compassionate quality within the attending, a sense of openhearted, friendly presence and interest). And mindfulness, it should also be noted, being about attention, is also of necessity universal. There is nothing particularly Buddhist about it. We are all mindful to one degree or another, moment by moment. It is an inherent human capacity. The contribution of the Buddhist tradition has been in part to emphasize simple and effective ways to cultivate and refine this capacity and bring it to all aspects of life.*

Modern applications of the general concept of mindfulness have built on both traditional skills of meditation and have also developed unique nonmeditative approaches to this human process of being mindful. A useful fundamental view is that mindfulness can be seen to consist of the important dimensions of the self-regulation of attention and a certain orientation to experience as Bishop and colleagues (2004) have proposed: (1) "the self-regulation of attention so that it is maintained on immediate experience, thereby allowing for increased recognition of mental events in the present moment" and (2) "a particular orientation toward one's experiences in the present moment, an orientation that is characterized by curiosity, openness, and acceptance." In the Dialectical Behavior Therapy approach, mindfulness has been described as "the intentional process of observing, describing, and participating in reality, nonjudgmentally, in the moment, and with effectiveness" (Dimidjian and Linehan, 2003a, 2003b). These and other authors acknowledge that mindfulness may also result in common outcomes, such as patience, nonreactivity, self-compassion, and wisdom. In Acceptance and Commitment Therapy, mindfulness "can be understood as a collection of related processes that function to undermine the dominance of verbal networks, especially involving temporal and evaluative relations. These processes include acceptance, defusion, contact with the present moment, and the transcendent sense of self" (Fletcher and Hayes, 2006).

A recent synthetic study of numerous existing questionnaires regarding mindfulness (Baer et al., 2006) reveals five factors that seemed to cluster from independently created surveys: (1) non-reactivity to inner experience (e.g., I perceive my feelings and emotions without having to react to them); (2) observing/noticing/attending to sensations, perceptions, thoughts, feelings (e.g., I remain present with sensations and feelings even when they are unpleasant or painful); (3) acting with awareness/(not on) automatic pilot/concentration/nondistraction (e.g., I (do not) break or spill things because of carelessness, not paying attention, or thinking of something else); (4) describing/labeling with words (e.g., I can easily put my beliefs, opinions, and expectations into words); (5) nonjudgmental of experience (e.g., I (do not) tell myself I shouldn't be thinking the way I'm thinking).

All of these, except for observing, were found to be the most statistically useful and reliable constructs in considering an operational definition of mindfulness. They seemed to reveal four relatively independent facets of mindfulness. Observing was found present more robustly among college students who meditated regularly. Observation was considered a learnable skill. Future research needs to clarify it as an independent facet. For now we will maintain observation in the five facets that Baer and colleagues delineated as we explore the nature of mindfulness and the brain.

At this point in the scientific endeavor to operationalize a clear definition for mindful awareness, the most parsimonious approach will be to build on the cumulative wisdom of the breadth of practitioners and researchers in the field. This will be our framework for exploring the ways in which this form of mindful awareness may involve the social neural circuitry of the brain as mindfulness promotes a form of internal attunement.

AWARENESS OF THE MIND ITSELF

Ultimately the practices that develop mindful ways of being enable the individual to perceive the deeper nature of how the mind functions. Though there are many ways to cultivate mindful awareness, each of them develops an awareness of the faculties of the mind, such as how we think, feel, and attend to stimuli. Mindfulness meditation, as one example, is thought to be especially important for the training of attention and the letting go of a strict identification with the activities of the mind as being the full identity of the individual.

Mindful awareness practices, or "MAPs" as we call them at the Mindful Awareness Research Center at UCLA (www.marc.ucla.edu), can be found in a wide variety of human activities. Historically, various practices have been developed for literally thousands of years in the forms of mindfulness meditation, yoga, Tai chi, and Qigong. In each of these activities, the practitioner is focusing the mind in a very specific way on moment-to-moment experience.

In almost all contemplative practices, for example, there is an initial use of the breath as a focal point in which to center the mind's attention. Because of this commonality of the breath across cultural practices, we'll be discussing the possible significance of breath awareness for the overall processes of the mindful brain. Mindful awareness is a human capacity not limited to one religious or contemplative practice, but practiced by and available to the full spectrum of our human family.

Mindfulness enables us to not only refine our awareness of the present moment, it opens an important window of the mind to come to know itself.

Mindful awareness involves awareness of awareness.

This reflection on the nature of one's own mental process is a form of "metacognition" in which "meta" signifies something reflected onto itself: thinking about thinking in the broadest sense. When we have "meta-awareness" this indicates "awareness of awareness." Whether we are engaging in yoga or centering prayer, sitting and sensing our breathing in the morning or doing Tai chi at night, each MAP develops this capacity to be aware of awareness.

Awareness of awareness is one aspect of what we can consider a form of reflection. In this way, mindful awareness involves reflection on the inner nature of life, on the events of the mind that are emerging, moment by moment.

COAL AND KIND AWARENESS

In addition to this reflective awareness of awareness in the present moment, mindfulness has the qualities that I describe with my patients using the acronym "COAL": we approach our here-and-now experience with curiosity, openness, acceptance, and love.

Imagine this situation. Let's say you've stubbed your toe badly and feel the intensity of the pain. Okay, you may say, I am "mindful" of that pain. Now if you say inside your head "What an idiot I was for stubbing my toe!" you can be sure that the suffering you'll experience will be greater than the pain you have emanating from your toe. You are aware of the pain, but are not filled with the COAL mind-set. In this case your brain actually creates more suffering by amplifying the intensity of the pain and belittling you for having the accident. This is all the difference between intensifying the distress versus coming to feel the pain without suffering.

Diane Ackerman told the story at our Mind and Moment gathering of poets, practitioners, and psychotherapists about a time when she had an accident in Japan and nearly died. She had been traversing down a cliff to study some rare birds on a small island and fell, breaking several ribs and being barely able to breathe. Her description of the event (Ackerman et al., 2006) reveals how she approached the moment-to-moment encounter with curiosity, openness, acceptance, and love. This mind-set enabled her to learn from the event, to gather the internal strength she needed to hold on, literally, and to not only survive in spite of the accident, but to thrive because of it. ·

This distinction between awareness with COAL and just paying attention with preconceived ideas that imprison the mind ("I shouldn't have hit my foot: I'm so clumsy." "Why did I fall off this cliff? What is wrong with me!") is the difference that makes all the difference.

This is the difference between being aware and being mindfully aware.

Cultivating mindful awareness requires that we become aware of awareness *and* that we be able to notice when those "top-down" preconceptions of shoulds and ought-tos are choking us from living mindfully, from being kind to ourselves. Top-down refers to the way that our memories, beliefs, and emotions shape our "bottom-up" direct sensation of experience. Kindness to ourselves is what gives us the strength and resolve to break out of that top-down prison and approach life's events, planned or unplanned, with curiosity, openness, acceptance, and love.

But can we actually cultivate such love for ourselves? Research into mindful awareness suggests that we can. Our approach to mindfulness as a form of relationship with oneself may hold a clue as to how this is accomplished. With mindfulness seen as a form of intrapersonal attunement, it may be possible to reveal the mechanisms by which we become our own best friend through mindful practice. Would you treat your best friend with kindness or hostility? Attunement is at the heart of caring relationships of all sorts: between parent and child, teacher and student, therapist and patient/client, lovers, friends, and close professional colleagues.

With mindful awareness, we can propose, the mind enters a state of being in which one's here-and-now experiences are sensed directly, accepted for what they are, and acknowledged with kindness and respect. This is the kind of interpersonal attunement that promotes love. And this is, I believe, the intrapersonal attunement that helps us see how mindful awareness can promote love for oneself.

Interpersonal relationships have been shown to promote emotional longevity, helping us achieve states of well-being and medical health (Anderson and Anderson, 2003). I am proposing here that mindful awareness is a form of self-relationship, an internal form of attunement, that creates similar states of health. This may be the as yet unidentified mechanism by which mindfulness promotes well-being.

MEDICAL APPLICATIONS

Sensing the profound importance of this power of mindfulness, Jon Kabat-Zinn began a project nearly thirty years ago to apply these ancient ideas in a modern medical setting. What began as an inspiration during a silent retreat led to Kabat-Zinn's approaching the medical faculty at the University of Massachusetts Medical Center where he taught. Could he take on the patients whose situations could no longer be helped by conventional medical interventions? Could he add anything at all to the recovery of those patients who were treated conventionally? Glad to have a place where these individuals might find some relief, the medical faculty agreed and the beginnings of the Mindfulness-Based Stress Reduction (MBSR) clinic were initiated (Kabat-Zinn, 1990, 1995).

The MBSR program brought the ancient practice of mindfulness to individuals with a wide range of chronic medical conditions from chronic back pain to psoriasis. Kabat-Zinn and colleagues, including his collaborator Richard Davidson at the University of Wisconsin in Madison, were ultimately able to demonstrate that MBSR training could help reduce subjective states of suffering and improve immune function, accelerate rates of healing, and nurture interpersonal relationships and an overall sense of well-being (Davidson et al., 2003).

MBSR has now been adopted by hundreds of programs around the world. Research (Grossman et al., 2004) has demonstrated that physiological, psychological, and interpersonal improvements occur in a variety of patient populations. With these consistent findings being so robust, and a rising interest in mindful awareness practices, it wasn't surprising that my own field of mental health would take note and integrate the essence of mindfulness as a basis for approaching individuals with psychiatric disorders.

DISCERNMENT AND MENTAL HEALTH IMPLICATIONS

Mindfulness has influenced a wide range of approaches to psychotherapy with new research revealing significant improvements in various disorders with reduction in symptoms and prevention of relapse (Hayes, Strosahl, and Wilson, 1999; Linehan, 1993; Parks, Anderson, and Marlatt, 2001; Marlatt and Gordon, 1985). Studies on depression (Mayberg, 2005) reveal that mindfulness techniques can alleviate symptoms of depression and lead to improvements in brain functioning that balance previously abnormal neural functioning. Mindfulness can also prevent relapse in cases of chronic depression in Segal, Williams, and Teasdale mindfulness-based cognitive therapy. (Segal, Williams, and Teasdale, 2002; Segal, Williams, Teasdale, and Kabat-Zinn, 2007). Similarly, mindfulness has been used as an essential part of the treatment of borderline personality disorder in Marsha Linehan's creative and effective Dialectical Behavior Therapy (DBT) (Linehan, 1993). Relapse prevention in individuals with substance abuse is also a part of the skills taught by Marlatt and colleagues (2001). The principles of mindfulness are also inherent in the application of contemporary behavior analysis in Steven Hayes's Acceptance and Commitment Therapy (ACT) (Hayes, 2004). One of the first studies to demonstrate that psychotherapy can alter the function of the brain utilized mindfulness principles in the treatment of individuals with obsessive-compulsive disorder (Baxter et al., 1992). In the past five years, several books (Hayes et al., 2004; Segal, Williams, and Teasdale, 2002; Germer et al., 2005) have been published that review the use of mindfulness and acceptance in the psychotherapy of a wide range of conditions from which people suffer, from eating disorders to anxiety, posttraumatic stress, and obsessive-compulsive disorders.

The general idea of the clinical benefit of mindfulness is that the acceptance of one's situation can alleviate the internal battle that may emerge when expectations of how "life should be" do not match how "life is." Being mindful entails sensing what is—even sensing your judgments—and noticing that these sensations, these images, feelings, and thoughts, come and go. If you have a COAL stance, the rest takes care of itself.

There is no particular goal, no effort to "get rid" of something, just the intention to be—and specifically, to experience being in the moment as one lets go of grasping on to judgments and goals.

Emerging from this reflective COAL mindful way of being is a fundamental process called "discernment" in which it becomes possible to be aware that your mind's activities are not the totality of who you are.

Discernment is a form of disidentification from the activity of your own mind: as you sift through your mind (being aware of sensations, images, feelings, and thoughts) you come to see these activities of the mind as just waves on the surface of the mental sea. From this deeper place within your mind, this internal space of mindful awareness, you can just notice the brainwaves at the surface as they come and go. This capacity to disentangle oneself from the chatter of the mind, to discern that these are "just activities of the mind," is liberating—and for many, revolutionary. At its essence, this discernment is how mindfulness may help alleviate suffering.

Discernment also gives us the wisdom to interact with each other with more thoughtfulness and compassion. As we develop kindness toward ourselves, we can be kind to others. By getting beneath our automatic mental habits, we are freed to engage with each other with a deeper sense of connection and empathy.

The clinical mental health implications of mindfulness have been explored in great detail in a number of texts and special journal editions that offer an excellent set of chapters and articles discussing various research and practical applications for aspects of mindfulness in psychotherapy. So this is not the goal here. Instead we'll be exploring the possible underlying neural mechanisms of mindful awareness that enable it to promote such a profoundly important sense of relief from suffering in our daily lives and in clinical practice. These mechanisms, as we've discussed, may be proposed to involve the social circuits of the brain that enable a sense of love and concern to develop for oneself. This intrapersonal attunement may help us understand the deeply transformative nature of mindfulness in our lives.

WHY THE MINDFUL BRAIN?

Why turn to the brain to explore mindfulness?

By exploring potential mechanisms in the brain that correlate with mindfulness, it becomes possible to see the connection between our common everyday view of mindfulness and the clinical use of reflective mindful awareness in medical and mental health practices. I propose that these sometimes intermixed modern uses of the term "mindfulness," while quite distinct in practice, actually share common neural pathways. Illuminating these neural mechanisms associated with cognitive and reflective mindfulness might then assist us in expanding our scientific understanding further, opening the doors for asking specific testable questions. Such neural insights may also shed light on how to design and implement practical applications of mindfulness in ways we haven't yet imagined. By revealing the ways in which mindfulness harnesses our social neural circuitry, we may be able to extend our understanding of its impact on physiological and psychological well-being.

Another important dimension of looking toward the mindful brain is that by understanding the neural mechanisms beneath mindful awareness, we may be in a better position to identify its universal human qualities and make it more accessible and acceptable to a broader audience. We all share the brain in common. Can you imagine a world in which this health-promoting, empathy-enhancing, executive-attention developing, self-compassion nurturing, affordable, and adaptable mental practice was made available in everyone's life?

We so need the wisdom of reflection in our individual and collective lives.

MINDFULNESS AND INTEGRATION

Why would mindfulness and secure attachment have similar outcomes? This question drove me to dive deeply into the nature of mindfulness to understand what they could share as common mechanisms.

The outcome measures for studies of secure attachment and the relationship between child and parent had markedly overlapping findings with those for mindful awareness practices. I found, too, that many of the basic functions that emerged in these two seemingly different entities were associated with a certain region of the brain, the middle areas of the prefrontal cortex just behind the forehead. These functions include regulating your body, balancing your emotions, attuning to others, modulating fear, responding flexibly, and exhibiting insight and empathy. Two other functions of this prefrontal region—being in touch with intuition and morality—had not been studied in attachment work but did seem to be an outcome of mindful awareness practices.

The proposal that my colleagues and I had made earlier (Schore, 2003a and 2003b, 1994; Cozolino, 2002; Siegel, 1999; Siegel and Hartzell, 2003; Solomon and Siegel, 2003) was that the relationships of secure attachment between parent and child, and the effective therapeutic relationship between clinician and patient/client, each promoted the growth of the fibers in this prefrontal area.

Prefrontal function is integrative. What this means is that the long lengths of the prefrontal neurons reach out to distant and differentiated areas of the brain and body proper. This linkage of differentiated elements is the literal definition of a fundamental process called "integration." For many reasons discussed elsewhere (Siegel, 1999, 2001, 2006), integration can be seen as the underlying common mechanism beneath various pathways leading to well-being.

How does attunement promote integration?

When relationships between parent and child are "attuned," a child is able to "feel felt" by a caregiver and has a sense of stability in the present moment. During that here-and-now interaction, the child feels good, connected, and loved. The child's internal world is seen with clarity by the parent, and the parent comes to resonate with the child's state. This is attunement.

Over time, this attuned communication enables the child to develop the regulatory circuits in the brain—including the integrative prefrontal fibers—that give them a source of resilience as they grow. This resilience takes the forms of the capacity for self-regulation and engaging with others in empathic relationships. Here we see that interpersonal attunement—the fundamental characteristic of what is called a "secure attachment"—leads to the empirically proven outcome measures we described above.

This list of nine prefrontal functions also seemed to overlap with what I was coming to learn about mindfulness practice. I presented this idea for the first time publicly to Jon Kabat-Zinn on a discussion panel (Ackerman et al., 2005) with much trepidation and excitement. I was not a meditator and knew no one in the mindfulness field. What if these ideas were a delusion, a fantasized hope for similarity that was way off the mark? Could it be plausible that an intrapersonal-form attunement of mindful awareness actually promoted the growth of these integrative middle prefrontal regions? Could this be the shared mechanism underneath the seemingly common outcome measures between mindfulness and secure attachment?

Fortunately, Jon Kabat-Zinn confirmed the accuracy of the observation of these as outcome measures. He went on to extend the idea that this list is not just about research-verified outcomes, but it is the process of mindful living itself. In fact, one can examine being mindful through a step-by-step immersion in each of these nine functions (Siegel, 2008).

In this exploration into the mind we examine what in the world mindful awareness, secure attachment, and prefrontal brain function could have in common.

As we'll see, much of the research on mindfulness meditation examines the attentional processes that are thought to be involved in this training of awareness. But if we apply the emerging findings of social neuroscience (Cozolino, 2006; Goleman, 2007) to a new understanding of mindfulness as self-relational, could these existing neural studies perhaps be seen in a new light? What would intrapersonal attunement correlate with on a scan? How would we picture the neural associations with "being your own best friend"? What would learning to befriend yourself feel like? And how could we approach helping others, and ourselves, in perhaps slightly new ways if we conceived of mindfulness as a way of having an attuned relationship—with your self?

"BRAIN" AND "MIND"

Whenever you see me write about "the brain" please remember that I always mean "the brain as an integrated part of the whole body." This reality changes the way we think about the relationship of "brain" to "mind."

Because the mind itself is both embodied and relational, our brains actually can be considered the social organ of the body:

our minds connect with each other via neural circuitry in our bodies that is hardwired to take in each others' signals.

To examine the relationship of the mind (regulation of the flow of energy and information) to the brain (neural connections and their complex patterns of firing), we need to be careful of certain preconceived ideas that might restrict our understanding and bias our thinking. The timing and location of neural activation correlate with the timing and characteristics of mental activity. If I show you a photograph and can monitor your brain's activity in a functional scanner, we'll see activation (usually increased blood flow in a functional MRI scan or electrical activity in an EEG) in the posterior part of your brain. The most accurate thing we can then say is that occipital lobe firing correlates with visual perception.

Why not say the neural activity created the visual perception? If we make causal phrases like this, the erroneous idea is reinforced that the mind is only created by the brain. But isn't that true? If we are cognitively mindful here, we need to be open to the truth that seeing the picture actually created the neural firing. The directional arrow goes both ways: the mind can actually use the brain to create itself.

Without cognitive mindfulness, we'd miss this bidirectional point. When we examine the nature of our evolution as a species, for example, we find that in the last forty thousand years our species has changed by way of cultural evolution. Culture is the way that meaning is transferred among individuals and across generations with groups of people. How this energy and information flow shifts its patterns across time is what cultural evolution involves. This reality of how we've changed as a species involves not the genetically driven evolution of our brains, but the *mental* evolution of how we collectively pass energy and information among each other across generations. This is the evolution of the mind, not the brain.

In fact, one can see that for the mind (regulation of the flow of energy and information) to occur, it needs to harness the activity of the brain.

The mind uses the brain to create itself.

I know this may seem different from what you may have read from other views. But this perspective actually is consistent with the scientific state of our understanding of how mind and brain are related to each other. There is no need to try to simplify the dimension of one reality into that of another. Mind is not "just" brain activity. Energy and information flow happens in a brain within the body and it happens within relationships.

To visualize this perspective we can say that "the mind rides along the neural firing patterns in the brain" and realize that this riding is a correlation with bidirectional causal influences.

Relationships among people involve the flow of energy and information, and thus utilize these riding patterns along neural firing as well. This interconnection among brain, mind, and relationships will be a triangle of reality that we'll be returning to again and again.

Here is an important point: relationships shape energy and information flow—as is happening now through these words in your mind. But the brain's activity also directly shapes how energy and information flow is regulated. Right now your brain may be activating certain firing patterns that distract you from paying attention to the reading. This would impair your ability to be mindfully aware at this moment in time. A friend may come into the room and also distract you, shaping how energy and information flow—the focus of your attention—is occurring at this moment.

In this way, we can imagine a *"triangle of human experience"* in which the three points represent mind, brain, and relationships. None of these three are reducible to the others. In fact, one can sense that the arrows of influence go in all directions—a tridirectional flow. The mind is how we regulate energy and information flow. The brain embeds the pathways of energy and information flow. And relationships are the way we share energy and information flow. This triangle represents three aspects of the one reality of human experience. A healthy life entails a coherent mind, integrated brain, and attuned relationships.

Attention to the present moment, one aspect of mindful awareness, can be directly shaped by our ongoing communication with others, and from the activities in our own brains. Indeed, the biggest challenges to being present are the patterns of activation in our brains we call "top-down" influences that continually bombard us with neural firing and mental chatter, keeping us from showing up in the moment. Mindful awareness is one way to promote a healthy triangle of our human lives in mind, brain, and relationships. As we move forward in our journey, we'll explore how we can be influenced by these neural patterns as the mind reaches toward being aware in the moment.

REFLECTION IN CLINICAL PRACTICE: BEING PRESENT AND
CULTIVATING THE HUB OF THE MIND'S WHEEL OF AWARENESS
The implications of our journey into the mindful brain point to the importance of our own reflective presence as individuals. Whether we are teachers or clinicians or everyday people, the ways in which we help others grow will be directly shaped by our own mindful presence. We can engage in "mindful practice" (R. Epstein, 1999) in the medical professions to create in ourselves a state of reflection and emotional availability that is at the heart of effective clinical work.

Mindful awareness can become a fundamental part of the mental health effort of psychotherapy to improve people's lives and reduce mental suffering in both direct and indirect ways (Germer et al., 2005; M. Epstein, 1995). Some approaches use formal mindfulness meditation techniques, such as MBSR (Kabat-Zinn, 1990) and MBCT (Segal et al., 2002), while others use applications of mindfulness skills such as ACT (Hayes, 2004) and DBT (Linehan, 1993). In these approaches the availability and empathy of the therapist that emerge with the therapist's own mindful presence may be a common source of healing in psychotherapy across the various "schools" and specific orientations. These may be considered the indirect effects of a mindful therapist on the patient's experience. Such indirect impacts may be seen to emerge from the empathic availability of the clinician to be mindfully present for whatever arises in the shared attentional field of the therapy experience. But teaching mindfulness itself, within formal meditation or other skill-building exercises, can offer patients useful capacities that can transform their relationships with themselves, reduce suffering from symptoms, and create a new approach to life itself.

Direct application of mindfulness skills teaches people how to become more reflective. The overall idea of these approaches, as we've discussed, is that the various facets of mindful awareness are cultivated. Such practices enable individuals to jettison judgment and develop more flexible feelings as they come to approach what may previously have been mental events they tried to avoid or to which they had intense aversive reactions. Becoming nonreactive and developing equanimity in the face of stressors support the view of mindfulness directly shaping the self-regulatory functions of the brain by promoting reflection of the mind.

Mindfulness is a teachable skill. In many ways this learning parallels the idea of mindsight: our capacity to see the mind in ourselves, and in others. Developing the circuits of mindsight, as with mindful awareness, can be done through reflective dialogues and skill building.

Reflective dialogues are the ways in which we focus our mutual attention on the nature of the mind itself within conversations with each other. As we use words to illuminate the mind, the linguistic representations serve as a finger pointing to the important dimension of our internal lives and develop our capacity for mindsight (see Siegel, 1999; Siegel, in press). Describing and labeling these mental events with words is a facet of mindfulness that these reflective dialogues can directly foster. Research has shown the capacity to label seems to balance the arousal of the right hemisphere with the activity of the left to create a more flexible integrated state.

As reflective dialogue becomes internalized, the individual can develop a new source of insight into her own mind. Life is transformed when mindsight is developed: being able to "be" with whatever arises is greatly helped by being able to "see" that what is arising is in fact a transient activity of the mind itself, not some fixed entity that can take over the person's life. Sometimes words can be of great help in setting the stage for seeing this dynamic and nonverbal world of the mind. These dialogues may be of central importance in helping children in families and schools and patients in therapy develop the reflective thinking needed to sense the mind itself. When offered with mindful learning principles (Langer, 1989, 1997, 2000) in mind—with the state of the learner, the conditional nature of learning, and the sensitivity to contexts and distinctions as a part of the dialogue—then reflective conversations can create new states of mindful awareness. As we help each other grow toward this open and receptive state, we can create the collective internal and interpersonal worlds of a reflective and awakened mind.

Dr. Peter Levine, author of *Waking the Tiger: Healing Trauma: The Innate Capacity to Transform Overwhelming Experiences*, asks the compelling question: What do meditation, sex, death, and trauma have in common, and how are they all related to enlightenment? Explaining his discoveries from decades of study, Dr. Levine provides compelling evidence about the interrelated nature of trauma and spiritual states, noting that the very brain structures that are central to experiencing trauma also mediate "mystical" and "spiritual" states. In a series of fascinating connections rooted in clinical research and science, he also uses animal behavior to analyze the nature of human trauma and spirituality.

Trauma and Spirituality[1]

PETER LEVINE, PH.D.[2]

If you bring forth that which is within you,
Then that which is within you
Will be your salvation.
If you do not bring forth that which is within you,
Then that which is within you
Will destroy you. —the Gnostic Gospels

In working with traumatized individuals for nearly forty years, I have been struck by the intrinsic and wedded relationship between trauma and spirituality. From my earliest experiences with clients suffering from a daunting array of crippling symptoms, I have been privileged to witness profound and authentic transformations. As these individuals mastered the traumas that had haunted them—emotionally, physically, and psychologically—unexpected "side effects" appeared. Seemingly out of nowhere, these surprises included ecstatic joy, exquisite clarity, effortless focus, and an all-embracing sense of oneness. In addition, my clients described deep and abiding experiences of compassion, peace, and wholeness. While many of these individuals realized the classic goals of enduring personality and behavioral changes, the transcendent "side effects" were simply too potent and robust to overlook. I have been compelled to follow these exciting and elusive enigmas with wonder and curiosity for many decades.

For this chapter, I've elected to chronicle this mysterious journey of inquiry: a passage which has been clinical, scientific, and personal (including an exploration of diverse spiritual traditions). About two months after the lunar landing in 1969, an unexpected event occurred that changed my worldview, in a way that seemed no less significant to me than the images of the Earth seen perched upon the moon's horizon. A chance encounter initiated an exploration into the nature of how instinctual reactions lie at the root of human trauma. It also brought to light the evolution of a therapeutic methodology.[3] This approach enrolled the organic processes of invigorating resilience and restoring natural equilibrium. It promoted self-healing and catalyzed transformations, which could be described as "spiritual."

This story began when a psychiatrist, aware of my keen interest in the nascent new fields of stress and mind/body healing, referred one of his patients to me. "Nancy," who had been suffering from frequent migraines, hyperthyroidism, and fatigue, was also plagued by chronic pain[4] and debilitating PMS. Her difficult life was further diminished by severe panic-anxiety attacks and "agoraphobia" that kept her tied to home.

I had been developing some body-oriented relaxation/stress-reduction procedures that the psychiatrist thought might be beneficial to her.[5] They were not. On the contrary, they led her straight into a major panic attack. At first I had helped her become aware of, and then learn to release, her chronically tense neck muscles. She seemed to be relaxing deeply. Her heart rate dropped and her (shallow) breathing deepened. However, moments later she became extremely agitated; her heart rate shot up, pounding wildly, to about 150 beats per minute. Her breath was rapid and she was gasping erratically. Then, abruptly, she froze in terror. As I watched helplessly, her face turned deathly white, her fingers icy blue. She appeared paralyzed and barely able to breathe. Her heart seemed to almost stop, dropping precipitously to about 50 beats per minute.[6] Fighting my own impending panic, I was at a loss as to what to do.

"I'm dying; don't let me die," Nancy pleaded in a small, taut voice. "Help me, help me . . . please don't let me die." Suddenly, in my mind's eye, a dream-like image appeared. A crouching tiger, preparing to strike, materialized out of the far wall of the room. "Run, Nancy . . . a tiger is chasing you," I commanded without thinking. "Climb those rocks and escape." Bewildered by my own outburst, I gazed in amazement as Nancy's legs began to tremble, then undulate in what appeared to be spontaneous running movements. Her whole body started shaking, first convulsively, then more softly. As the shaking subsided (over the better part of an hour), she experienced a feeling of peacefulness that, in her words, "held her in warm, tingling waves."

Later, Nancy reported that during the session she had seen nightmarish images of herself as a four-year-old child, struggling to escape the grasp of doctors who held her down in order to administer ether anesthesia for a "routine" tonsillectomy. Until that moment, she recounted, this event had been "long forgotten." To my utter amazement these unusual gyrations turned Nancy's life around. Many of her symptoms improved significantly and some disappeared altogether. The panic attack that occurred during the session was her last, and there were also dramatic improvements in her chronic fatigue, migraines, and menstrual symptoms (which I noted while following her for two more years until her graduation). In addition, she reported that she "felt more alive and happier than [she] could remember."

OBSERVATION

To acquire knowledge, one must study;
but to acquire wisdom, one must observe. —*Marilyn vos Savant*
(*"Highest IQ" since 1986, Guinness Book of World Records*)

The astonishing event with Nancy initiated a search that turned into my life's work. I was struck, of course, by the dramatic abatement of her symptoms, the intensity of her positive feelings, and her sense of aliveness and wholeness. I was also surprised by my "hallucination" and gripped by a curiosity about its effects on her physiological responses. I recognized that my vision, which prompted the spontaneous command for Nancy to run, was informed by some study material on predator/prey encounters from a class I was attending at that time. This zoology class in comparative animal behavior had been taught from the perspective of evolutionary biology and ethology (the scientific observation of animals in their natural environments). Simultaneously, I was developing a keen interest in brain physiology, most particularly those areas involved with stress and the autonomic nervous system. I realized I needed to learn more in order to make sense of Nancy's death-like descent, rapid recovery, and improbable transformation. I began a journey of a thousand steps by ensconcing myself deep in the musty stacks of the graduate library, learning what animal behavior and brain physiology might suggest about such vigorous resilience.

In the investigation that followed, I came across two formative scientific papers that laid a foundation for the dual pillars of my inquiry: naturalistic observation and the physiology of transcendent states. The first article was a transcript of the acceptance speech of the ethologist Nikolas Tinbergen, recipient of the 1973 Nobel Prize in medicine and physiology.[7] Tinbergen, whose life's work was to pioneer the observation of animals in their natural environments, implored scientists to observe human behaviors as they occurred naturally (as opposed to under the "controlled" conditions of the laboratory). As I continued to see other trauma sufferers in the years following Nancy, I was inspired to hold to this essential principle of "raw" observation of peoples' bodies. It echoed the message of my childhood baseball hero, Yogi Berra (the catcher for the New York Yankees, circa 1950s), who quipped, "You can observe a lot just by looking." And so, I did just that.

Because the formal diagnosis of trauma, as Post Traumatic Stress Disorder (PTSD in the *Diagnostic and Statistical Manual of Mental Disorders III)*, was still over a decade away, I didn't have a preformulated set of pathological criteria to distract me. I was freer to observe in the tradition of Tinbergen and the ethologists. From this vantage point, and without a premeditated list of symptoms, I was able to monitor my clients' bodily reactions and self-reports as I participated in their transformative process of healing. I began to recognize that as a group, they were manifesting physiological responses similar to reactions of the animal prey that I had been reading about. Observations of animals and discussions with ethologists[8], veterinarians, zookeepers, and wildlife managers confirmed my hypothesis that these responses represented the resolution of stress following predator-prey encounters. The highly charged reactions included shaking, trembling, and dramatic changes in temperature, heart rate, and respiration. In both animals and humans, I was to infer that these involuntary physiological reactions restored their equilibrium and promoted a relaxed readiness, an aptitude that is cultivated in Zen and martial arts such as aikido. The physiological reactions deactivated the intense arousal associated with the survival actions of "fight or flight."

My clients frequently had endured decades of frozen suffering before being able to restore their equilibrium. With support and guidance, they were able to "discharge" and "thaw," releasing powerful "survival energies." In sorting through these types of involuntary, energetic, and deeply moving experiences, I realized that their reactions manifested what was right and normal—rather than what was wrong and pathological. In other words, they exhibited innate self-regulating and self-healing processes, similar to animals in the wild. And as the animals went on about their business after such discharge reactions, so too did my clients re-engage into life with renewed passion, appreciation, and acceptance.

In addition to my role as observer, I learned to engage my clients in becoming aware of their bodily sensations and then tracking them during these spontaneous reactions. In our shared efforts, my clients were consistently able to engage and transform their traumas. At the same time, they frequently touched into a variety of experiences that I learned to appreciate as spiritual encounters, such as Nancy's feelings of aliveness, joy, and wholeness. In moving toward an understanding of this intrinsic relationship between trauma ("survival energy") and spirituality, I was excited to come across the second formative article, published in the prestigious journal *Science*, by Roland Fisher. Together with the Tinbergen transcript, a surprising and unexpected tenet emerged: that spiritual experience is welded with our most primitive animal instincts.

TRANSCENDENTAL STATES

Your deepest presence is in every small contracting and expanding,
the two as beautifully balanced and coordinated as bird wings.

—Rumi, "Bird wings"

Roland Fischer's article, titled "A Cartography of the Ecstatic and Meditative States,"[9] described a schema for showing the association of various parasympathetic and sympathetic (autonomic-instinctual) activities with mystical and meditative experiences. While the details of his work are well beyond the scope of this short chapter, suffice it to say that I suspected his view of the psychophysiological underpinning of various mystical states paralleled the range of "transpersonal" experiences that my clients were encountering as they unwound and released their traumas.

Trauma represents a profound compression of ("survival") energy: energy that has not been able to complete its meaningful course of action. When in the therapeutic session, this energy is gradually released (the term I use is "titration") and then redirected, one observes (in a softer and less frightening form) the kinds of reactions I observed with Nancy. At the same time, the numinous qualities of these experiences consistently integrate into the personality structure. The ability to access the rhythmic release of this bound energy makes all the difference as to whether it will destroy or vitalize us.

Primitive survival responses engage extraordinary feats of focused attention and effective action. The mother who lifts the car off of her trapped child mobilizes vast (almost superhuman) survival energy. These same energies, when experienced through titrated body-sensing, can also open to feelings of ecstasy and bliss. The ownership of these primordial "oceanic" energies promotes embodied transformation and (as suggested in Fischer's methodology) the experience of "timelessness" and "presence" known in meditation as "the eternal now." In addition, it appears that the very brain structures that are central to the resolution of trauma are also pivotal in various "mystical" and "spiritual" states.

In the East, the awakening of Kundalini at the first (or "survival") chakra has long been known to be a vehicle for initiating ecstatic transformation. In trauma, a similar activation is provoked, but with such intensity and rapidity that it overwhelms the organism. If we can gradually access and reintegrate this energy into our nervous system and psychic structures, then the survival response imbedded within trauma can also catalyze authentic spiritual transformation. In a practical sense, gradual therapeutic movement in this direction provides a vital resource for helping people engage back into life after the devastation of trauma.

As I began to explore the relationship between trauma-transformation and the Kundalini experience, I searched for confirmation of this connection. Around that time I met a physician named Lee Sannella in Berkeley, California. He shared with me a large compilation of notes he had taken about individuals who were experiencing spontaneous "Kundalini awakenings." I was intrigued by how similar many of these reactions were to those of my clients. Dr. Sannella's notes formed the basis for his valuable book, *The Kundalini Experience: Psychosis or Transcendence?*[10] This phenomenon has been described by great contemporary adepts such as Gopi Krishna.[11] In addition, the book by C.G. Jung titled *The Psychology of Kundalini Yoga*[12] (based on a 1932 seminar) gives an erudite exposition but concludes, ironically, that Kundalini is unlikely to ever be experienced in the West. However, Jung goes on to say: "The life of feeling is that primordial region of the psyche that is most sensitive to the religious encounter." The essence of religious experience is an act of feeling the animating force—spiritus— within the lived encounter. When my clients experienced this *elan vital* surging forth from within them, it was not surprising that they also encountered aspects of the religious experience.

Over the years I had the opportunity to show some videos of my clients' sessions to Kundalini teachers from India. These were wonderful exchanges. The yoga masters, with genuine and disarming humility, seemed as interested in my observations as I was in their vast knowledge and intrinsic "knowing."

"Symptoms" frequently described in Kundalini awakenings may involve involuntary and spasmodic body movements, pain, tickling, itching, vibrations, trembling, hot and cold alternations, changed breathing patterns, paralysis, crushing pressure, insomnia, hypersensitivity to environment, synethesia, unusual or extremes of emotions, intensified sex drive, sensations of physical expansion, dissociation, and out-of-body experiences, as well as hearing "inner" sounds such as roaring, whistling, and chirping. These sensations associated with Kundalini awakenings are often more forceful and explosive than those I observed with my clients. As I developed my methodology (called Somatic Experiencing®[13]), I learned to help clients gradually "touch into" their bodily sensations so that they were rarely overwhelmed. In general, focusing inward and becoming curious about one's inner sensations allow people to experience a subtle inner shift, a slight contraction, vibration, tingling, relaxation, and sense of openness. I have named this alternation of feelings of dread, rage, or whatever one likes to avoid, and "befriending" one's internal sensations, *pendulation* (an intrinsic rhythm pulsing between the experienced polarities of contraction and expansion/openness). Once people learn to do this, "infinite" emotional pain begins to feel manageable and finite. This allows their attitude to shift from dread and helplessness to curiosity and exploration.

The mystical text, the Hermetic Kybalion, says, "Everything flows, out and in; everything has its tides; all things rise and fall; the pendulum-swing manifests in everything; the measure of the swing to the right is the measure of the swing to the left; rhythm compensates." The application of this perennial philosophy to trauma is the very principle that allows sensations and feelings which have previously overwhelmed people to be processed and transformed in the present. In doing this, trauma transformed can approach Kabalistic enlightenment.

TRAUMA, DEATH, AND SUFFERING

Yea, though I walk through the valley of the shadow of death,
I will fear no evil . . . —Psalm 23

It would be an error to equate trauma with suffering, and suffering in turn with transformation. At the same time, however, in virtually every spiritual tradition suffering is understood as a doorway to awakening. In the West, this connection can be seen in the biblical story of Job, and magnificently in the Twenty-third Psalm. It is found as the dark night of the soul in medieval mysticism, and of course in the passion of Christ. In Buddhism an important distinction is made between suffering and unnecessary suffering. According to the Buddha, "When touched with a feeling of pain, the ordinary person laments . . . becomes distraught . . . contracts . . . so he feels two pains . . . just as if they were to shoot a man with an arrow and, right afterward, were to shoot him with another . . . so that he would feel the pains of two arrows . . ." Trauma sufferers are so frightened of their bodily sensations that they recoil from feeling them. It is as though they believe that by feeling them they will be destroyed or at least it will make things worse. Hence they remain stuck. In this way, they shoot themselves with the second arrow. With support and guidance, however, they are able to gradually learn to befriend and transform their trauma-based sensations.

In several Eastern (Buddhist and Taoist) traditions, four pathways are said to lead to spiritual awakening (Pema Chödrön). The first is death. A second route to freedom from unnecessary human suffering can come from many years of austere meditative contemplation. The third gateway to liberation is through special forms of (tantric) sexual ecstasy. And the fourth portal is said, by these traditions, to be trauma. Meditation, Sex, Death, and Trauma, in serving as great portals, share a common element. They are all potential catalysts for profound surrender.

Evidence suggests that the physiological root of trauma occurs when the organism is overwhelmed and immobilized.[14] This occurred when the four-year-old Nancy was terrified and held down for her tonsillectomy. These death-like states lie at the root of trauma. The ability to feel the physical sensations of paralysis (without becoming overwhelmed) is the key in transforming trauma. When we are able to "touch into" that death-like void, even briefly (rather than recoil from it), the immobilization releases. In this way the second arrow of unnecessary suffering is eliminated. The "standing back" from fear allows the individual to emerge from the strangulation of trauma. As people "experience into" the paralysis sensations (in the absence of fear), they contact the "mini-deaths" which lie at the eye of the hurricane, at the very heart of trauma. This visitation is an opportunity to enter the rich portal of death. It is well known that many people who have had near death experiences (NDEs) undergo positive personality transformations. With a therapist's help, traumatized individuals are encouraged and supported to feel into the immobility/NDE states, liberating these primordial archetypal energies while integrating them into consciousness.

In addition, the "awe-full" states of horror and terror appear to be connected to the transformative states such as awe, presence, timelessness, and ecstasy. They share essential psychophysiological and phenomenological roots. For example, stimulating of the amygdala (the brain's smoke detector for danger and rage) can also evoke the experience of ecstasy and bliss.[15] This seems to support an approach that guides individuals through their awe-full feelings of fear and horror toward those of joy, goodness, and awe.

Newberg and his colleagues[16] have, in their seminal book, *Why God Won't Go Away*, brought together a vast amount of research on the brain substrates underlying a variety of different spiritual experiences. The application of this type of brain research to trauma transformation is a rich area worthy of further research and exploration.

REGULATION AND THE SELF
As Below, So Above   —*The Kabilyon*

The autonomic nervous system (ANS) gets its name from being a relatively autonomous[17] branch of the nervous system. Its basic, yet highly integrated function has to do with the regulation of energy states and the maintenance of homeostasis. The ANS is composed of two distinctly different branches.[18] Its sympathetic branch supports overall energy mobilization. If you are physically cold, perceive threat, or are sexually aroused, the sympathetic nervous system increases the metabolic rate and prepares you for action. The parasympathetic branch, on the other hand, promotes rest, relaxation, gestation, nurturance, and restitution of tissue and cellular function.

When the level of activation of the sympathetic branch of the autonomic nervous system is very low, we are apt to be feeling somewhat lethargic. At moderate levels of sympathetic activity, we are generally doing or preparing to do something active.[19] This level of arousal is usually experienced as being alert, as well as pleasurably excited. In this realm there is typically a smooth back-and-forth shifting between moderate levels of sympathetic and parasympathetic activity serving a balanced physiological state called homeostasis. I call this flexible, seesaw, shifting range of arousal, "relaxed alertness." The following drama on an uplands meadow illustrates this:

A herd of deer grazes in a forest clearing. A twig snaps.
Instantly, the deer are alert, ready to flee into the forest. Each
animal becomes still. Muscles tensed, they listen and sniff
the air, attempting to pinpoint the source of the sound (ori-
entation). Deeming it insignificant, they return to leisurely
chewing on their afternoon repast, cleaning and nurturing
their young, and warming themselves in the early morning
sun. Another stimulus sends the animals back into the state of
alertness and heightened vigilance, once again ready to flee or
fight. Seconds later, again having found no actual threat, the
deer again resume their former activity.

By watching the deer carefully through binoculars, one can sometimes witness the transition from the state of activated vigilance to one of normal, relaxed activity. When the animals' instinct determines that they are not in danger, they may begin to vibrate, twitch, and lightly tremble. This process begins with a very slight twitching or vibration in the upper part of the neck around the ears and spreads down into the chest, shoulders, and then finally down into the abdomen, pelvis, and hind legs. These little "tremblings" of muscular tissue are the organism's way of regulating extremely high states of nervous system activation toward relaxation and quiescence. The deer move through this rhythmic cycle dozens, perhaps hundreds, of times a day. This cycle, between sympathetic and parasympathetic dominance, occurs each time they are activated.[20] The animals move easily and rhythmically between states of relaxed alertness and tensed vigilance. And while I try to minimize "zoomorphism" (the wholesale attribution of animal characteristics to humans), it is not difficult to imagine the profound difference in people's lives when they are no longer "stuck" in traumatic hypervigilance but are deeply at home with their energy shifts. They know (not from their minds but from their whole organisms) that whatever they experience not only will pass, but will enrich their lives, adding energy, passion, and focus.

In mammals, this capacity for self-regulation is essential. It endows the animal with the capability to make fluid shifts in internal bodily states to meet changes in the external environment. Animals with developed orbito-frontal systems have evolved the capacity to switch between different emotional states. This ability (known as affect-regulation) allows animals to vary their emotions to appropriately match environmental demands. According to Schore and others, this highly evolved adaptive function is the basis for the core sense of self in humans.[21] These same circuits in the orbito-frontal cortex receive inputs from the muscles, joints, and viscera. The sensations that form the inner landscape of the body are mapped in the orbitofrontal portions of the brain.[22] Hence as we are able to change our body sensations we change the highest function of our brains. Emotional regulation (our rudder through life) comes about through embodiment.

EMBODIMENT

For in my flesh I shall see God. —Book of Job

Cry for the soul
that will not face the body as an equal place . . . —Dory Previn song

Traumatized people are fragmented and disembodied. The constriction of feeling obliterates shade and texture, turning everything into good/bad, black/white, for us or against us.

It is the unspoken hell of traumatization. In order to know who and where we are in space and to feel that we are vital-alive beings, subtleties are essential. Furthermore, it is not just acutely traumatized individuals who are disembodied; most Westerners share a less dramatic but still impairing disconnection from their inner sensate compasses. Given the magnitude of the primordial and raw power of our instincts, the historical role of the church and other cultural institutions in subjugating the body is hardly surprising.

In contrast, various (embodied) spiritual traditions have acknowledged the "baser instincts" not as something to be eliminated, but rather as a force in need of, and available for, transformation. In Vipassana meditation and various traditions of Tantric Buddhism (such as Kum Nye), the goal is "to manifest the truly human spiritual qualities of universal goodwill, kindness, humility, love, equanimity and so on."[23] These traditions, rather than renouncing the body, utilize it as a way to "refine" the instincts. The essence of embodiment is not in repudiation, but in living the instincts fully as they dance in the "body electric," while at the same time harnessing their primordial raw energies to promote increasingly subtle qualities of experience.[24]

As the song by Dory Previn suggests, mystical experiences that are not experienced in the body just don't "stick"; they are not grounded. Trauma sufferers live in a world of chronic dissociation. This perpetual state of disembodiment keeps them disoriented and unable to engage in the here-and-now. Trauma survivors, however, are not alone in being disembodied; a lower level of disembodiment is widespread in modern culture.

A distinction is made in the German language between the word "korper," meaning a physical body, and "leib," which translates into English as the "lived (or living) body." The term "lieb" reveals a much deeper generative meaning compared with the purely physical "korper" (not unlike "corpse"). A gift of trauma *recovery* is the rediscovery of the living, sensing, knowing body. The poet and writer D.H. Lawrence inspires with this reflection on the living, knowing body: "Our body is how we know that we are alive, alive to the depths of our souls and in touch somewhere with the vivid reaches of the cosmos."

Trauma sufferers, in their healing journeys, learn to dissolve their rigid defenses. In this surrender they move from frozen fixity to gentle thaw and free flow. In healing the divided self from its habitual mode of dissociation, they move from fragmentation to wholeness. In becoming embodied they return from their long exile in the desert of trauma. They come home to their bodies and know embodied life, as though for the first time. While trauma is hell on earth, its resolution may be a gift from the "gods."

T.S. Eliot seems to have grasped this hero's journey of awakening through deep exploration in his epic poem "Little Gidding":

We shall not cease from exploration
And the end of all our exploring
Will be to arrive where we started
And know the place for the first time.

Can optimism be learned? Does it actually change our health and mental condition and produce happiness? Dr. Suzanne Segerstrom, author of *Breaking Murphy's Law: How Optimists Get What They Want from Life—and Pessimists Can Too*, shares her research about practicing behavior, the relation between thoughts, behaviors, and emotions, and how to build a more satisfying, optimistic life. In the following excerpt, she explores the findings that, while optimism can be traced to one's nature, or genes, it can also be developed through the way we direct our attention and the way we choose to live our lives day to day.

Doing Optimism

Optimists, Pessimists, and Their Potential for Change

SUZANNE C. SEGERSTROM, PH.D.

I recently had cause to read some Web log ("blog") entries by people with broken legs, and I was struck by how many of the bloggers on the site struggled through recovery. Many of them were preoccupied with either under-ambitious or frankly pessimistic ideas about recovery from a broken leg. Are pessimists with broken legs doing themselves a disservice with their blogs? Would they recover faster if they focused less on the roadblocks to their recoveries? I feel that they would. Furthermore, I have reason to believe that if they used their diaries somewhat differently, they could actually start to reverse the self-fulfilling prophecies of low expectations, and that the most pessimistic of them might even benefit the most.

Optimism can be defined from the bottom up as a collection of thoughts (positive expectations for the future) and behaviors (persistence, directing energy toward goals, and the like). The consequences of optimism arise from this collection of individual thoughts and acts: when people have positive thoughts about their futures, they are more likely to pursue goals that will make those futures come true. The message of my book, *Breaking Murphy's Law*, is that positive thoughts improve lives when they lead to positive behaviors, and those positive behaviors lead to building resources. Positive thoughts seem relatively easy to define (though, as we shall see, they are somewhat harder to bring into being), but what are positive behaviors? In my mind, whether a behavior is positive or not depends on whether it builds one of the four fundamental categories of human resources: basic (strength, health, energy), social (relationships, intimacy), status (knowledge, ability, power), or existential (giving to others, being part of something larger than yourself, a relationship to the divine). If what you are doing builds a resource, then it is positive; if not, then it is neutral at best or possibly negative. And, as we shall see, building resources makes people happier, more satisfied with their lives, and perhaps even healthier. So, optimism is important insofar as it leads people to be more engaged, persistent, and motivated in their positive behaviors, which leads to resource growth, which leads to happiness.

Whether you can become more optimistic, happier, healthier, and the like depends on which statement is truer:

1. Optimism and happiness come primarily from genes, and although the leopard can get a dye job, it cannot change its spots.

2. Optimism and happiness come from your daily choices.

What if pessimism were nothing more than a habit that you could change?

Changing your thoughts, behaviors, and emotions just because you want to isn't all that easy. Ask anyone who's tried to get physically healthier by exercising more, eating better, or quitting smoking. Often people make several attempts at change before it sticks. Therapists who help people change their behavior, whether physical behavior like lack of exercise or emotional behavior like avoidance or passivity, know it's not just a matter of willpower, although being determined to change certainly helps. Fortunately, psychologists have developed techniques that help people make difficult changes, and as it turns out, these methods can also be used to change pessimistic thoughts and behaviors. I'm not suggesting you change your essential nature to reap the benefits of optimism, however. It's like trying to teach a pig to sing: disappointing for you and frustrating for the pig. Nonetheless, there is evidence to suggest you can develop a more optimistic attitude, and if your "nature" is really just your habitual attitudes, then changing your habits could actually change your nature.

THE HABIT OF OPTIMISTIC THINKING

Richard joined a study of whether people could increase their optimistic thoughts because he felt anxious and worried all the time. A decade away from retirement, he was already anticipating that it would be a personally and financially difficult transition. Certainly, attention to threats and defensive pessimism can be helpful, but only when they initiate action, and in Richard's case, his vision of retirement was so pessimistic that there was no incentive to act. Perversely, although his pessimism did not motivate him to do anything about retirement, he *felt* that his worry and rumination were going to help him, and he was wary of more optimistic thoughts, claiming that such thinking created dangerous complacency and illusory hopes. Richard was correct to be skeptical of fantasy. Fortunately, the research that he participated in was offering an experimental treatment to make people more optimistic, not to get them to indulge in fantasy. In fact, he was encouraged *not* to fantasize.

Fantasies have the opposite effect on motivation and action that optimism does. Fantasies encourage people to linger on a dream, whereas optimism encourages people to act to achieve it.[1] Optimism involves consideration of the *contrast* between what is now and what could be: an optimistic Charlie Brown might think about the fact that he hasn't yet introduced himself to the little red-haired girl, the fact that he wants to meet her, and the odds of a successful meeting. Fantasy, on the other hand, involves immersion in an enjoyable but entirely simulated future world that doesn't admit the contrast between what is and what could be. If you're not aware of that discrepancy, you have no motivation to reduce it. As a consequence, when people only visualize already having what they want, they often disengage from actually trying to get it. If Charlie Brown wants to meet the cute little red-haired girl, sitting around imagining what it would be like to hold her hand or planning their wedding doesn't get him very far.

Beliefs such as "I'll just be disappointed if I think too positively," "I'll overlook something and fail," or "If I think too positively, I won't work hard" are not going to get you very far either. These beliefs are patently not true (optimists are not disappointed, they pay adequate attention to potential problems, and they work harder than pessimists) and they obviously inhibit attempts to have more optimistic thoughts. Richard's therapist suggested alternative thoughts about optimism, because until Richard let go of his optimism-suppressing beliefs, there was little possibility of actually starting to envision a more positive future. Once he substituted optimism-supportive beliefs, such as "optimism can decrease inertia" and "optimism can give you something to work toward," he was able to imagine his ideal retirement and consider the steps he would need to take to get there. Eventually, Richard admitted that "wishful thinking is not all undesirable." Faint praise, to be sure, but it reflected real change in psychological functioning: when tested at the end of the program, he and his fellow optimism trainees had more positive thoughts, felt more capable of solving problems, and generated more creative solutions to a real problem-solving task than people who had not been through the program.[2]

In addition to undoing optimism-suppressing beliefs and learning to imagine a more positive future, good optimism training addresses automatic attention. Optimists are automatically more attentive to positive aspects of the environment than are pessimists. Although *automatic* seems to imply "uncontrollable," automaticity is merely a function of practice. You can play a piece on the piano without thinking about where your fingers are or hit a tennis ball without thinking about what your elbow is doing only after consciously practicing the action over and over. If you have a bad habit, like biting your fingernails, the cure is to consciously substitute a better habit (even clenching your fists will do) until it automatically overrides the bad habit. When someone like Richard worries and ruminates, he is essentially practicing thinking about the negative aspects of his future and ignoring the positive. As a consequence, he develops the habit of pessimism. To undo this habit in pessimistic people, optimism training instructs people to deliberately focus on the positive, much as a nail-biter might deliberately clench his fists rather than bite his nails.

One simple way to train attention to the positive is to keep a log of three good things that happen each day. It's pretty safe to say that everyone experiences at least three good things— even if they are just little things—every day. Not everyone pays attention to them, though. Those who don't unfortunately miss the motivating and inspiring aspects of their lives, not to mention reminders of their progress and even their resources. Here are three positive things listed by an optimism trainee: seeing a pretty flower, being told he did a good job, and getting a good night's sleep. These are signs of a beautiful environment, professional progress, and energetic renewal, which are all resources that can lead to greater life satisfaction. Noticing these signs every day can help people to realize that they have more resources than they were aware of and to feel different about their lives.

In fact, this attentional change is one of the things that can lead to long-term changes in happiness, potentially allowing a person to escape the hedonic treadmill, psychological immune system, and other mechanisms that bring people back to their set points. A large study compared the effectiveness of several different one-week exercises on happiness six months later. The exercises included thinking about a time in the past when you were at your best, identifying your personal strengths (such as gratitude, kindness, modesty, or curiosity), using strengths in new ways, expressing gratitude to someone you have never properly thanked, or writing down three good things that happened each day. All these exercises made people feel happier, but for the most part that happiness dissipated over time. The "three good things" exercise, though, actually increased happiness over time, so that people who did that exercise got happier and happier over six months.[3] Why? First, people who did that exercise were more likely to keep doing it after their mandatory week ended. Second, as they did that, they probably got better at it. That is, over time, their attentional *habits* became more optimistic. Third, noticing the positive probably helped energize motivation to behave positively, leading to an upward spiral of attention to one's resources (positive thoughts), motivation, positive behavior, and resource growth. A simple exercise, but one with complex, positive, and lasting effects.

OPTIMISM FOR EEYORE

For the true pessimist (or even the die-hard skeptic), changing thought habits from pessimistic to optimistic may not be as simple as retraining attitudes in the way Richard did. It's always easier to build on an existing foundation than to start from scratch, and so optimism training might be most effective for people who are already somewhat optimistic and want to expand or maximize that optimism and less effective for people who just don't feel that optimism is "them." I was in school with a couple of graduate students who were dedicated to being more positive in their attitudes, and I mean, they really worked at it. I'm sorry to say, however, that I don't think it ever really "took," because the positive veneer they put on seemed to be so easily shattered. One of them was on the verge of dropping out of graduate school whenever an obstacle or difficulty arose, which was—not atypically for difficult graduate study—about once a year. His friends and professors were pretty good at talking him down from the metaphorical ledge, but it was hard to see him as a positive or optimistic person down deep. Another problem both people had was that they were chronic giver-uppers who would start relationships or projects and abandon them a short while later. As a consequence, they failed to grow the kind of academic or social capital that you really need to keep you away from the ledge during graduate study.

Perhaps part of the problem is that being positive is not enough to get the entire optimism system working. Some evidence for the missing piece comes from studies that asked people to write journal entries about important situations in their lives. Many people think of a journal as a place to express their deepest thoughts and feelings, and there is interesting evidence that when people write about their deepest thoughts and feelings, a number of positive outcomes can ensue: better health, better immune function, better mood, and so on.[4] Not all people improve through expressing their deepest thoughts and feelings, however, and emotional expression might not be good for people when their deepest thoughts and feelings are pessimistic. Instead of progressing toward a meaningful understanding of those thoughts and feelings, pessimists might get mired in rumination and depression. Rather than celebrating a return to weight bearing or appreciating lessons learned by breaking a leg, pessimists are likely to dwell on the deficits they experience and dire predictions about their futures. Fortunately for pessimists, although it is the typical use of a journal, you don't have to use a journal to explore the deepest thoughts and feelings you already have. You can use a journal to create new habits of thinking.

One possibility is to use the journal to refocus on the possibility of a positive future, which is sort of the journal equivalent of noticing three good things because it gets you in the habit of thinking positively about the future. In one example, HIV-infected women wrote journal entries that focused on a future in which their treatment regimens were simple[5]—one pill daily, which would be a significant improvement over the complex regimen currently available. Although very effective in reducing mortality, the currently available medication regimen involves taking a large number of pills on a strict schedule, some on an empty stomach, some on a full stomach, and so on. A simpler treatment regimen would significantly decrease the logistic burden of controlling HIV infection. Pessimistic women who focused on this positive possibility became more optimistic over the four weeks during which they were writing the entries.

You can also use a journal to better self-regulate; that is, to be aware of your goals, to behave in a way that is consistent with your goals, and to explore ways to overcome obstacles. Imagining not only what you want but also how you are going to get it—that is, substituting "mental simulation" (a mental practice of the steps you're going to follow) for fantasy—activates the self-regulatory loop and actually increases the odds that you'll get what you want.[6] This way of using a journal should be particularly helpful for people who are not very optimistic and therefore don't already do this on their own and who might get mired in negative thoughts and feelings if they were to focus on expressing them. In this example, college freshmen either (1) wrote about their deepest thoughts and feelings (expression), (2) wrote about their problems and challenges in college and ways they could cope with them (self-regulation), or (3) wrote about trivial aspects of college life (experimental control). As it turned out, the self-regulation task, writing about how to cope with challenges, had the most beneficial effects. When it came to feeling better, people at all levels of optimism felt better if they did the self-regulation writing task rather than expressing their emotions or describing trivia.[7] Optimists' health benefited from both self-regulation and expression, but pessimists' health benefited only from self-regulation and not from expression. Pessimists who expressed themselves had just as many visits to the doctor for illness as pessimists who focused on trivial topics.

The most interesting thing about these journal studies is that they were most effective for people who were the most pessimistic. On one level, this is unsurprising. After all, you wouldn't expect to dramatically influence the optimism level of someone who was already relatively optimistic. On another level, however, it's encouraging. Sometimes it's easier to build on an existing strength than to remedy a deficit—a new exercise program will be easier for a person who is already somewhat fit than for a person who is entirely sedentary. In the case of improving positive expectations and self-regulation, however, it appears to be possible to build from the ground up. By writing about their goals, ambitions, and plans to get there, the pessimistic bloggers might smooth the path to their own recovery and literally standing on their own two feet.

CHANGE YOUR LIFE AND YOUR THOUGHTS WILL FOLLOW
The true diehard pessimist might still be skeptical that changing thoughts is possible for her. In fact, someone who is that pessimistic in general would be very likely to be pessimistic specifically about the possibility of change. Fortunately, you don't always have to believe in change for change to occur. I have seen a book entitled *Change Your Thoughts and Your Life Will Follow*. But what if the opposite were also possible? Can you change your life and have your thoughts—that is, optimism—follow?

Therapists who treat phobias see this all the time. People who have spent a lot of time and energy talking about their phobias without seeing any improvement can be especially pessimistic because they perceive themselves as untreatable. When I did my clinical internship, I treated a man named Jake who had developed an unusual phobia of hearing sirens. He worked in his home office near a busy thoroughfare, so he would hear sirens several times daily. Unlike those who fear dogs, spiders, or heights, he did not believe that the feared objects, the sirens, were going to hurt him, but he felt assailed by the noise. The more the sirens made him feel this way, the more upset he would be by subsequent sirens, which created an upward spiral of agitation. He took steps to eliminate the noise such as trying to soundproof his home office, but this only muffled the noise, and the failure to eliminate it made him feel more out of control. By the time he got to me, he had been to see several therapists and had tried our clinic only on the insistence of his family doctor, who had known another of his patients to improve there. As a consequence of his experiences, Jake felt quite pessimistic that I would be able to help him.

Fortunately for both Jake and me, I didn't need him to change the way he thought or felt about the sirens to help him get over his phobia. I only asked him to change the way he behaved. Instead of trying to avoid the sirens, I instructed him to try to hear as many sirens as loudly and as often as he could, even to the point of buying his daughter a toy ambulance with a siren (needless to say, siren toys had not been allowed in the house). That is, instead of avoiding sirens, he was now supposed to approach them.

Your thoughts, behaviors, and emotions are interrelated. The critical aspect of this constellation is that what you think, how you feel, and how you behave all influence each other. When Jake thought about how the sirens were both intolerable and uncontrollable, he naturally felt anxious and irritable. In turn, his anxious and irritable emotional state made him think and behave differently. Emotions have signal value, and feelings of fear, anger, anxiety, and irritability signal threat. As a consequence, thoughts and attention will naturally be focused on potential threats in the environment. Left to their own devices, the thoughts and emotions will naturally spiral upward, as they had for Jake.

Now recall that Jake had also acted to reduce the impact of the sirens on his environment by soundproofing his office and forbidding toys with sirens in the house. This is not a surprising consequence of anxiety—after all, the point of feeling fearful of a saber-toothed tiger is not to induce you to go up and pet it (you might die trying). Unfortunately, however, the behaviors that arise from anxiety often either prolong or even create the feared outcome. For example, people who are insecure in their relationships often try to reassure themselves and cement their relationships by doing things like frequently asking their partners if they love them. This can, however, be perceived as nagging or clinging and can actually put the partner off. When the partner backs off, insecurity-driven behavior increases and the relationship gets on a downward spiral. Another example is the nervous speaker who tries so hard to look relaxed that she comes off as stilted. In both cases, the behavior that was intended to alleviate the problem actually creates it.

Unfortunately, the kind of behavior that Jake was pursuing to control his anxiety—avoidance of sirens—virtually eliminated the mechanisms that could actually change his anxious thoughts and alleviate his emotional distress. However, getting him to pursue exposure to the very thing that made him anxious, done properly, could be an incredibly effective remedy. Why?

On a very basic level, we might define it as effective because it undoes the problematic behavior. The definition of phobia includes avoidance of the feared situation that impairs the person's ability to live his life. If you can eliminate avoidance, impairment is decreased by definition: a person with social phobia is now talking to people at parties, a person with agoraphobia is now going to the grocery store. This is the psychopathology version of a bottom-up definition: what you do is the nature of your problem.

Exposure can, however, produce more benefit than behavioral change, because feelings and thoughts are linked to behaviors. The more experience people have with the situations they fear, the more they realize that the imagined consequences are not likely to come to pass and, if they do, they are not as catastrophic as feared. They become less anxious and fearful in those situations, which makes anxious thoughts and behaviors less likely. As thoughts and feelings become less anxious and anxiety provoking, exposure to the situations becomes easier, leading to greater cognitive and emotional change: an upward spiral that leads to overcoming fear.

In essence, when using exposure therapy, therapists are sending patients out into feared situations to collect data. If the sirens went all day, would you really go crazy? One of my favorite training experiences as a therapist was a workshop with the British psychologist Paul Salkovskis, an expert in treating anxiety disorders. In the workshop we watched a video of Salkovskis collecting data on the hypothesis of a patient with anxiety that any atypical behavior (like having a panic attack) would cause people to gather, sneer, point, and so on. Salkovskis did this by taking his patient to the mall. The patient gathered data by watching while Salkovskis did a Monty Pythonesque silly walk right through the middle of the mall. (How many people gathered, sneered, pointed, and so on? Try it for yourself sometime.)

Trying to change your feelings by changing your behavior has two advantages. First, behavior is easier to change than thoughts or emotions. Emotions are notoriously difficult to change through an act of willpower. In fact, if emotions have signal value, the ability to change them at will would actually be a pretty big design flaw in the human self-regulatory machine. What good would it be to voluntarily stop the hair on the back of your neck from prickling if, as a consequence, you missed the fact that a saber-toothed tiger was about an inch from said neck? People's emotions are a little bit like the mercury in thermostats: they indicate how things are going and what needs to be done to change them. Fear tells you, you are about to get eaten by a saber-toothed tiger, and you should get the heck out.

Being able to change emotion at will would be something like being able to change the room temperature reading on the thermostat without actually changing the temperature in the room. This would be pretty stupid, because not only would you still be too hot (or too cold), but you would actually stop doing anything about it because the gauge said everything was okay. If you could turn off fear at will, you might end up as lunch.

If your therapist tells you, "Don't worry, be happy," find a new therapist (if for no other reason than trying to be happier actually makes it harder to feel happy). Find one who will teach you ways to change your behaviors to escape the downward spiral. Don't worry about the emotions. They will take care of themselves.

Second, when you target behavior, you don't have to believe in the possibility of cognitive and emotional change for change to occur. It helps, but it's not necessary. Over a period of weeks, Jake's attitude toward the sirens changed. By actively pursuing exposure, he found that just listening to the sirens was not intolerable after all; he could tolerate as much noise as they could produce. He felt more in control and able to cope, and his anxiety decreased. Jake reversed the downward spiral he had been on by taking control of the behavioral part of the spiral and letting thoughts and emotions come along for the ride.

Behavior change may also be the best route to the benefits of optimism because it does not require the adoption of thoughts that for some people may feel foreign. The truest route to optimism is to act like an optimist until the positive feedback loop of behaviors, resources, and thoughts kicks in and starts growing optimism from the bottom up. That is, if you really want to develop optimism, "fake it till you make it." People can learn to be more optimistic by acting as if they were more optimistic. In this case, that means being more engaged with and persistent in the pursuit of goals. What are your goals? What is important to you?

Make a list of your goals or write a description of what you want yourself and your life to look like in a few months or years. Every once in a while, look at it. In the self-regulation study, students wrote in their journals on only three occasions. For only five minutes on each occasion, they listed three things that they could do to help them deal with the problems and challenges they were facing in the transition to college. Those five minutes, however, were critical to the benefit that accrued to their happiness and health. Even brief reminders about important goals and brief plans about how to go about reaching them can make a big difference. Get a little chalkboard or even a sticky note and write down three things you can do to help you get to your most important goal. Next week, evaluate whether any of them are working and whether they should be continued, modified, or replaced. This may be all the "journal" you need.

Behaving optimistically can also translate into trying one more time (or maybe more) when you feel like giving up, because that's what an optimist would do. Be ready for the possibility that you might succeed more than you expected. Also be ready for the possibility that you might not succeed even when you persist. See those as learning experiences: even if persistence doesn't pay off, you start to learn the signals that differentiate trying hard to get a date from stalking. Next time, you will be wiser. Keep it up long enough and you're on your way to optimistic behavior and all that comes with it.

TAPPING INTO YOUR INNER OPTIMISM
Each year my students and I interview each of the law students participating in our ongoing optimism-immunity research. The interview opens with a "warm-up" question, which was originally intended to let the students relax and get used to talking on tape before the hard questions start. We begin this way: "Tell me about why you decided to go to law school."

As we've found, students go to law school for all kinds of different reasons. Some enjoy the intellectual challenge, some want to use a law degree as a means to a career in another field such as government, some are going into the family business (everyone else in the family is a lawyer), and some want to be able to help and protect others using the legal system. Some even go to law school as a default professional degree—medicine wasn't appealing (all those sick people), and a PhD takes too long. Although all these students were working toward the same goal—to graduate from law school—that goal had very different origins for different students.

When you think about *what* goals you have, be sure to think also about *why* you have them. People have three basic psychological needs: competence (doing well), relatedness (connecting with others), and autonomy (acting freely).[8] When a goal arises from a person's own values and identity, it is called "self-determined." Self-determined goals provide their own reward and motivation because they meet autonomy needs (you are acting freely in adopting the goal). That is, goals you choose yourself are inherently rewarding. Macaroni art is not a good money-making proposition but, when intrinsically motivated, offers an opportunity for the exercise of creativity and skill (forms of competence) and autonomy. Goal pursuits that are extrinsically motivated—that arise from the pursuit of external rewards or punishments, to avoid guilt or shame, or because of rules (real or imagined)—can never offer the same reward.

Furthermore, people make better progress toward intrinsically motivated goals than extrinsically motivated goals and feel better while doing it. Students who are intrinsically motivated learn better than students who are extrinsically motivated. Churchgoers who are intrinsically motivated have greater well-being than those who are extrinsically motivated. Among our law students, we would expect that those who went to law school for intrinsic reasons (they enjoy the law, they want to help people) to be better adjusted and more successful than those who went to law school for extrinsic reasons (my husband wants me to make more money, Grandpa always wanted me to be a lawyer).

Providing external reasons for doing something can even undermine existing intrinsic motivation. In one classic demonstration of this effect, when children who were interested in drawing were told they could get a certificate by doing more drawings, they eventually lost interest in drawing, spending about half as much free playtime drawing after the certificate offer as before.[9] Children who were unexpectedly given a certificate or who did the extra drawings "for free" stayed interested in drawing. Once kids expected that they should get some kind of reward apart from their own enjoyment, they stopped being rewarded *by* their own enjoyment.

In adulthood, cultural messages about the importance of extrinsic rewards may also undermine our best motivations. When students start law school, most of them pursue academic goals because they think those goals are important and they find them enjoyable and stimulating. As law school progresses, however, a number of messages, explicit and implicit, begin to take a toll on these students. Students start hearing more and more about money and status and not as much about public service, intellectual stimulation, or other personal reasons for studying the law. Consequently, they start to pursue certain goals and pathways because of the money or status, because other people think they should, or because they would feel guilty if they didn't. Intrinsic motivation falls as much as 25 percent in the first few months of law school, a change that leads to a loss of well-being and an increase in physical symptoms such as insomnia and headaches. When law students' intrinsic interest in the law is supplanted by expectation of extrinsic rewards, they suffer.

Unhappily for those who become absorbed in extrinsic motivators for their behavior, this change in motivation works against them, since extrinsic motivation also predicts lower grades in law school, and lower grades means less ability to pursue the "status" careers.[10] The pursuit of extrinsically motivated goals may be self-defeating.

If you were to make a list of your goals, it might be tempting to idealize it:

- Write a guaranteed best-seller novel
- Run for Mrs. Jessamine County
- Keep up correspondence with three hundred best friends (reminder: buy more engraved notecards)
- Have four perfect offspring
- Teach four perfect offspring to play violin, viola, and cello for perfect offspring string quartet
- Host elaborate dinners for forty (reminder: dig wine cellar)

However, when you consider your goals, you do yourself a disservice if you edit yourself or try to limit yourself to what you think are good or admirable goals. If you want to learn macaroni art, don't leave it off the list. No one can tell you what your goals should be. Other people may have goals for you, but those are their goals and not necessarily yours. In fact, these two sets of goals are so distinct that people who study the self actually separate out two *possible selves*, which are people's views of what they might look like in the future: an "ideal" self that incorporates a wished-for future self based on one's own values and goals and an "ought" self that incorporates a future self based on other people's imposed wishes, values, and goals.[11] The goals that drive you may be either your own or other people's. Maybe other people have very good ideas for what you should be like, but the research evidence suggests that when it comes to happiness, your goals are better for you than other people's goals.

Like goal engagement, intrinsic motivation is something you may be able to maintain through a simple process of reminding yourself. Psychologist Ken Sheldon and his colleagues have suggested some strategies for increasing intrinsic motivation that may help you:[12]

1. *Own the goal.* Think back to the core value,
important resource, or ideal self that the goal expresses.
What does macaroni art do for you? Does it tap into
your desire to create? Does it allow you to unleash your
inner Impressionist?
2. *Make it fun.* Pursue the goal in a context you enjoy.
Find people, times, or settings that maximize enjoyment.
For example, while riding the stationary bike one day, I
was reading an interesting book.
3. *Remember the big picture.* If you have a relatively
narrow goal ("lose ten pounds"), what broader purpose
does it serve ("live a longer, healthier life")?

The first rule of doing optimism is pursuing goals. Optimism acts as a kind of permissive agent for all kinds of motivation, because the ability to see positive outcomes promotes all kinds of motivation. Pessimism can undermine intrinsic motivation via negative expectations for achieving competence, connectedness, and autonomy; likewise, pessimism can undermine extrinsic motivation, if the expectation is that external punishments are more likely than rewards. Because any motivation is clearly better than no motivation in terms of well-being and performance, optimism yields benefits in those areas. However, focusing the benefit of optimistic beliefs on self-determined, intrinsically motivated goals may further increase its power by channeling the resulting motivation into goals that will meet the basic needs of competence, connectedness, and autonomy.

For thousands of years, gratitude has been an essential element of spirituality, but can we measure how cultivating gratitude affects our quality of life, physically and mentally, in the short and long term? Can a disciplined approach toward recognizing gratitude in daily life actually affect mood and outlook, translate to emotions like love and joy, and even strengthen relationships? Does gratitude maximize pleasure in our lives? In the below essay, Dr. Robert Emmons, author of *Thanks!: How the New Science of Gratitude Can Make You Happier*, answers these questions and more.

Gratitude

The Science and Spirit of Thankfulness

ROBERT A. EMMONS, PH.D.

> *Gratitude is the secret to life. The greatest thing*
> *is to give thanks for everything. He who*
> *has learned this has penetrated the whole*
> *mystery of life—giving thanks for everything.*
> > *—Albert Schweitzer*

Gratitude is always praised. "Whatever you are in search of—peace of mind, prosperity, health, love—it is waiting for you if only you are willing to receive it with an open and grateful heart," writes Sarah Breathnach in the *Simple Abundance Journal of Gratitude*. Elsewhere in this volume, gratitude is referred to as "the most passionate transformative force in the cosmos." Another popular treatment of the topic refers to it as "one of the most empowering, healing, dynamic instruments of consciousness vital to demonstrating the life experiences one desires" (Richelieu, 1996). Lock-and-key metaphors are especially common; gratitude has been referred to as "the key that opens all doors," that which "unlocks the fullness of life," and the "key to abundance, prosperity, and fulfillment" (Emmons and Hill, 2001; Hay, 1996). The claims are impressive; the empirical evidence, until recently, scant.

How do these extraordinary claims fare when scientific lights are shined on them? Can gratitude live up to its billing? Before answering this question, we must first deal with some basic issues concerning the nature of gratitude, and its spiritual foundations.

WHAT IS GRATITUDE?

Gratitude has a dual meaning: a worldly one and a transcendent one. In its worldly sense, gratitude is simply a feeling that occurs in interpersonal exchanges when one person acknowledges receiving a valuable benefit from another. Much of human life is about giving, receiving, and repayment. In this sense, it, like other social emotions, functions to help regulate relationships, solidifying and strengthening them. Feelings of gratitude stem from two stages of information processing: (1) an affirmation of goodness or "good things" in one's life and (2) the recognition that the sources of this goodness lie at least partially outside the self. In gratitude, we humbly acknowledge the countless ways in which we have been and are supported and sustained by the benevolence of others.

Gratitude's other nature is ethereal, spiritual, and transcendent. Philosophies and theologies have long viewed gratitude as central to the human-divine relationship. As long as people have believed in a Supreme Being, believers have sought ways to express gratitude and thanksgiving to this Being, their ultimate giver. In monotheistic traditions, God is conceived of as a personal being that is the source of goodness and the first giver of all gifts, to whom much is owed. In these traditions gratitude is quite likely a universal religious emotion, manifested in the thank offerings described in ancient scriptures; in the daily ceremonies and rituals of Native Americans; in the contemporary praise and worship music of the evangelical tradition. For a person who has religious or spiritual beliefs, gratitude sets up a relationship to the Divine, the source from which all good comes. It is a relationship that recognizes the gift of life from the Creator. Choosing to live in that space of recognition puts one in a heavenly sphere of humility, awe, and recognition of how blessed one is to have the opportunity to learn, grow, love, create, share, and help others. The response to these gifts can be an overwhelming sense of humility, wonder, and desire to give thanks and to pass along the love that is activated within. There is a looking up and then out. A grateful person senses that they are not separate from others or from God. This recognition itself brings a deep sense of gratefulness.

Though the concept of a personally transcendent God is no longer applicable in nontheistic traditions, gratitude retains its spiritual nature. This fundamental spiritual quality to gratitude, which transcends religious traditions, is aptly conveyed by Streng (1989): "in this attitude people recognize that they are connected to each other in a mysterious and miraculous way that is not fully determined by physical forces, but is part of a wider, or transcendent context" (5). This spiritual core of gratefulness is essential if gratitude is to be not simply a tool for narcissistic self-improvement. True gratefulness rejoices in the other. It has as its ultimate goal reflecting back the goodness that one has received by creatively seeking opportunities for giving. The motivation for doing so resides in the grateful appreciation that one has lived by the grace of others. In this sense, the spirituality of gratitude is opposed to a self-serving belief that one deserves or is entitled to the blessings that he or she enjoys. Knowing the grace by which one lives is itself a profound spiritual realization.

Gratitude has been well established as a universal human attribute. Its presence is felt and expressed in different ways by virtually all peoples, of all cultures, worldwide. The fact that gratitude is universal across all cultures suggests that it is part of the fabric of human nature. A positive affirmation of life comes from a deep sense of gratitude to all forms of existence, a gratitude rooted in the essence of being itself, which permeates one's every thought, speech, and action. Gratitude, in this profound sense, is not simply a mere attitude, a deep feeling, or even a desirable virtue. It is as elemental as life itself. In many world ethical systems, gratitude is *the* compelling force behind acts of compassion because life is seen as a vast network of interdependence, interpenetration, and mutuality that constitutes being.

THE NEW SCIENCE OF GRATITUDE

Examinations of gratitude in the history of ideas come from a number of perspectives—philosophy, theology, and political economy, to name a few. Each of these is valid and valuable in its own right. However, only a scientific perspective can provide an evidence-based approach to understanding how and in what ways gratitude brings benefits into the life of the practitioner. Recently, the tools and techniques of modern science have been brought to bear on understanding the nature of gratitude and why it is important for human health and happiness. Empirical research can put to the test those extraordinary claims made about gratitude that I quoted at the beginning of this chapter.

RESEARCH ON THE BENEFITS OF GRATITUDE

A number of rigorous, controlled experimental trials have examined the benefits of gratitude. Gratitude has been scientifically examined at the level of an emotion by asking people to cultivate it through journaling exercises (Emmons and McCullough, 2003). Recent research has demonstrated that mood and health benefits can accrue from grateful thinking cultivated in this manner. In these experimental studies, persons who were randomly assigned to keep gratitude journals on a weekly basis exercised more regularly, reported fewer physical symptoms, felt better about their lives as a whole, and were more optimistic about the upcoming week compared to those who recorded hassles or neutral life events (Emmons and McCullough, 2003, Study 1). A daily gratitude journal-keeping exercise with young adults resulted in higher reported levels of the positive states of alertness, enthusiasm, determination, attentiveness, and energy compared to a focus on hassles or a downward social comparison (ways in which participants thought they were better off than others: Emmons and McCullough, Study 2). Participants in the daily gratitude condition were more likely to report having helped someone with a personal problem or having offered emotional support to another, relative to the hassles or social comparison condition. This indicates that, relative to a focus on complaints, an effective strategy for producing reliably higher levels of pleasant affect is to lead people to reflect, on a daily basis, on those aspects of their lives for which they are grateful. Other benefits have extended to the physical realm, including longer sleep and improved sleep quality and more time spent exercising for those keeping gratitude journals (Emmons and McCullough, 2003).

In these studies, participants in the gratitude condition are given the following instructions: "We want to focus for a moment on benefits or gifts that you have received in your life. These gifts could be simple everyday pleasures, people in your life, personal strengths or talents, moments of natural beauty, or gestures of kindness from others. We might not normally think about these things as gifts, but that is how we want you to think about them. Take a moment to really savor or relish these gifts, think about their value, and then write them down every night before going to sleep." A wide range of experiences sparked gratitude: cherished interactions, awareness of physical health, overcoming obstacles, and simply being alive, to name a few. This instructional set was in contrast with comparison conditions asking those in other randomly assigned groups to chronicle their daily travails or hassles or to reflect on ways in which they were better off than others.

In daily studies of emotional experience, when people report feeling grateful, thankful, and appreciative, they also feel more loving, forgiving, joyful, and enthusiastic. These deep affections appear to be formed through the discipline of gratitude. In this regard, it is interesting that the Greek root of the word enthusiasm, *entheos,* means "inspired by or possessed by a god." Importantly, the data showing that gratitude is correlated with beneficial outcomes is not limited to self-reports. Notably, the family, friends, partners, and others who surround them consistently report that people who practice gratitude seem measurably happier and are more pleasant to be around. Grateful people are rated by others as more helpful, more outgoing, more optimistic, and more trustworthy (McCullough et al., 2002).

Strikingly, our participants continued to keep gratitude journals long after the study ended, and when we contacted them months later they commented on the long-term benefits of being in the study. One individual told us that "Being forced, consciously, to reflect, contemplate, and sum up my life on a daily basis was curiously therapeutic, and enlightening. I was reminded of facets of myself that I very much like and others that could use improvement . . . I have tried to become more aware of my level of gratitude."

The benefits of gratitude were further confirmed in a recent study that compared the efficacy of five different interventions that were hypothesized to increase personal happiness and decrease personal depression (Seligman, Steen, Park, and Peterson, 2005). In a random-assignment, placebo-controlled Internet study, a gratitude intervention (writing and delivering a letter of thankfulness to someone who had been especially helpful but had never been properly thanked) was found to significantly increase happiness and decrease depression for up to one month following the visit. Results indicated that "participants in the gratitude visit condition showed the largest positive changes in the whole study" (Seligman et al., 417). Thus, the benefits of gratitude do not appear to be limited to the self-guided journal keeping methodology utilized by Emmons and McCullough (2003).

But cultivating gratitude in the short term is not the same thing as having the ability to feel grateful on a consistent basis. Gratitude is not just a transient emotion, but is also a virtue. Grateful people are more prone to the emotion, are prone to respond with gratitude to a wider range of beneficent actions, and are more likely to notice beneficence on the part of others—in particular more likely to respond to it with the emotion of gratitude rather than with alternative emotions like resentment, shame, or guilt. Grateful people are likely to agree with statements such as "It's important to appreciate each day that you are alive," "I often reflect on how much easier my life is because of the efforts of others," and "For me, life is much more of a gift than it is a burden." Items such as these come from personality questionnaires designed to measure trait levels of gratitude; in other words, to identify people who are by nature grateful souls.

Research has shown that dispositionally grateful people enjoy many of the same benefits that accrue from cultivating grateful thinking, namely enhanced psychological, physical, spiritual, and relational well-being (McCullough, Emmons, and Tsang, 2002).

WHY IS GRATITUDE GOOD? EXPLORING MECHANISMS

The research literature indicates that gratitude, measured either dispositionally or activated by specific tasks, is linked to improved well-being and general positive functioning. How does one account for the psychological, emotional, and physical benefits of gratitude?

Simply put, gratitude feels good. It is inherently positive. But there must be more to it than that. Gratitude implies a recognition that it is possible for other forces to act toward us with beneficial, selfless motives. In a world that was nothing but randomness, hatred, and injustice there would indeed be no possibility of gratitude. Being grateful to a Supreme Being and to other people is an acknowledgment that there are good and enjoyable things in the world to be enjoyed in accordance with the giver's intent. Good things happen by design. If a person believes in the spiritual concept of grace, they believe that there is a pattern of beneficence in the world that exists quite independently of their own striving and even their own existence. Gratitude thus depends upon receiving what we do not expect to receive or have not earned, or receiving more than we believe we deserve. This awareness is simultaneously humbling and elevating.

Gratitude maximizes pleasure. Gratitude maximizes enjoyment of the pleasurable in our lives. A well-established law in the psychology of emotion is the principle of adaptation. People adapt to circumstances, both pleasant and unpleasant. Our emotion systems like newness. Unfortunately for personal happiness, adaptation to pleasant circumstances occurs more rapidly than adaptation to unpleasant life changes. This is why even a major windfall, such as a huge pay raise, tends to impact happiness for only a few months. Once the glow fades, we return to the same happiness level we had before. Psychologists call this phenomenon hedonic adaptation. The only thing that can change it and prolong the increase in happiness is gratitude. Gratitude promotes the savoring of positive life experiences and situations, so that the maximum satisfaction and enjoyment are derived from one's circumstances. In helping people not take things for granted, gratitude may recalibrate people's "set points" for happiness—our baseline levels of happiness that appear to be primarily innate, driven by one's genes.

Gratitude protects against the negative. Gratitude also mitigates toxic emotions and states. Nothing can destroy happiness more quickly than envy, greed, and resentment. The German moral philosopher Balduin Schwarz identified the problem when he said "the ungrateful, envious, complaining man . . . cripples himself. He is focused on what he has not, particularly on that which somebody else has or seems to have, and by that he tends to poison his world" (Schwarz, 1999). Grateful people tend to be satisfied with what they have, and so are less susceptible to such emotions as disappointment, regret, and frustration. Moreover, in the context of material prosperity, by maintaining a grateful focus a person may avoid disillusionment and emptiness. The sense of security that characterizes grateful people makes them less susceptible to needing to rely on material accomplishments for a stable sense of self.

Gratitude strengthens relationships. Perhaps most important of all is that gratitude strengthens and expands social relationships. It cultivates a person's sense of interconnectedness. An unexpected benefit from gratitude journaling, one that I did not predict in advance, was that people who kept gratitude journals reported feeling closer and more connected to others, were more likely to help others, and were actually seen as more helpful by significant others in their social networks. Gratitude is the "moral memory of mankind," wrote noted sociologist Georg Simmel. One just needs to try to imagine human relationships existing without gratitude. By way of contrast, ingratitude leads inevitably to a confining, restricting, and "shrinking" sense of self. Emotions like anger, resentment, envy, and bitterness tend to undermine happy social relations. But the virtue of gratitude is not only a firewall of protection against such corruption of relationships; it contributes positively to friendship and civility, because it is both benevolent (wishing the benefactor well) and just (giving the benefactor his due, in a certain special way).

We also have evidence that people who are high on dispositional gratitude, the chronic tendency to be aware of blessings in life, have better relationships, are more likely to protect and preserve these relationships, are more securely attached, and are less lonely and isolated. People who have an easier time conjuring up reasons to be grateful are less likely to say that they lack companionship or that no one really knows them well. Our innate longing for belonging is strengthened when we experience and express heartfelt gratitude. Gratitude takes us outside ourselves, where we see ourselves as part of a larger, intricate network of sustaining mutually reciprocal relationships.

A healthy heart. Lastly, there appears to be growing evidence that gratitude and related states can impact physiological functioning and physical health. Activation studies are beginning to examine the physiological concomitants of gratitude and related positive emotional states. Researchers at the Institute of HeartMath in Boulder Creek, California, have developed a behavioral technique for inducing a positive emotion they call "appreciation" (McCraty and Childre, 2004). The technique entails in consciously disengaging from unpleasant emotions by shifting attention to one's physical heart, which they think most people associate with positive emotions, and focusing on feeling appreciation toward someone—appreciation being an active emotional state in which one dwells on or contemplates the goodness of someone. McCraty and Childre have found that heart rhythm patterns associated with "appreciation" differ markedly from those associated with relaxation (neutral emotion) and anger (negative emotion). Appreciation increases parasympathetic activity and also produces entrainment or coherence across various autonomic measures (e.g., heart rate variability, pulse transit time, and respiration rate), a pattern that is associated with improved cardiovascular health.

Relatedly, recent studies of autonomic nervous system activity during meditation have reported a pattern of mutual activation of both the parasympathetic and sympathetic systems that is associated with the subjective experience of a sense of overwhelming calmness as well as significant alertness. We bring this up here because the conscious activation of gratitude through the journaling exercise resulted in increased *calmness* and *alertness* (Emmons and McCullough, 2003). Other studies have found that certain meditative techniques do lead to an increased sense of gratitude and thankfulness (Gillani and Smith, 2001).

Coping with stress. As a prevailing orientation toward life, a sense of gratefulness can serve as a resource that a person can draw upon in times of need, including coping with stress and dealing with and recovering from physical illness. There is evidence that dispositionally grateful individuals are at less risk for depressive symptoms and other indicators of traumatic stress disorder following a major upheaval in their lives. The horrific events of September 11, 2001, provided an unprecedented opportunity for mental health researchers to study the human reaction to a large-scale national trauma. The first studies to appear focused predictably on negative effects: post-traumatic stress symptoms, anger, anxiety, depression, sleep disturbance. Even those not directly impacted by 9/11 experienced vicarious trauma upon repeated exposure to media images of the burning towers. But soon thereafter a study appeared that included the remarkable finding that in the aftermath of 9/11, the positive emotion of gratitude was the *second* most commonly experienced feeling by American adults. Only compassion was more frequently felt. Furthermore, those who previously had reported high levels of gratitude in their lives were less shattered by the tragedies of this day compared to those initially less grateful (Fredrickson and Tugade, 2002). The belief that tragedy can ultimately result in positive outcomes has been a mainstay of religious systems since the beginning of recorded time. Suffering can be a reason for gratefulness in that it shatters our illusions of self-sufficiency, causes us to be accountable, and teaches us what is truly important.

CULTIVATING GRATITUDE

The data are clear. Gratitude is good. Science has demonstrated that gratitude results in enhanced and sustained positive emotional experience and effective functioning. Yet despite all of the benefits that living a grateful life can bring, gratitude can be hard and painful work. It does not come easily or naturally to many. At least initially, it requires discipline. So this is the paradox of gratitude: while the evidence is clear that cultivating gratitude, in our life and in our attitude to life, makes us happier and healthier people, more attuned to the flow of blessings in our lives, it is still difficult. Practicing gratitude is easier said than done.

A number of evidence based-strategies have proven effective in creating sustainable gratefulness. In my book (Emmons, 2007) I offer ten prescriptions for raising one's gratitude consciousness. Space does not allow me to elaborate upon all of them here; I refer the curious reader to this book for more information.

What requires mentioning, however, is that all of the strategies converge on the importance of three principles: Attention, Interpretation, and Memory. This can be thought of as the AIM model of gratitude (see also Diener and Biswas-Diener, in press, for an application of AIM to happiness). In many respects, then, gratitude can be thought of as a mindfulness practice that leads to a greater experience of being connected to life.

Attention is noticing and becoming aware of blessings that we normally take for granted. It is tuning in to the many reasons for gratitude that already exist in our lives. Simultaneously, directing our attention this way in a focused manner blocks thoughts and perceptions that are inimical to gratitude, such as feelings of exaggerated deservingness or perceptions of victimhood. Focusing techniques that enhance attentiveness (such as mindfulness meditation) will be effective in increasing one's appreciation for the simple blessings of life and in banishing incompatible thoughts from consciousness.

Interpretation is the conscious decision to see blessings instead of burdens, contributions instead of curses. Grateful people have a way of interpreting reality that enhances and sustains a grateful outlook on the world. They describe their lives in terms of gifts, givers, fortune, fortunate, abundance, favors, even luck. They rarely mention regrets, disappointments, or deprivations. Trafficking in the language of thanksgiving, grateful people have little need to notice what they have missed out on because in their minds, they perceive that they have everything they need to be grateful, every minute of every day. This allows them to be less reactive to everyday life events, a prerequisite for smooth emotional functioning.

Finally, there is remembering. Grateful people draw upon positive memories of being the recipients of benevolence. This is why religious traditions are able to so effectively cultivate gratitude—litanies of remembrance encourage gratitude, and religions do litanies very well. The scriptures, sayings, and sacraments of faith traditions inculcate gratefulness by drawing us into a remembered relationship with a Supreme Being and with the members of our community. There is a French proverb that states that gratitude is the memory of the heart—it is the way that the heart remembers. The memory of the heart includes the memory of those we are dependent on just as the forgetfulness of dependence is unwillingness or inability to remember the benefits provided by others. In the end, those who live under an aura of pervasive thankfulness by holding on to memories of received kindnesses will reap the rewards of grateful living, whereas those who fail to remember and acknowledge their dependence on others will diminish their experience of life.

While nature has played a role in almost every religious and spiritual tradition in history, is there proof that nature can facilitate spiritual awakening, fulfillment, joy, and awareness? Dr. Sara Warber and Dr. Katherine Irvine lead us through an examination of nature's place in human health and spirituality and offer research that answers such questions as: Can gardens, vineyards, and farms aid and heal the mentally and physically ill? How important to our physical and emotional well-being is a sense of connection with nature? Can humans and plants communicate, and if so, does this prove a spiritual interconnectedness of humanity and the earth?

Nature and Spirit

SARA L. WARBER, M.D., AND KATHERINE N. IRVINE, PH.D.

Is nature spirit-filled? Are the contemplation of nature, and the immersion in nature, forms of spiritual practice? Does nature heal our bodies, our psyches, our minds, our spirits? If nature does heal, what is it about nature that heals us? Is this potential ability to heal our whole selves an important part of the argument for protection of natural areas? Does this possibility demand rethinking our relationship with Earth's other inhabitants? These questions are the impetus for the explorations shared here. Through examination of stories and cultural ways of life, this essay will look for evidence of spirit in nature. We will go on to explore history, theory, and research that investigates the possibilities of whole person healing and spiritual deepening occuring in nature, whether it be a nearby garden or a pristine wilderness area.

While a clear definition of spiritual health has yet to be developed, some common elements include having a sense of meaning or purpose and feeling connected to one's self, to others, and to a larger reality (Hawks, 1995; Zuefle, 1999). Seaward (1995) conceptualizes four practices necessary for nurturing a healthy human spirit: centering, emptying, grounding, and connecting. Centering involves taking time to quiet the mind, and is most often done in solitude. Emptying entails clearing the mind, letting go of residual thoughts and feelings from the day. Grounding is a time for reflection on what one has to offer the world and for cultivating creativity or inspiration, while connecting, the fourth practice, speaks to the importance of reconnecting with the wider world and sharing one's insight with others. We will explore how nature, whether in the intimacy of a garden or in the grandeur of an ocean vista, may be a place that fosters these processes, thereby nurturing our spiritual well-being.

We draw on stories, cultural wisdom, empirical research, and our own observations of recent trends and events to explore the notion that the natural world contributes to human well-being, especially spiritual well-being. We examine the history of healing gardens and their recent redis-covery by the health care industry. We discuss some of the theories about why time with nature is healing. We present experimental results of the benefits of interaction with the natural environment for people. And we examine research on humans' impact on nature in order to illustrate the recip-rocal relationship between people and nature. It is our hope that through research the reader might come away with a better understanding of the gut-level feeling, held by many, that our spiritual well-being, our very health, and quality of life are shaped and influenced by our interactions with the natural world.

NATURE AND HUMAN HEALTH

The notion that people are disconnected from the natural world is an ever-present theme in discussions about environmental degradation and the need for sustainable living patterns. Although native peoples the world over, those who trust ancient wisdom, recognize the importance of balance and harmony with nature as an integral part of personal and community health, many modern-day humans, sequestered within the self-made environment that daily grows more dominant, are often unaware of something lost. For some, however, a vague feeling of discontent pervades, a sense that something is missing; dis-ease precedes disease. Spring arrives and we all rush outside to feel the warmth of sun, to breathe the fresh, oxygen-rich air. The very term "outside" reveals a perception that humans are apart from rather than a part of nature. We have relegated ourselves to a life "inside." We are born into the human-built domain of hospitals. We live in houses, become educated, and work inside buildings. And then we end our lives in nursing homes and hospitals. The cost of such a way of living may very well be our own health in all its dimensions: physical, mental, emotional, and spiritual.

Many discussions of the relationship between the natural world and human well-being emphasize the potential for negative health effects, such as increased childhood asthma or links to cancer (Frumkin, 2001). Little attention is focused on what impact a lack of contact with nature might have on personal well-being or, conversely, how interaction with the natural world might promote well-being and health. Over the past decade, however, stories have begun appearing in the popular press (e.g., *Prevention, Ms. Magazine*) about the healing power of nature. Often written by or about an individual who has experienced a life-changing event (such as the loss of a loved one or a diagnosis of cancer), the story describes the vital role that spending time in the natural world played in their healing process. The "time in nature" might consist of creating and nurturing a garden, taking daily walks along a country road, or regularly watching the sunset. This interaction somehow provided a venue for reflection, an opportunity to gain perspective on life. The individual was able to reach a point where they could move forward with their life, often describing the experience as a process through which they began to feel whole again. Anne Morrow Lindbergh called this "a gift from the sea" (Lindbergh, 1977).

How might interaction with the natural world promote health and spiritual well-being? On a fundamental level, we rely on nature for the physical necessities of oxygen, water, food, and warmth. How else might nature-interaction influence our health? Take a moment to imagine the ways that one might experience a natural setting. Here are some of our own images. Visual—cloud patterns, the red of a robin's breast, movement of leaves in the wind, the flight of birds. Smell—freshly turned earth, fragrant flowers, salty sea air. Taste—berries eaten on a trail, a garden-grown tomato. Hearing—bird song, bullfrogs croaking, intermittent silence, water gurgling in a brook. Touch—wind touch on skin, the creature touch of fur, the flower touch of dandelion seeds, the water touch of rain.

As one experiences nature through these multiple sensory modalities, the body may change its rhythm, modulating the cascades of neurotransmitters or immune system warriors in such a way that health is enhanced. Additionally, these interactions may touch us at a deeper level that some call the spirit, inviting us to realign our actions with what is truly important to us. Cultural wisdom, history, theory, and research can provide insight into the potentially profound impact natural settings can have on these multiple levels of well-being.

GLOBAL CULTURAL PATTERNS

From a global view, other cultures, both past and present, inform our thinking about the relationship of humans and nature. In this section, we look at some examples of cultural principles that illuminate the spiritual connection of humans and nature, thus laying a foundation for a new appreciation of nature as a place filled with spirit. Many cultures identify humans and the land, and by extension, nature, much more closely with each other than commonly is done in the West. Concepts from Australia, Fiji, Africa, and the Americas, although widely scattered in geographic origin, create a trail that marks the deep interconnection between humans, nature, and place. This connection is grounded in the concept of a spirit-filled world, of which humans are one equal piece. In Marlo Morgan's fictional work, she succinctly describes aboriginal Australian thinking when the heroine explains, "My people . . . lived in oneness with the earth, all its creatures, and each other" (Morgan, 1999, 309). Later the character elaborates, "Every physical thing on planet earth comes from the One Divine Source and all are made from identical fragments of energy. We are one with all creation" (Morgan, 1999, 310).

This idea of interconnection is also present in Fijian culture. Richard Katz, in his anthropological work, *The Straight Path*, highlights the relationship of the people and the land with the ancestral or cosmological gods, known as the *Vu*. "[O]ne respects the land and the people and the traditions that govern both; ultimately one's respect is for the *Vu*, since land, people and traditions express the way and will of the *Vu*"(Katz, 1993, 28). He explains what he has been taught about the special connection between people and land:

> Vanua *literally means land, but also refers to the social and cultural aspects of the physical environment identified with a*

social group . . . For a vanua *to be recognized, it must have
people living on it and supporting and defending its rights and
interests. A land without people is likened to a person without
a soul. The people are the souls of the physical environment . . .
The land is the physical or geographical entity of the people
upon which their survival . . . depends. It is a major source
of life; it provides nourishment, shelter, and protection . . .
Land is thus an extension of the self. Likewise the people are
an extension of the land. Land becomes lifeless and useless
without the people, and likewise the people are helpless and
useless without the land to thrive on. (Ravuvu, 1987, 76)*

The Fijian principles admonish us to value and respect the land,
suggesting that we are nothing when not in relationship with the
land. This relationship is a reflection of the connection between
human, nature, and spirit. In Africa, Malidoma Somé explains a
similar worldview: "Our base is in the Spirit World . . . the indigenous mind sees Spirit or the potential for the existence of Spirit
in every object; we are hungry for instructions in navigating an
often-uncertain world" (Somé, 1998, 31). He goes on to explain,
"Human beings long for connection, and our sense of usefulness
derives from the feeling of connectedness. When we are connected—to our own purpose, to the community around us, and to
our spiritual wisdom—we are able to live and act with authentic
effectiveness" (Somé, 1998, 36). He further states that "To attend
to the world of Spirit . . . is to connect to the geography in which
you find yourself" (Somé, 1998, 36). These three cultures demonstrate how the land, and the natural elements associated with it,
are a reflection of spirit. Humans are likewise spirit, but no more
important than others. Humans are at their best when connected
to each other and the land and spirit source.

If we accept that spirit fills nature, then plants, present in
many natural settings, must also be filled with spirit. Somé

challenges us, asking: "What if they [the elements of nature] are not inanimate objects, as people in the West have been taught to believe, but rather living presences? How would we need to change if we granted to a tree the kind of life that we usually reserve for so-called intelligent beings?" (Somé, 1998, 47). An example of how we might live in relationship with plant spirits is the accord given to the *yaqona* plant (*Piper methysticum*, commonly known as Kava) by the Fijian people. *Yaqona* accompanies every ceremony; otherwise, the *Vu* are not present (recall from above that the *Vu* are the ancestral or cosmological gods). *Yaqona* is the "nourishment of the gods." Its exchange opens and closes all ceremony and underpins all material and social exchange. It can be offered as the whole plant, as dried roots, or as finely ground powder. "Though *yaqona* is literally a plant, it is in essence a spiritual messenger" (Katz, 1993, 47). While the exchange of *yaqona* takes place between humans, it is actually being exchanged by the *Vu* related to the people. *Yaqona*, when mixed with water, is a mildly psychoactive drink, producing congenial interaction, relaxation, and finally sleepiness. In traditional culture, its use is highly ceremonial and solemn, as befitting the connection to the *Vu*. An elder said, "The *Vu* speak through the *yaqona*. We must be wide awake in order to hear them" (Katz, 1993, 54). Many other cultures, including the native cultures of North America, acknowledge the spirit of plants, for example, by making offerings to the plant spirit when harvesting the plants (Peat, 1994; Warber, 2003).

Often times we wonder at the causes of sickness and the means for the return to health. In the Western worldview, there are known pathogens or altered biochemical processes that cause disease and known molecules to fight the pathogens and fix the biomechanisms of our bodies. This system has been remarkably robust in curing infection and addressing acute catastrophic conditions. But it has not been as successful in ameliorating chronic conditions with multifactorial causation, including the interplay of psychosocial issues with biologic disease. Many people find themselves searching beyond conventional Western medicine for the answers to their health challenges. Indigenous people often have another point of view about the basis for illness and healing. Somé explains, drawing on his indigenous African teachings:

> *Our relationship to the natural world and its natural laws*
> *determines whether or not we are healed . . . . Every tree, plant,*
> *hill, mountain, rock, and each thing that was here before us . . .*
> *has healing power whether we know it or not. So if something*
> *in us must change, spending time in nature provides a good*
> *beginning. This means that within nature, within the natural*
> *world, are all of the materials and tenets needed for healing*
> *human beings. (Somé, 1998, 38)*

He specifically describes an encounter with a tree's spirit during his initiation ritual. He felt a kind of deep love and connection with that spirit that could not be denied. For him, it was transformative and healing, reuniting him with nature and his village community after thirteen years of French mission schooling (Somé, 1998).

Somé's experience is echoed around the globe in a story told by South American trained shamana and pharmacist, Connie Grauds. She speaks eloquently of a new kind of medicine where we let the spirit of nature, of plants, enter into the healing process (Grauds, 2001). She tells stories where there is no ingestion of the plant and yet a healing shift occurs in the patient. One such story involves a woman with depression who had tried both conventional medicine and St. John's Wort (*Hypericum perforatum*), the best studied of herbal antidepressants. Following a momentary intuition, Grauds recommended that the woman volunteer at a retreat center garden. The woman's first assignment was to weed a large bed of lavender. Six hours later, she was a changed person. She began to incorporate more lavender into her life (i.e., color, smells, bath oils) but never ingested the plant and continued to grow in health (Grauds, 2001). It might be argued that it is, in fact, the spirit of lavender, not the biochemistry of lavender, that is healing this woman.

An ancient source of medicine wisdom is to ask plants for information and receive it telepathically or by other nonordinary means. This is documented by physicist F. David Peat in his book *Lighting the Seventh Fire,* which seeks to bridge the Native North American worldview and Western science. He reflects with wonder on a remembered world where animals and plants spoke to humans, teaching them of right behavior and medicinal uses of plants (Peat, 1994). In South America, shamans also have a spiritual relationship with the plants (Grauds, 2001). Don Antonio, Grauds's teacher from the Amazon rainforest, instructs her, "Stay close to nature. Silence yourself and listen. The plants have secrets to tell you. They can help you and your patients. When a shaman wants to learn the medicinal properties of any plant, he asks the plant, then listens closely, and the information comes directly from the plant itself" (Grauds).

From diverse cultures, we see united themes. According to these trends, plants and all of nature itself have spirit, humans can understand this spirit when they silence themselves, and listening to the spirits of nature brings healing that can be life changing.

A HISTORICAL PERSPECTIVE
In Western thinking, the idea that interaction with natural settings contributes to well-being has not been completely ignored. The intuitive sense that nature plays an important

role in human health and wellness is found in many disciplines. Frederick Law Olmsted, a landscape architect during the early part of the twentieth century, was known for his efforts to incorporate parks into cities and residential areas (Todd, 1982). Central Park, located in the heart of New York City, is perhaps the clearest example of Olmsted's belief in the importance of providing opportunities for people to get away from the stress of city living and rejuvenate themselves through interaction with a natural setting. Nature writers describe the subtle yet long-lasting effect that the sight of a sunset, the sound of a birdcall, or the taste of freshly picked raspberries can have on an individual's sense of connectedness with something larger than oneself (e.g., Williams, 1992). Transcendentalist writers wrote of the importance of living close to nature in order to remain healthy:

> *What is the pill which will keep us well, serene, contented?*
> *For my panacea let me have a draught of undiluted morning*
> *air. Morning air! If men will not drink of this at the fountain-*
> *head of the day, why, then, we must even bottle up some and*
> *sell it in the shops, for the benefit of those who have lost their*
> *subscription ticket to morning time in this world.*
> *—Henry David Thoreau (1892)*

Access to the natural world was once considered integral to health care and health care settings as well. In medieval times, nature was a prominent part of hospitals, which were often located adjacent to monasteries and provided courtyards for walking and sitting, as well as for growing medicinal herbs (Gerlach-Spriggs, et al., 1998; Griswold, 1996). As hospitals moved away from their affiliation with religious institutions, became more specialized, and emphasized efficiency, the natural world was relegated to the cosmetic, something to enhance the appearance of the building through, for example, potted plants located on the check-in desk.

Small pockets of the medical profession have, however, held on to the notion that the natural world may contribute to well-being. Some sanatoriums utilized gardens, vineyards, and farms in the care of the mentally ill (Warner, 1995). Hospices and long-term care facilities for individuals with incurable diseases (e.g., AIDS) continue to incorporate gardens and provide access to the natural world, recognizing the need to make the end of life as pleasant as possible (Gerlach-Spriggs et al, 1998). The field of horticultural therapy utilizes interaction with the natural environment as a way to modify behavior or reteach motor skills to, for example, individuals who have suffered a stroke (Simson and Straus, 1998). Perhaps coupled with the increased interest in complementary and alternative therapies, and the demand for health care that treats the whole patient, the healing power of nature is again playing a prominent role as clinical health care settings begin to reincorporate gardens into their design.

Called "healing gardens," "therapeutic landscapes," "restorative gardens," and "wellness gardens," these spaces at first glance appear to be merely a garden in a hospital. They are, however, making a profound philosophical statement. The word "healing" means making something whole, a restoring of integrity and balance (Merriam-Webster, 1967). The origins of the word "garden" lie in the Old High German word *"gart,"* which means enclosure (Griswold, 1996; Merriam-Webster 1967). Thus, a healing garden literally means an enclosure that enhances restoration and integration of all aspects of a human—physical, mental, emotional, social, and spiritual. These natural areas are designed to be places that are simple and orderly, in contrast to the often complex, seemingly chaotic internal environment of a health care setting. The gardens represent the cycles of life, stimulate the senses, and provide the solitude needed for quiet reflection. A well-designed garden "reduces stress and fosters a sense of well-being, empowerment, dignity, and promise" (Kamp, 1995).

These healing gardens in many ways symbolize a recognition that the outdoor spaces around a hospital should be considered as much a part of the therapeutic environment as the inside of the building. In many respects, these gardens are a reincarnation of the intuitive belief that interaction with the natural world is a vital part of the healing process and of being a whole individual. While research that explores the impact of these healing gardens is still in the early stages, theory and evidence from several different disciplines provide much food for thought as to how nature positively impacts human well-being.

A THEORETICAL PERSPECTIVE

Attention Restoration Theory, grounded in cognitive psychology, suggests that interaction with nature restores our ability to concentrate (Kaplan, 1995a). The theory draws on James's notion that there are two kinds of attention, voluntary and involuntary. Voluntary, or directed, attention is the brain's ability to focus and is thought to require conscious effort. It is the resource tapped, for example, when one needs to shut out distractions (e.g., voices, music) and focus on how to solve a particular problem; it is also a resource that can be depleted through constant use (Kaplan and Kaplan, 1989; Kaplan, 1995a). Involuntary attention is considered to be effortless, and is drawn to such stimuli as "strange things, moving things, wild animals, bright things, pretty things, metallic things, words, blows, [and] blood" (James, 1892/1984, 88).

A restorative environment is one that engages involuntary attention and allows directed attention to rest. It is hypothesized that the natural environment contains both content (e.g., trees, animals) and processes (e.g., wind in the tree, squirrel burying a nut) that are essential for this restorative process to occur (Kaplan and Kaplan, 1989; Kaplan, 1995b). Thus, an individual whose directed attention is fatigued—as occurs during prolonged work or when trying to assimilate the implications of diagnosis and prognosis while hospitalized—may be readily distracted, unable to learn new information, and easily overwhelmed by details. On the other hand, a restored individual would likely to be able to think clearly, to take in new information, and, ultimately, to function more effectively, whether in work-related activities or personal decision making (Kaplan and Kaplan, 1989; Kaplan, 1995a; Kaplan, 1995b).

The impact of stress on the body provides another way of conceptualizing the healing effects of nature. Many types of situations can contribute to feeling stressed, including life events (Turner and Wheaton, 1995), chronic strains (Perlin et al., 1981), daily hassles (Dohrenwend et al., 1984), and lifetime trauma (Breslau, 1999). Research has demonstrated that the body's physiological response is the same, regardless of the stressor (Selye, 1946; 1956). This "fight or flight" response includes increased blood pressure and heart rates and a redistribution of blood flow from the extremities to the vital organs (e.g., the brain) (Cannon, 1932). These physiological changes could, over time, be deleterious to the body (Kiecolt-Glaser and Glaser, 1995; McEwen, 1998). For example, chronic exposure to stress can reduce the immune system's ability to adequately defend the body against illness (Cohen et al., 1991). Learning how to cope with stress is thus an important element of human well-being. Several researchers hypothesize that interaction with the natural world may counteract these negative effects of stress (Ulrich et al., 1991; Parson et al., 1998).

A RESEARCH PERSPECTIVE

Given cultural ways of life that emphasize our spiritual connection with nature, historical leanings toward incorporation of gardens into the therapeutic environment, and theories that underpin these observations, we now turn to research to illustrate that science, too, supports the notion of beneficial interaction between nature and humans. At a fundamental level, people appear to have a preference for natural settings. Kaplan and Kaplan discuss a series of studies that, collectively, illustrate that views dominated by nature (e.g., trees) are more highly preferred over those consisting of primarily human-made structures (e.g., buildings). This research has been conducted and replicated with different populations (Kaplan and Herbert, 1987), across different age groups (Balling and Falk, 1982), and in different geographical locations (Orland, 1988; Sullivan, 1994). Some researchers theorize that this affinity derives from our evolutionary history; settings dominated by nature are more characteristic of those in which humans evolved (Appleton, 1996; Kaplan, 1987; Kellert and Wilson, 1993; Wilson, 1984). We might also argue that the affinity is because these nature views link us to kindred spirits, to an expression of the divine.

Studies suggest that not only are nature-dominated settings preferred, but they also seem to positively affect a variety of health-related outcomes. In a study of the post-operative recovery process, Ulrich (1984) found that patients with a window view of nature (versus those with a view of another building) had shorter hospital stays, used less pain medication, had fewer minor complications (e.g., headache, nausea), and experienced more positive emotional states. Another study demonstrates that healing gardens also reduce pain and emotional distress (Sherman et al., 2004).

Measures of stress have also been utilized to explore the healing power of nature. A study of work-related stress found that individuals who viewed pictures of natural settings following a stressful event experienced a decrease in blood pressure, heart rate, and muscle tension. Those who viewed images of the human-made environment showed no recovery or a slower recovery using the same measures (Ulrich et al., 1991). Similarly, Parsons' group (1998) found that individuals who viewed a simulated drive through predominantly human-built environments had greater physiological symptoms of stress (i.e., blood pressure, heart rate) than those who viewed nature-dominated scenery. Interestingly, individuals who viewed natural scenery showed a lower stress response to a second stress event, suggesting that interaction with the natural world might immunize individuals to subsequent stressors.

Interaction with natural environments also appears to affect one's overall assessment of a situation. For example, a window view of nature was shown to contribute to job satisfaction (Kaplan et al., 1996; Kaplan et al., 1988) and increased residential satisfaction (Kaplan, 1983; Sheets and Manzer, 1991). Additionally, a series of studies done with gardeners found a positive link between gardening and life satisfaction (Kaplan and Kaplan, 1989). When asked to identify the contribution of spending time in the garden to overall well-being, 57 percent of householders in Perth, Australia indicated it was very or most important (ARCWIS, 2002). Garden access in the city has been shown to reduce self-reported sensitivity to stress (Stigsdotter and Grahn, 2004). These findings are interesting in light of Lazarus's (1966) emphasis on the perceptual element of the experience of stress. He proposes that an individual's response to a situation or event is shaped by how it is perceived by the viewer; if a setting is perceived as potentially harmful, one will react physiologically as if it is. The above-mentioned studies suggest that the presence of nature can shape how a setting is perceived, which may influence one's level of stress in addition to one's emotional well-being.

Studies of healing gardens suggest that they promote positive changes in mood (Cooper et al., 1999; Whitehouse et al., 2001). Grahn and colleagues (2007) have demonstrated the value of these spaces for individuals with severe burnout, while Detweiler and Warf (2005) illustrated the use of gardens for motivating post-stroke patients through difficult periods of rehabilitation treatment. In the field of horticultural therapy, the activity of gardening has been used as part of the healing process for children with learning disabilities. Participation in gardening was found to increase self-esteem and self-confidence as well as decrease aggression and depression (Aldridge and Sempik, 2002, as cited in Brown and Grant, 2005). Conversely, a lack of access to gardens is associated with increased self-reported levels of depression and anxiety (Macintyre et al., 2003).

Several studies support the idea that natural environments are mentally restorative for individuals. In a study of women recovering from breast cancer surgery, Cimprich (1992; 1993) found that those whose standard care routine was coupled with time spent in nature were better able to focus and were more likely to start new projects. In a separate study, students with a nature view were better able to concentrate during exam time than those with a view dominated by buildings (Tennesen and Cimprich, 1995).

Social well-being also appears to be influenced by nature. One comparison study of long-term care facilities with and without gardens demonstrated a significant difference in the incidence of violent behavior among Alzheimer's patients. Over a two-year period, the two facilities with gardens showed a decrease in violent behavior of 19 percent, compared to a 691 percent increase among the three facilities without gardens (Mooney and Nicell, as cited in Stevens, 1995). A provocative set of studies in urban public housing shows that having a window view of nature (e.g., a tree, a small garden) correlated with reduced domestic violence and greater interaction with neighbors (Coley et al., 1997; Sullivan and Kuo, 1996; Taylor et al., 1998). These findings suggest that the presence of nature may also impact the "health" of social groups in addition to that of the individual.

There is also evidence for a spiritual dimension to interaction with nature. When it comes time to think about issues in one's life, Herzog and colleagues (1997) find that people make a distinction between natural and human-built environments. Natural environments were rated higher as places that would foster reflection. Recent research shows that in urban settings, public green spaces such as parks do indeed facilitate contemplation and that this ability to reflect is enhanced in more biologically diverse green spaces (Fuller et al., 2007). Interaction with nature has also been found to support spiritual well-being within the work setting. In a study of the effect of work breaks in nature on hospital nurses, Irvine (2004) found that nurses who took nature breaks reported feeling refreshed, relaxed, and energized upon return—almost as if they were starting the day over again. Additionally, those who took breaks in nature had a significantly greater sense of wholeness than those who took breaks inside.

Studies of forested landscapes illustrate similar spiritually related findings. In a study of privately owned forestland, owners perceived their land as a place of refuge, a place in which to reconnect with themselves following a day at work (Irvine, 1997). Participants in outdoor challenge and wilderness programs often describe feelings of wholeness, of connectedness to a larger whole, and of being more in tune with what is important to them (Kaplan and Kaplan, 1989; McIntyre and Roggenbuck, 1998; Fredrickson and Anderson, 1999; Heintzman, 2000). In a study of retreat programs conducted in a natural setting,

participants felt more connected to the web of life, more connected to nature, and reported an increase in the ability to
reflect (Warber et al., 2007). One physician describes his own
outings in nature as "wilderness therapy," stressing how essential they are for his ability to stay focused and in the present
moment when meeting patients (Cumes, 1998). Interestingly,
the U.S. Forest Service is sponsoring research to explore how
these spiritual benefits of nature-based recreation (e.g., camp-
ing, hiking) may help guide the management of public parks
(Driver et al., 1996; Dustin, 1994).

EFFECTS OF HUMANS ON NATURE
The preceding sections illustrate both theory and research
suggesting that the presence of nature can indeed have an
effect on the health and well-being of humans. Is it possible
that people can affect the well-being of plants and nature,
beyond their well-known ability to destroy critical habitat?
Several researchers have explored this reverse relationship
with intriguing results.

Much like people, plants are made up of approximately two-
thirds water. Anyone with a garden or house plants knows that
water is essential for the health of plants. Water is drawn up
through the roots of plants, into the stem, and out to the leaves
where it eventually departs through openings in the leaves into
the surrounding air. In an indirect way, the water provided by
a person to an edible plant is ultimately returned to the person. Japanese researcher Masaru Emoto has explored the effect
of human words and thoughts on the formation of crystals in
water (Emoto, 2004). He has found that water forms beautiful
crystals when exposed to words such as "love," "gratitude,"
or "thank you." On the contrary, words such as "fool," or
"do it" resulted in poorly formed crystals or no crystals at all.
Emoto has also explored the effect of music (e.g., classical,

heavy metal) and electromagnetic waves on the formation of crystals in water with similar results. He has also looked at the ability of water from different sources (e.g., city water system, spring water) to form crystals. If people's words affect the water within the plants, then likely they will affect the plants as well. Might our words also affect other elements of nature?

People also affect plants through touch. Many of us have heard of, or perhaps experienced, the effect of touch on the leaves of certain plants, such as mimosa (*Mimosa pudica*). When touched, the leaves visibly drop to a limp position. This discovery was made by a pioneer in the study of plants, Jagadish Chandra Bose, a versatile scientist from India who conducted intricate research during the early part of the 1900s (Shepherd, 1999). Using self-designed instrumentation, he demonstrated not only the visible response to touch but also the invisible responses of plants to other forms of intervention, such as heat, light, gravity, and electricity (Bose, 1906; 1913). More recent evidence indicates that physical contact with plants by humans, such as stroking or rubbing stems, leaves, or flowers, will "turn on" the expression of so-called "touch genes" (Braam, 2005). This has implications for plant survival: insurance of pollination (as in hand-pollinated tomatoes, *Lycopersicon esculentum*), trapping of insects that devour plants (as in insectivorous plants), and even climbing of plants on human-placed stakes to ensure greater exposure to light.

The reactions of plants to events in their environments were further explored by Cleve Backster. An expert in polygraphs, or lie detectors, Backster used polygraphs to measure plants' reactions to events. He demonstrated the reaction of plants to human intention (e.g., the intention to burn a leaf), activity occurring in a plant's territory, death of nonhuman forms of life (e.g., brine shrimp), and the presence or absence of a plant's caretaker (Backster, 2003). Although controversial, in part due to a lack of replication of these studies, Backster's findings suggest plants may react, in ways we do not yet understand, to humans in their surroundings.

Another provocative area of research comes from the field of energy medicine. Biofield energy healing is based on the premise that an individual can channel energy for use in healing. Therapeutic Touch, practiced by nurses world wide, and Reiki, a modern adaptation of an ancient Eastern tradition, are two such examples. Grad (1963, 1964) demonstrated an effect of therapeutic touch on corn plants (*Zea mays*). Plants exposed to therapeutic touch grew more vigorously than plants that were not. Again, this adds evidence to the notion of a reciprocal relationship between humans and nature. Nature affects us positively for our well-being and we, too, can affect the nature around us. If all of life is spirit-filled then mindful interconnection may benefit us all.

SUMMARY AND A CALL TO ACTION

Looking out a window, walking to a neighbor's home, an excursion to a remaining wild area—each of these activities has the potential to place an individual in contact with some element of the natural world. While subtle, the natural world appears to touch us on many different levels, influencing our physical, emotional, mental, social, and spiritual well-being. And we, in turn, affect the spirit-filled nature around us. Nature somehow entices us to experience the world at a different pace, slower than the pace of cell phones, faxes, and beepers. The myriad sounds, textures, and colors re-awaken us to the sensuous side of life. We may be reminded of people, places, dreams that were once a part of our life, or hopes for the future. By encouraging us to reflect on these threads to the past, present, and future, we have an opportunity to move beyond our dominant way of being, limited by the constraints of the time-space construct of the material world. When we have that moment with nature—a treetop peeking out from above a building, a bird singing, the flow of water in a stream—we cease to be bounded. We experience interdependence and connectivity; our spirit is unified with the greater whole; we experience ourselves as whole; we are transformed; and on some level, we heal. Interaction with nature may no longer be a luxury, something we do if we have time or while on vacation. It may be a vital, necessary part of being whole persons. With this knowledge, each of us can begin to create actions that will alter our collective vision of human life, health, and the interconnectedness with all of Nature.

DAWN OVER THE POND

The pale glow at the intricate nonlinear edge of darkness transforms itself. Pink-blue light grows high into the sky. The jagged mass of blackness becomes discernable as green cascades, jumbles of trees and shrubs. Deep down into the center of the mass, smoke or spirits rise up from the flat reflection of the pond. Doves call, reminding me of childhood summers in the rose-filled backyards of my grandparents' tiny midwestern town. Life was full and simple; I was surrounded by love. In the now-time, the doves are joined by hundreds of other birds, sending their wake-up calls, their prayers out into the world. I drink this all in with my eyes, nose, breath, ears. I am immersed in this place and its spirit like one in water. I am water in water. The bag of my body is just that—a flimsy bag, not a solid container that separates me from the world around me. I merge; I slow my rhythms; I enter spiritual space. I begin to heal.

Sara L. Warber, M.D.

Is the outer world of the environment a reflection of the inner world of humanity? Can our thoughts and intentions actually change the pH balance of water? If so, is this a viable way to combat the environmental decline of the earth? Sharing the results of some ground-breaking experiments, Sandra Ingerman, author of *How to Heal Toxic Thoughts: Simple tools for Personal Transformation*, offers some ways to use spirituality to change the very composition of water, and possibly save the planet.

Medicine for the Earth

SANDRA INGERMAN

Rivers have always reminded me of the magic of life. My love for rivers has led me to wonder whether or not it is possible to reverse river pollution. This question in turn leads me to work toward the reversal of all environmental pollution. As a shamanic healer, I have always known that pollution in the outer world is a reflection of our inner state of consciousness. In the following essay, I'll share the results of research I have done about the ability to change the quality of water by changing this internal state of consciousness.

SHAMANISM AS A JOURNEY OF CHANGE
Shamanism is the first spiritual practice of humankind, dating back at least 40,000 years. The core method in shamanism

is the shamanic journey, a way to access spiritual information by traveling into nonordinary reality and engaging with compassionate spirits who offer direct revelation that answers questions and provides healing help.

I started practicing shamanism in 1980, and my personal practice led me to explore with the spirits the issue of reversing environmental pollution. One of the most important messages I have received in my twenty years of journeying is that it is not what we do, but who we *become,* that changes the world and our environment. Harmony within creates harmony without. So the true work is learning how to change our thoughts, attitudes, and belief systems. We have to work with "the alchemy of the soul" to change our inner environment, which is reflected back to us in the outer world. The literal definition of alchemy is "working within and through the dense darkness inside." This is big work, and involves committing to engage in spiritual practices all day, every day.

Stories from the Bible, the Kabbalah, and various Taoist, Hindu, yogic, alchemical, Egyptian, and shamanic works show that miracles were once an everyday occurrence. I researched many spiritual traditions for clues to how miracles were performed by ancient cultures, mystics, and saints. As I read about miracles, a formula of the elements that seem to be part of all of them came to me: a hologram. The elements cannot be taken separately but must combine to create transmutation. In my experiments with polluted water, I am partaking in what alchemists might have called transmutation, otherwise known as the ability to change the nature of a substance. I believe that in order to effect environmental change we must learn to change toxic substances into neutral ones. The formula I arrived at is: intention + union + love + focus + concentration + harmony + imagination = transmutation.

For miracles to happen, we must hold a strong intention of what we want to see happen. Intention requires concentration to create action. We must also be able to maintain a focus on our short-term and long-term goals.

All miracles involve union with a divine force. In the Bible, when Jesus instructs his followers "to heal in my name," the true Aramaic translation of this is "to know God and heal as God does." This means one must have union with the creative force of life for true healing to take place. The Indian guru, Sai Baba, is known for his miraculous acts and healing abilities. He says, "The only difference between me and you is I know who I am and you don't." In other words, he knows he is divine.

Love is an essential ingredient in all miracles, because techniques don't heal, only love does. Where there is an open heart, there is the energy to bring through miraculous and magical energy. Love is the great transformer.

I have already mentioned harmony as it is known in the practice of alchemy—harmony within creates harmony without. Disharmony creates disease; harmony creates beauty and health.

Imagination is another key in performing the miracle of transmutation; we must be able to envision an environment that is pure and clean and supports all of life. Caroline Casey, an American astrologer, says, "Imagination lays the tracks for the reality train to follow." With our imagination we have the ability to sculpt our world.

Adding to this formula, there are other principles to remember. As we change our perception we change our reality. In order to change our perception and create the reality of a clean environment, we must be able to see the beauty in all things. To do this we must live in a state of appreciation and gratefulness.

There are two phases of the work. One is to learn how to recognize that we are more than our bodies, our thoughts, and our past experiences. We are spiritual light and we are divine at all times.

In our egoic states we perceive ourselves as separate from each other and the rest of life. We are not separate; rather we are connected to one source and a web of life. Imagine one of your fingers dropping to the floor and thinking it can have an independent life without being connected to your body. That is what is happening today. Humankind is acting like separate fingers that have forgotten the connection to their original source of life.

Life circumstances and our relationships with others trigger negative thoughts and feelings. While it is important to acknowledge our thoughts and feelings, it is also important to acknowledge the energy behind our thoughts and feelings that we can send out to others and into the environment. In shamanic cultures it is understood that there is a difference between expressing anger and sending anger.

It is healthy to have a range of thoughts and emotions. Our task is to learn how to transmute or transform the energy behind our thoughts and emotions into love and light. In this way we can feel the depth of our feelings but not create any harm by doing so.

We must again recognize, as all ancient cultures did, that words are vibration. And when we speak aloud we send a vibration out into the universe that will manifest back on others and us.

You might remember how when you were a child you used the word "abracadabra." This is actually Aramaic, "abraq ad habra," and it literally translates to "I will create as I speak."

In my book *How to Heal Toxic Thoughts,* I teach readers how to work with the transmutation of negative states of consciousness and how to work with the power of words. This is the first phase of the work I have been doing with the environment.

The second phase is gathering in community to perform alchemical ceremonies to reverse the pollution that we have created. Alchemists did not actually change lead into gold. I believe the practice of alchemy was about changing lead *consciousness* into golden light *consciousness*. As we begin to change our consciousness and get in touch with the light inside us, we can effect great changes in our outer world. It is who we become, not what we do, that changes the world. Just as our experiments changed the content of the water molecules, by working together, we can change the environment as we change ourselves. This is the approach we took in our experiments: All life is made of light. We are all light. Everything is light. In remembering this, we can transmute everything in our outer environment, and everything that we take in, into pure healing light.

All spiritual traditions teach that everything manifests on a spiritual level before manifesting on the physical. During this time when so many of us feel disempowered, it is crucial to understand that we have power right now to create change on the planet by incorporating spiritual practices into our lives.

EXPERIMENTING WITH INTENTION

My book *Medicine for the Earth: How to Transform Personal and Environmental Toxins* goes into detail about the discoveries I made while working to understand how spiritual practices can affect the environment (more about this below). After I wrote the book, I started some scientific experiments to verify whether the practices I wrote about would truly transmute toxins. I began by intentionally polluting deionized (pure, mineral-free) water with ammonium hydroxide, a common and dangerous pollutant in our environment. As ammonium hydroxide is a strong base, it is easy to check its presence using pH strips. Over the years, I have worked with many groups of students to test whether the pH of the water decreases when we perform a ceremony I will describe below. I have worked with numerous groups in the United States since 2000, and I have repeated the experiment in England, Austria, and Switzerland. Every time, the pH of the water has changed, moving between 1 and 3 points toward neutral. From a scientific point of view, this would be seen as impossible, but I have replicated the results time and time again.

THE CEREMONY

The key ingredient is the ceremony, in which we use visualization to change the pH of the water we are working on. The ceremony takes place in a circle, at whose center is an altar where we place whatever substance we are working on (water, food, soil, etc.). We begin with a great deal of conscious preparation, including a cleansing with the smoke of burning sage and other traditional rituals. Then each participant begins to tone, or sing, a sound that to them represents the light of truth within each of us. After a certain period of time we end the ceremony and check the water for changes in the pH.

Here is an analogy to help to explain the magnitude of the changes we have observed in pH levels after performing this ceremony. Imagine a 1,000 square foot room with white wall-to-wall carpeting. Now imagine that the carpet has a huge grape juice stain that covers the entire 1,000 square feet. That completely stained carpet corresponds to a pH of 11. If the pH is reduced from 11 to 10, it's as though *900 square feet of the carpet have been cleaned*, leaving 100 feet stained. If the pH changes from 11 to 9, 990 square feet of the carpet have been cleaned. Every change in pH is an exponential change to the tenth power. In each experiment we have done, the water has changed a pH of 1 to 3 points toward neutral.

THE EQUIPMENT

After these initial experiments, I started using a gas discharge visualization (GDV) camera. A GDV allows one to capture the physical, emotional, mental, and spiritual energies emanating to and from an individual, plant, liquid, powder, or inanimate object and translate those energies into a computerized model. It measures and evaluates the energy of the auric field and integrates that information into a computer-generated report with pictures. This camera enables us to document the change in energy of the substances present inside our circle. To change the variables in the experiment, we put food (a peach and crackers) and soil in the circle instead of water.

When we took a photo with the water at a pH of 11.5, there was just a slight image of light, which was barely noticeable. A photo of the same water at a pH of 10 showed what looked like a star shining in the night star sky. When the water had a pH of 9.5, the starlight image was all the stronger. I found this interesting because in my invocation before our ceremonies, I use the words "Let's shine our light, reflecting the beauty of the night sky."

The photo of the peach was equally compelling. The peach came from a tree in my garden. Santa Fe had been in extreme drought when the peach had been growing, and I had thus been doing spiritual work to help all the trees on my five acres of land. As I could not physically give them the water they needed, I walked around each day visualizing each tree in its divine light and perfection.

When we took the first picture of the peach before the ceremony, the light it was emitting looked good. But it looked even better, and significantly brighter, after fifty people performed the ceremony I have described. This taught me about the power of working in a group versus working alone.

I soon began to get reports from people present at the ceremonies who were experiencing profound healing on an emotional and/or physical level as a result of being present for the circle. This did not surprise me, as we humans are made up mostly of water.

We soon started to invite people to lie in the middle of the circle along with the water or other substances we were testing, and these people subsequently reported the alleviation of many different symptoms. One woman who had been struggling with lupus and needed a service dog to help her walk started hiking without the aid of her dog the day after being in the middle of our circle. The ceremony was years ago and she has been hiking without any aid ever since. Other people have reported that their problems with depression and anxiety have cleared up after the experiment. A wide variety of ailments seem to be improved through this process, and those who have kept up the practice of performing ceremonies like this regularly have experienced real, long-term change.

Throughout these experiments, we have received positive feedback from people involved with the research. In 2005, I joined with the University of Michigan's integrative medicine department to conduct a pilot research study with heart attack patients to measure the effects of these spiritual practices.

During these group ceremonies, we perceive everyone and everything in the room as divine. On a physical level someone may have an illness, but on a spiritual level we recognize their divine perfection. In this way we stimulate the radiance of each being to shine forth. In quantum physics it is said that a lower frequency attunes to a higher frequency, and not the reverse. For example, if you enter into a room and there is a person full of light and love who is beaming, shining, and smiling, you will feel yourself lifted up by this energy. In the same way, when divine radiance is shining in a room it jump-starts the radiance of every substance or person present.

It is important to note that in our ceremonies we have not tried to manipulate the environment. We have not focused on the substances (water, food, or soil) within our circle. Instead, we intentionally focus on divine light, perfection, and oneness.

In doing so, we change our inner consciousness, which changes the other objects around us (like the pH of water). Through these experiments, we have found that our outer world will reflect back to us the inner changes that we make. This way of perception goes back to the ancient and esoteric principle of "as above, so below; as within, so without."

To find a local Medicine for the Earth teacher in your area, please visit www.medicinefortheearth.com. To find a local shamanic teacher in your area, please visit www.shamanicteachers.com.

To read Sandra's monthly Transmutation News, please visit www.shamanicvisions.com/ingerman.html. This website is translated into eight languages. To read more articles on shamanism and Sandra's work, please visit www.sandraingerman.com.

The visions presented by many spiritual ancient texts, of a universe reflecting human consciousness or united by a universal field of energy, have long been scorned by science. Now, many researchers are investigating how these beliefs hold up in the scientific understanding of reality, and how they might inform future scientific inquiry into the nature of the universe. Gregg Braden, author of the bestselling books *The Divine Matrix* and *The God Code*, addresses such questions as: Can widespread intention and prayer change events on a global scale? Can science help us understand the divine wisdom of our DNA? How do the universal field of energy and molecules of matter react to our innermost experiences? Is God found within the body?

The Power and Promise of Spiritually Based Science

GREGG BRADEN

The following chapter will examine new developments in science as they relate to ancient spiritual beliefs. Scientific discoveries validating the universal essence that connects all things, and our heart-based power to influence the world through that essence—the very foundation of spiritual empowerment—invite us to reexamine the way we think of science and spirituality today. In doing so, we gain life-affirming insights into ourselves and a renewed confidence to meet the tests of our future.

Since the birth of the scientific method three hundred years ago, modern science has been based on the belief that we are insignificant in the overall scheme of things. It has written us right out of the equation of nature, reality, and even life. Now, the same science that has discounted our role in the past is finding that consciousness, and our role in consciousness, provide the missing link to understanding everything from the behavior of the atom to the birth of the universe.

For the first time ever, we have the means to explore the possibility that we're born with the power to reverse disease, redefine aging, and even change reality itself, by embracing our role in consciousness.

While such a revelation may require a huge leap in traditional scientific acceptance, it comes as no surprise to those steeped in the wisdom of our most ancient and cherished spiritual traditions. The reason: for at least seven thousand years those traditions have described precisely the same concepts, only in the nonscientific language of another time.

As we find ourselves faced with the greatest challenges in recorded history, we may also discover that it's the marriage of modern science with the wisdom of our spiritual past that solves the mysteries of our existence, and perhaps even holds the key to our survival. If we have the courage to honor both ways of knowing, where can such wisdom lead? It's already happening and the answer may surprise you.

TAPPING THE MOST POWERFUL FORCE IN THE UNIVERSE
"There are beautiful and wild forces within us."

With these words, St. Francis of Assisi described the mystery and power that lives within every man, woman, and child born into this world. The Sufi poet Rumi further described the magnitude of our power by comparing it to a great oar that propels us through life. "If you put your soul against this oar with me," he begins, "the power that made the universe will enter your sinew from a source *not outside* your limbs, but from a holy realm *that lives in us.*"[1]

Through the language of poetry, both Rumi and St. Francis express the great secret of what has been called the most powerful force in the universe—our power to create the conditions in our heart (feelings and beliefs) that change the reality of our world. It's our ability to tap this power that carries us beyond the obvious experiences of our everyday world. Ironically, it's this very secret that was lost through the editing of the Judeo-Christian spiritual texts in the fourth century.[2]

The lost *Gospel of Thomas*, discovered in 1945 as part of Egypt's Nag Hammadi Library, offers a beautiful example of how the instructions for such a miraculous power were preserved. In the controversial pages of this Gnostic text, identified as a rare record of Jesus's own words, the master shared the key to living in this world without being a victim of it. He described how the union of thought and emotion—two related inner experiences—can be focused into a single potent force that molds our outer reality to the belief-waves of our heart. In verse 48 of the text, for example, we are told "If the two [thought and emotion] make peace with each other in this one house [our body], they will say to the mountain 'Move away' and it will move away."[3]

While I used to believe that such admonitions were simply metaphors for the power that lives within us, I now believe that our inner ability to change our outer world is factual. Although these simple instructions may seem to lack the technical credibility that we expect from a scientific paper today, recent discoveries have validated the power of such mystical texts. We now know, for example, that when we combine thought and emotion, they create a feeling in our heart, the very organ associated with the spiritual qualities that seem to make us who we are. Late in the twentieth century, scientists also documented that *it's our heart* that produces the strongest electrical and magnetic fields in our body—ten times stronger electrically and five thousand times stronger magnetically than those of our brain![4] And it's these powerful fields that extend *beyond* our heart to influence the atoms of the world that surrounds us. So when we have a feeling, we're actually creating patterns of energy that interact with the very stuff that the universe is made of!

This is the crux of the wisdom described in the passages from the Gospel of Thomas, as well as in records preserved in some of the most magnificent, pristine, isolated, and remote locations remaining in the world today. From the high-altitude monasteries of the Tibetan plateau, Egypt's Sinai peninsula, and the Andes Mountains of Peru to the oral traditions of native peoples throughout the Americas, it's the knowledge of how to hone our heart's focus into a potent force in our lives that has been preserved as a well-kept secret.

At this point you may be asking yourself the same question that I found myself asking as a senior computer systems designer working in the defense industry over twenty years ago. If such a power actually exists, and if we all have that power within us, then why doesn't everyone *know* that we have it? Why don't we all use it every day? The bulk of my adult life has revolved around my search to answer precisely this question—to know who we are and how the knowledge of our past, combined with the best science of today, can help us to become better people and create a better world.

From huge cities like Cairo and Bangkok to remote villages in Peru and Bolivia; from ancient monasteries in the Himalayas of Tibet to the world's oldest Hindu temples in Nepal, throughout my experience of each culture, a dual theme has emerged. First, each tradition describes the web or "net" of a universal essence—a pure space where all things begin. Second, they preserve the instructions of how we may communicate with this essence to change our bodies and our world. Interestingly, while these themes have been in direct conflict with the scientific beliefs of much of the past three hundred years, each one is now remarkably aligned with the new discoveries of the late twentieth and early twenty-first centuries. And it's these understandings that have underscored a powerful reality regarding what we now know about our world.

SCIENCE AND SPIRITUALITY: TWO PATHS TO THE SAME REALITY
Historically, the scientific way of thinking has discounted the wisdom that we find in ancient, indigenous, and spiritual traditions. The bottom line is that science and spirituality have been viewed as incompatible. The thinking has been that we must choose to study one way or the other to understand how the universe works, but never both of them combined. Now we know that to make such a choice can actually become the barrier to the very understandings that we search for. And here's the reason why.

Science is a way of describing our world, a language if you will, and a good one at that. Science and the scientific era are typically acknowledged as beginning in the 1600s when Newton formalized the mathematics that seem to describe our everyday world. For over two hundred years, Newton's observations of nature were the foundation of the scientific field now called *classical physics*.

Along with additional theories of electricity, magnetism, and relativity, classical physics has been tremendously successful in explaining the large-scale things that we see, such as the movement of planets and galaxies, and apples falling from trees. It's served us so well, in fact, that we've been able to calculate the orbits for our satellites, and even to put a man on the moon. But as well as this view of the world has served us, *the best scientists of our time openly admit that our scientific knowledge is incomplete*. And, in some instances, it's absolutely wrong.

During the early 1900s, advances in science revealed places in nature where Newton's laws just don't seem to work:

places like the very small world of the atom. It was in the sub-atomic world that scientists began to see things that could not be explained by classical physics. This is important because the places where the scientific ideas break down are the very places that form the essence of our bodies and our world! A new kind of physics—*quantum physics*—had to be developed with the new rules that would explain the exceptions.

In their attempt to describe the universe and our role in it, scientists who subscribed to classical physics as the only laws of nature suddenly found themselves locked into an impossible situation that has led to a series of incomplete theories. We can say this with certainty because those theories, some proposed over twenty years ago, have yet to unify the forces of nature and provide an accepted explanation for the mysteries of the very small world (the quantum world) and the very large realms of the universe.

To merge the two kinds of physics into a single unified description of the universe, something is missing: something that fills the empty space between things in the universe. Although traditional science has not allowed for that "something," spiritual traditions have. While it's called by many names, the missing link in the unified physics falls under the umbrella that we think of as *consciousness*. Consciousness, and our role in it, is quickly becoming the new frontier in exploring the way the universe works. And this is where the spiritual traditions of our past come in. Without the use of technology and equations, they tell us in no uncertain terms just what the new discoveries are pointing to: that we are part of, rather than separate from, all that we experience and that we play a powerful role in the universe.

So today we find ourselves in an interesting position where modern science is just arriving at the point where the spiritual traditions of our past began! With the acceptance of what quantum experiments are showing us, the question is less about whether or not we affect our world, and more about how much we do so and how to create the effects of healing, peace, and joy in a predictable way.

Although science has yet to answer these questions, the scientific method is only one way to describe how the universe works. There are other ways—other "languages"—that do so very well. And they have been in existence much longer than science! The discovery that everything in our world is part of a universal field of energy is a perfect example. While science has debated the existence of such a field for three hundred years, the spiritual texts of the Hindu traditions, for example, use the field's existence as a starting point, and have explored what the field means in our lives for over seven thousand years!

This is a beautiful illustration of how the marriage of science and spirituality—specifically the knowledge of science and the wisdom of spiritual traditions—can become the bridge to a powerful new way of seeing the universe and our role in it.

KNOWLEDGE AND WISDOM: EQUAL PARTS OF A GREATER POWER

Knowledge is the bridge that connects us with everyone who has ever lived before us. From civilization to civilization and lifetime to lifetime, we contribute the individual stories that become our collective history. No matter how well we preserve the information of the past, however, the words of these stories are little more than "data" until we give them the meaning that allows us to apply what we know. It's the way we apply what we know of our past that becomes the wisdom of the present.

The way we think of prayer illustrates what I mean here. For thousands of years, those who have come before us preserved the *knowledge* of our inner ability to change our outer world through certain forms of prayer. The secret, however, is not found in the words of the prayers themselves. Just as the power of a computer program is more than the language in which it's written, we must search deeper to know the true power of our inner experience—the thought, feeling, emotion, and belief—that is awakened by the words of the prayers.

It may be precisely this power that the nineteenth-century mystic George Gurdjieff discovered as the result of his lifelong search for truth. After years of following ancient clues that led him from temple to village, and teacher to teacher, he found himself in a monastery that remains secret even today, hidden in the mountains of the Middle East. There a great master offered the words of encouragement that made his search worthwhile. "You have now found the conditions in which the desire of your heart can become the reality of your being." I can't help but believe that the conditions described by Gurdjieff's teacher were based on the knowledge of how the universe works, and the practical wisdom of how to apply such knowledge in our lives.

Gurdjieff's experience illustrates why the combination of scientific knowledge and spiritual understandings is so appealing. Together, each serves as part of a greater whole: in this case a more complete understanding of our role in the universe. In this way, the scientific facts validate the inner power that our spiritual traditions imply.

When we allow each way of knowing to serve us in the way that it is designed—the science that tells us *how things work,* and the spiritual traditions that tell us *how to apply* such knowledge—together they may hold nothing less than the wisdom needed to survive what the experts are calling the greatest challenges in human history and to embrace the promise of our future!

FRAGMENTS OF THE WHOLE

If we accept what our two great ways of knowing—*science and spirituality*—have shown us in their respective languages, they both tell us precisely the same thing: that we are powerful architects of reality living in a world that is soft and malleable, and that changes in our presence. From the words of the great masters themselves, such as Buddha, Jesus, and the yogi Milarepa to the landmark Double Slit Experiment of 1909, repeated at Israel's Weissman Institute of Science in 1998 (*Nature*, February 1998), *both spiritual and scientific traditions are describing different aspects of the same thing—our relationship with the universe—*and doing so with a clarity that leaves little doubt as to what they are saying. *The key is that they tell us in different ways.* And this is where things get really interesting.

In the traditional way that science has thought of the universe, the theories that explain why things "are" have been based on forces that can be seen, or at least measured. While we know that additional forces such as consciousness do exist, because they cannot be measured they've been discounted as a significant factor in the way things seem to work. And this line of thinking has led to two beliefs that have separated us from a deeper understanding of the universe. It's only recently that these assumptions have been proven false.

> *False Assumption 1: Based upon the famous Michelson-Morley experiment performed in 1887, science has portrayed the space between "things" as empty. This landmark experiment was duplicated in 1986 with better equipment under the auspices of the U. S. Air Force* (Nature, 1987) *and yielded positive results in tests of the universal field, and proves that this assumption is simply not true!*
>
> *False Assumption 2: Based on the belief that space is "empty" and that there is nothing to carry inner experiences, such as feeling and belief, beyond our bodies, science has portrayed them as having no effect upon the world. And this has been proven absolutely false, as well* (Bulletin of the Lebedev Physics Institute, 1992).

The new discoveries cited above, published in leading-edge, peer-reviewed journals, reveal that we're bathed in a field of intelligent energy that fills what used to be thought of as empty space. Additional discoveries show that this field responds to us—*rearranges itself*—in the presence of our heart-based feelings and beliefs. Even with the proof, the new discoveries have yet to be universally accepted.

Regardless of who accepts them or how they're received, the experiments demonstrate beyond a reasonable doubt that we're part of the world, and affect it in ways that we're only beginning to understand. And this fact changes everything that we thought we knew about the way things work. They demonstrate what the ancient traditions have always held as the foundation of our existence: that a change in our world begins with a change in ourselves.

THE PROMISE OF A NEW WISDOM:
EXAMPLES OF MARRYING SCIENCE AND SPIRITUALITY
Clearly we don't know all that there is to know about how the universe works and our role in it. While new studies will undoubtedly enable greater understandings, we don't have to wait that long to reap the benefits of what, to many people, is a very strange way of thinking of the world. If the merger of science and spirituality can truly yield powerful new ways of thinking of the world, then we should be able to experience those benefits now, and we have!

Following are two examples of the kind of discovery, and the magnitude of the impact that such discoveries can have in our lives today. The discovery of a text message in the DNA of all life is very personal and provides an unprecedented window into the question of our origins, while the documented influence of a relatively few people creating peace in a broad geographic area offers a personal way to participate in a global issue. The fact that both have already been proven offers a glimpse into the magnitude of what awaits as we allow ourselves to see the universe through the new eyes of a greater wisdom.

EXAMPLE I: THE CODED MESSAGE
IN THE DNA OF LIFE—THE GOD CODE

Perhaps one of the most powerful examples of where the marriage of science and spiritual traditions can lead is the remarkable discovery of a lost code in our DNA—*a message that can be read like the letters on a page*—and a clue to our past that we have carried since the time of our origins. The discovery of the message resulted from a twelve-year-long project and became possible only after crossing the traditional boundaries that have separated spiritual traditions from scientific knowledge. In other words, it was only by considering the theme of a five-thousand-year-old text (the Sefer Yetzirah) through the eyes of modern science that the message in our DNA could be read.

The bottom line to this discovery is that both the ancient and modern accounts of life's origins use different languages to describe the same principles: both describe DNA using words and numbers. *The key is that while the words have changed over time, the numbers have not.* Applying this discovery to the biology of cells, the familiar elements of hydrogen, nitrogen, oxygen, and carbon that form our DNA may now be replaced with key letters of the ancient languages. Through a process that is detailed in *The God Code* (Hay House, 2004), when we do so, we discover that each of the 50 trillion or so cells of our body carries the literal words of a timeless message. *Translated, the message reveals that the precise letters of God's ancient name are encoded in every cell, of every life.*

The message literally reads:
YH VG, *translating to* "God within the body."

The meaning of the message:
Humankind is one family, united through a common heritage,
and the result of an intentional act of creation.

Preserved within each cell of the six billion-plus inhabitants of our world, the message is repeated, again and again, to form the building blocks of our existence. This ancient message from the day of our origins—*the same message*—exists within each of us today, regardless of race, religion, heritage, lifestyle, or belief. The code is so universal that it produces the identical message when translated into either the Hebrew or the Arabic language! And the statistics show that this message is no accident. The odds of this sequence forming by chance are only 1 in 234,256! When combined with the meaning of the message itself they suggest that something more than chance or coincidence is responsible for the code.

It may be no accident that such a powerful message of unity is revealed now, in the first years of the new millennium. The discovery of a universal message, including God's ancient name, within the essence of all life demonstrates that we are related not only to one another, but to all life, in the most intimate way imaginable. With such tangible proof of a common bond, we're given a reason to look beyond the issues that may have separated us in the past, and a place to begin when our differences seem insurmountable.

EXAMPLE 2: PERSONAL PEACE REFLECTED
IN A REGIONAL WAR

I suspect that future generations will see our time in history as the turning point when the conditions of the world forced us to discover how the universe really works, and accept our interactive role in it, to survive what we've created. The key to tapping our power to influence reality lies in our ability to embrace the two landmark discoveries described above. The first is the fact that the universe, our world, and our bodies are made of a shared field of energy and the second is the fact that our inner experiences of feelings, emotions, and beliefs directly influence what happens in the shared field.

The scientific validation of these two principles gives new meaning to ancient accounts that sound strikingly similar. From the ancient Indian Vedas, believed by some scholars to date to 5000 BC, to the two-thousand-year-old Dead Sea Scrolls, a general theme suggests that the world is actually the mirror of things that are happening in a deeper reality of consciousness. Commenting on the new translations of the Dead Sea Scroll fragments known as *The Songs of the Sabbath Sacrifice*, for example, its translators summarize the content, stating "What happens on earth is but a pale reflection of that greater, ultimate reality."[5]

While the idea of an ever-present field of intelligence is nothing new, modern physicists have now elevated the concept to a higher level of acceptance. Perhaps renowned Princeton University physicist John Wheeler, who was a contemporary of Albert Einstein, best described the revolutionary physics of an energy that connects all of creation. He proposed that consciousness is more than a by-product of the universe, suggesting instead that we live in what he calls a "participatory" universe. "We are part of a universe that is a work in progress," he said. "We are tiny patches of the universe looking at itself, *and building itself.*" The implications of Wheeler's statements are vast. In the language of twentieth-century science, he reiterated what ancient traditions stated millennia ago: it is consciousness that creates!

And this is where it becomes clear how a change that we make within us can become such a powerful contribution to our world. Scientific studies support these principles and show that when peace, for example, is experienced *within* a group of people through meditation and prayer, the effects of peace are measured *beyond* the group.

In 1972, 24 cities in the United States with populations over ten thousand experienced meaningful changes in their communities when as few as 1 percent of the population (100 people) participated in communal prayer and meditation. These and similar studies led to a landmark study, the International Peace Project in the Middle East, which was published in the *Journal of Conflict Resolution* in 1988.[6] During the Israeli-Lebanese war of the early 1980s, researchers trained two hundred people to *feel* peace in their bodies rather than simply to think about peace in their minds or pray *for* peace to occur.

On specific days of the month, at specific times of each day, these people were positioned throughout the war-torn areas of the Middle East. During the window of time that they were feeling peace, terrorist activities stopped, crimes against people declined, emergency room visits declined, and traffic accidents dropped. When the people stopped their feelings of peace, the statistics reversed. These studies confirmed the earlier findings; when a small percentage of the population achieved peace within themselves, that peace was reflected in the world around them.

While these and similar studies obviously deserve more exploration, they show that there's an effect here that's beyond chance. The quality of our innermost beliefs clearly influences the quality of our outer world. While this is certainly an empowering way of seeing the world, it is also a very different way for the Western mind to think. It's clear that for the mirror of our world to reflect positive, life-affirming, and lasting change, we must give the mirror something with which to work! Rather than forcing the world to bend to our wishes, this relationship promises that when we change our feelings about the world, our changes become the blueprint of our reality.

Through these two very different examples, we find the common thread that makes them important to the ideas presented here. Both became possible only by crossing the traditional boundaries between science and spirituality. As powerful as each example is in its own right, I can't help but believe that they offer only a glimpse into what we'll find as we allow ourselves to embrace a more holistic way of thinking.

WHY HERE? WHY NOW?

In the first years of the twenty-first century, we find ourselves in a situation that no humans are believed to have ever faced, with threats of war, disease, dwindling resources, and climate change that no humans have ever had to address. While our ancestors certainly dealt with some of these problems individually, it's the sheer magnitude that each of these conditions poses today, *and the fact that they are all happening at the same time*, that places us in a situation unprecedented in our past.

Recent studies, such as those reported in *Scientific American*'s special issue titled *Crossroads for Planet Earth* (September 2005), state: "The next 50 years will be decisive in determining whether the human race—*now entering a unique period in its history*—can ensure the best possible future for itself" (author's italics). The consensus of the special issue underscores the theme of the journal: we simply can't continue with the way we use energy, the direction of technology, and an ever-expanding population if we expect to survive into the next century. Complicating all of these problems is the growing threat of a world war (perhaps a nuclear war) that is driven, at least in part, by the competition for the same disappearing resources that defined the essays.

If we can accept the powerful evidence that consciousness itself, and our role in consciousness, are the missing links in the theories of reality, then everything changes. Suddenly we become part of, rather than separate from, all that we see and experience. It writes us—all of humankind—right back into the equation of life and the universe. Such healed wisdom also writes us into the role of solving the great crises of our day, rather than leaving them to a future generation or simply to fate. We may well discover that by giving ourselves permission to cross the boundaries that have separated science and spirituality in the past, we also open the door to the most powerful discoveries of our future—discoveries that will answer our oldest questions, solve our deepest mysteries, and perhaps assure our survival.

This is precisely where our willingness to marry our two great ways of knowing—science and spirituality—into an even greater wisdom may prove to be one of the powerful turning points in human history. Discovering that we are architects of our reality, *with no less than the power to rearrange the atoms of matter itself*, we can ask: what problem cannot be solved and what solution could possibly be beyond our reach? It all comes down to what we know about the universe, what we accept as our role in it, and how we apply what we've learned to the great tests of our time.

PART 2

Biology, Psychology, the Brain, and Quantum Physics

Neuroscience, Epigenetics, Energy Psychology, Quantum Physics, Eudaimonics, Buddhism, and the Brain

How do biology and the evolving science of epigenetics interface with current evidence about consciousness and the subconscious mind? Who is actually "running the show" in our brains? These are the questions Bruce Lipton, author of several books including *The Biology of Belief: Unleashing the Power of Consciousness, Matter, and Miracles*, examines in the following essay. Lipton leads us from new discoveries about cellular biology to the true ability of the subconscious mind and its relationship with mindfulness.

Revealing the Wizard Behind the Curtain

The "New" Biology and Epigenetics

BRUCE H. LIPTON, PH.D.

There is a "new edge" biology in town and it's radically reframing our understanding of life. Frontier science is recognizing that there is a lot more to life than just a bio-chemical machine controlled by genes. Amazing advances in cell biology and biophysics are invoking the role of mind and spirit as the creative force controlling the character of our lives. Recently described biochemical pathways have now revealed the mechanisms by which thoughts, attitudes, and beliefs create the conditions of our body and the external world. An awareness of these biological breakthroughs is fundamental for healing ourselves and our planet. Through a personal understanding of how consciousness interfaces with biology, we are offered the key to realizing personal growth and impacting global transformation.

Since Watson and Crick's discovery of the genetic code in 1953, the public has been programmed with the conventional belief that DNA "controls" the attributes passed down through a family's lineage, including dysfunctional traits such as cancer, Alzheimer's, diabetes, and depression, among scores of others. As "victims" of heredity, we naturally perceive ourselves as being powerless in regard to the unfolding of our lives. Unfortunately, the assumption of being powerless is a path that leads to personal irresponsibility: "Since I can't do anything about it anyway . . . why should I care?"

By the 1970s, the notion of *genetic determinism* led scientists to believe that life's programs were encoded in the genes. They thus set out to map the human genome, hoping that in revealing that code, they would find the key to finally preventing and curing human illness. The project was well underway when cell biologists began to uncover a paradigm-shattering view of how life really works. Their revolutionary research has led to an entirely new branch of science known as *Epigenetics* (Watters, 2006). Epigenetic science has shaken the foundations of biology and medicine to its core, for it reveals that we are not "victims," but in fact "masters" of our genes.

The prefix *epi-* means "over or above." Currently, students in high school and basic college biology courses are programmed with the now outdated notion of *genetic control,* the belief that genes primarily control the traits of life. In contrast, the new science of *epigenetic control* reveals that life is controlled by something "above" the genes. Exciting new insights concerning what that *something* "above" the genes is provides a gateway to understanding our proper role as participatory creators in the unfolding of our lives.

SOMEWHERE BEYOND THE GENES

Epigenetic science focuses upon the mechanisms by which environmental signals regulate gene activity. Protein "switches" in the cell's membrane respond to environmental signals by relaying "secondary" signals into the cell's cytoplasm. Some membrane-derived signals regulate the cell's physiologic functions (e.g., digestion, respiration, and excretion); other membrane signals are directly sent to the cell's nucleus where they control gene activity (Lipton, 2005).

This is far different from the conventional belief that genes turn themselves "on" and "off." Genes are not *emergent* entities, which means genes do not control their own activity. Genes are simply molecular "blueprints" (Nijhout, 1990). In contrast, epigenetic mechanisms are functionally analogous to "contractors" that select appropriate gene blueprints needed for the construction and maintenance of the body. Genes do not *control* biology . . . they are *used* by biology.

The traditional notion that the genome represents "read-only" programs has given way to a new reality wherein epigenetic mechanisms modify the readout of an individual's genetic code. The power of epigenetics is revealed in the fact that epigenetic mechanisms edit the readout of a gene and are able to create over thirty thousand different variations of proteins from the same gene blueprint (Silverman, 2004)! Depending on the nature of the environmental signals, the same gene can be modified to produce either healthy or dysfunctional protein products. In other words, one can be born with healthy genes but through a distortion in epigenetic signaling, can develop a mutant condition such as cancer (Kling, 2003). On the positive side, the same epigenetic mechanisms enable individuals born with potentially debilitating mutations to create normal, healthy proteins and functions from their inherited defective genes (Waters and Jirtle, 2003).

Epigenetic mechanisms modify the readout of the genetic code; consequently, the genome represents "read-write" programs wherein life experiences can actively redefine an individual's genetic traits. As organisms interact with the environment, their perceptions engage epigenetic mechanisms to fine-tune genetic expression so as to enhance their opportunities for survival. This environmental influence is dramatically revealed in studies of identical twins. At birth and shortly after, these siblings express almost the same gene activity from their identical genomes. However, as they begin to experience life, their personal individualized experiences and perceptions lead to the activation of profoundly different sets of genes (Fraga, 2006).

This revised version of science emphasizes the reality that we actively control our genetic expression moment by moment throughout out our lives. We are "learning" organisms, and our life experiences can become incorporated into our genomes and passed to our offspring. Rather than perceiving of ourselves as helpless victims of our genes, we must now own the empowering truth that our perceptions and responses to life dynamically shape our biology and behavior. Now let's take a look at how those all-powerful perceptions are actually shaped.

FROM THE MICROCOSM OF THE CELL
TO THE MACROCOSM OF THE MIND

Most of the trillions of cells forming bodies such as ours have no direct perception of the external environment. Liver cells "see" what's going on in the liver, but don't directly know what's going on in the world outside the skin. The function of the brain and nervous system is to interpret environmental stimuli and send signals to the cells that integrate and regulate life-sustaining functions of the body's organ systems.

Evolution accommodated increases in brain size, allowing organisms to dedicate vast numbers of nerve cells for cataloging, memorizing, and integrating complex perceptions. The ability to remember and select among the millions of experienced perceptions acquired in life provides the brain with a powerful creative database from which it can design and integrate complex behavioral repertoires. When put into play, these behavioral programs endow the organism with the characteristic trait of *consciousness*. In this case, the term *consciousness* is used in its most fundamental context: *the state of being awake and aware of what is going on around you.*

Many scientists prefer to think of consciousness as something an organism either has or does not have. However, the study of evolution suggests that consciousness mechanisms evolved over time. Consequently, the character of consciousness would likely express itself as a gradient of awareness from "less conscious" in primitive organisms to the unique character of *self-consciousness* manifest in humans and other higher vertebrates. *Self-consciousness* endows one with the quality of simultaneously being both a participant and observer in the unfolding of one's life.

The expression of *self-consciousness* is specifically associated with a small evolutionary adaptation in the brain known as the *prefrontal cortex*. The prefrontal cortex is the neurological platform that enables us to realize our personal identity and to experience the quality of "thinking." Monkeys and lower organisms do not express self-consciousness. Monkeys looking into a mirror will never realize that they are looking at themselves; they will always perceive the image to be that of another monkey. In contrast, neurologically more advanced chimps looking in the mirror recognize the mirror's reflection as their own image.

An important difference between the brain's *consciousness* and the prefrontal cortex's *self-consciousness* is that conventional *consciousness* enables an organism to assess and respond to the immediate conditions of its environment that are relevant at that moment. In contrast, *self-consciousness* enables the individual to factor in the consequences of their actions not just in the present moment, but also as to how they will impact the future.

Self-consciousness, which incorporates a reasoning individual ("self") in the decision-making process, enables us to be cocreators, not merely responders, to environmental stimuli. While conventional *consciousness* enables organisms to participate in the dynamics of life's "play," the quality of *self-consciousness* offers an opportunity to be not just an actor, but also an audience member and even a director. *Self-consciousness* provides an individual with the option for self-reflection, and the ability to review and edit their character's performance.

As significant as it is to our own identity, *self-consciousness* is actually just a small part of what we call the *mind*. While the self-conscious mind is engaged in self-reflection, someone has to be minding the store; enter the *subconscious mind*. In conventional parlance, the brain's mechanism associated with automated stimulus-response behaviors is referred to as the *subconscious* or *unconscious mind*, because this function requires neither conscious observation nor attention. Subconscious mind functions evolved long before the prefrontal cortex. Consequently, organisms unable to express self-consciousness are fully able to operate a body and navigate the challenges of a dynamic environment. In a manner similar to lower organisms, we too can cruise on "automatic pilot" regulating our physiologic and behavioral functions without need for advice or other input from the *self-conscious mind*.

WHO'S RUNNING THE SHOW?

The *subconscious mind* is an astonishingly powerful information processor that can record perceptual experiences (programs) and forever play them back at the push of a button. Interestingly, many people only become aware of their subconscious mind's push-button programs when their own "buttons are pushed" by the actions of others.

Actually, the entire image of pushing buttons is far too slow and linear to describe the awesome data processing capacity of the subconscious mind. It has been estimated that the disproportionately larger brain mass providing the subconscious mind's function has the ability to interpret and respond to over 40 million nerve impulses per second (Norretranders, 1998). In contrast, the diminutive self-conscious mind's prefrontal cortex only processes about forty nerve impulses per second. As an information processor, the subconscious mind is *one million times* more powerful than the self-conscious mind.

In contrast to its computational wizardry, the subconscious mind has only a marginal aptitude for creativity, best compared to that of a precocious five-year-old. While the self-conscious mind can express free will, the subconscious mind primarily expresses prerecorded stimulus-response "habits." Once a behavior pattern is learned—such as walking, getting dressed, or driving a car—those programs become automatic habits in the subconscious mind, meaning you can carry out these complex functions without paying any attention to them.

While the subconscious mind can run all internal systems *and* chew gum at the same time, the much smaller self-conscious mind can juggle only a small number of tasks simultaneously. Although its ability for multitasking is physically constrained, the trained self-conscious mind is quite adept at "single-tasking." It is the organ of focus and concentration. It was once thought that some of the body's involuntary functions, such as the regulation of heartbeat, blood pressure, and body temperature, were beyond the control of the self-conscious mind. However, yogis and other adept practitioners have clearly demonstrated that the mind can indeed control presumed "involuntary" functions. Most of us have experienced how mind controls such functions when we become excited, happy, or sad while watching a movie or awaken from a scary dream, wet with perspiration and our hearts pounding. A vivid imagination controls autonomic functions as much as real events.

The subconscious and self-conscious minds work as a marvelous tandem tag team. The subconscious mind's role is to control every behavior that is not attended to by the self-conscious mind. For most of us, the self-conscious mind is so preoccupied with thoughts about the past or the future, or engaged with some problem in our imagination, that we leave the day-to-day, moment-to-moment "driving" to the subconscious mind. Cognitive neuroscientists reveal that the profoundly more powerful subconscious mind is responsible for 95 to 99 percent of our cognitive activity and therefore controls almost all of our decisions, actions, emotions, and behaviors (Szegedy-Maszak, 2005).

The most powerful and influential behavioral programs in the subconscious mind were acquired during the formative period between gestation and six years of age. Now here's the catch—these life-shaping subconscious programs are direct downloads derived from observing our primary teachers: our parents, siblings, and local community. Unfortunately, as psychologists are keenly aware, many of the perceptions acquired about ourselves in this formative period are expressed as limiting and self-sabotaging beliefs (Lipton, 1998, 2001).

Unbeknownst to most parents, their words and actions are being continuously recorded by their children's minds. Since the role of the mind is to make coherence between its programs and real life, the brain generates appropriate behavioral responses to life's stimuli to assure the "truth" of the programmed perceptions.

Let's apply this understanding to real-life behavior: Consider that you were a five-year-old child throwing a tantrum in a department store over your desire to have a particular toy. In silencing your outburst, your father reprimands you with his *often-repeated* response, "*You* don't deserve things!" You are now an adult and in your self-conscious, thinking mind you are considering the idea that you have the qualities and power to assume a position of leadership at your job. Remember, while in the process of entertaining this positive thought in the self-conscious mind, programs in your more powerful subconscious mind are automatically managing all of your behaviors. Since your fundamental behavioral programs are those derived in your formative years, your father's rebuke that "you do not deserve things" may become the subconscious mind's automated directive. So while you are conjuring up wonderful thoughts of a positive future and not paying attention to the current moment, your subconscious mind automatically engages self-sabotaging behaviors to assure that your reality matches your program of "not deserving."

THE SUBCONSCIOUS MIND: THE INVISIBLE PILOT

When the self-conscious mind is engaged in thought, it rarely observes the automatic behaviors generated by the subconscious mind. Consider the significance of this common reality: Let's say you have a friend Mary whom you've known since childhood. Being familiar with her and her family so long, you recognize that Mary's behavior closely resembles that of her mother. Then one day you casually remark, "You know, Mary, you're just like your mom." Mary backs away in shock, indignant that you could even suggest that she was like her mother! "How can you say something so ridiculous?" she demands.

The cosmic joke is that everyone else can see that Mary's behavior resembles her mom's *except* Mary. Why? Simply because when Mary is engaging the subconscious behavioral programs she downloaded in her youth from observing her mom, her self-conscious mind is preoccupied in thought and she's not paying attention. At those moments, her automatic subconscious programs operate without observation; hence they are *unconscious*. Only rarely do we observe our unconscious behavior—and it is usually a shock when we do.

Consequently, most of our personal and cultural problems arise from the belief that we are running our lives with our conscious desires and aspirations. *"This is what I want from life. I want to do all these wonderful things."* Yet our lives usually don't match our intentions; as a result there is a tendency to think, *"I can't get the things that I want . . . the world is not providing them. The Universe is against me!"* Generally, the reason we fail to get what we desire is not because the Universe does not want us to succeed, but because we undermine our own efforts with "invisible" limiting behaviors. Unfortunately, our fundamental subconscious programs were acquired by observing the behavior of others (e.g., parents, family, community, TV), people who may not share our personal goals and aspirations. While our conscious minds are trying to move us toward our dreams, unbeknownst to us, our subconscious programs may be simultaneously shooting ourselves in the foot and impeding our progress.

We have all been shackled with emotional chains wrought by dysfunctional behaviors programmed by the stories of the past. However, the next time you are talking to "yourself" with the hope of changing sabotaging subconscious programs, it is important to realize the following information. The subconscious mind is simply a "record-playback" mechanism that downloads experiences and programs them as "behavioral tapes." There is no thinking, conscious entity controlling subconscious programs; this autopilot mind is basically a stimulus-response reflex mechanism. Using reason to communicate with your subconscious mind in an effort to change its behavior would essentially have the same influence as trying to change a program on a cassette tape by talking to the tape player. In neither case is there an entity in the mechanism that will respond to your dialogue.

Positive affirmations and positive thinking are not that effective in reprogramming limiting beliefs. Positive thoughts are generated by the conscious mind, a tiny processor that controls the system less than 5 percent of the time. If programs in the subconscious mind do not support the intentions of the conscious mind, which will win out? Positive thinking is a good idea, much better than negative thinking, yet while one is engaging the conscious mind to create positive thoughts, the subconscious mind with its limiting and self-sabotaging programs is running the show! Consequently, positive thinking does not necessarily improve the situation for most people.

FROM THE BLAME GAME TO RESPONSE-ABILITY

One of the most important points to make is that subconscious programs are *not* fixed, unchangeable behaviors. We have the ability to rewrite our limiting beliefs and in the process take control of our lives. However, to change subconscious programs requires the activation of processes other than engaging in a running dialogue with the subconscious mind.

One of the more ancient processes of taking control of your life is to be fully present and use your creative conscious mind to control behavior, rather than rely on the "autopilot" habitual programs downloaded into your subconscious mind. For example, the next time you are driving and come to a stoplight, pause for a moment and listen to the monologue that is continuously emanating from your mind. Most of the information is either a rehashing of the past or expectations about your future.

Psychologists suggest that most of these thoughts are negative and redundant, with 95 percent of them arising from perceptions programmed in the subconscious mind. As mentioned earlier, the function of the brain is to create coherence between its programs and the life you experience. When you have the opportunity to "listen" to your thoughts, realize that their content is greatly influencing your future expectations. Increasing consciousness by being an observer of your thoughts is a foundational principle of Buddhism.

Amazingly, the power of thought is also fully recognized by the principles of quantum physics, a science that acknowledges the participation of the observer in the creation of reality. This profound conclusion is originally derived from many experiments that attempted to identify the "true" character of Nature's fundamental building blocks—were they made of immaterial *waves* (energy) or were they physical *particles* (matter)? This is an "either-or" solution since something cannot be both physical *and* nonphysical. The surprising answer to their quest: if the scientist created an experiment that registered particles, they were particles; if the scientist created an experiment to detect waves, they were waves. Simple conclusion: "The observer *creates* the reality!" This role of mind in creating reality was recently underscored in the prestigious scientific journal *Nature*. In an article entitled "The Mental Universe," Richard Conn Henry, professor of physics at the Johns Hopkins University, concludes, "The universe is immaterial—mental and spiritual. Live and enjoy" (Henry, 2006). It is a scientific reality that thoughts influence the material world!

When the *subconscious mind* provides for most of our thoughts, then our lives are primarily shaped by our developmental experiences, including behaviors and attitudes acquired from others (e.g., parents, family, and community) (Lipton,

2001). However, if we keep our self-conscious mind focused upon the present moment, rather than letting it wander into the past or future, we can actively control our mind by using thoughts that empower ourselves and lead us to our desired intentions and aspirations.

Interestingly, you may have actually experienced the spectacular consequences of living from the *self-conscious mind,* and it was probably the happiest, healthiest, and most energetic period of your life. It was when you fell in love and experienced the "honeymoon effect," a period where you were fully present and very self-conscious of your attitudes and behaviors. Your self-conscious mind was "running the show" to assure that you were presenting yourself in the qualities you aspire to, rather than allowing the expression of habitual traits programmed into your subconscious mind. These new insights from biology and physics provide a scientific recognition of the powerful, life-affirming consequences of the Buddhist spiritual practice known as *mindfulness.*

Other approaches to rewriting limiting or sabotaging subconscious programs include clinical hypnotherapy and a new field of diverse modalities, collectively called "energy psychology," that identify and rapidly rewrite limiting belief programs in our subconscious minds. For more information on how to rewrite our subconscious programs, review the Resources selection at www.brucelipton.com.

THE OLD STORY IS THE NEW STORY

The conclusions of the "new edge" biology provide a radical departure from our conventional beliefs of how life works. In contrast to the notion of being a genetically driven biochemical automaton, the new insights reveal that it is the mind that controls genes, which in turn shape our biology and behavior. The self-conscious mind, associated with our individual identity and the manifestation of thoughts, is guided by our own personal beliefs, desires, and intentions.

Here's what is important for now: As we recognize our ability to change our programming, we evolve from passive victims to responsible cocreators. In the process, we are afforded the opportunity to respond to life, not merely react to it.

Once we realize that our past behaviors were predicated on the invisible operation of the subconscious mind—whose programs are derived from other people's beliefs—we are afforded the opportunity to forgive ourselves. Our invisible behaviors are programs primarily derived from others, who in turn were programmed by others, backward through time. Perhaps instead of original sin, we should be talking about "original misperception." In any case, neither we nor our parents, nor their parents, were aware that we were primarily controlling our lives using behavioral programs derived from others.

In this regard, it is important to remember this: ALL of the people we have ever engaged with over our lifetime were also responding using invisible behavioral programs downloaded into *their* infant subconscious minds. Consequently, they too were personally unaware of their own invisible participation and contributions that may have impacted our lives.

Based upon the scientific insights on the nature of how the mind works, the "new" biology implores us to heed the advice of all the great prophets to forgive all of those that have transgressed against us. We have all been shackled with emotional chains wrought by dysfunctional behaviors programmed by the stories of the past. Through forgiveness, we unshackle ourselves and others, allowing us all to let go of the old story.

It is of profound importance to the evolution of humanity that these new insights reach the public. Efforts to bring peace into the world are truly impeded because most citizens are unconsciously responding to cultural wrongs that were perpetrated generations ago on their ancestors. From this perspective, it behooves us to step back and reconsider our emotionally charged notions concerning blame, guilt, victims, and perpetrators. These labels can only be legitimately applied to situations in which the participants are fully cognizant of the programming and operation of their self-conscious and sub-conscious minds and yet still engage in destructive behaviors.

In studying the life and teachings of Jesus, it is clear that He was innately aware of the mechanics of consciousness and employed it in controlling His own biology and behavior. This is why Jesus emphasized that were it not for our (limiting) beliefs, we all could do the miracles He did, and perhaps, even better than He did them. He was on target when He declared that we could renew our lives with our beliefs. And most importantly, He saw the reality of forgiveness as the most important path toward peace. If enough of us performed this simple "local" act, we would indeed advance global evolution.

How do the ideas of psychologists, neuroscientists, and philosophers compare to those of the Dalai Lama? Dr. Daniel Goleman, author of bestsellers such as *Emotional Intelligence,* chronicled the eighth meeting of the Dalai Lama and a diverse group of Western scientists in his book *Destructive Emotions: A Scientific Dialogue with the Dalai Lama,* from which the following article is excerpted. At the conference, called the Mind and Life Institute, the group discussed the nature of consciousness and the transformation of destructive emotions. In this excerpt, one of the scientists, the late Dr. Francisco Varela, who specialized in the deep philosophical questions of neuroscience, engages in a dialogue with the Dalai Lama about the sequence of the mental activity of a moment, from perception to action, and how such scientific findings correlate to Buddhist epistemology.

The Brain's Melody

DANIEL GOLEMAN

Dr. Francisco Varela mapped out two complementary goals he saw in the research agenda for the Mind and Life Institute, his own work focusing on the dynamics of mental activity within a moment's time, while Richie Davidson explored lasting changes in the brain over a much longer time span: months or even years.

"For example, when anger arises, there is a refractory period where you just have time to catch the anger arising and try to suppress the action that will follow. It follows that you need to understand very precisely the dynamics of the emergence of that state. You need to understand in great detail a moment of experience. How does a moment of consciousness, a moment of cognitive activity, a perception, or an emotion actually arise?

If we understood it better, then we could clarify how to apply that understanding to work with it. But very little is known about the minute details of how it arises."

At this, the Dalai Lama perked up; he had a keen personal interest in just this question. Though the ensuing presentation seemed quite esoteric to many in the room, from the Dalai Lama's perspective it was to be one of the richest parts of the entire week.

Varela continued: "When we perform a cognitive act—for example, we have a visual perception—the perception is not the simple fact of an image in the retina. There are many, many sites in the brain that become active. The big problem, Your Holiness, is how these many, many active parts become coherent to form a unity. When I see you, the rest of my experience—my posture, my emotional tone—is all a unit. It is not dispersed, with perception here and movement there.

"How does that happen? Imagine that each one of the sites in the brain is like a musical note. It has a tone. Why a tone? Empirically, there is an oscillation. The neurons in the brain oscillate all over the place. Each goes *whoomph*—(his arms rising as in an expansive gesture)—and then *ffhhh*—(falling in deflation). The *whoomph* is when different places in the brain oscillate, and these become harmonized. When you have a wave here and another there, from different parts of the brain, several become synchronized, so they oscillate together.

"When the brain sets into a pattern—to have a perception, or to make a movement—the phase of these oscillations becomes harmonized, what we call phase-locked. The waves oscillate together in synchrony."

"Am I right in understanding your metaphor," the Dalai Lama asked, "that each of these oscillations is like a different tone and when they are combined together you create music?"

"You create music, exactly," Francisco agreed. "Many patterns of oscillations in the brain spontaneously select each other to create the melody; that is, the moment of experience. That's the *whoomph*. But the music is created with no orchestra conductor. This is fundamental."

Francisco mimed a conductor, waving his arms in the air. "You don't have a little man in there saying, 'Now you, and you, and you.' It doesn't work that way. So again, to understand the large-scale integration of the whole brain, the basic mechanism is the transitory formation of synchronous groups of neurons that are distributed widely. This was a beautiful discovery that gives us an account of how a moment of experience can arise."[1]

FAMILIES IN THE BRAIN

Here the Dalai Lama donned his familiar debater's hat as the scientific interlocutor: "Does this process vary from individual to individual? Would it be faster in some cases? Is it stable? Does it depend on age?"

"Those are very good questions, Your Holiness," Francisco replied. "It's probably very constant. There seems to be a universal law of how the brain works—we see the same thing even in animals. However, the specific patterns that arise certainly change from individual to individual depending on their learning and their unique history. Quite frankly, the answer to that is still unclear.

"If you put electrodes on different parts of the brain, you can measure oscillating signals. Then you put another electrode on another part of the brain, and what you see is another oscillation—a *whoomph*. And they enter into synchrony: they start and stop together. That's the basic mechanism."

The Dalai Lama asked, "Within one specific brain location, will there be a difference in what can be detected, depending on how far apart you put the two electrodes?"

"Absolutely," Francisco said. "We use a cap of electrodes that covers the brain. We are interested here in locations that are

No-perception
condition

Perception
condition

really far apart because we're interested in the large-scale integration. The small scale is a different story—where the neurons are so tightly together they are almost inevitably synchronous because they are interconnected. They are like a family because they are so close together. But the question is, can a family here in Dharamsala have synchronicity with a family in Delhi? That's the analogy. That's a different story because it requires they have a mechanism to get synchronized."

Then Francisco showed a slide of an extremely high-contrast black-and-white image that on first glance seemed to be just a set of blotches, but with more scrutiny suddenly revealed itself to be the face of a woman.

"Do you see it now?" he asked. "Once you see it you cannot stop seeing it, right? These are called moony faces, like the man in the moon—in other words, high-contrast faces. They're not easy to see, but most people can immediately detect them with a little attention.

"These faces are easily recognized when they are presented right side up." Then, showing the same image upside-down, he asked, "But now, do you see a face there? Very few people ever do. The upside-down stimuli are much more difficult to read. For the purpose of the study, we call the first image the perception condition—people eventually see the face—and the more difficult one the nonperception condition, because people usually don't recognize it at all."

THE ANATOMY OF A MOMENT IN THE MIND

At that, Francisco displayed a chart showing the sequence and timing in his experiment deconstructing a moment in the mind.[2] While volunteer subjects in Francisco's Paris lab had their EEG measured, they were simply asked to press a button the instant they could recognize an image. The sequence occurs with extraordinary rapidity, so fast that it must be tracked in milliseconds—thousandths of a second.

As the chart showed, during the first 180 milliseconds, when the black-and-white pattern is presented, the person's mind begins to stir into action. The act of recognition takes place from 180 to 360 milliseconds after the initial presentation— that is, by about the end of the first third of a second. The person's brain goes back to resting from that act of recognition during the next sixth of a second. The movement—the person pushing the button—occurs during the following sixth of a second. The whole sequence ends before three-quarters of a second has elapsed.

"When it starts, there's about a tenth of a second where nothing happens. I like to think of it as everybody's trying to get started, going *rrr-rrrrrr,*" he said, making the noise of an engine revving up. "Everyone is trying to make allies to form the synchronous groups," he pointed out, referring to the first head on his chart, where there were barely any connecting lines—and the image had not yet been recognized.

On the second head, there were suddenly many cross connections, indicated by black lines, as alliances were made by brain cells in disparate areas. "Then the groups begin to form; there is a pattern that emerges. This is truly a case of emergence, because nobody told them to be synchronous—say, between this electrode and that electrode. They self-synchronize with each other. That corresponds, we know from all kinds of other evidence, to about one-third of a second after the stimulus—to the moment the person actually recognizes a face.

"From that moment of recognition on, you can see lots of green lines, which mean the opposite of synchronous. Everything in the brain is going out of synchrony. Everybody is oscillating on their own. The whole *whoomph* is now going *poof,*" he said, waving his hands wildly around his head. "In other words, the brain says, 'Erase that oscillation pattern.'"

The Dalai Lama had been listening with particular attentiveness, gently rocking back and forth in his chair. Now he asked, "Could you conceive a study where instead of showing a visual stimulus, you have an auditory stimulus—a sound? Then could you see these processes—in the second stage this synchrony, and in the third this dissynchrony? And then compare that dynamic to the visual stimulus, to see if there's the same pattern in the third stage?"

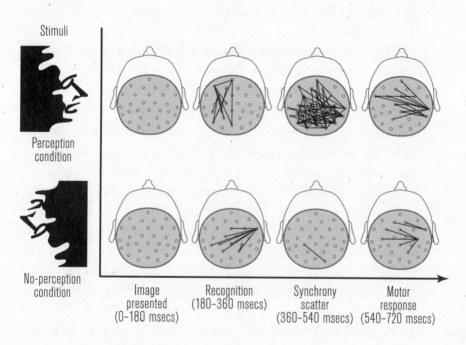

"We have done that experiment," Francisco replied, "and you will see the same patterns. We have done experiments with audition, with memory, with conflict of attention between visual and auditory. The answer is always the same: you have one particular pattern at the moment of the arising of the perception, and then you have a moment of recognition, and then you have a new pattern being formed at the moment of the action, which is pushing the button.

"Another set of synchrony arises in a new group of neurons as the person remembers that he has to push a button. The recognition arises, and then *poof,* the dissynchrony. Then the person remembers to push the button, and that needs a new pattern or synchrony in a new pattern of neurons."

"It's almost as if once a synchrony is formed, the role of those neurons is finished," the Dalai Lama observed.

"That's right—they are transient. And that's what I like. It's like the transience of mental factors." Francisco was referring to the basic elements that compose each moment of awareness in the Buddhist Abhidharma model of mind. "They come and they go, and they correlate to transient patterns in the neurons. That was clearly a big discovery for me. The brain actively undoes itself; it creates a gap where the transition from one moment to the next is actually marked. There is recognition and then action, but they are punctuated.

"It's like saying 'perception, comma, action,' rather than a continuous flow. This is systematic; we have seen it in all kinds of different conditions."

TIMING THE MIND

Francisco's results accord with those of other researchers who have been timing the fine movements of the mind. Benjamin Libet, a neurosurgeon at the University of California at San Francisco Medical School, found, for example, that electrical activity in the motor cortex begins about one-quarter of a second before a person is aware of his or her intent to move a finger. And there is another full quarter second between the awareness of the intention to move the finger and the beginning of the movement itself. Like Francisco's work, Libet's unpacks otherwise invisible, fine-grained components that in our experience seem a single, solid event: the recognition of a face, the movement of a finger.

The Dalai Lama pursued such an unpacking of a moment's mental activity in his next question: "The measuring device you use seems highly sensitive, to milliseconds. So is there still a gap between the initial exposure and the recognition if you show a photograph of a face that is so familiar that the person would instantly recognize it without having to actually think about it or recall from memory?"

"We have actually done that, and the answer is that the gap shortens but it is still there," Francisco replied.

At this point there was a heated discussion in Tibetan on the issue of whether there is an initial phase of nonconceptual awareness before memory and other aspects of cognition create Francisco's *whoomph*. The Dalai Lama, pleased at this opportunity to explore a topic of high personal interest to him—the distinction between conceptual and nonconceptual processes in the mind—continued, "Would you agree that this would indicate that the first moment is nonconceptual, purely a visual perception that apprehends the form in question, and the second is conceptual, which recognizes, 'Oh, this is that'? This seems to corroborate Buddhist psychology."

"Which leads you to decide to push the button," Francisco said. "It's only when I say 'Oh, I recognize that' that it leads to the moment of decision, where you then push the button. So it is a conceptual moment. The first one is just the pattern being perceived, without the conceptual process."

The Dalai Lama pushed on, intrigued by the implications he saw: "Would you agree that this corroborates a point in Buddhist psychology, that the first moment is a purely visual perception that is nonconceptual and the second moment, no matter what its duration might be, is when the conceptual mind apprehends, 'This is that'? For example, as I look at Alan Wallace here, I immediately recognize his face without having to figure it out. Grossly speaking, it seems like it's instantaneous, but in fact—"

"In fact it's at least two hundred milliseconds," Francisco interjected.

"This is exactly the Buddhist point of view," the Dalai Lama continued. "Even though, grossly speaking, it seems to be instantaneous, in reality it's not instantaneous. First there's an impression, and then the labeling—the conceptual recognition—and it's a sequence."

"Absolutely," Francisco agreed. "Typically, under normal conditions you cannot compress a mental moment to less than a hundred and fifty milliseconds. Even when it's something that's virtually immediate."

This is, in fact, a key point in Buddhist epistemology. The first moment of, say, a visual cognition is pure perception—a raw percept without a label—but shortly thereafter comes a mental cognition, the murmur of a thought, drawing on memory and enabling one to recognize and label the visually perceived object for what it is. Realizing that the first moment of cognition is nonconceptual and that those thereafter are conceptual offers a gateway, an opportunity for inner liberation, in the Buddhist model. This insight into the nature of our ongoing construction of reality represents a necessary step (though not in itself a sufficient one) toward freeing the mind from the inertia of mental habit.

As we entered this territory in our discussion, we left behind most people in the room, including many of the scientists. But the Dalai Lama was keenly interested to hear what science had found about what happens during the arising in the mind of a moment of experience, and to see how these findings fit with Buddhist models as described in the texts he was familiar with. This was a rare opportunity to hear a detailed scientific description of the process, and he found striking parallels between the scientific and Buddhist views, the two versions largely supporting each other.

Can neuroscience trace brain function accurately enough to understand what happens when enlightenment is achieved? Some Buddhist meditators seek a state called *kensho,* in which, for a brief moment of selfless insight and wisdom, they are able to perceive the existential essence of all things; can such seemingly mystical experiences be tracked by science? In the following essay, Dr. James Austin, acclaimed neurologist and author of *Zen Brain, Selfless Insight: The Meditative Transformations of Consciousness,* discusses recent developments in neuroscience, including new information about refining meditative attention, and an incredibly detailed new understanding of the path to enlightenment.

Selfless Insight-Wisdom

A Thalamic Gateway

JAMES H. AUSTIN, M.D.

> *How can you even hope to approach the truth*
> *through words . . . ?*
> *You approach truth through the Gateway of the Stillness*
> *Beyond All Activity.*
> —*Chan Master Huang-po (died 850)[1]*

INTRODUCTION

It happened before daybreak. He had been meditating all night under a pipal tree. Afterward, his followers were so impressed by the spiritual "awakening" that had transformed him that they referred to it as a tree of enlightenment (a Bodhi tree).

His first sermon began with a prescription: a practical eight-fold path for living one's life free from suffering. His teachings later evolved into a cultural movement the world would call Buddhism. When monks in China simplified this meditative approach to enlightenment, they called it "Chan." When their system of meditative practices arrived later in Japan, it would be pronounced "Zen."

Recently, researchers in the neurosciences have become keenly interested in the inherent potentials of Buddhist meditative training to awaken extraordinary states of consciousness and to transform traits of character.[2-5] How could such a "peak" experience of enlightenment arise in the human brain? These pages provide an oversimplified interpretation.[6] Whereas states of "spiritual awakening" also occur on the path of Zen, they are regarded rightly as the *beginning* of true practice. Few would resemble the momentous culmination that only after a rigorous six-year quest had overcome Siddhartha, and helped transform him into the person history would then call the Buddha, meaning "the awakened one."

ENLIGHTENED STATES ON THE LONG PATH OF ZEN

Zen training emphasizes a mindful, attentive, introspective approach to meditation. This system of practice becomes a kind of nonthinking, *clearly:* a style that carries its clarified awareness into each present moment of everyday living. After years of practice on such a meditative path, after the trainees have passed through the superficial levels of absorption, their consciousness can open up briefly into deeper, wordless, alternate states.

In the extraordinary state called kensho, meditators see into the existential essence of things during a brief moment of selfless insight-wisdom. What is such wisdom? It includes the profound comprehension of "the way all things *really*

Table I. **The Attentive Art Of Meditation**

CONCENTRATIVE MEDITATION	RECEPTIVE MEDITATION
A more effortful, sustained attention, focused and exclusive.	A more effortless, sustained attention, *un*focused and inclusive.
A more deliberate, one-pointed attention. It requires *voluntary,* top-down processing.	A more open, universal, bare awareness. It expresses *involuntarily* modes of bottom-up processing.
More Self-referential.	More other-referential.
May evolve into absorptions.	May shift into intuitive, insightful modes.
"Paying" attention.	A bare, choiceless awareness.

are." Its salient insights into the nature of ultimate eternal reality are accompanied by a dissolution of all egocentric concerns, yielding an unparalleled impression of release. Satori is a term often reserved for much deeper and more advanced states of realization.

ZEN CULTIVATES ONE'S POWERS OF ATTENTION

Meditation is an attentive art. Like any other skill, it must be practiced regularly in order to become effective. Formal meditative training cultivates, exercises, and refines one's attentive capacities. In general, there are two generic categories of meditation: concentrative and receptive (table I).

They are mutually reinforcing. Concentrative attention is a voluntary, top-down practice. One begins by focusing on the simple movements of breathing in and breathing out. After intensive practice, concentration can evolve toward a one-pointed mode of attention.

Receptive meditation, in contrast, draws on involuntary, bottom-up, *thought-free* mechanisms. It is a bare universal awareness, so open and inclusive that it can notice *any* stimulus. Later, it develops the capacity to shift spontaneously into moments of intuition, comprehension, and lesser insights.

OUR TWO NORMAL SYSTEMS OF ATTENTION

As you read these lines, you are looking *down* and paying close attention to one page of the book that you are holding in your hands. Yet when the bright planet Venus captures your attention, you will be gazing *up* into the sky above the distant horizon. Different regions over the *outer* (lateral) surface of the cortex represent these two systems of attention. Each serves distinctive needs, and each attends preferentially to external events in a different part of space.

- The dorsal attention system directs our more voluntary, "executive" types of focused attention (table II).
- Its networks are distributed higher up (more dorsally).[7] Note that they tend to pursue a *parietal-frontal* course. We use these top-down functions to (1) selectively tune in to prior cues and make fine-tuned adjustments to actual sensory stimuli as they start to come in and (2) continually monitor incoming data in order to respond to their potential conflicts in a relevant manner.
- Our ventral attention system becomes more involved during receptive meditation practices. It remains on standby alert, poised to detect *any kind of unknown stimulus* that might arrive unexpectedly. Note how its bottom-up functions respond automatically to fresh needs to disengage attention and to reorient it to a separate event. Its networks are distributed lower down over the cortex and pursue a *temporal-frontal* course.

OUR TWO NORMAL VERSIONS OF SELF/OTHER REALITY

"Anatomy is destiny," said Freud. Anatomical connections explain why when we first look at an apple, the upper and lower networks each synthesize their own different versions of it (table III).

Table II. **Representations and Responses of the Dorsal and Ventral Attention Systems**

	THE DORSAL ATTENTION SYSTEM FOR TOP-DOWN ATTENTION	THE VENTRAL ATTENTION SYSTEM FOR BOTTOM-UP ATTENTION
MOSTLY LATERAL ANATOMICAL REPRESENTATION	Symmetrical, on both sides. Mostly upper bi-frontal-parietal	Right-sided, predominantly. Chiefly lower parietal-temporal-frontal
RESPONDS ATTENTIVELY TO	Each side responds to the opposite side of the environment.	The right side responds to both sides of the environment, L > R.
MODES OF ORIENTING	More voluntary, intentional, executive, task-driven.	Strongly "stimulus-driven." Reflexive, automatic.
FLUCTUATES SPONTANEOUSLY	Yes, reciprocally with mostly medial frontal-parietal regions.	Yes, reciprocally with mostly medial frontal-parietal regions.
MAJOR MODULES	Intraparietal sulcus (IPS) Frontal eye field region (FEF)	Right temporoparietal junction (TPJ) Right ventrolateral frontal cortex (VFC)
RESPONDS MOST ACTIVELY TO	Prior cues denoting "what-where-when."	Salient task-relevant targets in unexpected locations. Fresh needs to disengage attention and to reorient it.
"EXECUTIVE OVERLAP" THAT CAN INTEGRATE THE TWO SYSTEMS	Right prefrontal cortex; in the middle and inferior frontal gyrus.	

The representations of these two attention systems are defined here by their spontaneous, intrinsic activity. The subjects are resting passively. Their eyes are: either open and looking at a cross-hair; or are open in dim light; or are closed. No task is superimposed; no stimuli are being added. Adapted from reference 7.

- Our egocentric point of view is *Self*-referential. This version always receives first priority, because we refer its images of external things back toward the physical axis of our Self. Therefore, this Self-centered processing is inherently private, subjective, and personal. It's *our* own version. *We are attached to it.* These are only some of the important reasons for spelling our Self with a capital S throughout this essay.

- The allocentric perspective is *other*-referential (allo means other). This version automatically views its target as a separate *object, "out there."* Its resources easily identify as an apple the distant fruit it observes. Any kind of this other-centered processing is inherently impersonal. It is an object-oriented version, so detached that it seems objective.

In brief, our dorsal, parietal lobe networks tend to be oriented more toward nearby interests that are close at hand—such as a book. Their vital sensory avenues are proprioception and touch. Our physical Self-image engages these functions when it reaches down to turn the page. In contrast, the interests of our ventral temporal lobe networks tend to be oriented more toward identifying what *other* stimuli mean at a distance, things that reside out there, detached, and far *outside* our skin. Their two sensory avenues, vision and hearing, warn of distant events and serve survival functions.

During ordinary kinds of perception, we quickly fuse the two versions—Self and other—into what seems like only one image in "our" own "mind's eye." Having awarded supremacy to our personal mode of interpretation, we overlook the fact that it embraces a covert, objective version of attentive processing. However, the original differences between these two versions remain crucial for the purposes of this essay. Soon, they will help clarify how a self*less* mode of experience unfolds suddenly, on the long path of meditative training.[8]

THE PSYCHIC SELF AND ITS LIABILITIES

Many associations representing our *physical* Self-image (our soma) are referable to the convex outer surface of the superior parietal lobule (shown in figure 2). In contrast, where do

Table III. **The Two Major Processing Streams**

	EGOCENTRIC PROCESSING STREAM (Self-relational)	ALLOCENTRIC PROCESSING STREAM (Other-relational)
MAIN THEME	Spatial processing in relation to the personal Self. Inherently more subjective.	Object processing in relation to other things in the environment. Inherently more objective.
INITIAL COURSE	Occipital → parietal.	Occipital → inferior temporal.
MAJOR CROSSROADS	Superior occipital region; superior parietal lobule; angular gyrus.	Inferior occipital region; fusiform gyrus; parahippocampal gyrus; superior temporal gyrus.
ADJACENT AVENUES AND INTERACTIONS	Proprioception and touch. "Where is it?" pathway. Localization in space.	Vision and hearing. "What is it?" pathway. Object identification and semantic interpretation.
METRICS	More absolute, and action oriented.	More relative and abstract.
OPERATIONAL ASPECTS	Faster and more accurate.	Slower and less accurate.
NEARBY LOCAL ATTENTION RESOURCES	Higher, in posterior intraparietal sulcus.	Lower, in superior temporal sulcus.
EARLY THALAMIC CONTRIBUTIONS TO EACH STREAM	Dorsal tier of pulvinar subnuclei, lateral posterior and lateral dorsal thalamic nuclei.	Ventral tier of pulvinar nuclei.
ORDINARY LEVEL OF ACTIVITY	The sovereign Self dominates the mental field.	More passive, subliminal contributions.
MENTAL FIELD DURING KENSHO	Self processing is deactivated or bypassed.	Other is overtly manifested. Meaning is amplified.

many abstract cognitive functions arise that contribute to our *psychic* sense of Self? These functions are represented chiefly on the brain's *inner* surface. Often such notions relating to the *I-Me-Mine* functions of our psyche arise in either (1) the medial prefrontal region or (2) the medial posterior parietal region.

Others draw on (3) the inferior parietal lobule over the brain's lateral surface.

Neuroimaging studies reveal a striking fact: *even when normal subjects seem to be passively resting, these same three Self-referential regions remain unusually active* (figure 1).

Indeed, PET scans show that by their high metabolic activities, these regions are three of the most significant "hot spots" in the resting brain.

What makes our Self-referential sites so active at rest? Let us venture a plausible explanation: each psychic Self has its own long narrative history; the Self-preoccupied regions continue to consolidate our personal story. These sites seem to actively keep a kind of personal journal. In it, we record the circumstantial details that summarize each event in terms of its particular timing, setting, and emotional atmosphere. Why would we bother to maintain such a personal journal? In part, because someday its database of remembered experience might help us survive a future crisis.

But memories have a downside. They generate a constant flow of recurrent thoughts and stimulate plans for the future. This "stream" of consciousness contaminates our field of consciousness whenever we try to meditate. Meditators use the phrase "monkey mind" to describe the way our thoughts leap from one trivial topic to the next. Yet the least of our problems are these random, discursive mind-wanderings. Covert longings and loathings cause our biggest problems. These deeply conditioned likes and dislikes distort our interpersonal behaviors and cause incalculable human suffering. Where do such biased, dysfunctional opinions come from?

LIMBIC CONTRIBUTIONS TO OUR PSYCHIC LIABILITIES

Most pejorative biases are referable to the cognitive dissonances, emotional valences, and hardwired instinctual drives

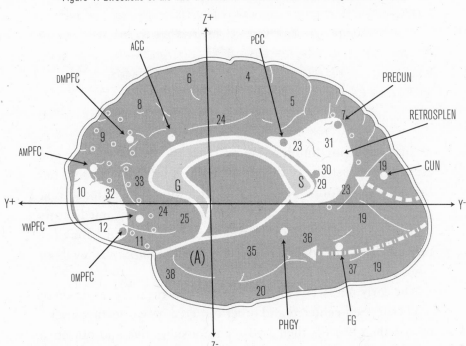

Figure 1. **Directions of the Two Streams in a Medial View of the Right Hemisphere.**

This view represents the inside surface of the right side of the brain. One large white area at the viewer's left (and its halo of small circles) occupies much of the medial prefrontal cortex. Here, normal subjects show high levels of metabolic activity in PET scans even when they are resting passively. At right, the other large white area represents our second major metabolic "hot spot." It lies deep in the medial parietal region near the splenium (S) of the corpus callosum. This extensive region includes the precuneus, retrosplenial cortex, and the posterior cingulate cortex.

The short, curved white dashed line suggests one of the medial branches of the dorsal egocentric stream. Its course takes it along the pathway that provides Self-relational answers to "Where is it?"-type questions. Lower down is the longer, gray arrowheaded, dashed and dotted line. This represents the major initial, ventral direction of the allocentric stream. This pathway runs along the undersurface of the temporal lobe. It provides other-relational answers to different questions of the "What is it?"-type.

Starting at the left, in the frontal lobe, mPFC refers to four subdivisions of the medial prefrontal cortex: orbital, ventral, anterior, and dorsal. Elsewhere, aCC= anterior cingulate cortex. pCC= posterior cingulate cortex. PRECUN= precuneus. RETROSPLEN= retrosplenial cortex. CUN= cuneus. FG= fusiform gyrus. PHGY= parahippocampal gyrus.

The gray curved area in the center represents the corpus callosum. Its fibers cross over to link the two hemispheres. G refers to its genu; S refers to its splenium. The lines of the vertical (Z) and horizontal (Y) axes suggest how the height and width of their coordinate sites are measured.

arising from our limbic system. True, the hypothalamus and amygdala infuse lively dynamic qualities into our psyche, but limbic polarizations also keep us continually agitated. Long-term, mindful, introspective training can help meditators find responses that yield affirmative results, avoid behaviors proven to be maladaptive, and arrive at harmonious levels of emotional balance and stability.

The early milliseconds are crucial in this regard. During these, the brain's Self-centered and other-centered networks first attend to and then process their two separate subjective and objective versions of the world. Table III and figure 1 indicate where key distinctions reside between these two cortical versions of reality. But the pivotal gateway for the two processing streams begins down in our thalamus and *lower subcortical* pathways, not in the higher levels of thought-filled cortex discussed thus far.

THE THALAMUS

Thalamus is an old term. It dates from the ancient Egyptian or Greek descriptions of an anteroom or chamber. The left and right halves of the thalamus, poised deep in the center of our brain, interact with their corresponding partners up in the cortex. Thus, the whole thalamus serves not just as a simple stopover for impulses traveling on their way *up* to the cortex. Instead, thalamic functions exert an early major, dynamic, preconscious influence on the basic ways we perceive, feel, think, and behave.

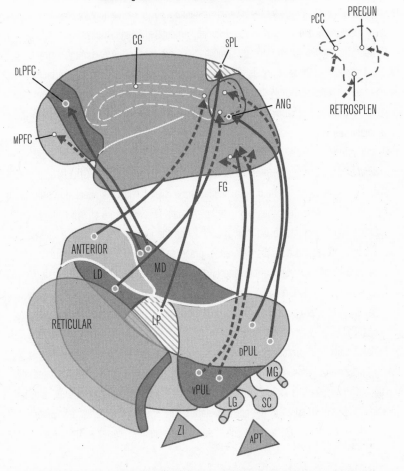

Figure 2. **Thalamo-Cortical Contributions to the Dorsal Egocentric and Ventral Allocentric Streams.**

This composite view shows the normal interconnections between the thalamus and the cortex. For convenience in viewing, only left-sided structures and ascending pathways are shown. The arrows interconnect the left thalamic nuclei with their cortical targets both on the outside and inside of the left hemisphere. Pathways predominate from the dorsal tier of thalamic nuclei. Thus, at bottom right, one path leads up from the *dorsal pulvinar* (dPUL) to the angular gyrus (ANG) on the *outer* cortical surface. A second path from this dorsal pulvinar leads up to the *precuneus*

(PRECUN). Every dashed arrow-line indicates a medial path that is projecting to the *inner* cortical surface. Other projections from the *lateral posterior* (LP) nucleus supply the *superior parietal lobule* (sPL). These associations help to anchor the subliminal sensate impression that we exist as a physically articulated image, a physical Self.

In front, the *medial dorsal* (MD) thalamic nucleus projects to the prefrontal cortex (PFC). It supplies both its entire outer, dorsal lateral (dL) and its medial (m) surfaces (suggested by cross-hatching). In the back of the brain, the other deep *medial* region (both are illustrated in figure 1) is shown here enlarged at the top right. Projecting to this large region are two other adjacent dorsal nuclei of the limbic thalamus (dashed lines). Thus, the *anterior nucleus* projects up to the posterior *cingulate cortex* (pCC), whereas the *lateral dorsal nucleus* (LD) projects to the *retrosplenial cortex* (RETROSPLEN).

Note that fewer pathways from the thalamus are shown serving the allocentric processing stream. However, some messages from the *ventral pulvinar* (vPUL) are shown rising first through the region of the *fusiform gyrus* (FG) on the undersurface of the temporal lobe. These contribute to our other-referential processing as they continue forward through the rest of the temporal lobe and on up toward the superior temporal gyrus.

Three important inhibitory nuclei are shown, artificially detached, at the bottom. They are: the large *reticular nucleus,* the small *zona incerta* (ZI), and the small *anterior pretectal nucleus* (aPT). *The superior colliculus* (SC) in the midbrain relays its coarse, reflexive visual and related polymodal messages quickly through both the dorsal and ventral pulvinar to the amygdala and beyond. Two sensory relay nuclei of the thalamus are also indicated at the bottom right. One, the *lateral geniculate nucleus* (LG), is our major avenue for relaying conscious visual information to the occipital cortex. The other is the *medial geniculate nucleus* (MG). It relays most auditory information to the auditory cortex in the temporal lobe.

The largest thalamic nucleus is the pulvinar (please see figure 2). The pulvinar's vital role is to confer *salience.* How do we grasp the essence of a particular stimulus event and instantly assign attentional resources to it? The pulvinar helps by separating the key figure in the visual foreground from the surrounding pattern of incidental items in the background.

A major distinction between Self and other begins early. Its coding starts in the relay which speeds visual impulses up from the superior colliculus (SC, in the bottom of figure 2). This reflex-ive relay into the pulvinar serves as our primal "hot-line" circuit. Detecting a signal of potential interest, the pulvinar instantly sends this message on to the amygdala. The amygdala is the vital entry point for the subconscious resonances of fear that we compound in the form of angst throughout the rest of the limbic system. It lies deep in the medial temporal lobe (A in figure 1).

THE DORSAL AND VENTRAL NUCLEI OF THE PULVINAR

The pulvinar's subnuclei are arranged into an upper and lower level. This anatomical division into a dorsal and ventral tier is not only physiologically efficient but also especially relevant to the central theme of this essay. Why? Because it relates not only to our dorsal and ventral cortical systems for attention outlined in table II. It is also significant in terms of those two separate versions for Self-referential and other-referential processing summarized in table III. In brief, the multiple distinctions between upper and lower levels help clarify how the impression of insight-wisdom arises when the Self drops out.

- The Dorsal Nuclei: In figure 2, the two arrows start in the dorsal pulvinar and follow up into the parietal lobe. One important egocentric path will interact with the angular gyrus (ANG) on the outside of the inferior parietal lobule. The other will interact with the precuneus (PRECUN) on the *inside* surface of the posterior parietal lobe. Figure 2 shows that the next nucleus of the dorsal thalamus is the lateral posterior nucleus (LP). This LP nucleus interacts with the whole superior parietal lobule (SPL), a major framework for the associations underlying our sense of a physical Self image.

What do these interactions between the dorsal thalamus and the parietal cortex normally accomplish? They incorporate various higher-order functions of our Self-centered soma into dynamic 3-D topographical mergers. One can envision their joint efforts as helping us to "imagine" extending parts of our own body out into the matrix of our environment, helping us to "embody it" there as an agency in outside space, and enabling us to act in the outside world with a memorable subjective sense of Self-referent precision and attachment.

- The Ventral Nuclei: Notice that the two other arrows rising up from our ventral pulvinar pursue a different course. They illustrate how this ventral version of other-referential processing relays forward throughout the *lower* occipital temporal pathway. This ventral stream is designed to inject the portent of salience into the processing of an other-centered version of incoming visual and auditory information. Recall that this allocentric pathway is designed to identify objects perceived "out there" in a detached, objective manner. No intrusive Self enters into the picture when this path observes "things as THEY really are."

THE IMPLICATIONS OF HAVING THREE
LIMBIC NUCLEI IN THE DORSAL THALAMUS

The dorsal thalamus is unique. It contains three more separate nuclei, each devoted to limbic system functions. Figure 2 shows these three limbic nuclei lining up just in front of the lateral posterior (LP) and dorsal pulvinar nuclei. They include:

- The large medial dorsal thalamic nucleus (MD). Figure 2 shows that this MD nucleus interacts with both the inside and outside parts of the prefrontal cortex (mPFC; dlPFC).
- The anterior thalamic nucleus. It interacts with the posterior cingulate cortex (PCC) and with the entire length of the long cingulate gyrus (CG).

- The lateral dorsal nucleus (LD). Contributions from this LD nucleus enhance the metabolic and functional activities of the retrosplenial region and adjacent medial cortex.

Each of these limbic nuclei down in the dorsal thalamus relays up the results of its own interactions with the limbic system to influence the ways particular parts of our cortex respond emotionally. Which cortical regions receive such affect-laden responses, and how will they be stimulated?

It is no accident that the white areas of figure 1 already illustrate the two largest targets. These are the same medial Self-referential "hot spots," normally activated by their connections with the limbic thalamus regions that maintain the highest resting metabolic activities in the whole cortex.

A skeptic might say: tables II and III indicate only that some functional anatomical overlap exists between our top-down voluntary system of parietal-frontal attention, the large network serving our stream of Self-centered processing, and these five nuclei, all in the dorsal thalamus. Can this overlap explain how a meditator could shed such biased Self-centering, cut the longings and loathings coming from an overconditioned limbic system, and become more self*less*?

It can, as soon as we consider the pivotal *inhibitory* functions of three other nuclei, shown at the bottom of figure 2. Their role in selflessness is fundamental: to block the links that connect the entire dorsal thalamus with its counterparts up in the cortex. When they cut these bidirectional attachments, they delete the upper level psychic and somatic association functions of the Self.

SUBCORTICAL SOURCES OF INHIBITION

How might meditators view the functions of such inhibitory nuclei? In a sense, as guardians of that thalamic "Gateway" through which will pass their nascent psychic and somatic associations. Eleven centuries ago, master Huang-po was aware that the road toward the Gate meant becoming free of all willful thoughts that were Self-directed from the top down. Indeed, he had cautioned: meditators "would not be on the right road towards such a Gate until they had abandoned all thoughts of seeking for something, and their minds had become motionless."[9] When did Huang-po conclude that the meditator's sudden, major comprehension would finally arrive? "Only after the mind was purged of all the clutter of conceptual and discriminatory thought-activity." In Zen traditions, the phrase *mushin* ("no-thought") refers to the innocent clarity of such a preliminary stage on the threshold of awakening.

Our largest inhibitory gate, by far, is the reticular nucleus of the thalamus (figure 2). Its enveloping layer of nerve cells releases GABA, an inhibitory neuromessenger. It can inhibit all of these nuclei of the thalamus. Playing the role of a selective blocker, the reticular nucleus shields the other thalamic nuclei from overfiring. Acting almost like an insulating blanket, it also stops their cortical hot spots from becoming "overheated." Our two other GABA nuclei are the zona incerta (ZI) and the anterior pretectal nucleus (APT). Each can exert a similar potent inhibitory influence.

How do these three inhibitory nuclei negate the functions of the higher-order thalamic nuclei? They shift the critical frequency rates of the synchronized oscillations that normally shimmer back and forth between the thalamus and cortex. Whereas *in*-phase oscillations normally unify and enhance thalamo-cortical functions, GABA inhibition renders oscillations so grossly disorganized and *out-of*-phase that they become physiologically ineffectual.

WHAT HAPPENS WHEN A DORSAL THALAMUS SHUTS DOWN? Ordinarily, the first priority of any sovereign Self is to attend to its own Self-referential attachments. It matters less how such physiological biases might be expressed in dysfunctional social behavior. However, suppose this profound shift were to occur:

an acute change in one's mental set that "demagnetized" the old internal compass and blocked its conventional egocentric bias. Now, perception could be free from those polarized tendencies. No longer would incoming messages, pointing *inwardly,* be granted exclusively Self-centered priorities. A freshly receptive mental field could open *outwardly* instead.

Why does this liberated perception now seem to register so clearly inside this novel dimension of *other-*consciousness? Because it has been freed from elaborate limbic associations. No longer do its old *I-Me-Mine* modes of overconditioning reverberate up through the dorsal thalamus.[10] As soon as the old Self-centered processing stops, *other-referential processing instantly takes over as the sole operating mode of consciousness.*

This is not a new idea. The ancient Pali term for this unconditioned state of non-I is *anatta.* Zen traditions speak of this version of consciousness as a state of "no Self."

OBJECTION: DOES ANY NORMAL PRECEDENT EXIST FOR SUCH A MAJOR SHIFT INTO OTHER-REFERENTIAL PROCESSING?
Similar remarkable shifts recur normally several times a minute on their own intrinsic cycle. This phenomenon was discovered only when researchers stopped assigning tasks to their subjects and simply monitored them *for several minutes continually* with the aid of functional magnetic resonance imaging.[11] Under these *passive* conditions, the fMRI signals showed that similar networks in the normal *resting* brain also underwent similar *reciprocal* shifts in their "functional connectivity." These shifts recurred *spontaneously,* alternating between our two normal modes of Self/other processing. Researchers recently observed the two modes tilting back and forth three to four times a minute in an almost seesaw-like manner. When other-referential networks *in*creased their activity, shifts occurred simultaneously in the *opposite* direction. These *de*creased (de-activated) the Self-referential network (and vice versa).

Moreover, *similar normal shifts are prompted whenever our attention turns outward*. These normal shifts occur either when we direct attention in a top-down (executive) manner toward various ordinary external goals, *or* when attention reacts to an external stimulus in a reflexive, involuntary manner (table II). In each instance—whether top-down attention is activated by one's intent, or bottom-up attention is suddenly activated by capture—both the *medial* frontal-parietal regions and the inferior parietal lobule are *de-activated* and get slightly "cooler." Note that these same regions (the ones that become "cooled" whenever attention is activated) are our major Self-referential "hot spots" at rest (figure 1).

Repeated observations confirm that our two networks—Self-relational versus other-relational—respond *reciprocally*. Seesaw changes recur on both sides of the brain whether the shifts are generated spontaneously at rest (that is, on the basis of some intrinsic rhythm, several times a minute), or are prompted by directing attention during a top-down executive decision, or are driven when attention reacts automatically to some extrinsic stimulus.

So what? The bilateral, reciprocal, seesaw nature of the fMRI shifts suggests that a plausible explanation lies in some deep *central* mechanism, perhaps involving the thalamus (and influenced by its connections to the brainstem). Furthermore, one type of shift has other intriguing implications for meditators. This is the particular stimulus-driven kind that *de*-activates Self-relational regions. This is the kind that is normally prompted whenever attention reacts to a surprising external event in a reflexive manner (table II, at right).

THE IMPLICATIONS OF TRIGGERING STIMULI
THAT PRECIPITATE KENSHO

For centuries, the annals of Zen have emphasized this important fact: extrinsic sensory stimuli can suddenly trigger kensho.[12] When an unexpected trigger strikes deep in a long-term meditative context, the prelude has usually been years of preparation. Regular training, in receptive meditation in particular, has been setting the stage for the brain to react with an increased amplitude of reciprocal responses. Let a triggering stimulus now abruptly capture attention, and the Self-referential networks are poised to topple over into a major, simultaneous deactivation (table III, at left).

THE SIGNIFICANCE OF GAZING UP INTO THE DISTANT SKY

Several lines of evidence suggest that a possible physiological basis underlies an ancient legend. According to this legend about Siddhartha's awakening, his final transformation was triggered by his glimpse of a bright "star" in the Eastern sky before dawn. This description of a bright heavenly body fits the planet Venus.

Our upper fields of vision exhibit a selective processing advantage when they react quickly to stimuli using an other-centered frame of reference. These visual fields, located above the horizontal, are most efficiently serviced by the "What is it?" version of allocentric processing inherent in temporal lobe functions (table III, at right).

The description of a later Buddhist awakening experience is also noteworthy. It hints at a similar physiological response, one precipitated in association with gazing up toward stimuli that were entering the *upper* visual fields. The lines are by Shabkar (1781–1851), an enlightened sage in the Tibetan Buddhist tradition.[13]

I raised my head, looking up
And saw the cloudless sky.
I thought of absolute space free from limits,
. . . Then experienced a freedom
Without center, without end.

IN CLOSING

This essay outlines some long-range benefits of refining one's powers of attention. An extended program of mindful meditative training cultivates enhanced attentive reactions to a triggering stimulus. The results could enable meditators to drop their old maladaptive Self-referential bias and *simultaneously* open up into a major fresh allocentric state of consciousness. Let both our first and last words on this topic be reserved for Master Huang-po. He had cautioned that a "full understanding can come to you only through an inexpressible mystery."

As Andrew Weil said of Les Fehmi's teachings about honing attention and healing the mind, "The techniques . . . can make a life fuller, more enjoyable, and more productive." Fehmi's work rests on the basic idea that the way we pay attention in daily life can play a critical role in our health and well-being; he calls this way of paying attention "Open Focus." Fehmi is a pioneer in the development of neurofeedback and the director of the Princeton Biofeedback Center. In the following adapted excerpt from his book *The Open-Focus Brain: Harnessing the Power of Attention to Heal Mind and Body,* Fehmi, with coauthor Jim Robbins, shares what he has discovered about synchronous alpha brainwaves and how this understanding can be used to change conscious awareness and quality of life. Can we generate alpha brainwaves at will in our daily life? Can this lead to tranquility and transcendent experiences?

Sweet Surrender

Discovering the Benefits of Synchronous Alpha Brainwaves

LES FEHMI, PH.D., AND JIM ROBBINS

In the 1960s, Joe Kamiya, a researcher at the University of California at San Francisco's Langley-Porter Psychiatric Institute, stumbled onto the fact that alpha brainwaves offered a path to feelings of well-being, even transcendence. Other researchers found the same thing. Though the hype of alpha training got ahead of the research—and gave biofeedback a bad name—a half century later, those who believed humans could be taught to voluntarily control their brainwaves in the service of transcendence were shown to be right.

A Zen student once asked his teacher, fifteenth-century Zen master Ikkyu, to sum up the highest wisdom. The master responded to this enormous question with a single word scratched in the sand: "Attention." The student wasn't satisfied and asked him to elaborate. Ikkyu wrote, "Attention. Attention. Attention."

I started to formulate my ideas about attention when I was an assistant professor of psychology at the State University of New York at Stony Brook in the late 1960s. My initial research had nothing to do with helping people to relax or feel better. As a graduate student at UCLA, I had researched visual perception in macaque monkeys and found that a fundamental principle of how the brain communicates with itself is something called synchrony—when the brain's electrical activity, or brain waves, are synchronized in one or more areas of the brain.[1] The greater the ability to enter into and exit synchrony in brain-wave activity, the better the brain performs its tasks.

This is true no matter what the frequency. Over the course of a day, our brains naturally move in and out of synchrony, but we can actually train ourselves to achieve greater control of synchrony. At SUNY Stony Brook I wanted to study the role of synchrony in the human nervous system to see if it would lead to greater subtlety, clarity, speed, and scope of information processing and perception. Since synchronous activity is most prominent when the brain is in a relaxed but alert state, I needed to find a way for human subjects to enhance this activity. Early research had proven that people could control their brain's electrical activity with the help of feedback. But as I experimented on myself, I realized I was on to something more important than just the study of synchrony.

Commercial EEG-biofeedback instruments weren't available in 1967, so I designed and built my own. Connected to a pen-and-ink EEG and an oscilloscope, in a soundproof room, I sat upright in a comfortable chair. A sensor was attached just above the inion (the bump on the back of the head). During twelve two-hour sessions over the course of the next four weeks, I struggled in every way imaginable to produce alpha waves (8–12Hz). I tried with eyes closed and tried with eyes open. I filled the room with negative ions, incense, music, and different-colored lights. None seemed to create much alpha.

Finally, in the thirteenth session, I was exasperated and gave up and accepted the fact that it was simply impossible for me to create more than baseline alpha on demand. Fortunately I was still connected when I gave up. The second I deeply accepted my failure, the EEG registered high-amplitude alpha production, five times the amplitude and abundance I had been producing before. I got rhythm! I couldn't believe it. I had been trying too hard and didn't know it. By surrendering I had slipped into alpha—the alert, wakeful relaxation that had eluded me. Even though I had learned you couldn't control it, at least not force it, I still wanted to, and every time I tried to produce it I was frustrated and couldn't. As my experiment continued, I found that I could increase the duration and amplitude, or power, of my alpha. After a few hours in alpha some curious and wonderful changes started to happen. My muscle tone softened, and I moved with a newfound effortlessness and fluidity; sometimes I felt like I was gliding when I walked. Anxiety evaporated. I felt extraordinarily present, centered, poised, open, lighter, and freer, more calmly energetic and spontaneous. I laughed and smiled more. Untoward events no longer threw me the way they had before. Arthritic pain in my joints subsided. My senses improved, vision and hearing foremost among them. Colors were more vibrant. I could pick up the subtle scent of perfume long after someone had walked down a hallway. I not only heard sounds I hadn't noticed before but also became more aware of the silence in which the sounds occurred. My obsessive-compulsive style mellowed, and I taught complex graduate-level courses with newfound ease. Friends and family responded positively. I was more aware of the bigger picture.

Yet I didn't feel as if I had lost my edge; indeed, the things I had been doing—teaching and researching—came more easily and more clearly than before. I was in the zone. There was a feeling that I had come home after a long absence, home to who I really was. The feeling lasted for many months, and with more training it could be refreshed. I felt strongly that this is the way life was meant to be. And from an evolutionary point of view it made a great deal of sense. Chronic depression, anxiety, and a host of other physical and psychological problems are not the natural state of human beings. Nor are they necessarily the result of a brain that is somehow fundamentally flawed. Instead they are the result of "operator error." Alpha isn't magical—it just seems that way because we've forgotten how to access it, increase its amplitude, and prolong it. When someone learns to operate their central nervous system the way it was designed to be operated, however, and includes abundant low-frequency synchrony, things run more smoothly and efficiently and don't break down as often. We are equipped with a rapid and sensitive emergency response to assure survival. But we are also equipped with a process of restoration and recovery, a way to lay down our burden: by generating low-frequency synchrony.

THE LESSON OF BIOFEEDBACK

I wasn't the first to discover the power of alpha. That distinction belongs to Dr. Joe Kamiya, a now-retired professor of psychology from UC San Francisco's Langley-Porter Psychiatric Institute and a friend. In 1965, he was researching the ability of people to recognize what frequency range their brain was in. Kamiya wired each student volunteer to an EEG, and as the student lay in a darkened chamber, the professor spoke to him by intercom and watched as the young man's EEG tracings were scribbled on paper. "Keep your eyes closed," Kamiya told him softly. "Listen to a series of tones." After each tone sounded, the subject was to guess if he felt he was producing a particular brain wave that Kamiya was watching for on the EEG recorder. That was all the information the student would get. By watching the tracings of the EEG, Kamiya knew if it was alpha being produced, but the subject did not. When the subject said "yes" or "no," Kamiya would answer "correct" if he was in alpha or "wrong" if he wasn't. During the first session the subject seemed to be guessing. But by the third and fourth sessions he could easily tell when he was in alpha almost every time. By the fourth session the young man correctly guessed his brain state four hundred times in a row. The experiment ended only when the subject thought he was being tricked with so many "yes" answers and purposely gave the wrong answer. Kamiya was flabbergasted that the young man could recognize his EEG frequency so successfully.

Following up, Kamiya wanted to see if the student could generate alpha at will. "Go into the alpha state when you hear a bell ring once," the young man was told. "If it rings twice do not go into alpha." The student was perfect. Over the next few months he and others demonstrated adroit control over their brain waves. What would later capture the public's imagination about Kamiya's work, however, was not the fact that people could learn to control their EEG, but the benefits some subjects claimed after they spent hours generating alpha: they felt refreshed, clear, relaxed, and centered in a way they had never experienced before. Colors took on a new richness and the world seemed fresher. They felt less depressed and less anxious. It was a "eureka" moment for Kamiya. "Instead of gulping a tranquilizer," he wrote in a 1968 *Psychology Today* article about the experiments, "one might merely reproduce the state of tranquillity that he learned with the kind of training used in our studies."

Kamiya's article led to a tremendous outpouring of interest in EEG biofeedback, with many proclaiming it a shortcut to enlightenment that would transform society. Other researchers built their own biofeedback technologies and manufacturers rushed equipment—much of it flawed—to market. The hype, however, got ahead of the science and many of the claims made by some manufacturers and researchers were exaggerated. Meanwhile, other researchers, who wanted to debunk these claims, used faulty methodologies in their studies or simply denounced the benefits of alpha training without evidence. But the response people had to generating alpha was a very real phenomenon, as many subsequent studies showed.[2] Unfortunately, in part because of too many exaggerated claims, these later studies were largely ignored. The transcendent experiences of Kamiya's students corresponded precisely to what I had experienced. But there was one other change I noticed. In addition to those feelings, I noticed that the brain-wave training broadened my attention; I took in the world visually in a very different way. I now perceived larger scenes without focusing on any one element and with much less effort. I went back to some of the writings of Hans Berger, who discovered the existence of the brain's electrical output and who, in the 1930s, reported on the association between alpha and a state of relaxed attentiveness. But it wasn't just visual. My awareness of the room I was in, my feeling and sense of it, was also much bigger. It was my first inkling of Open-Focus attention.

So, at the time, two critical discoveries had emerged. First, it dawned on me that producing alpha caused my attention to shift from narrow to diffuse, thus opening my awareness. Second, I realized that subjects could relax and produce abundant alpha not only with eyes-closed biofeedback but also by changing the way they paid attention in an eyes-open state. Changing the way they paid attention manifested in the EEG. And when they attended in full Open Focus, they not only produced alpha, but a very specific kind called phase-synchronous alpha.

Phase synchrony means not only that many parts of the brain are producing alpha but that these waves are also rising and falling in unison. This means that a large number of cells are working together—an especially powerful type of synergistic cortical activity. While high-frequency, nonsynchronous beta activity is like the chatter of an auditorium full of high school students engaged in separate conversations, the synchronized, uniform lower frequency generated across the whole brain by open styles of attention is the equivalent of the same group of students singing together.[3] Though it is made only of light, a laser beam is powerful enough to use as a cutting torch because the light waves are in phase. Dr. William Tiller, professor emeritus of engineering at Stanford University, writes: "If we could somehow take the same number of photons emitted by [a 60-watt] lightbulb per second and orchestrate their emission to be in phase with each other . . . the energy density at the surface of the lightbulb would be thousands to millions of times higher than the present photon energy density at the surface of the sun."[4] Soldiers marching in lockstep are in phase synchrony; this phenomenon is so powerful that soldiers have to break cadence when they cross a bridge or they can destroy it. And, although less visibly dramatic than these effects, learning to create phase-synchronous alpha brain waves is an extremely efficient way to release stress. Once I had recognized the tremendous potential of synchronous alpha, the focus of my research became finding a way to help others produce those brain waves as quickly as possible. It had taken me twelve two-hour sessions before I was able to let go during the thirteenth session and increase alpha amplitude and duration. That was simply too long, and many people would give up before they experienced the release. And it defies verbal instruction. The only way it could be learned efficiently was through experience.

MUCH ADO ABOUT NOTHING

Nothing is more real than nothing. —*Samuel Beckett*

In 1971, I discovered a shortcut. In research experiments student volunteers were exposed to a number of relaxation methods as their EEG was monitored to see which exercises produced the most phase-synchronous alpha. Some were asked to visualize peaceful scenes and locations. Some listened to their favorite music. Others tried fragrances, negative-ion generation, and colored lights. Some of these things had a mild alpha-enhancing effect; most had very little impact. One day I tried a standard twenty-item relaxation inventory. During the first few questions—imagine a dewdrop on a rose petal or a cascading waterfall, for example—their EEG manifested little change. Then I asked, "Can you imagine the space between your eyes?" Boom. The pens scribbled the symmetrical waves of high-amplitude alpha. A subsequent question was, "Can you imagine the space between your ears?" Again, boom, high-amplitude alpha appeared instantly. When either of these "space"-related questions was asked, subjects almost invariably generated a significant increase in alpha brain synchrony in the brain sites being monitored. No other question or imagery brought about such profound changes in the EEG. "Objectless imagery"—the multisensory experience and awareness of space, nothingness, or absence—almost always elicits large amplitude and prolonged periods of phase-synchronous alpha activity.

"Nothing" is not merely nothing. Nothing, in fact, is a great and robust healer and is critical to the health and well-being of our nervous system. Space is unique among the contents of attention because space, silence, and timelessness cannot be concentrated on or grasped as a separate experience. It slips through, permeates your attention, through all your senses. Seeing, hearing, tasting, feeling, smelling, and thinking of space, basking in it—while simultaneously experiencing time-lessness—is a powerful way to let go, the most powerful way that I know.

Simply by watching EEG activity, I discovered the robust effects of the awareness of space on the central nervous system in my own way. But I was certainly not the first to realize that being aware of space or nothing has value. I've since found other examples of perceiving space and nothingness as a goal of meditation. One Eastern mystic wrote that it was important to "attain a state of mind in which even though surrounded by crowds of people, it is as if you were alone in a field extending for tens of thousands of miles." The Japanese have a philoso-phy of *ma*—the ability to see the space between objects as well as the objects themselves. Other traditions use guided visual meditations on mandalas, in which practitioners focus on the space between the lines of the sacred symbols. All of these "technologies" no doubt slow cortical rhythms and relax the central nervous system; certainly they deserve further study and research.

Indeed, work by several researchers would later show that phase-synchronous alpha is the hallmark of veteran meditators.[5] What I'd done, in effect, was to discover some of the Western correlates of Eastern spiritual disciplines and describe them in the language of psychology and physiology. Since a sustained awareness of space is key to Open-Focus attention, I recorded a series of exercises to guide people through different kinds of objectless imagery, asking them to imagine space first between and around body regions and then through them, extending lim-itlessly in every direction. For example, I ask listeners to imagine space in, around, and through their eyes, neck, head, and hands (which leads to a release of those areas) and ultimately space extending limitlessly in every direction. When people gently direct their awareness to it and imagine feeling space, the brain responds immediately, dropping into whole-brain synchronous alpha. Connected to instruments that show them when they are in synchronous alpha, subjects can learn to change very quickly; some notice positive changes in mood, tension, and anxiety— all widely reported effects of alpha—in a single half-hour session.[6] And long-term effects included improved memory, clearer thinking, and heightened creativity.[7]

What is the physiological mechanism underlying the sudden and powerful effect on the brain of imagining space, silence, and timelessness? Part of it may be that the brain is very active when it is making sense out of the world. When it is processing sense objects—either physical or imagined—it uses high-frequency, desynchronized beta activity in order to make that processing possible. Electrical signals move through the brain at speeds exceeding a hundred miles an hour in many different and disparate regions. For example, research at Princeton University on monkeys found that when the eyes of the animal locate an object, not only do the visual centers get busy, but there is also activity elsewhere. Neurons rapidly fire in the ventral premotor cortex, which coordinates muscle activity with what the animal sees, hears, and feels, a firing that continues well after the object is gone. In fact, the parts of the brain responsible for sense perception and voluntary action become activated when we simply imagine objects and actions. EEG research shows that when athletes imagine performing their sport, for example, the brain activates in the same regions as when they are actually performing.[8]

When the mind is asked to imagine or attend to space, however, there is nothing—no-thing—to grip on to, to objectify and make sense of, no memories of past events or anticipation of future scenarios. The brain is allowed to take a vacation. This is presumably why cortical rhythms slow quickly into alpha, and later into theta, and the same brain that was racing moments before becomes a stress-reducing brain and a quiet mind. The imagination and realization of space seems to reset stress-encumbered neural networks and return them to their original effortlessly flexible processing. Then, after this "vacation," overall performance is enhanced. Even as it relaxes the brain's attention mechanisms, imagining space opens the scope of attention very quickly. And while imagining space most prominently affects our vision, it opens the other senses as well. In fact, just closing one's eyes causes a prominent increase of synchronous alpha over the whole brain, not only in the visual system. This suggests that synchrony's role is a more general and fundamental one, like attention. In my experience, object-less imagery is the quickest way to get into an open focus, and an awareness of space is a powerful tool to teach people to access and maintain alternative styles of attention. We can also transfer this awareness of space to everyday life. Moreover, if we pay attention to stress in an open style as it occurs, it doesn't accumulate and stay bottled up; it is immediately experienced and released to go through on its merry way. If we are not only aware of the things around us, but also admit an awareness of space, silence, and a sense of timelessness as the ground of our experience, we have the ability to lead a much less stressful life.

Once we are fully capable of flexible attention, we can readily move into alternative forms of brain activity when emergency functions aren't needed, just as the lioness does after the hunt. Presumably the lioness that fixes on a single object of prey, one gazelle among a herd, chases and brings down the animal in narrow-objective attention. During the hunt the targeted gazelle was foreground, and all other gazelles besides the chosen one were rendered peripheral background—even though they might be physically closer. Narrow focus played its role—it induced a surge of adrenaline, increased blood flow to the large muscle groups, and increased heart rate to support stalking, chasing, and the takedown. When the chase ends, the lioness's attention moves out of narrow focus and increases diffuse attention where there is no longer a strong distinction between figure and ground. If the herd of gazelles remains, the lioness now sees all of them, as well as the other elements of the landscape, equally. It is an attentional shift away from emergency function. The sympathetic nervous system quiets and parasympathetic function increases. The lioness moves toward a multisensory awareness, feeling the sun on her back again and aware of the scents and sounds around her. Muscles relax, hormonal flows adjust, and blood flow is redistributed. The body normalizes. The physiological and mental recovery that occurs with whole-brain synchrony and its attentional correlates is the basis for the clinical approach that I have used with clients for the last thirty years.

In neuroscience, the best quality of life is often defined as "peak performance"—meaning that when we are able to function without illness, disease, or injury, we can then pursue happiness and spiritual fulfillment. Neurofeedback treatments are aimed at discovering how to allow patients to achieve their peak performance, and pursue happiness, without hindrance. Neurofeedback can be used to treat many health conditions, including epilepsy, attention deficit disorder, head injuries, addictions, autism, and depression, with no drugs or side effects. In his book *A Symphony in the Brain,* author Jim Robbins explores the historical development of neurofeedback; in the following excerpt, he focuses on the controversial Low-Energy Neurofeedback System (LENS), addressing such questions as: Can the results of neurofeedback be proven? Can the LENS treatment actually help patients achieve their peak performance, and if so, should it be used even if we don't understand exactly how it works?

Weird Stuff

Low-Energy Neurofeedback System (LENS)

JIM ROBBINS

Many neurofeedback practitioners don't speak of diagnoses or cures, but of peak performance. Everyone can improve, no matter what their problem or where they start. That may mean sharper memory, or being happier, or experiencing feelings of spiritual transcendence. While neurofeedback has steadily gained credibility in the last five years, one new kind of brainwave training instrument is extraordinarily powerful in helping people reach their peak—and controversial, especially within the field.

A young woman shuffled into Mary Lee Esty's office in Chevy Chase, Maryland, one day, carrying a scrapbook. She took a Polaroid photo of Esty, put it in the scrapbook, which was jammed with other photos, notes, and scraps of paper, and underneath the photo of Esty wrote the therapist's name and why she was important. The woman was the victim of a serious head injury and had virtually lost her short-term memory. Just like the lead character in the film *Memento,* she could not remember what happened long enough to function and had to keep a record.

She had been riding in a car with her boyfriend in California when he failed to negotiate a curve and they plunged over an embankment. Her trauma was almost unimaginable. Years later, in addition to the memory problems, she had precious little energy and was awake only in three two-hour intervals each day. The rest of the time she slept. She had severe dysautonomia—her body could no longer regulate its temperature, and even in the middle of a muggy Washington, DC, summer she wore a wool sweater and wool socks and wrapped herself in a blanket. Her speech was halting and it would take long, painful seconds for her to iterate a sentence. She lost a quarter of her field of vision, common in brain injuries.

After her fourth treatment of Low-Energy Neurofeedback System, or LENS—a total of less than twenty seconds of feedback—she came to see Esty, a therapist.

"I did my laundry today," she said.

"Great," said Esty.

"You don't understand. I did my laundry *today*. It used to take me five days."

One morning, further along in treatment, she woke up with a sharp pain behind her eyes, as if, she said, someone was poking it with a pipe cleaner. The next morning the same thing happened. The third day her field of vision normalized and stayed that way. In the course of twenty-five sessions, she went on to regain almost all of her function, including the normalization of her body temperature, speech, and memory.

This rapid success and treatment of a problem for which there is no other treatment was accomplished by LENS. It is in a class of neurofeedback by itself—if indeed it is neurofeedback. Instead of just feeding the user back his or her own brain waves, as is the case with most systems, it also feeds back a tiny bit of electrical frequency to the brain. The dose is in infinitesimal shards of a microwatt—a dose of electricity so low it's considered homeopathic. (Homeopathy is the dilution of a substance to the point where there may be no molecules of it left—but somehow it engages the immune system.)

Instead of sessions in which the brain works to create feedback that lasts a half hour or more, the feedback from the LENS system lasts less than one second. One second! It seems absurd. When I wrote the first edition of *A Symphony in the Brain,* I considered including the story of LENS and Len Ochs, who founded the system. He's one of the old guard of neurofeedback, has a good reputation, and is smart and articulate and full of dry and often self-deprecating humor. But every time I saw him and asked him what he was doing, he would shake his head and laugh and say, "weird stuff, really weird stuff." Writing about neurofeedback at the time was weird enough; in the end I felt it would only muddy the picture to include a system that was unique and was routinely referred to as weird by its own developer.

Och's stuff is still, even by neurofeedback standards, weird. But it is also extraordinarily powerful and within the field top people have been migrating to LENS over the last few years, using it alone and integrating it with other kinds of neurofeedback and other interventions. The time has come for the technique to receive more attention.

For one thing, practitioners of LENS, some of the most capable in the field, have amazing stories to tell, even by the standards of neurofeedback's amazing stories, especially in the area of head injuries, one of the most intractable of problems to treat. Secondly, a thorough book on LENS has been published, called *The Healing Power of Neurofeedback: The Revolutionary LENS Technique for Restoring Optimal Brain Function,* by Dr. Stephen Larsen, who uses the approach. There are also two published studies. And there is controversy brewing about LENS.

At the International Society for Neurofeedback and Research conference in San Diego in September 2007, I caught up with Len in his hotel room. I asked him to hook me up for a session on the LENS system, which, like most neurofeedback these days, runs on a laptop computer. He pasted a sensor on my scalp, on the front of my head, fiddled around with his computer, and in a matter of less than five minutes pronounced me done. I felt nothing. As is the case with other systems, I hadn't had to look at a screen and make a race car go with my brain waves or do any other tasks.

"That's it. If you see God tell him I said hello," Len said dryly.

We chatted for a while, and then I left. While I didn't glimpse the deity, the next day I did experience a classic "clean windshield effect," an experience in which the sun seems more golden, the colors richer, the Mediterranean breezes of southern California more sensuous. Whether it was the single session of neurofeedback or the fact that I was in a gorgeous, sunwashed environment is hard to say. But I feel as if LENS and Len played a role.

Ochs, who is sixty-five and lives in Walnut Creek, California, is one of the founders of the neurofeedback movement. In high school he was a self-confessed science geek who toured a medical school and saw researchers doing intercranial cell stimulation in rats in what he realized was biofeedback, which was coming on to the scene at the time. He saw an article about neurofeedback by George Von Hilsheimer, a pioneer practitioner, in the *Whole Earth Catalog,* and started doing it on his own with an early device called the Autogenic 120.

Ochs fell in love with operant conditioning. In 1975, he became a counselor at Rensselaer Polytechnic Institute in Troy, New York, and used neurotherapy for his students. "I had every kind of biofeedback I could get my hands on," he said. He also used it himself. "Neurofeedback reduced my drowsiness during the day and improved my sleep," Ochs said. "For every ten minutes of neurofeedback I did I dropped an hour of sleep at night. It was impressive." In 1977, he read C. Maxwell Cade's landmark book, *The Awakened Mind: Biofeedback and the Development of High States of Awareness,* and got interested in Cade's biofeedback device, called a Mind Mirror. A technophile, Ochs built his own with a Heathkit minicomputer kit. He also designed computerized EMG and EEG feedback technology.

In 1990, Ochs and a collaborator, Dr. Harold Russell of Dallas, Texas, developed feedback technology that was called EEG-driven stimulation, or ESD, a combination of feedback and stimulation. Instead of just feeding back the brain's electrical signal to the user, the system included light-emitting diodes in a pair of glasses that stimulated the brain. Like neurofeedback, it was used to treat pain, anxiety, and other similar issues.

Because of the stimulation, which drives the EEG rather than teaching the brain to make the changes, it was more powerful than other approaches, but the light proved too much for some people, and Ochs covered it with tape in order to dim it. People were still sensitive to the light and Ochs continued to reduce the light's intensity until it was completely covered with black electrician's tape. Even though they couldn't see the light they could sense it. It was a lesson in sensitivity.

In 1997, Ochs bought a J&J I-330c2—the first neurofeedback instrument with a standard computer microprocessor. It was the inadvertent beginning of LENS.

Ochs was treating a client in Chicago who had fibromyalgia, a debilitating problem of fatigue and extreme muscle pain. The client had done quite a few sessions with the light-fitted glasses on. With his earlier lesson in sensitivity, he wondered if it was overstimulating her and he took the glasses off and moved them across the room to diminish the effects of the stimulating light.

What came next was a totally unexpected "aha" moment, one that defied all of Ochs's plans and work. "The wires to the glasses turned out to be an antenna carrying the electromagnetic signal from the computer," Ochs said, still in awe of the unexpected turn of events. When the glasses sat on the person's head the signal was too close, too much, or not the right frequency. Every session had wiped her out and sent her to bed. When he took off the glasses the wire stretched, and the signal strength got weaker and apparently more appropriate. It was the right frequency. "Instead of her going to bed, which she did after every session, we went for a walk," he said. "It was amazing." The client continued to improve.

Ochs scratched his head. After much pondering he realized that the EEG signal was being processed with a Digital Signal Processor (DSP) chip, an off-the-shelf crystal clock that regulates the timing of instructions to the computer chip. These chips gave off an 11-megahertz signal and that little bit of frequency was traveling up the EEG electrode wires to the site on the scalp that was being trained. Together with feedback—and they need to be delivered in tandem or the approach doesn't work—it was a totally new invention. "A wacko system," as Ochs called it.

The feedback frequency of LENS is just off the dominant brainwave frequency. If the dominant frequency coming from the brain is 10 hertz, for example, the feedback will be 10.50. Then the tiny amount of power goes to the same site and the feedback rides on the tiny bit of stimulation.

Known as "disentrainment" therapy, when the stimulation is just off the dominant frequency it seems to break up existing neuronal patterns and reset them at a different level. When synchronous brain waves are presented with similar but not identical synchronies, it tries to assimilate that frequency and moves to the other frequency. In essence, the brain is nudged out of its default frequency, or moved, as Tansey might put it, out if its parking spot. Ochs thinks the subtlety and timing of the signal catches the brain and the ego off guard and a person's defenses never have a chance.

It was an accidental discovery, a kind of serendipity similar to Barry Sterman's discovery of the treatment for seizures in cats exposed to rocket fuel. Chance favors the prepared mind, and Ochs' mind was prepared to recognize and capitalize on such an anomaly.

He started using the new approach, and its efficacy, he says, was off the charts. "It did it so fast, I was worried," he recalled. "I was frightened. The results were so good." Head-injured patients years after their injury, for example, well beyond the time when they would get any natural gains, were getting an 80 percent improvement in the first week of brain wave training. After just seconds of brain-wave training.

Ochs was tickled and disturbed at the same time. "I had always sworn never to do anything that didn't make sense," he said. "And this didn't make sense but something good was happening. It was also eerie and uncomfortable."

I asked Ochs if he had any idea what the radio waves were doing to the brain. "None," he said. "They may effect glial cells or vascular cells but we don't know." Could it be dangerous? No, he said. The microwattage of the signal is tiny, "smaller than the radio waves around us."

Stephen Larsen, who wrote the only book about LENS, hypothesizes that it works faster than other kinds of neurofeedback in part because the radio waves go deep into the brain. "They penetrate everything," he said. They go into the whole brain, through six layers of cortex, the understory, and the brain stem. It breaks up pockets of coherence, so the brain is not locked into a monolithic response. It's more nimble and it moves quickly through its capabilities."

The big difference between what LENS does and other systems is "the speed at which it often operates," he says. "It's like time-lapse photography where the pumpkin vines grow in fifteen minutes and you go, 'Holy smoke, how did that happen?' Some of the changes are slow and gradual and some are nonlinear and rapid."

In a session a therapist using the system records from twenty-one sites on the brain in the standard places and creates a map, ranking the sites according to the healthiest of amplitude. Starting with the healthiest sites, the treatment progresses to those that are most deviant from the norm. A client is not given much instruction or asked to do anything: simply, according to therapist Larsen, to "be inwardly attentive, with closed eyes, while the lights are flashing, and when we are done, tell me what you experienced. If you feel any discomfort or unfamiliar sensations during the treatment that feel disturbing, let me know and I will stop the session." The sensor for feedback is on the brain for about four minutes.

Ochs says that using LENS takes considerable therapist skill, and is not just a matter of hooking someone up. "There's a careful match of the feedback and the person being treated," he said. "How sensitive are they? How strong?" Changes happen so quickly that they need to be told how to deal with changes. "What if their life is suddenly not ruled by anxiety when they have been ruled by anxiety all their lives? That's a big change and people need to deal with it."

The LENS approach is different—and seems to be one of the ways neurofeedback is trending—in that the process is not training the brain to a specific frequency. "I don't want to tell the brain what to do," Ochs said. "I want to disrupt the malfunctioning of the brain and let the brain reorganize the way it thinks it should. It's like taking the log off the railroad track," says Ochs, and allowing the train to travel again. That is, he is not telling the train how fast to go, but simply removing what he calls the auto-protective mechanisms of the brain to let it operate on its own. Stress, whether emotional or physical, seems to freeze certain parts of the brain into place and they stay there until they are disrupted.

And the more severe the injury, says Ochs, the better LENS seems to work. "It treats problems especially well that come on suddenly," says Ochs, like a head injury or post traumatic stress disorder (PTSD).

The intervention is being used to treat autism, fibromyalgia, depression, insomnia, fatigue, dizziness, anxiety, Asperger's syndrome, chronic pain, headache, traumatic brain injury, ADHD, stroke, PTSD, and other problems. Because it requires no engagement from the patient, the technique is even being used on animals. Stephen and Robin Larsen use it on horses, dogs, and other animals at their Stone Mountain Clinic in upstate New York. "We even treated a rooster named Gustav Klimt, who is from Brooklyn," said Larsen.

Larsen acquired a new dog named Gandalf from an animal rescue shelter in Connecticut, an animal who had been confined to a kennel and treated horribly. They were looking for an emotionally damaged dog so they could treat it. "The dog displayed fear biting and fear barking," said Larsen. Larsen and his wife and partner Robin Larsen wanted to see what they could do for such a neglected animal. They did a brain map and it showed an attachment disordered dog, "a brain map that looked like an adoptee from a former Communist country."

After a series of treatments, the animal is normal. "You meet this dog and it is nice and gentle," says Larsen. "And the brain map reflects the changes."

There is of course the oft-heard criticism that it is the placebo effect. But the changes last, practitioners say. And there are responses that seem to illustrate placebo has nothing to do with it.

Larsen tells a story about a Vietnam veteran who was doing sessions with LENS. While the actual feedback lasts only a second, the wires are fixed to the scalp for anywhere from ten to thirty minutes. As Larsen observed, the traumatized veteran sat in the chair. When the one second of feedback was discharged automatically—it was invisible to the client—he writhed in his chair. In that second, he later told Larsen, he heard mortar fire and screaming, a flashback from his Vietnam war experience.

LENS does cause some mild abreaction, something like the Peniston flu, though the problems are transient. Esty usually sees the reaction after the first treatment. "Headaches, fatigue, or nausea and dizziness," she says. "They are mild usually, and they usually pass the next day."

There are some metrics of the efficacy of LENS. The *Journal of Head Trauma Rehabilitation* published a study of twelve patients and their outcome in 2001 that found significant improvement. Based on patient outcome statistics, Esty says of the 1,400 clients she has worked with since 1994, 67 to 72 percent of those see positive outcomes.

LENS threw the field of neurofeedback into controversy when it emerged: a controversy that lingers—because it is, as Ochs plainly and often states, a wacko system. Critics of LENS respect Ochs and his work and others who use the system, but they harbor serious doubts about LENS on a number of levels. "It could be placebo," says Joel Lubar, who admits the approach confuses him. "We don't know whether (the electrical signal) penetrates the scalp, the skin, the muscle, and other coverings."

It is not, says Lubar, neurofeedback. "It's passive," he says. "The patient has no awareness. Neurofeedback, on the other hand, is an active learning process and the client needs to engage."

"I don't know what to make of it because I can't explain it," says Sterman. "I can't promote it until I understand it. It can't be magic. You need a theoretical model to show how it might be working. That isn't there yet."

Both Sterman and Lubar cite LENS as an approach that they believe could hurt the neurofeedback field's efforts to earn scientific credibility.

No matter how small the electricity, Ochs's system is different from standard neurofeedback. Neurofeedback has always been able to get around claims that it is a medical device because biofeedback, which mirrors biological activity, has an exemption. But the notion of inputting wattage, no matter how small, is different.

Esty's world was upset in 2006 when a client filed a complaint with the Maryland Board of Physicians. Esty used LENS on a patient who seemed pleased with the outcome. The patient later suffered an anxiety attack, blamed it on Esty, and complained to the board that Esty was practicing medicine without a license. The board ordered Esty to cease her practice. That outcome has been challenged, however, and is not yet settled.

"In eighteen years I've never seen anybody damaged," said Ochs. "I've seen people surprised and upset and get restless or sleepy, but these are the stages people have to go through to get better."

Ochs, Esty, Larsen, and the others in the LENS field mirror the frustration of the field of neurofeedback as a whole that an intervention as powerful as LENS is still not taken seriously by enough people, either by clinicians, researchers, or potential clients. There seems to be not just a scientific barrier, but an emotional one, that keeps people from not only moving outside of their comfort zone but even thinking about it. Ochs tells a story of a race car driver who came to see him. He sat in his office and described his injuries. When he finished, Ochs told him six sessions would go a long way toward helping him. Shocked, the driver stood up and said Ochs had "just made a mockery out of my injury and everything I have been through." He walked out.

Ochs has just developed a new system based on LENS that he is testing. The tests, he says, are extremely promising. He won't offer many details but he says, "It's not any stronger. But its exponentially more efficient and precise. And it's as different from LENS as LENS is from traditional neurofeedback."

Physical, emotional, and mental hurdles can prohibit the free and easy pursuit of a better, more fulfilling spiritual life. Conditions like post traumatic stress disorder (PTSD) or limits on physical abilities like a frozen shoulder or paralyzed movement can become barriers for many as they seek better lives. New evidence in science is questioning the origins of these problems through energy psychology and epigenetic medicine. In the following essay, Dr. Dawson Church, author of several books including *The Genie in Your Genes: Epigenetic Medicine and the New Biology of Intention*, shares his most recent findings about how science can clear away obstacles that stand in the way of spiritual progress by altering energy fields in the body to cure physical limitations and psychological stress. He also explores what happens when energy psychology methods are used on healthy people.

Psychological Clearing as Prelude to Soul Emergence

DAWSON CHURCH, PH.D.

"An atheistic, communist Darwinian," muttered my grandfather darkly, knitting his brow as he summarized all that was wrong with my black sheep great-uncle Chetwynd Montague. As a boy, I was kept far away from this dark force, lest I be infected by proximity with Chetwynd's dangerous ideas. My grandfather was an evangelical Christian of the most unchristian variety: dour, rigid, opinionated, and unforgiving. In my mind's eye, I can still see his scowling face and tightly crossed arms as he contemplated the sins of the world, with the theory of evolution topping the contemporary list. An indiscriminate discriminator, he was prejudiced against every race, nationality, and color with the grudging exception of his own. Born in the first decade of the twentieth century, my grandfather was one of a generation of Christians humiliated by the failure of their unbending opposition to staunch the tide of Darwinism that engulfed the literary, cultural, and scientific life of Great Britain, her colonies, and eventually, much of the world.

How quaint my grandfather's stance seems to me today, as I read, conduct, and write about scientific research—study upon study upon study—that affirms the role of consciousness in sciences from biology to sociology. I find myself moving effortlessly between Buddhists meditating and psychologists practicing mindful therapy; between biologists having transcendental experiences and ethicists finding lessons in unicellular organisms; between Anglicans singing the liturgy and energy medicine practitioners clearing the chakras; from physicists describing dark matter to Vedantists studying the *Gita*. Never do I experience a moment of conflict, or a sense of anything but unity between the diverse worlds of science and spirit, for spirit informs the scientific quest, while the scientific quest validates the most authentic messages of spirit.

This unity is demonstrated by surveys of the spiritual practices and beliefs of scientists conducted during the last decade. An article that appeared late in 2005 in *Science and Theology News,* entitled "Spirituality Soars Among Scientists," surveyed over sixteen hundred scientists from twenty-one institutions. To measure spirituality, the survey used indicators such as prayer, scripture reading, yoga, and meditation. It found rapidly rising rates of spiritual practice in the ranks of elite teaching institutions. The fastest rate of increase was in the "hard" or empirical sciences such as physics, biology, and mathematics, rather than "soft" sciences such as psychology and sociology.[1] Another survey found that over three-quarters of medical doctors believe that miracles occur today, and that two-thirds of them believe that prayer is important. These beliefs were not confined to any one religion; the trend was evident in all faiths.[2] To many scientists, God has become a hard fact rather than a soft fancy.

BELIEFS AND YOUR IMMUNE SYSTEM

You cannot get the right answers until you ask the right questions. The way experiments are set up has a big effect on the results they provide. If you design a questionnaire to determine the degree of psychopathologies such as traumatic stress, depression, and schizophrenia in subjects, you will find what you are looking for. But you will not find out how ethical, joyful, altruistic, or devout those subjects are.

Only very recently have scientists begun to ask the right questions when it comes to spirituality. At the Behavioral Medicine Institute at the University of Miami, researcher Gail Ironson has done several large-scale studies with AIDS patients examining the link between belief and the immune system. Specifically, she measured the concentration of a type of white blood cell called CD4 or T-helper cells in the bloodstreams of her subjects. These cells form part of the front line of defense for our immune systems.

She discovered that those patients who believed in a *punishing* God lost CD4 cells at more than twice the rate of those who believed in a *loving* God.[3, 4] Her studies showed an enormously strong link between spirituality and the robustness of the immune system.[5] As we design more such experiments to measure the effects of consciousness—such as belief, faith, prayer, visualization, and affirmation—on our bodies, we are finding that what you believe has a huge impact on your health and longevity.

BETWEEN IRAQ AND A HARD PLACE

Lieutenant Barry Gomez served in the Iraq War. He suffers from posttraumatic stress disorder (PTSD). He has many common symptoms of PTSD, including headaches (up to five a week), insomnia, rectal bleeding, and frequent involuntary flashbacks to memories of some of the terrible sights he witnessed in Iraq. Here's how Lieutenant Gomez tells his story:

> *After my medical discharge in 2003, I returned to West Virginia to find that my now ex-wife had become addicted to crack and I had no home, car, or anything to call mine. Friends tried to help but unfortunately, I suffer from an extreme amount of pride, so I asked no one for help. I slept on benches for two months until I saved enough money to secure an apartment.*
>
> *While in the service, I was a leader of men. After my separation, I was lost and unsure of the future. I was depressed and at one point suicidal. My dreams are of burnt bodies talking to me and to this day the smell lingers in my mind, causing me to vomit. I don't sleep for fear of dreaming and sometimes when I do fall to sleep, my final thought is, will I wake in the morning or will all this finally be over?*[6]

Note how in the lieutenant's story there's a strong link between the images in his mind, the sensations in his body, and his degree of emotional stress. The connection between unresolved emotional trauma and disease is one of the most well-established links in medicine. In one study, done at HMO Kaiser Permanente, which has over nine million members, 17,400 adults were examined for this link. The Adverse Childhood Experiences study found that patients with a high degree of childhood emotional wounding had elevated rates of:

Cancer
Heart disease
High blood pressure

Stroke

Diabetes

Bone fractures

Depression

Smoking

Illicit drug use

People with large amounts of adverse childhood experiences were thirty times more likely to attempt suicide, five times more likely to be depressed, and three times as likely to smoke. And speaking of smoke, the distinguished authors of the study compared the efforts of Western medicine to a heroic fire crew trying to extinguish a burning house by directing their hoses at the smoke, while ignoring the flames.[7] Emotional trauma is the flame from which the smoke of much physical disease springs, a correlation that has been reaffirmed by numerous other studies.

But while medical professionals have been aware of the problem, until recently they lacked the tools to reverse emotional trauma rapidly and reliably. Today, new research brings good news for Lieutenant Gomez and others like him. He's enrolled in a study designed and sponsored by Soul Medicine Institute and held at Marshall University medical school that treats PTSD sufferers with energy psychology.

YOUR PSYCHOLOGY BECOMES YOUR PHYSIOLOGY

Energy psychology is a group of therapies that holds out the possibility of rapid change, even for conditions and beliefs that have stubbornly resisted transformation by other means. These therapies make tiny changes to the electromagnetic energy grid of the body by tapping, massaging, or rubbing key points on your *meridians,* energy pathways identified thousands of years ago in China. When a subject *vividly recalls* a past trauma and then applies an energy therapy, the emotional trauma attached to the memory is often extinguished—immediately and permanently. Energy psychology is commonly used for pain, for phobias, for anxiety, for depression, and for PTSD.[8] It is now undergoing clinical trials in Great Britain's National Health Service, as well as in several universities and medical schools in North America.

With energy psychology, therapists now have a powerful tool kit to fight the fire, and extinguish the kindling below the smoke. Studies at Soul Medicine Institute are showing remarkable physical healing resulting from the alleviation of emotional trauma.

In one of several related experiments, we asked a simple research question: If we know that unresolved trauma contributes to physical disease, what happens to a physical disease when you discharge emotional trauma?

To find out, we used a very simple physical measure. We recruited people with stiff and frozen shoulders. Many of our subjects had suffered from shoulder limitations for years, and sometimes decades. A stiff or frozen shoulder might not sound too bad if you don't have one, but our subjects described functional limitations ranging from not being able to brush their teeth without help to not being able to raise their hands high enough to drive a car.

What would happen to a frozen shoulder, we wondered, after an energy psychology treatment? If a shoulder that had been locked at, for instance, only 50 degrees out of a possible 130 degrees for over ten years improved to 70 degrees, while untreated shoulders did not show a similar improvement, we would have evidence that the emotional energy treatment was having a physical effect on the body.

When subjects arrived at the clinic for our shoulder study, an occupational therapist used a measuring device called a goniometer to measure the range of motion in each shoulder to within three degrees. We also gave them a psychological health questionnaire to fill out and noted the severity of their pain.

Then we gave them a very brief treatment with emotional freedom techniques, or EFT, the most commonly used form of energy psychology. The treatment lasted just half an hour. That seems like an impossibly short time to affect a shoulder that might have been frozen for many years; but remember, when you change the energy field, you change the underlying matter, too. Think about iron filings suspended in a pattern between two magnets. When you change the position of a magnet, the iron filings move immediately. You don't have to push them around with a finger to achieve this effect; matter conforms to the energy patterns in which it exists. Your cells are the same way; change your energy field and the molecules of your body are affected.

One cool autumn afternoon at a bookstore in Marin County, California, I gave a lecture and signed copies of *The Genie in Your Genes*. I had an hour to talk, and with just five minutes left, I asked if any member of the audience had a problem they would like to work on.

One woman in the audience had a shoulder issue. Tall, fit, raven-haired, and articulate, she was brave enough to walk up to the front of the room and tell everyone her story. She said she had had her problem for seventeen years. She raised her arm forward and sideways to demonstrate, and the furthest she could lift it was about a foot from her hip. She told us that seventeen years before she worked in a tiny office where she had to reach behind her to pull out the file cabinet drawer, which would jam. This affected her shoulder, and it had been the same ever since. She also described some problems with her young daughter that had occurred around the same time.

With just a few moments left for my demonstration, I worked on her with EFT, targeting both her limited range of movement and the issues with her child. I then asked her to raise her arm again. Her eyes opened wide as her arm now lifted about three feet from her hip in both dimensions. I've grown used to this look of wide-eyed wonder over the years of doing this work, and it always reminds me of the human joy of having a problem removed.

The initial results of the frozen shoulder study at Soul Medicine Institute have been equally provocative. Initial tests show subjects regaining around 20 degrees of movement. Those given no treatment showed little or no improvement. When we retested people a month later, their shoulders had regained even more movement. Finding the emotionally traumatic events and releasing this stuck energy is like changing the magnets. The iron filings then naturally fall into a healthier shape. It was gratifying to see the change in the lives of the people we treated. Some even gained a greater range of movement in their previously frozen shoulder than they had in the normal shoulder![9]

How is this type of healing linked to spirituality? What is the link between healing our emotional wounds and living from our souls?

When we're tugged this way and that way by our emotional reactions to triggering events, our attention is constantly absorbed in them. We wake up in the morning and start the day by getting triggered by our domestic partners, by our children, by the weather, by thoughts of the workday ahead.

On our commute, we're triggered by the behavior of other drivers or passengers, by the news of the day (invariably bad), by worries about the future or regrets about the past. When we get to work, our emotions are tugged hither and yon by the "good" and "bad" things happening in our work life. "Good" things elate us while "bad" things deflate us.

When we get home, we turn on the TV and our emotions are then pulled and pushed by the programs we watch. We sleep, dream, and repeat the process, adrift on a sea of emotional waves. The sound track of emotional ups and downs leaves us little time to reflect, to contemplate, to discover, or to create. All these beneficial activities require unplugging from the sensory cacophony around us.

Our stress response, the "fight or flight" syndrome, is engaged whenever we're negatively emotionally triggered. When we're stressed, a cascade of hormones floods our body, from adrenaline to cortisol, getting us ready for emergencies that may never materialize. The genes that provide our cells with the code to build these stress hormones are called into action, and, within seconds, start doing their job. Stressful emotions, thoughts, and situations are epigenetic triggers. *Epi* means *above;* the term *epigenetic* indicates influences from outside the cell that activate our DNA. Emotional trauma sends an epigenetic signal activating our stress genes to start constructing cortisol and other biochemical building blocks of survival.

But this high stress level is no longer useful for our survival. It's an evolutionary relic that is shortening our lives, not lengthening them, causing disease, not saving us from it. The list of the effects of having high cortisol levels in our systems for prolonged periods makes depressing reading. It includes:

High blood pressure
Reduced memory and learning
High blood sugar
Heart disease
Diminished cell repair
Accelerated aging
Slower wound healing
Reduced bone repair
Decreased circulating immune cells
Diminished immune antibodies
Death of brain cells
Reduced muscle mass

Decreased skin cell repair
Increased fat deposits around waist/hips
Osteoporosis

Most of the Iraq veterans we've studied who have PTSD have elevated cortisol levels. Every flashback they have calls forth the fight-or-flight response from their bodies, along with a rush of cortisol and other stress biochemicals. Energy psychology releases that stress. It sends an epigenetic signal to our stress genes, saying, "Danger's passed, everything's OK, you can stand down now." And they do. After just four one-hour sessions with an energy psychology specialist, the veterans' cortisol levels plummet. Their physical symptoms begin to disappear. Lieutenant Gomez says: "Recently I participated in a study administered by . . . Soul Medicine Institute. I see the improvement within myself. I have learned to control the vomiting, I've increased my sleep, and the anxiety attacks have lessened. I hope that other vets will find help and do so faster than I did. I have learned that it doesn't make me weak to ask for help."

These improvements are typical of a decreased cortisol response. Those who have worked with Lieutenant Gomez have been deeply moved by his story. We've now started a new online initiative called the Iraq Vets Stress Project (www.stressproject.org) to hook them up with therapists who offer energy psychology treatments. Psychiatrists estimate that perhaps 200,000 Iraq vets and their families may have PTSD, so the challenge to our society is daunting. Only treatments that are able to rapidly offer help to big groups of people are going to be able to address a social problem of this magnitude.

WHAT ABOUT HEALTHY PEOPLE?
One intriguing question that occurred to me recently was: What happens when you use these same methods not with sick people,

but with well ones? What happens when you take people who are already peak performers, and address emotional issues that might still be holding them back?

In early 2006, a young baseball player for Oregon State University (OSU) learned energy psychology from Greg Warburton, a local therapist who also uses these techniques with veterans. He taught the technique to another player, and both surged ahead in their playing ability. The OSU baseball team went on to win the national college championship. Impressed, many other members of the team learned the methods, and OSU won the championship in 2007 for an unprecedented second consecutive year.

The athletic director heard the story, and this led to an his inviting me to visit OSU and perform a randomized controlled double-blind trial (that's science-speak for the highest possible standard of proof) of energy psychology with the men's and women's basketball teams. The conditions were challenging; the therapists, veteran sports psychologists Greg Warburton and Stacey Vornbrock, were asked to produce an increase in athletic performance in *just fifteen minutes of treatment*. Imagine being a therapist working under such conditions: an athlete whom you've never met before walks into your office, and you're expected to create rapport, surface their emotional issues, treat them, and improve their performance as judged in rigorous scientific conditions, in just one quarter of an hour.

The criteria we measured were the height to which the athletes could jump, and also how many free throws they were capable of dunking in the basket.

The results were stunning. Seven of the athletes in the energy psychology group jumped at the same height or higher after treatment, compared to four in the sham treatment group, though the results as a whole were not statistically significant. But it was on the measure of free throws that energy psychology treatment really shone. The group that got energy psychology treatment had their performance increase by 21 percent, while the group that got a placebo or fake treatment declined by 17 percent over the two-hour course of the session. Data analysis showed that there was less than one possibility in thirty that such a result could have occurred purely by chance.[10] This study gave me the first hard numbers showing that, when applied to healthy people, these methods could increase the performance of even peak performers.

THE UNIVERSE IS SPEAKING TO YOU

What do people turn their attention to when they're no longer dogged by ill health, inner and outer emotional wars, and psychological stresses? What happens when we cut away all the tangled vines and gnarly clawed roots of past emotional drama, revealing an open, uncluttered plain of being? My experience is that the calm, peaceful open space created by such pruning is a fertile seedbed for soul and spirit.

When your ears aren't filled with the chatter of reactivity and the cacophony of negativity, and your life is free of stress-generated mindless actions and the prolonged cleanup operations that result from the subsequent mess, then the still, small voice of spirit may be heard. The music of the universe becomes louder and louder in the silence generated by the absence of charged auto-chatter, and we are able to hear the whispered instructions of the soul, the rustle of angel wings, and the divine harmony of the spheres. A composer might hear uplifting music; a mechanic might make an adjustment leading to a perfectly tuned engine; a teacher might intuit the needs of a troublesome child's soul; and a scientist might conceive a research project asking a new question that leads to healing for many people.

Imagine if the whole world were healed. Imagine if all emotional traumas were tapped away, and everyone's physical health blossomed. Imagine if we no longer had to deal with all the challenges that rush at us as the result of the unhealed emotional wounds of others, and we were all free to play our own creative harmonic music. Imagine if war and poverty vanished, as social traumas (which are nothing more than individual traumas writ large) disappear, as the urge to strike and hurt others dissipates in the experience of divine love. Twenty years ago, I could not even imagine such a world. Today, I expect us humans as a species to achieve it within my lifetime.

On the seventh day of the week, I kneel at the altar rail and commune with spirit. The other six, I read papers, exchange e-mails, and receive inspiration from the brilliant minds of researchers. Both acts are sacraments, equally sacred. Both are worship. The scientific paper is the mind of God in evidence, the sacrament is the heart of God in action. For both, I am profoundly grateful, for as we integrate every experience into the act of being, they are one.

Understanding how positive and negative emotions develop, and how they shape our ability to be happy, can be central to a fruitful spiritual practice. In the following essay, Dr. Rick Hanson focuses on the intersection between psychology, neurology, and Buddhism, reviewing seven significant, scientifically proven facts about the brain. He explores such questions as: Is the brain more inclined toward positive or negative emotions? Is it possible to train your brain to focus on positive emotions and experiences and, if so, can that heighten the joy in life? How does our brain change, and can you use your mind to change your brain to benefit your whole being, and other beings, too, even the whole wide world?

Seven Facts about the Brain That Incline the Mind to Joy

RICK HANSON, PH.D.

In a way, the methodologies of Buddhist thought and science are essentially similar.
—The Dalai Lama

We all want to be truly happy. The question is, *how*?

From the perspective of both Western psychology and the world's contemplative traditions, the "how" of happiness—and less anxiety, sorrow, frustration, disappointment, and anger—always involves changing the mind in some ways. For example, in Buddhist practice one sees into the mind, the seat of clinging in all its forms, ever more deeply, in order to increase the causes of happiness and reduce the causes of suffering, ultimately to the point of complete Awakening.

But what does it mean, *actually*, to transform the mind? (I use the word "mind" in the ordinary sense, as the realm of awareness, thoughts, feelings, sensations, images, desires, personality patterns, etc.) It is very exciting these days that an integrated answer to that vital question is emerging from the growing intersection of three historically separated fields: psychology, neurology, and contemplative practice.

For example, in the past few years, scholars working in what's called "contemplative neuroscience" have made discoveries about attention, cultivating positive emotions, and controlling craving that support the development of virtue, concentration, and wisdom; besides being sources of happiness and valuable in their own right, these are the three pillars of Buddhist practice. Further, the growing synergies between science and contemplative training are a vital resource for a world poised on the edge of the sword, since the way it tips will depend a lot on whether enough people become more skillful at managing the reactive patterns of their minds, and thus, their brains.

As one illustration of this synergy—and how it can help you personally, and those you care for and about—let's explore seven facts about your brain, and how to use them to turn your mind increasingly toward peacefulness, contentment, and joy.

1: THE MIND AND THE BRAIN ARE MAINLY (PERHAPS ENTIRELY) A SINGLE SYSTEM.

Most neuroscientists think that our thoughts and feelings, darkest passions and loftiest dreams, poetry and imagery, chess gambits and baseball statistics and recipes and quilt patterns and earliest memories of snow—and all the other textures and aromas and shades of being alive—require and are produced by nervous system activity.

While there could well be a mysterious transcendental *Something* infusing objective and subjective reality, whose influence is subtle, profound, and full of grace (which is my personal belief), the wonders of the mind may not require an extraordinary (call it mystical) basis in addition to the brain itself.

To be sure, it is not unreasonable to think that an extraordinary phenomenon could require an extraordinary explanation. For example, seeing the extraordinary differences between humans and other animals, many people concluded that we must have been created by an extraordinary God. But today, it's understood that humans evolved by ordinary causes, notably DNA molecules and survival of the fittest, unfolding via zillions of organisms over several billion years. A *lot* of ordinary causes can produce an extraordinary result.

Similarly, when you take an ordinary synapse (basically, a simple on-off switch) but then multiply it by 500 trillion or so, usually firing many times a second, with tremendous interconnectivity . . . well, you can get extraordinary results, like understanding these sentences, or cultivating lovingkindness, or becoming aware of awareness itself. As the capabilities of the brain become even better understood over the next hundred years, most (if not all) of our experiences—the rich soil of the path of practice—will likely be revealed as entirely enabled by the physical brain, and not due in any way to extraordinary mystical factors.

For me, this view is not mechanistic or stifling. It makes you profoundly grateful for evolution's gift of the brain, sensitive to your responsibilities to shape it over time, and inspired by its potential for extraordinary goodness, love, and realization. So I bow to the Transcendental, but for the purposes of this essay, will stay inside the framework of Western science.

Within that frame, *everything* we are aware of, including our own sense of self, is considered to have a one-to-one correspondence with underlying physical brain structures and processes.

Just as a letter to friend or a picture of a sunset on your computer requires and represents an underlying pattern of magnetic charges on your hard drive.

This integration of mind and brain has three profound implications.

First, it means that *as your experience changes, your brain changes*. It changes both temporarily, millisecond by millisecond, and it changes in lasting ways. For example, researchers have found that:

- Different mental activities change brainwave patterns
- People who meditate have more of the vital neurotransmitter, serotonin
- The brains of pianists are thicker in the areas of fine motor function
- The brains of meditators are thicker in the regions engaged with sensory awareness and with the control of attention
- The brains of taxi drivers in London are thicker in the regions that are key to visual-spatial memories
- Repeated experiences of depression create marked changes in the brain that make a person more vulnerable to depression in the future

Second, *as your brain changes, your experience changes*. For example, as most of us have experienced in everyday life, caffeine makes you feel stimulated and alert while alcohol makes you feel relaxed and even sleepy. More technically, studies have found that:

- Activating the left frontal regions leads to a sunnier outlook and more positive mood, while strokes in those areas leave patients particularly irritable and depressed
- Surges of the neurotransmitter dopamine feel very pleasurable (why dopamine is associated with addictions)

- Damage to a cubic centimeter or so of tissue in a particular place on the left side of your brain can leave you able to understand language but incapable of generating it, while damage just a few centimeters away will have the opposite effect
- Electrically stimulating portions of the brain can trigger memories or even out-of-body experiences

And this research is mainly less than twenty years old. Consider how the invention of the microscope in the early 1600s opened up an entire new world in its revelation of all the "tiny beasties" found in a teardrop or a bit of pond water. Yet it still took four hundred years to develop the modern understanding of molecular biology and evolution.

Comparable technologies for peering into the brain have been around for only a few decades, and the scientific understanding of that organ is roughly comparable to the state of biology in, say, the early 1800s. Just imagine what will be understood four hundred years from now . . . or even forty.

This intimate intertwining of mind and matter, psyche and soma, self and brain, may seem off-putting and reductionistic at first. To put it a little graphically: "What do you mean? I'm just the *meat*?!"

Yet for me, this oneness of mind and brain actually provokes an incredible sense of awe, as well as gratitude that we have inherited the results of 3.5 billion years of evolutionary refinement of the machinery underlying the mind. That appreciation takes one to a sense of responsibility to make the most of one's life, to not waste this incredible, jaw-dropping gift of human consciousness.

This is the third profound implication of the integration of mind and brain, a fantastic opportunity for well-being, psychological growth, and contemplative depth: in hundreds of ways, large and small, you can deliberately *use your mind to change your brain to benefit your whole being*—and everyone else whose life you touch.

2: "NEURONS THAT FIRE TOGETHER, WIRE TOGETHER."
This famous saying, from the work of the Canadian psychologist Donald Hebb, explains how learning occurs in the brain, whether it's a newborn rooting for the nipple, a toddler acquiring language, a schoolchild figuring out fractions, a manager getting better at running meetings, or anyone getting clearer about what causes suffering for oneself and others. Learning is *everything*. Humans have the longest childhood of any animal on the planet because we have so much to learn, and it doesn't stop when we get out of high school. Even though our culture (and conventional education) idolizes words and verbal thought, most learning is nonverbal, emotional, or sensorimotor. For example, for someone starting to go deeper in meditation, there is a subtle learning of how to establish a steady awareness of attention itself, a growing competence and skillfulness at encouraging a gentle grounding in the body and quieting of the mind.

Hebb's insight was that we learn through the strengthening of connections between simultaneously firing neurons in the extraordinary network of the brain. Neurons with synapses to each other—tiny gaps full of a rich soup of neurotransmitters where they come oh-so-close together—which fire at the same time, become more responsive to each other. It's as if they're saying: "We're in synch with each other, so let's get more connected." This same process occurs in existing circuits, too. Every time one activates as a whole, the connections within it are reinforced.

This strengthening happens both during brief intervals of time through ephemeral electrochemical ebbs and flows and over longer periods, as physically observable changes occur in the brain. These include:

- Increased synaptic connections among neurons (synapses are the junctions between neurons: tiny gaps that function like microscopic switches, on/off)

- Increased thickening of the glial cells, the "scaffolding" tissues that support neurons
- Greater density of blood vessels bringing oxygen, glucose, etc. to neurons

3: FLEETING EXPERIENCES LEAVE LASTING TRACES IN THE BRAIN.

Since the mind and brain are one, the flow of information in the mind causes a corresponding flow of electrochemical activation through the neuronal circuitry of the brain. In other words, the fleeting "stream of consciousness" leaves behind lasting marks on your brain, much like a spring shower leaves a trail of little furrows on a hillside.

This means that your experiences are important: not just due to their brief effects on your momentary, subjective quality of life, but also because they produce enduring changes in the physical structures of your brain. And these alterations in your brain will then affect your well-being, functioning, and sometimes your physical health for days and decades to come. Which of course will affect others besides yourself.

Your experience really, really matters. Which is a scientifically substantiated rationale for being kind to yourself and creating the causes of more beneficial experiences for yourself and fewer harmful ones.

4: MOST CHANGES IN THE TISSUES OF THE BRAIN ARE IN IMPLICIT MEMORY.

There are two kinds of memory:

- Explicit: Recollections of specific events and factual knowledge
- Implicit: Emotions, body sensations, relationship paradigms, sense of the world, and behavioral strategies

Implicit memory is visceral, felt, powerful, and rooted in the fundamental and ancient—reptile and early mammal—structures of your brain. The inner atmosphere of your mind (what living feels like for you) depends greatly on what is stored in your implicit memory.

If in a physical sense "we are what we eat," in a psychological sense we are what we *remember*, especially *implicitly*—the slowly accumulating registration of lived experience. That's what we have "taken in" to become a part of ourselves. Just as food becomes woven into the body, memory becomes woven into the self.

5: UNFORTUNATELY, THE BRAIN EMPHASIZES NEGATIVE EXPERIENCES.

It's the negative experiences that signal the greatest threats to survival. So our ancient animal and human ancestors that lived to pass on their genes paid a *lot* of attention to negative experiences.

Consider 80 million years or so of mammal evolution, starting with little rodent-like creatures dodging dinosaurs to stay alive and have babies in a worldwide Jurassic Park. Constantly looking over their shoulders, alert to the slightest crackle of brush, quick to freeze or bolt or attack depending on the situation. Just like any mouse or squirrel you might see in the wild today: the quick and the dead.

Today, that same neurological circuitry is loaded and fully operational as you drive through traffic, argue with your mate, hear an odd noise in the night, or get an unexpected letter from the IRS.

First, the amygdala—the switchboard that assigns a feeling tone to the stimuli flowing through the brain (pleasant, unpleasant, and neutral) and initiates a response (approach, avoid, move on)—is physically primed to label experiences as frightening and negative. In other words, it's built to *look* for the bad. For example, when someone—a parent, friend, lover, or boss—gives you feedback, doesn't your mind go to the hint of criticism surrounded by praise? (Mine sure does.) It gets signals from an adjacent node in the brain called the hippocampus, which compares current perceptual information to memories of previous threats and whenever it discerns a match—BOO! it shouts to the amygdala, "Warn the whole town!"

Second, when an event is flagged as negative, the amygdala and its neighbor in the brain, the hippocampus, store it carefully for future reference. Forever after, the hippocampus-amygdala circuit compares current perceptual information to the record of old painful events, and if there are any similarities, alarm bells start ringing. Once burned, twice shy. In short, your brain doesn't just go looking for what's negative; it's built to grab that information and never let it go.

Sure, we can notice positive experiences and remember them. But unless you're having a million-dollar moment, the brain circuitry for what's positive is like a notepad compared to a high-speed computer hard-drive for what's negative. When you look back on a typical day, what's usually more prominent in memory: the dozens of mildly pleasant moments, or the one that was awkward or worrisome? When you look back on your life, what's more memorable: the ten thousand pleasures and accomplishments, or the handful of losses and failures?

Third, the negative generally trumps the positive; consider how a single bad event with a dog is more memorable than a thousand good times. Speaking of dogs, the studies on learned helplessness from Martin Seligman and his colleagues illustrate this point in haunting ways: it took only a short time to induce a sense of helplessness in the dogs, whose brain circuitry for emotional memory is in some ways similar to our own. But it took an extraordinary effort to get them to unlearn that training. It's as if mammals, including ourselves, are predisposed to believe the worst about the world and themselves, and to doubt the best.

As a result, your own personal training in the negative—whatever it's been—can't help but leave lasting changes in your brain that shape your view of the world and yourself, and your personality and interpersonal style and approach to life. (In extreme cases, if a person has a serious history of trauma or depression, the hippocampus can actually shrink 10 to 20 percent, impairing the brain's capacity to remember positive experiences.) Your brain is like velcro for negative experiences and teflon for positive ones.

All that can lead to more of the negative showing up on your radar, either because you are scanning for it preferentially or unwittingly increasing the odds of it coming your way. Which, in a vicious cycle, can make you even more inclined to see or cause the negative in the future—even though the actual facts are that the vast majority of the events and experiences in your life are neutral or positive! Every day, the minds of most people render verdicts about their character, their life, and their future possibilities that are profoundly unfair.

Besides the implications for everyday life, the brain's built-in negativity bias wears on spiritual inclinations and activities. In terms of Buddhist practice, for instance, this bias feeds the Five Hindrances of greed, ill will, sloth and torpor, restlessness and remorse, and doubt. It also saps motivation for right effort, the spiritual equivalent of learned helplessness. And it undermines *bhavana*—the cultivation of wholesome qualities—by downplaying good lessons and experiences, by undermining their storage, and by making it harder to recollect positive states of mind so we can find our way back to them.

What to do about this?

6: YOU CAN HELP EMPHASIZE AND STORE POSITIVE
EXPERIENCES THROUGH CONSCIOUS ATTENTION.
As you know from school (and this is corroborated by hundreds of studies) you remember something best when you make it as vivid as possible and then give it heightened attention over an extended period.

That's exactly how to register positive experiences in your implicit memory, which will slowly but surely change the interior landscape of your mind.

Three simple steps:

1. Help positive events become positive *experiences*:
   - Pay extra attention to the good things in the world and in yourself. For example, notice things that go well, or people who treat you kindly, or when you succeed at something. As we know, it is ignorance, fundamentally, that leads to suffering—and not seeing the good that is actually present is a kind of ignorance.
   - As a mindfulness practice, focus on the sensations and the feelings in a positive experience since they are the pathway to emotional memory.
   - Deliberately create positive experiences for yourself. Examples include acts of generosity, evoking compassion, or recalling a time when you were happy.
2. Savor the experience as a kind of concentration practice; keep your attention on it for many seconds while letting it fill your body and mind.
3. Sense that the experience is *soaking* into you, registering deeply in emotional memory. You could imagine that it's sinking into your chest and back and brainstem, or imagine a treasure chest in your heart.

These three steps usually take half a minute or less, and with practice you'll get even faster. Every day, there are many opportunities for noticing and absorbing good experiences. Any single instance won't make a big difference, but as the days and weeks add up, the mounting pile of positive implicit memories will provide more resources for coping—and practice—and brighten your inner landscape.

Because "neurons that fire together, wire together," momentary *states* become enduring *traits*. These traits then become the causes of more wholesome states, which nourish your traits further in a positive cycle. To paraphrase Mathieu Ricard: if you take care of the minutes and the hours—the days and years will take care of themselves.

7: POSITIVE EXPERIENCES HAVE MANY IMPORTANT BENEFITS.

In general
- Emotions organize the mind as a whole, so positive feelings and their related body sensations, thoughts, and desires have global effects.
- Positive experiences lower the stress response in your body by dampening the arousal of the sympathetic nervous system (the "fight or flight" wing) and by activating the parasympathetic nervous system (relaxed and contented). For example, positive feelings reduce the impact of stress on your cardiovascular system.
- They increase psychological resilience.
- They lift mood and protect against depression.
- They promote optimism—another bulwark against depression.
- Over time, positive experiences help counteract the effects of trauma or other painful experiences. When you remember something painful from your past, your brain first reconstructs that memory (including its emotional associations) from a few key elements, and then it reconstitutes it in storage *with tinges of your state of mind when you recalled it the last time*. This means that if you recall an event repeatedly with a dour, glum cast of mind, then your recollection of it will be increasingly shaded negatively. Alternately, if you recall it repeatedly with a realistically upbeat state of being, then it will

gradually come to mind more and more with a more neutral quality: you will not forget the facts of whatever happened, but their emotional charge will slowly fade—and that can be a great relief.

- They highlight key states of mind so you can find your way back to them in the future. So you can more readily tap into peace, contentment, strength, well-being, lovingkindness, etc.
- They reward you for doing things that aren't always easy (like acting with unilateral virtue even when others are being difficult) and thus support your ongoing motivation.

For children

- All of the benefits above apply to kids as well.
- In particular, children who are in the spirited range of temperament really benefit from deliberately slowing down to take in positive experiences, since they tend to move along quickly to the next thing before the previous good feelings have had a chance to consolidate in the brain.
- Similarly, children in the anxious/rigid range of temperament also benefit from consciously soaking in good feelings, since they tend to ignore or downplay the evidence for those positive experiences.

For contemplative practice

- Positive experiences promote steadiness of mind, necessary for any fruitful meditation.
- They support the deep states of absorption that are both blissful and profoundly insightful. For example, the high levels of dopamine associated with joy help keep the "gate" of awareness shut to being flooded by new experience, and thus support concentration.

- They build confidence in the fruits of one's efforts. Conviction is a major engine of practice and perseverance; for example, in Buddhism, it is one of the factors of enlightenment.
- Fundamentally, you are cultivating wholesome qualities in your mind and heart, and both crowding out and replacing negative ones.

HOW BRAIN SCIENCE CAN SUPPORT SPIRITUAL PRACTICE

To be sure, scientific ideas and methods are not *necessary* to fulfill any path of awakening, including the one laid out by the Buddha—the one I know best. But the emerging map of the mind and the brain can *support* practice in numerous ways.

First, knowing more about the brain/mind deepens conviction (faith), which is one of the factors of enlightenment in Buddhism, since scientific developments confirm many ancient (and modern) spiritual teachings. For example, researchers have found that the activities of "self" are scattered throughout the brain, constructed from multiple sub-systems, and activated by many prior causes: there is no coherent, stable, independent self looking out through your eyes; in a neurological sense, self is truly "empty." For many Westerners, science is the benchmark authority for what is true, and when it is in harmony with their spiritual or philosophical beliefs, that reduces the hindrance of doubt.

Second, neuropsychology can explain *why* traditional practices work, and help you focus on their key elements. For instance, rapture and joy, which are traditional factors of meditative absorption, involve high levels of the neurotransmitter dopamine. Your brain also uses pulses of dopamine to open the neuronal gate that allows new material into the field of attention. But when you're full of rapture and joy, any new surges of dopamine make little difference since their levels are *already* near their maximum. As a result, the gate of attention is harder to open, and you're more able to remain focused on the breath.

Third, brain science can highlight which of the hundreds of traditional methods are likely to be most effective for individual needs. This helps intensify practice, especially for householders who don't have the benefits of the all-surrounding environment and close guidance of monastic life.

The great variety of brains and thus minds is a diversity issue in its own right, which underscores the value of the appropriate individualization of practice. For example, there is a wide range of temperaments, and for a person who's naturally spirited, understanding and normalizing the hungry-for-stimulation systems in his or her brain can lead to emphasizing certain forms of meditation in the development of steadiness of mind (e.g., tracking the breath as a whole rather than at just one spot), and to becoming more self-accepting.

Fourth, the developing brain/mind map can suggest new and effective methods to build upon established practices. For instance, some teachers are drawing on the research literature in attachment theory, empathic attunement, and mirror neurons to refine the methods of interpersonal mindfulness. (For more examples, please see our website, www.wisebrain.org.)

Of course, any scientific enhancements of traditionally skillful means must be balanced by virtue and wisdom. Further, the ultimate fruit of practice—oneness with God, enlightenment, nirvana, or whatever it is for you—transcends all methods. Nonetheless, every contemplative tradition also teaches that the highest attainment always requires a dedicated training of mind and heart, which means a transformation of brain and body. Even if the apple falls by grace, its ripening comes from water, sunlight, and fertile ground.

PITFALLS

The meeting between science and contemplative practice brings many gifts and opportunities, but also some potential pitfalls, and understanding these will help you sift out the information that is personally useful:

- *Getting neurologically reductionistic.* While simplifications are sometimes clarifying, they need to be held in perspective. If you find yourself reading about the amygdala and fear, mirror neurons and empathy, oxytocin and lovingkindness, high-frequency brain waves and meditative concentration, etc. . . . no matter how accurate that material is, it's always more complicated than that.
- *Glamorizing science.* As the Buddha said, "See for yourself." The ultimate test of your practice is whether it *works*—and it probably has for millions of people for thousand of years. No contemplative tradition needs the endorsement of science to prove its validity.
- *Over-generalizing from group data to individuals.* In the press and even the scientific literature, you'll sometimes find statements like these: "Men have stronger visual-spatial abilities" or "Meditators react better to stress." Yes, the average man could be slightly better at visual tasks than the average woman. But it's *not* correct to equate everybody in a group with its average, and then make categorical statements about all its members. Many women are more visually adept than many men . . . just as many meditators can get pretty stressed out!
- *Overvaluing the physical.* For example, genetic factors usually account for less than a third to a half of our personality, intelligence, happiness, satisfaction with relationships, lifetime earnings, or spiritual growth. The rest is due to the influences of our own self-direction and the ways we interact with our environments—which is very, very hopeful. And since the normal brain can hold both horrible and wonderful thoughts, emotions, and wants, it's the

contents of mind that usually count most, not the physical organ that enables them.

Further, appreciating the integration of mind and brain does not mean reducing mind *to* brain. To be unavoidably technical: mind is patterns of information represented by patterns of matter. Since much mental information can be represented by any suitable neural circuit—much as a picture can be represented by any available RAM on your computer—it is functionally independent of its physical substrate. Second, this independence enables thoughts (and other aspects of mind) to be the fundamental cause of other thoughts; the brain carries thoughts but it does not necessarily *cause* them. And third, mind can cause changes in matter through its representations in matter; for example, immaterial thoughts of gratitude are embodied in cascading physical processes which can trigger physical circuits that dampen the release of stress hormones.

KEY FEATURES AND FUNCTIONS OF YOUR BRAIN

- It's shaped by evolution; the main genetic differences between humans and chimpanzees focus on the brain, particularly its social, emotional, linguistic, and conceptual abilities
- 3 pounds, 1.1 trillion cells, including 100 billion "gray matter" neurons
- Always "on": 2 percent of the body's weight uses about 25 percent of its oxygen
- Average neuron has about 1000 connections (synapses), 100 trillion in all
- Synapses firing 1 to 100 times a second
- Regions linked by brain waves synchronized within a few milliseconds
- Extremely interconnected network full of circular loops
- Number of possible brain states: 1 followed by a million zeros
- An organ that learns from experiences through lifelong changes in its structure
- The most complex object known in the universe

The underlying neurology of your mind is great for survival, but it poses a fundamental challenge to well-being: positive experiences typically roll through it while negative experiences get immediately flagged, stored carefully for quick access, and recalled with great power. But you can override those tendencies in simple and effective ways each day by focusing on positive experiences, valuing them, and helping them sink in. Through thought alone, you can create and strengthen wholesome circuits in your brain, for the benefit of yourself and all beings.

The deliberate internalization of positive experiences illustrates the oneness of the brain and the mind, and the power of using the mind to change the brain. It is a deeply wise and wonderful undertaking: *happiness is skillful means.* And happily for happiness, this undertaking is aligned with our deepest nature: always already awake, benign, and quietly inclined to joy.

Quantum physics puts forth the idea that we potentially have an ability to create our own reality. This is an exciting principle, but few understand the inner workings of the actual science involved. Dr. William Tiller of Stanford University, author of *Psychoenergetic Science: A Second Copernican-Scale Revolution,* illustrates the evolution of traditional science and the new frontier of science as it relates to energy. In the following essay he introduces us to what he calls the "ladder of understanding," which guides us toward a greater understanding of psychoenergetic science and ultimately his hypothesis connecting consciousness, intention, and spirit interaction, as they exist within (and outside) our current scientific model. Using the language of scientific equations, psychoenergetic science, and deltrons, he answers questions such as: How does quantum physics lead toward a definition of our personality self, the spirit domain, and our emotions? How much choice do we have in our own reality?

Toward a Reliable Bridge of Understanding Between Traditional Science and Spiritual Science

WILLIAM TILLER, PH.D.

INTRODUCTION

To understand science within the context of this anthology, think of nature as radiating to us on many uniquely different bands of information. Over the past four hundred years, traditional science has learned a great deal about one of these bands, the electromagnetic band, and almost nothing about any of the other bands. It is certainly not the time to be writing books about "The Theory of Everything"! We are a slowly evolving species and we need to develop a science that encompasses all of these bands of nature's informational radiations.

When we ask ourselves why we care about a scientific understanding of nature, we realize that humankind is concerned with scientific inquiry because people want to understand the milieu in which they find themselves. They want to engineer and reliably control, or cooperatively modulate, as much of their environment as possible to sustain, enrich, and propagate their life. Following this path, the goal of science is to gain a reliable description of all natural phenomena so as to allow accurate prediction (within appropriate limits) of nature's behavior as a function of an ever-changing environment. As such, science is incapable of providing us with absolute truth. Rather, it provides us with *relative* knowledge, internally self-consistent knowledge, about the relationships between different phenomena and between different things.

The goal of engineering, on the other hand, is to build upon this fundamental understanding in order to generate new materials, devices, structures, attitudes, moralities, philosophies, etc., for producing tangible order, harnessing the latent potential in nature's many, many phenomena, and expanding human capabilities in an ever-changing environment.

As we reflect upon our world and upon the humankind that populate its surface, one soon perceives that there are several categories of phenomena and information wherein we need to gain reliable understanding in order to enhance our life's journey. These might be classified as (1) things of the physical, (2) things of the psyche, (3) things of the emotion, (4) things of the mind, and (5) things of the spirit. In addition, we also need a meaningful perspective or reference frame from which to view these different categories of phenomena and information. Ultimately our understanding of all these phenomena and all this information must be internally self-consistent. Since we are an evolving species, growing in understanding via a bootstrap process, a useful metaphor for what we need is a "ladder

Figure 1. A metaphorical description of the "ladder of understanding."

of understanding" that guides us from the simple to the more complex (in the sense of levels of integration of different categories of infrastructure).

Thus, figure 1 represents our metaphorical "ladder of understanding" that we must build by our efforts and climb upon, rung by rung, as we evolve to higher states of beingness. In what is to follow, the overall map of the territory needing serious exploration will be laid out. However, the major focus, from a scientific perspective, will be on the bottom two rungs of figure 1.

TRADITIONAL SCIENCE, THE BOTTOM RUNG

From an overly simplistic viewpoint, one can say that, for the past four hundred years, establishment science has dealt with multiple aspects of the metaphorical reaction equation

$$\text{Mass} \quad \leftrightarrow \quad \text{Energy} \qquad\qquad (1a)$$

with each term being convertible to the other via Einstein's $E = mc^2$ relationship where E = Energy, m = Mass and c = the velocity of electromagnetic (EM) light through physical vacuum.

In the 1600s, René Descartes realized that a clear division between mind and physical matter or between soul and body was needed in order to gain a system of fundamental knowledge about our outer world. Thus, he proposed a real compartmentalization of thought between "natural philosophy," wherein consciousness was *not* an experimental variable of relevance, and "theology" where it was. Over time, it became an *unstated assumption* of physics that "no human qualities of consciousness, intention, emotion, mind, or spirit can significantly influence a well-designed target experiment in physical reality." Thus, in equation 1a, consciousness is not allowed as a significant experimental variable, so equation 1a is a convenient approximation to the behavior of nature.

Unfortunately, over time, physicists have forgotten that this was just a useful assumption that was fairly valid in the 1600s and 1700s. Because of this assumption, we learned how to develop a reliable methodology and set of procedures for the conduct of scientific experiments in the simplest of cases— where the biofields of the experimenters were relatively weak and thus they only negligibly perturbed the experimental outcomes. One of the upsides of the assumption was the discovery and engineering utilization of many natural laws. One of the downsides to almost total acceptance of this assumption is that the philosophical worldview of establishment science has become almost totally reductionistic and materialistic.

This approach by science has held sway through its classical mechanics (CM) era and into the almost one hundred years of the quantum mechanics (QM) era; however, today, both QM and our reference frame (RF) for viewing these aspects of nature appear to be significantly flawed.

As presently formulated mathematically, QM is a quantitatively precise theory whose mathematical RF is four-dimensional spacetime within the classical electric particle velocity limits from zero to c and involving the four fundamental forces discovered by science to date of (1) gravity, (2) Maxwellian electromagnetism, (3) the long-range nuclear force, and (4) the short-range nuclear force. This theory has been remarkably successful for particle physics, small atoms, molecules, and photons at very low temperatures. However, many of the outcomes from today's QM experiments require weirder and weirder explanations. This seems to be a clear sign that the present conceptual model of QM has reached the limits of its useful modeling capabilities.

PSYCHOENERGETIC SCIENCE, THE FIRST AND SECOND RUNGS
Returning to equation 1a, experimental research of at least the past decade shows that human biofield effects are no longer of insignificant magnitude[1-5] in a well-designed target experiment and that psychoenergetic effects from humans require an expansion of equation 1a to at least the form

Mass ↔ Energy ↔ Information ↔ Consciousness (1b)

When we ask what consciousness does rather than what it is, one immediately realizes that it manipulates information: information in the form of numbers, alphabetical letters, jigsaw puzzle pieces, and, most generally, symbols. For the past sixty years, establishment science has recognized the existence of a quantitative relationship between information in units of bits and the thermodynamic quantity, entropy, in units of calories per unit temperature.[4] For the past hundred and fifty years, entropy has been a very important contribution to the Gibbs Thermodynamic Free Energy, G, given by

$$G = PV + E - TS \qquad (2)$$

where P = Pressure, V = Volume, E = Energy, T = Temperature, and S = Entropy. It is changes in G, ΔG, that drives all the processes in nature that we have so far discovered. Thus, all terms in ΔG (PΔV, VΔP, ΔE, TΔS and SΔT) are equally important in producing significant changes in our world. The terms PΔV and VΔP were very important in the steam engine era and in today's era of refrigeration and heat pumps (compressors). The term ΔE has gained great popularity as particle physicists have accelerated electrons, protons, neutrons, etc. to high energies and smashed them into various material targets. The term SΔT is important in future geothermal energy conversion while the term TΔS is important to the change in informational content from a natural process inherent in equation 1b. One can see from this the intimate bridge that exists and connects energy and information in equation 1b.

To put the foregoing in perspective, let us consider what I call the "silver colloid" metaphor.

If one takes a beaker of water with some bacteria in it and then shakes some silver colloid particles into the water, we know that the bacteria will probably be killed via the bactericidal action of the silver particles. The general conclusion that has been drawn from this observation is that the physical contact between silver and the bacterium is a necessary condition for killing the bacteria. This, in turn, has led to the assumption that pharmaceuticals do their work in the human body via contact-types of chemical reactions and this has led to what is labeled as today's *chemical medicine.*

What is not so well known is that, if one takes a fluorescent tube with silver electrodes and then focuses the output light from the ignited tube onto the beaker of water containing bacteria, one also kills the bacteria. Such an experiment shows that it is *not* physical contact between silver and the bacterium that drives the killing process. Rather, it is one or more different frequencies of photons from the EM emission spectrum of silver that entangles with the EM carrier wave from the fluorescent tube's axial discharge, and is transported to the beaker of water, that is/are the actual killing mechanism involved in the demise of the bacteria. Pursuing this line of research will inevitably lead to tomorrow's *energy medicine.*

Over the past decade, this author and his colleagues have shown that one can imbed a specific intention, from a deep meditative state,[3] into a simple electronic device and have that device, in turn, "condition" a laboratory space wherein the proper experiment is running to test the efficacy of this intention procedure. This procedure has been highly successful with four uniquely different target experiments.[3] Replication of one of these target experiments in ten other laboratories in the U.S. and Europe shows that this is a viable procedure for killing the bacteria and will ultimately lead to the day-after-tomorrow's *information medicine*.

THE EXPERIMENTAL PICTURE

Expanding on the previous paragraph, from our recent intention-host device research,[3-5] we have discovered a second, unique level of physical reality that is quite different from our normal, electric atom/molecule level. This new level functions in the physical vacuum within the "empty" space between the fundamental particles that make up the electric atoms and molecules. The "stuff" of this coarse physical vacuum level appears to consist of magnetic information waves. We have discovered that it is the physics of this magnetic information wave substance that is modulatable by human mind, human emotions, and human intentions in general, rather than our familiar electric atom/molecule substance.

These two uniquely different kinds of charge substance appear to interpenetrate each other, but under normal conditions, they do not interact with each other. We call this *the uncoupled state* of physical reality. This is illustrated in figure 2a. Here, the black balls represent the electric substance and the smaller white balls represent the magnetic substance. Metaphorically, the black lines joining the black balls represents that they are interacting with each other and, since nothing connects the white balls

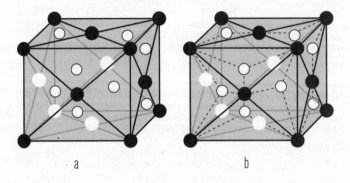

a   b

Figure 2. The physical reality metaphor: (a) the uncoupled state and (b) the coupled state.

with the black balls, this represents that they are not interacting with each other.

Via the use of an intention-host device,[1,3] (1) the indwelling consciousness of the space can be activated, (2) the EM symmetry state of the space can be lifted to a significantly higher level than normal, and (3) the space can be tuned to create a unique material property change. This occurs because now, the magnetic information wave substance is interacting with the electric, particulate substance to produce *the coupled state* of physical reality. This is illustrated in figure 2b where the dashed lines connecting the white balls to the black balls represent that they are interacting with each other.

In equation form, these two states of physical reality can be represented by

$$Q_M(t) = Q_e + \alpha_{eff}(t)Q_m \qquad (3)$$

Here, Q_M is the total magnitude of measurement of a particular material property, Q_e is the normal value expected from

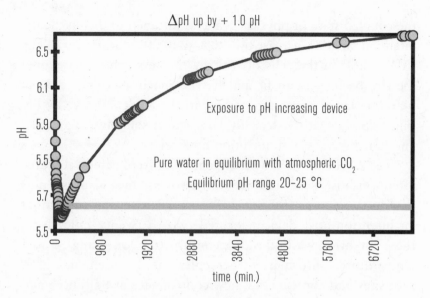

Figure 3. Plot of pH rising one full pH unit due to exposure to a pH-increasing intention-host device.

the electric atom/molecule level, Q_m is the value coming from the magnetic information wave level as modified by the specific intention, α_{eff} is the coupling coefficient between these two kinds of substance and t = time ($0 \leq \alpha_{eff} \leq 1$). When $\alpha_{eff} \sim 0$, the term on the right disappears and our normal physical reality, where $Q_M = Q_e$, is restored. However, when α_{eff} is of significant magnitude, Q_M changes upward or downward, or is unchanged, depending on the sign and magnitude of Q_m.

We have utilized this new procedure to (1) substantially change pH of the same type of water in equilibrium with air either up or down by one full pH unit, with a measurement accuracy of ±0.01 units and with no intentional chemical additions (figure 3 illustrates data from a ΔpH=+1 unit experiment), (2) increase by ~25%, with p<0.001, the in vitro thermodynamic activity of a specific liver enzyme, alkaline phosphatase, via a thirty minute exposure of the enzyme to a space already "conditioned" to the coupled state of physical reality and tuned to this particular intention, and (3) increase by ~20% (p<0.001) the in vivo [ATP]/[ADP] ratio in the cells of fruit fly larvae so that they would thereby become more fit and have a much shorter (~20% at p<0.001) larval development time to the adult fly stage by lifetime exposure of the fruit fly larvae to a suitably conditioned and tuned space via an intention-host device.

The ΔpH=+1 unit experiment was replicated at three intention-host sites (Arizona, Missouri, and Kansas) plus three control sites (the same measurement setup but without an intention-host device) located two to twenty miles from these intention-host sites. To confirm this long-range, room temperature, information entanglement between intention-host sites and control sites, new control sites at Baltimore and Bethesda (1,500 miles away) were successfully utilized.[4] Later, control sites in London, U.K., and Milan, Italy, successfully showed very long range (6,000 miles) information entanglement between sites, indicating that a newer type of information channel than standard electromagnetism was being utilized.[4,5]

During this period, we learned how to experimentally measure the excess thermodynamic free energy for the aqueous H^+-ion, δG^*_{H+}, between a room that was conditioned via an intention-host device to the coupled state of physical reality relative to the room's normal, uncoupled state, condition.

Figure 4 shows such data for both an intention-host device site (Payson, Arizona) and two very distant control sites (U.K. and Italy). We have found such data for all the sites in the replication experiment, whether it was an intention-host device site or a control site, and the magnitude of δG^*_{H+} was unexpectedly large (comparable to the average, room temperature thermal energy).[5]

As a last pair of important experimental observations concerning the coupled state versus the uncoupled state of physical reality:

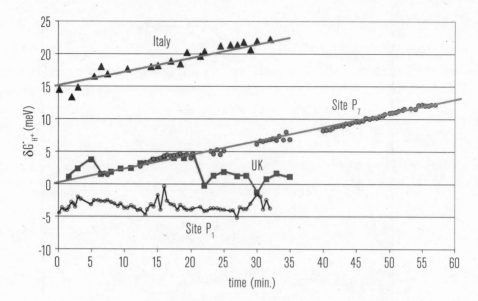

Figure 4. $\delta G'_{H^+}$ vs. time at four diverse sites.

1. We found that a key experimental signature for a space being at the *coupled state* compared to the *uncoupled state* was the pH response of water to a north magnetic pole of a magnet facing the water vessel versus the south magnetic pole of the magnet facing the water vessel. For the uncoupled state, because only magnetic dipoles are present, one should not expect any difference in the pH-response and, indeed, none is experimentally observed. However, for the coupled state, figure 5 shows that the south pole makes the water more alkaline while the north pole makes the water more acidic.

2. When the strength of various muscle groups of the human body are tested via kinesiology and also submitted to either the north pole or the south pole of a bar magnet being brought into the near-field (within 1 to 2 centimeters of the body points) of the local acupuncture points, one finds that (a) the south pole strengthens the muscle while the north pole greatly weakens the muscle. Because such a direct current magnetic field-polarity effect is observed for humans, and

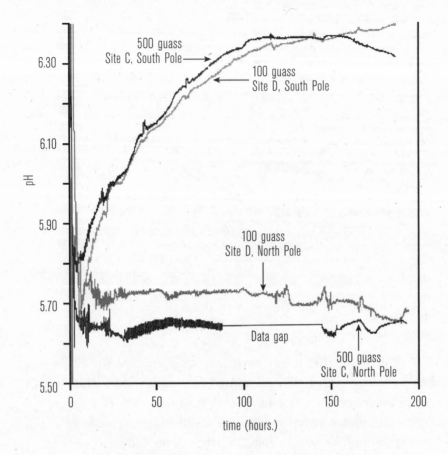

Figure 5. pH changes with time for pure water for both N-pole up and S-pole up axially aligned DC magnetic fields at 100 and 500 gauss.

perhaps all vertebrates, this means that the acupuncture meridian/chakra system of humans is already at *the coupled state of physical reality*. This means that sustained, focused intention by humans can activate this unique human body system at the vacuum level of physical reality to very high levels of output and, in turn, the majority of the body, which is always at the uncoupled state, can be raised to very high levels of performance and capability. It means, in principle, that all humans have the inherent capability to convert themselves to adepts, masters, and avatars. The choice is ours!

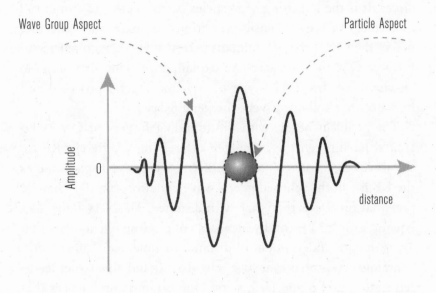

Figure 6. The de Broglie particle/pilot wave concept of the 1920s, for which he won a Nobel Prize, proposed that every particle had a pilot wave envelope enclosing it and moving at the particle's velocity. This was eventually to be called "the wave particle duality of QM."

THE THEORETICAL PICTURE

Quantum mechanics (QM) is today's paradigm of physics and its reference frame (RF) is spacetime. Both QM and its RF have serious limitations that can be partially illustrated by considering Louis de Broglie's particle/pilot wave concept of the 1920s (see figure 6) which became one of the essential cornerstones of the QM foundation.

It is now known that all of today's QM mathematical formalism can be calculated provided one assumes *the simultaneous existence of matter as both particle and wave.*[6] However, the pilot wave drawn in figure 6, which is continuous on the size scale of the particle, is not the type of wave that humans cognitively perceive. The waves that we see and hear in the world around us are all *modulations of particle densities or modulations of particle fluxes.* It is the bunching of particles (such as electric atoms and molecules) to create density variations in space and time that makes the waves that we humans perceive. Further, no particular form of QM in use today can explain something like "remote viewing"[7] or any other type of psychoenergetic process—and humans are all about psychoenergetic process!

The problem began with the founding fathers of QM, who should have taken the large step of creating a different RF for the waves than for the particles. Because they used spacetime as the RF for both, Schroedinger's wave equation can only handle potential functions that vary with distance. This very important equation for QM is totally incapable of treating phenomena that are seemingly independent of distance or time, e.g., information, consciousness, intention, love, etc. To expand this issue, let us return to figure 6 and look at two important consequences that come from applying simple QM and simple relativity theory concepts to this spacetime de Broglie concept.[8]

Calling the particle velocity in figure 6, v_p, and the velocity of the wave components that enter and leave the wave group as it moves along with the particle, v_w, one finds that

$$v_p v_w = c^2. \tag{4}$$

From relativity theory, we know that $v_p \leq c$, always. Thus, $v_w \geq c$, always. This $v_w > c$ result troubled physicists in the early days of QM because of the relativistic constraints, so they labeled such waves "information waves," thinking that therefore they could not transport energy and could be neglected. However, considering the discussion surrounding equations 1b and 2, one realizes that this is a wrong assumption because information of any type can transport thermodynamic free energy in the form of negentropy. The additional dilemma that this yields for us is that we have slower-than-EM light stuff interacting with a different kind of faster-than-light stuff that is a no-no for relativity theory (RT).

To escape from the foregoing dilemma, two new theoretical additions must be created: (1) a new RF that can independently treat electric particles and magnetic information waves and (2) a coupler type of substance, from beyond the reach of today's relativistic mechanics, that allows interaction to occur between these two uniquely different kinds of "stuff."

The new proposed RF is a duplex RF wherein there are two reciprocal, three-dimensional subspaces, one of which is our normal (x,y,z)-space, direct-space or D-space for short. The reciprocal subspace, or R-space for short, is a frequency domain (a spatial frequency where $v_x=2\pi l/x$, $v_y=2\pi m/y$ and $v_z=2\pi n/z$ with l, m and n being unknown integers because, at a core level, we are dealing with a spatial diffraction process.[2,3] The time coordinate is of a basically different nature and is not as involved with the diffraction event so that $\omega_t=2\pi/t$. Thus, this duplex RF should be considered as a unique member of the general seven-dimensional space. In the *uncoupled state* it would be labeled as a [(x,y,z,); $(v_x,\ v_y,v_z,v_t)$]-space or as a [(x,y,z,t); $(k_x,\ k_y,\ k_z,\ k_t)$]-space where k is a wave number (k = v).

This particular duplex RF has many important characteristics. One of these is that the (x,y,z,t)-subspace is ideal as an RF for electric particle substance traveling at $v_p<c$ while the $(k_x, k_y,\ k_z,\ k_t)$-subspace is ideal as an RF for magnetic information waves. Leaving out time-aspects for the moment, figure 7 illustrates how the uncoupled state electric particle and magnetic information wave might be pictured in this duplex RF.

A second very important characteristic associated with the *reciprocal nature* of these two subspaces is that a substance quality in one subspace has a conjugate, equilibrium quality in the other subspace that is given quantitatively by modified Fourier transform pair relationships.[5] However, for the uncoupled state, there appears to be no kinetic process path whereby this equilibrium condition can be achieved. In spite of this limitation, it is

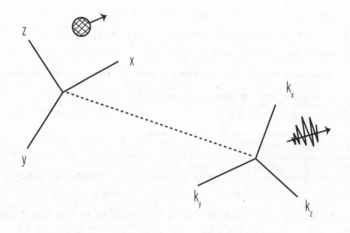

Figure 7. Adoption of the 7-dimensional duplex space as a basis for physical reality would produce a particle and wave simultaneity viewpoint with the RF of the particles being direct space (D-space or (x, y, z, t)-space or spacetime). The RF for the waves is labeled reciprocal space (or R-space) or (k_x, k_y, k_z, k_t)-space.

interesting to note that, mathematically, the particular Gaussian-shaped, R-space amplitude pattern, F(k), shown in figure 8b, has an inverse Fourier conjugate in D-space, given by f(x) shown in figure 8a, that is also of Gaussian envelope shape that looks remarkably like the de Broglie pilot wave of figure 6. Here, we also see that the D-space wavelength, λ, of the de Broglie wave packet is inversely proportional to the R-space, Gaussian location at spatial wave number (frequency) k_0. In addition, the half-width of its D-space Gaussian envelope, $2(\sigma)$, is inversely related to the half-width of its R-space Gaussian amplitude profile, $2(1/\sigma)$. Here, we see how the reciprocal relationship between these two sub-spaces expresses itself in conjugate qualities. Table 1 expands this "mirror principle" that appears to exist between equilibrium conjugate qualities for this particular choice of duplex RF.

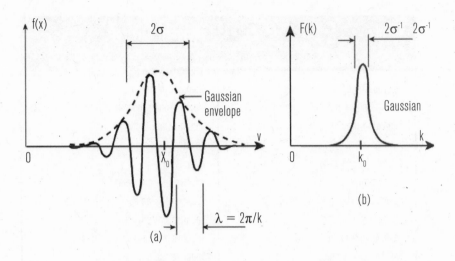

Figure 8. (a) A wavegroup; (b) transform of a wavegroup.

The foregoing sets up the basic framework needed for expanding QM while maintaining both the de Broglie particle/pilot wave complex and Planck's experimental discovery that energy exchanges between atoms and molecules do not occur in continuous steps but rather in discrete steps of magnitude $\Delta E = h\upsilon$ where υ is the frequency of the wave aspect in figure 6 and h is Planck's constant. To allow the $v_w > c$ magnetic information wave to actually interact with the $v_p < c$ electric particle, in seeming violation of relativity theory, I have proposed the existence[2] of a higher-dimensional substance, labeled *deltrons,* that exist outside the constraints of relativity theory and are able to travel at velocities greater than, less than, and equal to c. Further, these postulated deltrons can interact with both electric particles, magnetic information wave substance, and massless entities. Thus, they can act as the coupling medium between electric particles and magnetic information waves as illustrated in figure 9 so they can transform figure 7 into figure 10. Here, it is the deltron-deltron interaction that creates the coupling and allows these two types of substance to form

PHYSICAL Direct Space and Direct Time	CONJUGATE PHYSICAL Reciprocal Space and Reciprocal Time
Electric Monopoles	Magnetic Monopoles
Forms atoms, molecules, etc.	Forms atoms, molecules, etc.
Allopathic medicine	Homeopathic medicine
Positive mass	Negative mass
Velocity $< c$	Velocity $> c$
Positive energy states	Positive energy states
E_p increases as velocity increases	E_E increases as velocity increases
Positive entropy, S_p	Negative entropy, S_E
Positive free energy, $G_p = H_p - T_p S_p$	Negative free energy, $G_E = H_E - T_E S_E$
Positive temperature	Negative temperature
Electromagnetism	Magnetoelectrism
Gravitation	Levitation
Body sensory systems delineated	Body sensory systems not delineated
Photons at velocity c	Photons at velocity $c' \gg c$ ($\sim 10^{10} c$)
Fastest in vacuum	Slowest in vacuum
Slows down in dense material	Speeds up in dense physical matter
Faraday cage screening	Screening by magnetic cage

Table 1. Some "Mirror Principle" conjugates between D-space and R-space.

the *coupled state* of physical reality discussed earlier in this chapter (see figure 2).

The cornerstone of this new model is still the de Broglie particle/pilot wave of figure 6. However, now the picture involves (1) an R-space, magnetic, information wave, Gaussian-shaped profile centered at wave number, k_0, (2) a D-space, electric particle, with or without mass, centered at x_0 and (3) sufficient activated deltrons to form an

{E – Particle // Deltrons // ME – Pilot wave}   (5)

complex in D-space. Here, ME stands for magnetoelectric which is the R-space "mirror principle" conjugate of D-space

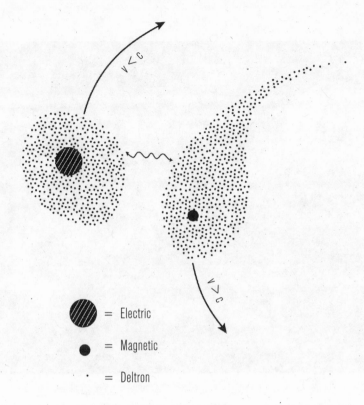

$v < c$

$v \lesssim c$

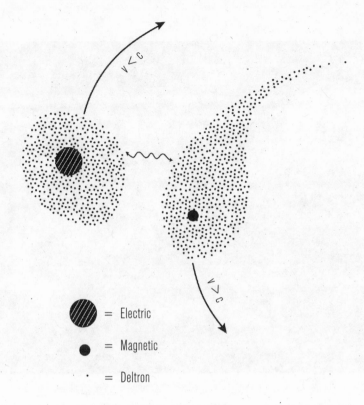

$\bigcirc$ = Electric

$\bullet$ = Magnetic

$\cdot$ = Deltron

Figure 9. A higher-dimensional level of substance, labeled deltrons, falling
outside the constraints of relativity theory and able to move at velocities greater
than and less than c, acts as a coupling agent between the electric monopole
types of substance and the magnetic monopole types of substance to produce
both electromagnetic (EM) and magnetoelectric (ME) types of mediator fields
exhibiting a special type of "mirror" principle relationship between them.

electromagnetic waves. Movement of R-space magnetic charge
in figure 8 to the left of k_0 causes the ME pilot wave to move to
larger values of x_0, while the deltron coupling drags the E-particle
with it to larger values of x_0.

Through the introduction of deltron-coupling to our evolving theoretical picture, one has begun to climb our "ladder of
understanding" illustrated in figure 1, not only from the bottom rung to gain a beginning grasp of the second rung but also

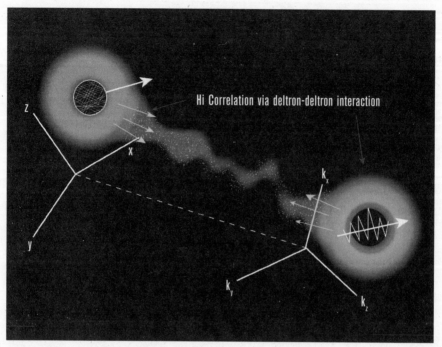

Hi Correlation via deltron-deltron interaction

Figure 10. Illustration of how deltron-deltron coupling (α_{eff}) allows the
two unique levels of physical reality to interact with each other.

to begin to dimly perceive the third rung (natural home for the
deltrons) and sense the higher rungs (natural home for intentions). Figures 11a and 11b illustrate my conceptual picture
of our duplex RF embedded in a higher-dimensional construct
consisting of three unique domains.

These are the emotion domain (8–11 dimensional), the mind
domain (12–14 dimensional), and the spirit domain (15 and
above dimensional). I am presently conceiving of these three
higher-dimensional domains as frequency domains but with different kinds of substance "stuff" operating in each domain and
with some type of coupler medium operating between domains.
Since these domains are well beyond any time and distance limitations, sympathetic resonance between these higher domains
and R-space is expected to readily occur.

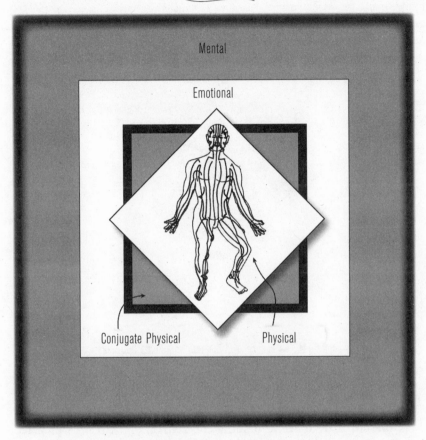

Figure 11a. A structural representation of our RF with the duplex space in the center. If one counts the entire duplex space as a 4-space, then the entire multidimensional representation is a 7-space. If, instead, we count the duplex space as a unique member of the general 8-space, then our RF is eleven-dimensional.

My working hypothesis is that specific human intentions begin at the level of spirit, as indicated in figure 12. A specific intention is thought to imprint a unique pattern of information on the mind-lattice nodal network.[2] This, in turn, both activates in-dwelling deltrons and imprints a highly correlated information pattern on

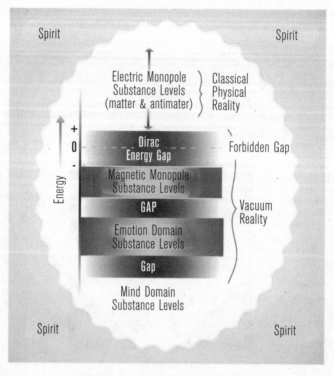

Figure 11b. An energy level diagram embracing both classical physical substances and "unseen" vacuum substances.

the nodal structure of R-space. Once the specific intention imprint is present in R-space and sufficient deltron activation is in place, the intention's D-space equilibrium conjugate can develop. This is how I think the specific intentions were imprinted into our intention-host devices that ultimately led to the robust experimental results described earlier with our four target experiments.[3]

PUTTING ALL THIS TO WORK IN EARTH-BASED LIFE

In the context of this essay, my personal bias is that we are all spirits having a physical experience as we ride the river of life together. Our spiritual parents dressed us in these biobody-suits, put us in this playpen that we call a Universe in order to

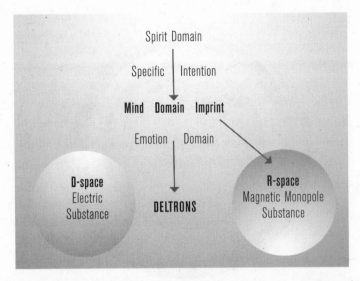

Figure 12. Human consciousness, and specifically human intention, can activate this deltron population, and thereby modulate this electric/magnetic monopole substance coupling, so as to alter the specifics of the EM state of the space wherein an object rests, and thus the experimentally measurable properties of that object.

(1) grow in coherence, (2) develop our gifts of intentionality, and (3) become what we were intended to become—co-creators with our spiritual parents. My working hypothesis is that we are all spirits having a physical experience. To effectively have this experience, we need a suitable structural interface with the spacetime world. That became a *biobodysuit* constructed from the substance complex presented by equation 5. That type of biobodysuit is what we put on when we are "born" into spacetime and it is what we take off when we appear to die in spacetime. In between, when we are manifesting what we call "life," this biobodysuit contains what I label our *personality* self. However, I feel that the *whole person* is much, much more than this!

My current metaphor for the whole person may be visualized as a sphere composed of three concentric zones that are at least weakly coupled to each other as illustrated in figure 13.

Figure 13. A metaphor for the whole person. I like to visualize a sphere composed of three concentric zones that are at least weakly coupled to each other. The outermost two layers are the personality self. The middle three layers are the soul self. The core region is the high spirit self (or the God Self).

The outermost zone is made of two layers of very different kinds of materials (electric particles and magnetic information waves) and constitutes the *personality self* mentioned above. The middle zone consists of three concentric layers, each constructed from uniquely different kinds of materials, and is labeled the *soul self*. The third, innermost zone I label the High Spirit Self, the "God self," or the *source self*, whichever label one is comfortable with. Thus, the whole person is made up of three very different selves!

In the personality self, the outermost layer of electric material interfaces, via our five physical senses neural circuitry, with what we call the outer world: the earth, our solar system, our galaxy, the cosmos. In the adjacent, magnetic information wave layer, some type of sensory system must exist by which our personality self interfaces with our soul self. Certainly a part of this system is our acupuncture meridian/chakra system, a part is what we call "the human unconscious," and a part encompasses all the psychic senses. This two-layer body is thought to be an evolved form of a basic animal species indigenous to the planet which, in our case, is from the chimpanzee/ape families.

The soul self, consisting of the still higher-dimensional domains of emotion, mind, and an aspect of spirit, is thought to be the entity that is importantly evolving in this overall process. It is much more durable than the personality self and is the repository of all the key experiences from a long succession of personality selves. Interaction between the personality self and the soul self is thought to *genetically* alter the personality self body, making it an increasingly resonant vehicle for the soul self to interface with the spacetime world. However, at all stages of this complex uplift process, vestiges of the basic animal instincts and drives seem to be present to varying degrees in the personality self. The personality self appears to have a somewhat independent will and habit structure that is distinct from the soul self, but it can entrain to that of the soul self with ever increasing degrees of coherence.

The overall construct of figure 13 looks like a type of two-stage step-down transducer/transformer between what we label God and one of God's inventions: "spacetime nature perturbed by the presence of freely willed, evolving humans." Consciousness exists at each stage with much more existing at the soul self stage than at the personality self stage. My working hypothesis is that consciousness is a *byproduct*, or emergent property, of spirit entering dense matter. Further, it is felt that spirit can only attach to dense matter if new infrastructure has been developed there to which it may attach. This appears to be one of the main jobs of living our daily lives: to build infrastructure into the various individual layers of our whole person self. It is important for us all to remember that *we are the product of our process, we collectively choose our process, and we are built by those choices.*

It is time to end this chapter even though there are many important items left undiscussed. The issues raised here can be further explored in my books.[2-5] However, I wish to close by expanding equation 1 to include one more term that seriously connects our soul self to our source self :

Mass $\leftrightarrow$ Energy $\leftrightarrow$ Information $\leftrightarrow$ Consciousness $\leftrightarrow$ Love   (1c)

Love is the source of all creation and we humans have much to learn about the full meaning of that word.

How have the practices of psychology, transpersonal psychology, and parapsychology approached consciousness and self-consciousness? Praised by Lynne McTaggart as "one of the world's experts on altered states of consciousness," Dr. Charles Tart provides in the following essay a guide through these three disciplines as they approach the questions: What is the nature of human consciousness? Does consciousness have properties of its own, or is it simply an epiphenomenon of the physical brain and nervous system?

Consciousness

A Psychological, Transpersonal, and Parapsychological Approach

CHARLES TART

It has long been fashionable to speak of humanity as a tool-making species. This is accurate but, unfortunately, we tend to then concentrate on the secondary tools, the physical, external machines, and ignore the primary and ultimate tool—human consciousness, our own minds.

What is the nature of human consciousness, especially its more profound aspects? I shall approach this question from three related perspectives that represent major aspects of both my scientific research and my personal life as a Westerner. (My personal life is included in this statement of approach because we cannot ignore the mind of the scientist when it comes to studying the mind, as we can in so many more external disciplines.) The three perspectives are those of ordinary psychology, transpersonal psychology, and parapsychology. I shall briefly discuss each of these perspectives in turn, with comments on its primary implications for understanding consciousness.

ORDINARY PSYCHOLOGY

I begin first with ordinary, mainstream psychology, an area long dominated by two approaches, the behavioristic and the psychoanalytic. Behaviorism insists that externally observable behavior (material phenomena) is the only proper subject matter of a scientific psychology. It has given us useful research tools in some areas, but its dismissal of experience as a legitimate research topic has made it far too narrow. The psychoanalytic/psychopathological approach, drawn from observations of and therapy with the mentally ill, has been very useful in dealing with mental illness, and has cast much light on ordinary activities of consciousness, especially socially hidden kinds of pathologies. Unfortunately, this second mainstream approach tends to see almost all human activity as pathological, giving us a lopsided view.

Classical behaviorism is no longer of great importance in psychology, partly because of its shortcomings, but mainly through having been largely displaced by contemporary cognitive psychology. Cognitive psychology was inspired by digital computers, and its primary function is to explain consciousness in terms of simpler, nonconscious subsystems, to reduce it to information-processing procedures in a physical system, whether that system be a digital computer or a biological one.

As a result of the dominance of behavioristic/cognitive and psychoanalytical approaches, humans tend to be seen as nothing but some combination of robots and instinctively driven animals, whose raw instincts are barely held in check by civilization. These views do not encourage exploration of the deeper levels of consciousness, for they suggest that all we will find there are animalistic and primitive impulses that are best left alone.

These two dominant psychological schools are very much in harmony with the materialistic view of man that still dominates Western intellectual thought, a view that, when it masquerades as science, I and sociologists of science have called "scientism," a rigidity and pathology of thought that takes the success of the physical sciences and their current findings as a total system of thought. It is called scientism or scientistic because of its resemblance to various other dogmatic religious and political systems, rather than having the continual openness to new data and ideas that proper scientific inquiry should have.

To illustrate the effects of scientism in Western life, some years ago I devised an experiential exercise to use in workshops, a "belief experiment" I called the Western Creed. Its purpose was to make people aware of the implicit and hidden assumptions that Western civilization and scientism have instilled to varying degrees in all of us, even people who think they have a spiritual orientation to life. I will just describe the Western Creed exercise today, as it is usually too emotionally powerful to actually do with people unless time is allowed to work with the feelings arising from it. Just hearing it described will give you some feeling for it, though.

I ask people to participate in a "belief experiment," a twenty-minute period where they will believe the words we later say as much as possible and will try to observe and later share their emotional reactions to them. I stress that they participate emotionally, rather than intellectually, from the heart rather than the head, because it is the emotional aspects of their beliefs that are of prime importance in their lives.

Then I use the power of social pressure and conformity to intensify the effects of participation. I don't know how universal this is, but in the United States we are trained as children in school to stand in a martially rigid position of attention, in orderly rows and columns, put our right hands over our hearts, and recite the pledge of allegiance to the American flag in unison.

I have participants take that physical posture and recite the Western Creed together. This Creed takes the same external form as the Nicene Creed in Christianity, but its content is based on currently popular scientistic beliefs, put in a form to make their emotional connotations clearer. Incidentally, I want to assure you that this is not an attack on Christianity, only an educational exercise.

Here is the creed the participants read aloud together:

I BELIEVE—in the material universe—as the only and ultimate reality—a universe controlled by fixed physical laws—and blind chance.

I AFFIRM—that the universe has no creator—no objective purpose—and no objective meaning or destiny.

I MAINTAIN—that all ideas about God or gods—enlightened beings—prophets and saviors—or other non-physical beings or forces—are superstitions and delusions.—Life and consciousness are totally identical to physical processes—and arose from chance interactions of blind physical forces.—Like the rest of life—my life—and my consciousness—have no objective purpose—meaning—or destiny.

I BELIEVE—that all judgments, values, and moralities—whether my own or others—are subjective—arising solely from biological determinants—personal history—and chance. —Free will is an illusion.—Therefore the most rational values I can personally live by must be based on the knowledge that for me—what pleases me is Good—what pains me is Bad.—Those who please me or help me avoid pain are my friends—those who pain me or keep me from my pleasure are my enemies.—Rationality requires that friends and enemies be used in ways that maximize my pleasure—and minimize my pain.

I AFFIRM—that churches have no real use other than social support—that there are no objective sins to commit or be forgiven for—that there is no divine or supernatural retribution for sin or reward for virtue—although there may be social consequences of actions.—Virtue for me is getting what I want—without being caught and punished by others.

I MAINTAIN—that the death of the body—is the death of the mind.—There is no afterlife—and all hope of such is nonsense.

Now I have not asked you to actually perform this belief experiment, but I suspect that some of you, from just hearing the description, are feeling some of the depression, nihilism, and negativity that participants commonly experience. I think of this as a "sadder but wiser" psychological exercise, for participants discover that many of these beliefs are indeed part of their makeup and affect their lives. They never made any conscious decisions about whether they wanted their beliefs to be like this; they were just conditioned into them as part of being modern Westerners.

Ordinary psychology is a source of much useful information about and research methodology for studying consciousness, but it is usually carried out within the implicit scientistic paradigm of our times. In spite of these limitations, there are a number of findings relevant to understanding consciousness that we can draw from it. To note just three:

1. The totality of mental functioning is greater than the part we experience as the contents of our conscious mind.
2. There are personal psychological distorting mechanisms, such as the classical defense mechanisms of psychoanalysis or needs for personal approval, that warp our observations of the contents of consciousness, as well as our observations of the external world and other people.
3. There are culture-specific emotional and cognitive investments in various beliefs and worldviews that similarly warp our observations.

This brings me to the second perspective I apply to studying the nature of consciousness: transpersonal psychology.

In the 1950s, a new kind of patient began coming to see psychotherapists. Your ordinary patient comes because she or he can't function well in ordinary life. They may experience too much stress, have unsatisfactory personal relationships, be too shy or too resentful, etc. These new patients should have been perfectly happy by ordinary social criteria, for they functioned well and had the social rewards that are supposed to produce happiness: things like fulfilling relationships, good sex lives, respect in the community, good jobs, and lots of money and material things. Their complaints were things like "Is this all there is to life?" Or "I'm bored with just getting richer, isn't there something more?"

These "existential neurotics," as they were called, wanted more meaning than Western society was able to provide.

INTERMEDIATE STEP: HUMANISTIC PSYCHOLOGY

This led to the creation of a small but important new branch of psychology, a "third force," humanistic psychology. People who functioned especially well, rather than psychiatric patients, were studied by psychologists like Abraham Maslow. New, heretofore largely neglected psychological topics such as authenticity, peak experiences, love, and creativity became legitimate areas of study. Culturally "normal" successful psychological functioning was shown to be subnormal, compared to what humans could learn to be. Considerable emphasis was put on practical application of these ideas, primarily as new forms of emotional and bodily education, and we had encounter groups, for example, where otherwise ordinary people learned to live much richer emotional lives.

By and large, though, humanistic psychology did not really question the reigning materialistic, scientistic paradigm. We were still nothing but material processes, with no inherent reasons for living other than the accidentally acquired biological drives that pushed us on, and with everything ending in meaningless death.

TRANSPERSONAL PSYCHOLOGY

My second perspective on consciousness, transpersonal psychology, the fourth major force in psychology, evolved from humanistic psychology in the 1960s. "Trans" comes from Latin roots which mean beyond: beyond the "persona," the social mask, the ordinary self, the personal. All through history, women and men have had experiences that convinced them that we are far more than our ordinary selves. Consider this minor "mystical experience," described in one of Yeats's poems, "Vacillations."

> My fiftieth year had come and gone.
> I sat, a solitary man,
> In a crowded London shop,

An open book, an empty cup
On the marble table top.
While on the shop and street I gazed,
My body of a sudden blazed,
And twenty minutes, more or less,
It seemed so great my happiness
That I was blessed and could bless.

That is not the way we ordinarily feel about ourselves, but a feeling of being an intimate part of and "channeling" something much greater than our ordinary selves, "trans" our personal.

As a fuller example, consider the full-blown mystical experience of Maurice Bucke, a nineteenth-century physician. He described it in the third person, trying to be as accurate and objective about it as he could.

It was in the early spring at the beginning of his thirty-sixth year. He and two friends had spent the evening reading Wordsworth, Shelley, Keats, Browning, and especially Whitman. They parted at midnight, and he had a long drive in a hansom (it was in an English city). His mind deeply under the influences of the ideas, images and emotions called up by the reading and talk of the evening, was calm and peaceful. He was in a state of quiet, almost passive enjoyment. All at once, without warning of any kind, he found himself wrapped around as it were by a flame colored cloud. For an instant he thought of fire, some sudden conflagration in the great city, the next he knew that the light was within himself. Directly afterwards came upon him a sense of exultation, of immense joyousness, accompanied or immediately followed by an intellectual illumination quite impossible to describe. Into his brain streamed one momentary lightning-flash of the Brahmic Splendor which has ever since lightened his life; upon his

*heart fell one drop of Brahmic Bliss, leaving thenceforward
for always an after taste of heaven. Among other things . . .
he saw and knew that the Cosmos is not dead matter but a
living Presence, that the soul of man is immortal, that the
universe is so built and ordered that without any peradventure
all things work together for the good of each and all, that
the foundation principle of the world is what we call love
and that the happiness of every one is in the long run absolutely certain. He claims that he learned more within the few
seconds during which the illumination lasted that in previous
months or even years of study, and that he learned much that
no study could ever have taught.*

*The illumination itself continued not more than a few
moments, but its effects proved ineffaceable; it was impossible for him ever to forget what he at that time saw and knew,
neither did he, or could he, ever doubt the truth of what was
then presented to his mind . . .*

To say that Bucke was beyond, trans, his ordinary self, is to put
it mildly.

Transpersonal psychology is the study and application of these
experiences that seem to take us beyond our ordinary, biological, and material selves. Still in its infancy, it draws heavily on
older spiritual traditions for stimulation. Young as it is, we can
still draw a number of important points from it for understanding human consciousness. In the realm of human experience, a
qualification whose importance I will discuss below, we may
say that it is possible for humans to experience:

1. A huge widening of the sense of self and
   consciousness that makes ordinary consciousness
   seem, by comparison, a very narrow and limited
   manifestation of a greater totality of Self.

2. An amusement and loving tolerance for the pretentiousness of the ordinary self in taking itself as the supreme manifestation of intelligence.

3. Various kinds of new knowledge, "transcendent knowledge," which make ordinary knowledge relative rather than absolute. These transcendent kinds of knowledge are often state-specific, i.e., they are not remembered or understood very well in ordinary consciousness, but make perfect sense in the altered transpersonal states of transcendence. The content of such knowledge usually concerns questions of ultimate value and purpose, and constitute "emotional" as well as intellectual "knowledge."

4. Even the briefest kinds of transpersonal experiences may enormously transform the remainder of the experiencer's life. An example is the absolute conviction brought back by many who have had near-death experiences (NDEs) that the primary purpose of life is to learn to love: that if you haven't learned to love, your life has not been of much value.

5. Absolutely convincing knowledge that the universe is an intelligent, living organism, in a mind dimension that includes material phenomena as a subset, and that this Intelligence makes the universe inherently loving and meaningful, in spite of apparent horrors on the ordinary level. We are an inherent part of that Intelligence, not a meaningless accident.

PARAPSYCHOLOGY

Note that in giving a brief overview of considerations for understanding consciousness from a transpersonal perspective, I qualified them as phenomena in the realm of human experience. Now we must deal with the main reaction that those caught in the scientistic paradigm usually have to the transpersonal. This reaction would be something like, "The import of these transpersonal experiences is obviously factually false, conceptually nonsensical, and probably psychopathological: human consciousness is nothing but the operation of the human brain. Consciousness, the human brain, is confined within the skull and body, with only indirect, sensory contact with the external world and others, and when the brain dies, consciousness dies. At worst, these transpersonal experiences foster delusion and superstition; at best they might be necessary opiates to soothe those who cannot face the reality of our material mortality." From the scientistic paradigm, transpersonal society can never be more than the study of illusions.

Parapsychology, a field of psychology literally *para,* beyond or alongside of ordinary psychology, is my third perspective on the nature of consciousness, as it is of vital relevance to this criticism.

It is somewhat daunting to try to summarize more than a hundred years of scholarly and scientific study in a few paragraphs, but I will try.

Parapsychology began with "psychical research," a primarily scholarly but retrospective study of spontaneous human experiences of acquiring information about distant events when no plausible sensory or physical mechanisms seemed able to account for them. For example, a mother who seldom recalled dreaming might suddenly have a terrifying dream of her son being killed and later receive a telegram that her son, in a distant country, had unexpectedly been killed in an accident at that time.

Although one can build a moderately convincing case for unknown information transfer mechanisms from the better cases of this sort, there are inherent problems of the reliability of witnesses, distortions of memory, occasional hoaxes, and evaluating precisely just what "coincidence" is in this approach. Parapsychology is the term generally applied to the body of procedure and knowledge built up when active laboratory research began to solve the above problems. I should also note that, unfortunately, the term "parapsychology" has become one popularly used to cover everything mysterious, but I speak here only of serious scientific parapsychology.

Over the years stringent laboratory methods gradually developed, employing elaborate safeguards against fraud, double-blind procedures, and conservative statistical evaluations of results. To make a long story short, four basic psi phenomena, as they are now termed, had enough research with significant outcomes (dozens to hundreds of studies each) done on them that I consider them proven to exist beyond any reasonable doubt. These are three forms of extrasensory perception (ESP), namely telepathy, clairvoyance, and precognition, and one form of physical action on the material world, psychokinesis (PK). There may be other genuine forms of psi phenomena, but we will stick with these basic four here.

Although psi phenomena usually manifest weakly and unreliably in the laboratory, we can conclude the following. Given what we scientifically know about the nature of the material world and reasonable extensions of that knowledge, in the absence of any known or readily plausible physical information transfer mechanisms:

1. People can sometimes pick up the conscious mental contents of another's mind: telepathy.
2. People can sometimes directly cognize the state of the distant physical world when it is currently unknown to any other human: clairvoyance.
3. People can sometimes accurately predict future events that are inherently unpredictable due to random processes determining their outcome: precognition.
4. People can sometimes affect the outcomes of physical processes simply by wishing for a desired outcome: psychokinesis.

Without having the time to argue it in detail, the consideration for understanding consciousness that is readily drawn from the above is:

Since these empirical data show properties of consciousness that do not seem to be reducible to physical variable with our current physical understanding or reasonable extensions of it, they indicate that consciousness must be investigated as a factor in its own right and with real properties of its own, not just as an epiphenomenon of physical brain and nervous system properties.

Note that this is a pragmatic approach and a conservative scientific approach. I am one of those scientists who believe data are primary and theory secondary. We have data that do not fit scientistic, physicalistic models. While we could have some kind of "religious" faith that perhaps someday they will be explainable in terms of some future physics quite unlike the one we know, that is faith, not a proper scientific approach.

CONCLUSIONS

Now we have the scientific basis to deal with the criticism that transpersonal psychology is about nothing but illusions. Of course it is—some of the time. Ordinary psychology has shown us innumerable mechanisms by which people fool themselves and each other. On the other hand, the data of parapsychology show us that sometimes there is a very real way in which the "mind" "transcends" the "brain." I put all three critical words in quotation marks to emphasize that while this statement is correct in general, our understanding of what exactly this means is still very crude, and great amounts of open-minded research are needed to flesh this statement out.

These considerations for understanding human consciousness are not simply intellectually interesting, but of great import to our and our planet's survival. The "Me first!" ethic fits easily with the dominant scientistic worldview. Who cares about the meaningless lives and meaningless fates of a bunch of other meaningless biological accidents, other people, compared to my pleasure?

The traditional values of the world's great religions say we should care, and exhort us to live moral lives and be kind to our neighbors, but they have become value systems seemingly left behind in the modern world, apparently "proven" to be just superstitions by scientism, so we can't count on those traditional sources of values to create the attitudes that can reorient us to a compassionate, global perspective. Religion is just conditioning, exhortation, meaningless words to too many people.

If you look at the sources of the great religions, however, you discover transpersonal experiences by the founders of them. If you look at transpersonal psychology, you see that such life-transforming experiences of love, unity, and compassion are a basic part of human potentials, not just things that happened to a few people long ago. And if you look at the data of parapsychology, you see that the scientistic basis for automatically rejecting such transpersonal experiences is fallacious.

There is considerable hope for humanity as conscious beings, and there is a lot of excitement awaiting us as we discover exactly what that means!

More and more scientific research is being done on the effects of meditation on the brain, but how much can a CAT scan really tell us about happiness? Is a Buddhist monk's brain registering the same kind of happiness as a hedonist's? Can we really say that meditation makes you happier? In the following excerpt from his book *The Really Hard Problem*, Owen Flanagan, a professor of philosophy at Duke University, comments on the developments in and implications of recent neuroscientific research into happiness, including the work of Richard Davidson and Daniel Goleman, and the various studies done with Buddhist monk Matthieu Ricard, and charts a course for the future of this promising field of inquiry.

The Meditating Monk and Neurophenomenology

OWEN FLANAGAN

Everyone wants to be happy—to attain what the Greeks called "eudaimonia," to be a "happy spirit." But people disagree about what happiness is, about what the word "happiness" even means. One wonders: Is there such a thing as true happiness, and if there is, are there methods to attain it? I answer "yes" to both questions. An empirically informed philosophy of happiness, what I call eudaimonics, exists and can help us find the way. Let me explain.

In my 1992 book *Consciousness Reconsidered*, I proposed use of a method for studying the mind/brain. I called it "the natural method" and recommended it as the right method to adopt if one is a naturalist about mind. The basic idea is to triangulate a subject domain by coordinating phenomenological data with psychological and behavioral data and both with neuroscientific data. Francisco Varela called his almost identical method "neurophenomenology." That is a sexier, catchier name, so I will use it. The work on the meditating monk is an instructive example of how profitable the method can be. Since more is involved in happiness, positive mood, well-being, and eudaimonia than what is going on in the brain, the task is eventually, or even at the same time, to make surmises about which causes and condition in genes, fetal development, upbringing, education, moral and spiritual commitments, and the social world in general are correlated with various brain indices of well-being.

Starting in the early 1970s, three young graduate students met in Cambridge, Massachusetts. Richard Davidson and Daniel Goleman were PhD students in psychology at Harvard; Jon Kabat-Zinn was a PhD student in molecular biology at MIT. They met because they were all interested in the practice of meditation. Very quickly, Davidson and Goleman set to publishing some work on the relation of prefrontal cortical activity and positive and negative affect, at least one on the connection of meditation and positive affect. Before their studies, there were some good data indicating that first-person subjective well-being (SWB) reports linked to differential activity across prefrontal cortex (PFC). Leftward activity (LPFC) was correlated with positive affect; rightward activity (RPFC) with negative affect. One background theory that might explain this hemispheric difference, and that has received increased support over the years, is this: PFC is important, maybe the most important area, when it comes to hatching plans and executing action, either approaching a goal or withdrawing from an aversive situation that is undesirable. LPFC is more active when we are going after what we want. Activity in RPFC increases when we want to escape what is undesirable.

The prefrontal lobes are relatively recently evolved structures (in ancestors of *Homo sapiens*) and have, as I have said, long been known to be important in foresight, planning, and self-control. The confirmation of the fact that prefrontal cortices are also crucially implicated in emotion, mood, and temperament is exciting because it lends some insight into *one* area where a well-functioning mind coordinates cognition, mood, and emotion. How exactly the coordination is accomplished is something about which little is known at this time.

In any case, thirty years after Davidson, Goleman, and Kabat-Zinn made their first foray into studying the relation between PFC and meditation, and thus at the time I wrote "The Colour of Happiness" (2003), this view of the role(s) of PFC was fairly well entrenched. I surmise, based on the science, that it, or something in its vicinity, is true.

In 2000, Matthieu Ricard, an experienced Buddhist monk (born and raised in France), was brought to Madison, Wisconsin, where Davidson's Center for Affective Neuroscience is housed, and his brain was studied. Lo and behold, Matthieu's left prefrontal cortex lit up brightly (thus the editor's choice of the word "colour" for the title of my article). Indeed, his left side lit up brightly and more leftward than that of any other individual tested in previous studies (approximately 175 subjects). It was literally off the charts. However, none of the earlier studies involved people meditating while the scanning was underway. (In the meditating monk's case, most of the meditation was on compassion and loving-kindness.) Scientific problems related to different tasks performed by Matthieu and the previous 175 subjects did not prevent various media sources from announcing that scientists had established that Buddhist meditation produces "true" happiness. Indeed, I was asked repeatedly whether Matthieu was the happiest person ever studied, and even whether he was the happiest person on earth. One could imagine this line of conversation culminating in the question "Is Matthieu the happiest person ever to exist?" (If that happens, I will say "Yes.")

If you are even slightly tempted to let your thoughts roam in this direction, stop and consider these obvious facts: being "leftmost" PFC-wise is not in any way like "being the tallest." Whoever is the tallest is the tallest, but whoever is the leftmost, despite being the leftmost, isn't the happiest, no matter what standard of happiness one is using. The consensus in neuroscience is that, for most and perhaps all complex mental states, individual brains "do the same thing" in sometimes very different ways, and at somewhat different locales. Suppose two people both think "that patch is red" in response to the exact same red patch stimulus. Assume that both are "having the exact same thought," although it must be said even this assumption is controversial. We might after all experience red a bit differently, perception of red things might cause different associations, and so on. Bracket these worries. Assume that whatever else goes on when each of these two individuals think "that is a red path," both think that much, and each thinks the thought in the same way as far as that red patch goes. If so, there will be brain activation in each individual that is that thought or is the neural correlate of that thought. But no one expects two different brains to have exactly the same thought (assuming they are) in a way that is subserved by perfectly identical neural activation. The consensus is that the exact same thought can be realized (indeed is likely to be realized) in different brains in somewhat different ways. The same goes for phenomenologically identical or very similar emotional states.

For all we currently know, the subject who tests twenty-fifth or thirty-fifth or even seventieth from the leftmost point so far plotted might be, according to all the evidence taken together— phenomenological, behavioral, hormonal, neurochemical—the happiest person ever tested. Left-side prefrontal activity is a reliable measure of positive affect, but no one has asserted, let alone confirmed, that among the group of "lefties," the left-most individual is the happiest. One problem is due to the fact that the concepts of "positive mood" and "affect," even more so "happiness," are not fine-grained enough, nor sufficiently well operationalized by the scientists who use them, for us to know what specific kind of positive mood or emotional state is attached to a lit-up area.

The important point is that for all anyone currently knows at this point, a happy life whose source is family might light up the brain in the same way as a happy life whose source is virtue or even money. One can control for this, of course, by being careful about the phenomenological and psychological-behavioral aspects of the neurophenomenology. Suppose that Donald Trump's, Rupert Murdoch's, and Hugh Hefner's LPFC light up just as Matthieu's did, with the ratio of LPFC to RPFC activity the same. We know that the causes and constituents of their "happiness" are different from Matthieu's and thus it seems that one ought to say that the happiness itself is different in kind. That is, even though the brain at this level of analysis doesn't reveal what the differences are, there are big differences. From a naturalistic perspective, these had better show up, at least as encoded, somewhere.

So we say that despite substantial LPFC profiles among this foursome, both the causes of their happiness, and the contents of their happiness (what their happiness is about), are different. Let me explain what I mean by "about-ness." Philosophical talk of the aboutness of mental states origi-nates in what Franz Brentano (adopting ideas from Thomas Aquinas) called "intentionality" (from the Latin *intendo* = to aim at). Feeling yucky might not be about anything, but believing [snow is white] is *about* the color of snow. So even if

A is happy to +9 *about* the fact that [she is very rich] and B is happy to +9 about the fact that she [directs an AIDS orphanage], they are happy in different ways. The *content* of their happiness is different even if the *degree* of their happiness is the same. There are no brain imaging or scanning techniques that (as of now) distinguish among contents. All information about *content* needs to come from first-person and third-person narratives and the like.

This much shows that a state of happiness is not to be typed or classified solely by neural markers in PFC. This is where other measurement tools come in handy since SWB ratings, if fine-grained enough, will show obvious differences between what matters to Hugh Hefner and what matters to Matthieu. And mattering and what I call content are related in a way I will leave unspecified, but that issue is worth working out precisely.

In any case, "happiness" is a polysemic term; it has many different meanings. For this reason, when discussing the topic I almost always revert to superscripting, so there is happiness[Buddha], happiness[Aristotle], happiness[Local hedonist club], happiness[Marquis de Sade], happiness[standard American = happy joy-joy-click-your-heels]. Aristotle pointed out that everyone says eudaimonia is the greatest good while meaning different things by the term. The same situation obtains today. Even those who say that happiness is what they want more than anything else may well mean different things by "happiness" or, what is different, may overrate happiness colloquially understood as happiness[standard American = happy joy-joy-click-your-heels].

The point about overrating happiness entails that even if one goes along with the superscripting strategy it doesn't remove all the problems. Individuals might legitimately claim that, even though they judge their lives as very meaningful as, say, an Aristotelian, or a Buddhist, or a Christian, feeling happy is not even an issue. And thus ascribing happiness[Aristotle] or happiness[Buddha] misses the point.

Was the Buddha happy? Was Jesus happy? Was Confucius (Kongzi) happy? The answers do not seem obviously yes according to common contemporary usage of the term "happy." When I ask my students these questions, they are unsure what to say. Many will say it doesn't matter or that is not the point. They are on to something.

On the other hand, no one who seeks happiness[Local hedonist club], happiness[Marquis de Sade], or happiness[standard American = happy joy-joy-click-your-heels] will say that happiness is not the issue, not what matters. It matters to them. In the Buddhist case, equanimity is one of the four noble illimitables (the other three are compassion, lovingkindness, and appreciative or sympathetic joy—being happy for the successes of others). "Equanimity" describes an abiding condition of "heart/mind" (this is the right translation for all Asian terms that we might wish to translate as "mind"). Equanimity, whatever exactly it names, might be said (like flow) to be intermediate between anxiety and boredom. It might in certain cases feel blissful, but it might not. As far as my own linguistic intuitions go, words like "equanimity" and "serenity" are not, even in American English, in the same family as happiness[standard American = happy joy-joy-click-your-heels].

In any case, as I have indicated, before the study of the meditating monk there had been a number of excellent studies on positive affect and the brain. This research showed that there was a distinction between basal (baseline) and tonic (variable) reports of "well-being" or "positive mood" as reported first-personally and as measured in PFC. The still-dominant view is that each person has a characteristic baseline ratio of LPFC:RPFC activity, and then various experiences (or stimuli) result in changes (which some say "overlay" the basal condition). Thus when subjects are shown pleasant pictures (say, sunsets), scans (PET or fMRI) or skull measurements of activity (EEG) reveal increased left side activity in prefrontal cortex.

Whereas when subjects see unpleasant pictures (say, a human cadaver), activity moves rightward. Furthermore, people who report themselves generally to be happy, upbeat, and the like, show more stable left side activity than individuals who report feeling sad or depressed in whom the right side of prefrontal cortex is more active.

Positive mood has two faces. Subjectively, phenomenologically, or first-personally, it reveals itself in a way that an individual feels, and about which she typically can report (although subjects commonly report difficulty describing exactly what the positive state is like). Objectively, the subjective feeling state is reliably correlated with a high degree of leftward prefrontal activity. Thus we can say that *if* a subject is experiencing happiness or, what is possibly different, is in a good mood, then left prefrontal cortex is or gets frisky, or bright, or even colorful depending on whether you use EEG, fMRI, or PET.

Most people (70 to 80 percent) report themselves to be happy as opposed to not so happy, sad, or depressed. Davidson found that in a normal population (of undergraduates) prefrontal lobe activity is distributed in a fashion that corresponds to the phenomenology, a left-leaning hyperbola. Those who are very happy are fewer than those who are pretty happy, but both groups are larger than *les misérables*.

I take it that any finding to the effect that Buddhist practitioners are happier than most would be a statistical finding that significantly more than, say 25 percent, are in the first, very happy group. Since the neurophenomenological curve reveals that in a normal undergraduate population approximately 18 percent fall into the "very happy" group, then a finding that 25 to 30 percent in that group for a representative sample of Buddhist practitioners would be statistically astounding. A somewhat lower percentage would still be impressive. As I write, the data don't exist but studies are under way. The Wisconsin group has a big research program under way studying adepts, and Alan Wallace and his colleagues in Santa Barbara are undertaking a long-term study of shamatha meditation (training in sustained voluntary attention) and its effects on happiness.

There are many people watching this research closely. And most of those I know are betting that the greater happiness hypothesis will be confirmed. I'm not sure. Let me explain why.

Matthieu radiates happiness. I am not sure how much he values happiness, but I know he values virtue and wisdom more. But he is, there is no doubt about it, a very happy man. Most of the Buddhists I know, however, will say that happiness is *not*, in almost all its usual senses, what matters. Wisdom and virtue are what matters, and being wise and virtuous typically brings equanimity. The next time I see Matthieu, I will ask him what he thinks. I predict he will say this too, despite the fact that he is very happy—by my standards, at least.

So Matthieu is very happy and equaniminous, and he is "off the charts" LPFC-wise. But he is just one individual. What should we expect in studying other adepts, Buddhist monks who have practiced meditation for many years or secular Western practitioners of mindfulness practice? I suspect we will find this: subjectively, if we listen carefully, we will hear them reporting that they are happy (if they are willing to use the word at all) meaning serene and equaninimous, not happiness-standard American = happy joy-joy-click-your-heels. One reason for my confidence in saying this is that I know enough about Buddhism to know that if there is such a thing as happiness[Buddha], which Buddhists would endorse as desirable, it will involve two aspects:

1. a stable sense of serenity and contentment (not the
   sort of happy-joy-joy-click-your-heels feeling state
   that is widely sought and promoted in the West as the
   best kind of happiness)

2. that this serene and contented state is caused or
   constituted by enlightenment or wisdom and virtue or
   goodness as these are characterized within Buddhist
   philosophy

Regarding the current state of research, there are in fact no
scientific studies yet on Buddhism as a lived philosophy and
spiritual tradition, in any of its forms, and happiness. What
we do have are a few scientific studies that involve examining
meditators—mostly experienced Tibetan Mahayana practitioners from France, America, and Northern India, or individuals
new to the practice of Zen and mindfulness meditation. What
has been found is interesting and important:

- Mindfulness practices lower stress and cause relaxation.
  Cortisol flow, the "natural killer," is contained, moderated,
  regulated. This helps with health and longevity.
- Mindfulness practice increases the number of influenza
  antibodies in meditators relative to controls, both of whom
  have been given flu shots.
- Mindfulness practice among adepts produces widespread
  synchronized gamma oscillations. This is rare in subjects who
  do not practice mindfulness, but such activity bespeaks of a
  mind/brain that is active, attentive, and very well focused.
- Adepts doing compassion meditation report increased
  intensity in a way that maps nicely onto increasing gamma
  activity and increased global synchrony of gamma.
- Matthieu is excellent—better than anyone ever tested—at
  controlling his startle response. The bets are that other very
  experienced adepts, as well as experienced mindfulness
  practitioners, will be able to do so as well.
- Matthieu and three other experienced meditators are "off the
  charts" when it comes to reading facial "micro-expressions."

The findings just mentioned have nothing directly to do with measuring happiness, and in this way are utterly different in kind from the PFC work. There is one exception: Davidson and Kabat-Zinn reported mood improvements as well as increased influenza antibodies. Nonetheless, all these studies show the worth of certain mindfulness practices. Supposing that researchers return to their initial devotion to testing for "happiness," and assuming that we eventually succeed at measuring the effects of different types of practice on happiness, we need to be extremely clear about what sort of happiness, if any, the practice aims at or promises. This requirement is a general one for doing good science in this area. If one wants to study ordinary Americans, Aristotelians, utilitarians, Trappist monks, secular humanists, scientific naturalists, or members of the local chapter of the "Hedonist Club," one will want their experts to specify the kind of happiness they claim to seek or to achieve. And one will want information on what aspects of their form of life they think lead to attaining their theory-specific form of happiness. Only with such information at our disposal can scientists construct experiments to "look and see" if the kind of happiness sought is attained and whether the practices thought to produce that kind of happiness are causally implicated in its production. Such work will involve a mother lode of careful anthropological and sociological analysis as well as psychology and neuroscience.

We also need much more philosophical work in which different theory and tradition-specific conceptions of "true happiness" receive articulation. We know that Aristotle, Epicurus, Buddha, Confucius, Mencius, Jesus, and Mohammed all put forward somewhat different philosophical conceptions of an excellent human life, with somewhat different conceptions of what constitutes true happiness. With these different conceptions well articulated, we can look at brain activity within and across advocates and practitioners of different traditions to see what similarities and differences our mappings reveal. The same strategy should work for negative emotions and destructive mental states. Get well-honed first-person reports from subjects on the negative states they experience and then look for brain correlates. With such data in hand we can then test Buddhist techniques, say, meditation on compassion, which are thought to provide antidotes for anger, hatred, and avarice. Along with first-person reports on any experienced change in mood or emotion, we can look and see what, if anything, reconfigures itself brain-wise. We can do the same for practices from other traditions. Eventually, we will want to coordinate such studies with the ever-deeper knowledge of the connections among virtue, mental health, well-being, and human flourishing, allowing science and philosophy to speak together about what practices seem best suited to make for truly rich and meaningful lives. At this distant point, with an array of conceptions of excellent human lives before us, as well as deep knowledge of how the brains of devotees of these different traditions look and work, we should be able to speak much more clearly about the nature(s) and types of happiness and flourishing than we can now.

The more theory-specific conceptions of virtue, well-being, and flourishing that we have, so much the better will our understanding be of the constituents of happiness, if, that is, "happiness" stays on our radar as what matters most, all things considered. Overlapping consensus on the components of these things will, no doubt, reveal itself. Differences in conceptions of virtue, well-being, and flourishing will also reveal themselves. The overlaps and the differences can be discussed and debated at the philosophical level from a normative ethical perspective, and the scientists can chime in, wearing philosophical hats if they wish, but equally important, telling us how the brains of practitioners from different traditions light up, which neuro-chemicals rise and fall, and so on.

Intertheoretical conversation such as I am envisioning will put us in the exciting position of being able to (a) have a better idea of the fine-grained states we are looking for and (b) compare different theories in terms of the goods they claim to produce and hopefully do, in fact, produce. For those of us who are convinced that Buddhism is a noble path to wisdom, virtue, and happiness[Buddha], and especially at this time when some scientists claim to be reaching pay dirt in the empirical exploration and confirmation of what many Buddhist practitioners already claim to know, it is necessary to speak with maximal precision about what practices, Buddhist and others, are thought to produce what sorts of specific positive states of mind and body. Overall, this sort of inquiry provides a truly exciting, unique, and heretofore unimagined opportunity for mind scientists, practitioners, and philosophers from different traditions to join together in a conversation that combines time-tested noble ideals with newfangled gadgetry to understand ourselves more deeply and to live well, better than we do now.

PART 3

Investigating the Science of Spiritual Practices

Meditation, Prayer, Distant Healing,
Qigong, Reiki, and Other Practices

Neuroscience continually offers new information about brain activity and development. In the following excerpt from her book *The Intention Experiment: Using Your Thoughts to Change Your Life and the World,* Lynne McTaggart gathers scientific evidence about concentrated focus and meditation, and how these two practices affect the brain. Can concentrated attention permanently enhance the brain's reception? Does the brain revise its "hardwiring" throughout life, and if so, can meditation rewire the brain? McTaggart gathers an impressive array of data as she works her way through a study of intention "masters," and paints a fascinating neurological picture of the state of intense focus, or "peak attention" reached by many healers and experienced meditators.

Entering Hyperspace

LYNNE MCTAGGART

Richard Davidson, a neuroscientist and psychologist at the University of Wisconsin's Laboratory for Affective Neuroscience, is an expert in "affective processing": the place where the brain processes emotion and the resulting communication between the brain and body. His work came to the attention of the Dalai Lama, who invited him to visit Dharamsala, India, in 1992; a science buff, His Holiness wished to understand more about the biological effects of intensive meditation. Afterward, eight of the Dalai Lama's most seasoned practitioners of Nyingmapa and Kagyupa meditation were flown to Davidson's lab in Wisconsin. There, Davidson attached 256 EEG sensors to each monk's scalp in order to record electrical activity from a large number of different areas in the brain. The monks were then asked to carry out compassionate meditation. The meditation entailed focusing on an utter readiness to help others and a desire for all living things to be free of suffering. For the control group, Davidson enlisted a group of undergraduates who had never practiced meditation and arranged for them to undergo a week's training, then attached them to the same number of EEG sensors to monitor their brains during meditation.

After fifteen seconds, according to the EEG readings, the monks' brains did not slow down; they began speeding up. In fact, they were activated on a scale neither Davidson nor any other scientist had ever seen. The monitors showed sustained bursts of high gamma-band activity—rapid cycles of 25 to 70 hertz. The monks had rapidly shifted from a high concentration of beta waves to a preponderance of alpha, back up to beta, and finally up to gamma. Gamma band, the highest rate of brain-wave frequencies, is employed by the brain when it is working its hardest: at a state of rapt attention, when sifting through working memory, during deep levels of learning, in the midst of great flashes of insight. As Davidson discovered, when the brain operates at these extremely high frequencies, the phases of brain waves (their times of peaking and troughing) all over the brain begin to operate in synchrony. This type of synchronization is considered crucial for achieving heightened awareness.[1] The gamma state is even believed to cause changes in the brain's synapses, the junctions over which electrical impulses leap to send a message to a neuron, muscle, or gland.[2] That the monks could achieve this state so rapidly suggested that their neural processing had been permanently altered by years of intensive meditation. Although the monks were middle-aged, their brain waves were far more coherent and organized than those of the robust young controls. Even during their resting state, the Buddhists showed evidence of a high rate of gamma-band activity, compared with that of the neophyte meditators. Davidson's study bolstered other pieces of preliminary research suggesting that certain advanced and highly focused forms of meditation produce a brain operating at peak intensity.[3] Studies of yogis have shown that during deep meditation their brains produce bursts of high-frequency beta or gamma waves, which are often associated with moments of ecstasy or intense concentration.[4] Those who can withdraw from external stimuli and completely focus their attention inward appear more likely to reach gamma-wave hyperspace. During peak attention of this nature, the heart rate also accelerates.[5] Similar types of effects have been recorded during prayer. A study monitoring the brain waves of six Protestants during prayer found an increase in brain-wave speed during moments of the most intense concentration.[6]

Different forms of meditation may produce strikingly different brain waves. For instance, yogis strive for anuraga, or a sense of constant fresh perception; Zen Buddhists aim to eliminate their response to the outer world. Studies comparing the two find that anuraga produces heightened perceptual awareness—magnified outer focus—while Zen produces heightened inner absorption: magnified inner awareness.[7] Most research on meditation has concerned the type that focuses on one particular stimulus, such as the breath or a sound, like a mantra. In Davidson's study, the monks concentrated on having a sense of compassion for all living things. It may be that compassionate intention—as well as other similar, "expansive" concepts—produces thoughts that send the brain soaring into a supercharged state of heightened perception.

When Davidson and his colleague Antoine Lutz wrote up their study, they realized that they were reporting the highest measures of gamma activity ever recorded among people who were not insane.[8] In their results they noticed an association between level of experience and ability to sustain this extraordinarily high brain activity; those monks who had been performing meditation the longest recorded the highest levels of gamma activity. The heightened state also produced permanent emotional improvement by activating the left anterior portion of the brain—the portion most associated with joy. The monks had conditioned their brains to tune in to happiness most of the time.

In later research, Davidson demonstrated that meditation alters brain wave patterns, even among new practitioners. Neophytes who had practiced mindfulness meditation for only eight weeks showed increased activation of the "happy-thoughts" part of the brain and enhanced immune function.[9]

In the past, neuroscientists imagined the brain as something akin to a complex computer, which was fully constructed in adolescence. Davidson's results supported more recent evidence that the "hardwired" brain theory was outdated. The brain appeared to revise itself throughout life, depending on the nature of its thoughts. Certain sustained thoughts produced measurable physical differences and changed its structure. Form followed function; consciousness helped to form the brain.

Besides speeding up, brain waves also synchronize during meditation and healing. In fieldwork with indigenous and spiritual healers on five continents, Krippner suspected that, prior to healing, the healers all underwent brain "discharge patterns" that produce a coherence and synchronization of the two hemispheres of the brain, and integrate the limbic (the lower emotional center) with the cortical systems (the seat of higher reasoning).[10]

At least twenty-five studies of meditation have shown that, during meditation, EEG activity between the four regions of the brain synchronizes.[11] Meditation makes the brain permanently more coherent—as might prayer. A study at the University of Pavia in Italy and John Radcliffe Hospital in Oxford showed that saying the rosary had the same effect on the body as reciting a mantra. Both were able to create a "striking, powerful, and synchronous increase" in cardiovascular rhythms when recited six times a minute.[12]

Another important effect of concentrated focus is the integration of both left and right hemispheres. Until recently, scientists believed that the two sides of the brain work more or less independently. The left side was depicted as the "accountant," responsible for logical, analytical, linear thinking, and speech; and the right side as the "artist," providing spatial orientation, musical and artistic ability, and intuition. But Peter Fenwick, consultant neuropsychiatrist at the Radcliffe Infirmary in Oxford and the Institute of Psychiatry at the Maudsley Hospital, gathered evidence to show that speech and many other functions are produced in both sides of the brain and that the brain works best when it can operate as a totality. During meditation, both sides communicate in a particularly harmonious manner.[13]

Concentrated attention appears to enlarge certain mechanisms of perception, while tuning out "noise." Daniel Goleman, author of *Emotional Intelligence*,[14] carried out research showing that the cortices of meditators "speed up," but get cut off from the limbic emotional center. With practice, he concluded, anyone can carry out this "switching-off" process, enabling the single mode of the brain to experience heightened perception without an overlay of emotion or meaning.[15] During this process, all of the power of the brain is free to focus on a single thought: an awareness of what is happening at the present moment.

Meditation also appears to permanently enhance the brain's reception. In several studies, meditators have been exposed to repetitive stimuli like light flashes or clicks. Ordinarily, a person will get used to the clicks, and the brain, in a sense, will switch off and stop reacting. But the brains of the meditators continued to react to the stimuli—an indication of heightened perception of every moment.[16]

In one study, practitioners of mindfulness meditation—the practice of bringing heightened, nonjudgmental awareness of the senses' perceptions to the present moment—were tested for visual sensitivity before and immediately after a three-month retreat, during which time they had practiced mindfulness meditation for sixteen hours a day. The staff members who did not practice the meditation acted as a control group. The researchers were testing whether the participants could detect the duration of simple light flashes and the correct interval between successive ones. To those without mental training in focusing, these flashes would appear as one unbroken light. After the retreat, the practitioners were able to detect the single-light flashes and to differentiate between successive flashes. Mindfulness meditation enables its practitioners to become aware of unconscious processes, and to remain exquisitely sensitive to external stimuli.[17] As these studies indicate, certain types of concentrated focus, like meditation, enlarge the mechanism by which we receive information and clarify the reception. We turn into a larger, more sensitive radio.

More and more people see their spiritual health as an integral part of their overall mental and physical well-being, and many are beginning to ask health care providers to include a greater spiritual element in the treatment of illness. But how much hard evidence is there of the health benefits—or dangers—of spiritual practice? Can the benefits of yoga, meditation, or faith healing be scientifically proven? Does going to church regularly lessen your risk of certain diseases? In recent history, the biomedical world has focused primarily on biological models of health and disease. In the essay to follow, Dr. Andrew Newberg, author of *Why We Believe What We Believe: Uncovering Our Biological Need for Meaning, Spirituality, and Truth,* provides a wealth of recent research that indicates a growing need to consider spirituality in the efforts to advance health and medicine.

Spirituality, the Brain, and Health

ANDREW NEWBERG, M.D.

INTRODUCTION

If we are going to fully understand the relationship between spirituality, the brain, and health, we have to begin with a strong reliance on research and take care in interpreting information and data in the proper way. This chapter will review what we currently know about the relationship between spirituality, the brain, and health, drawing from the growing evidence reported by researchers over the past two decades. This has been a most exciting time for research in this field, since we now have the tools and the expertise to evaluate this relationship in more detail than ever before. But as much as we are getting to know, there is still so much more for us to find out.

The relationship between religion and health has cycled between cooperation and antagonism throughout history. Some of the most advanced civilizations of ancient times, such as the Assyrians, Chinese, Egyptians, Mesopotamians, and Persians, equated physical illnesses with evil spirits and demonic possession. Treatment was aimed at banishing these spirits. Since then, physicians and other health care providers have been viewed by religious groups as everything from evil sorcerers to conduits of God's healing powers. Similarly, physicians', scientists', and health care providers' views of religion have ranged from interest to disinterest to disdain.

In recent years, interest in understanding the effects of religion on health has grown among the medical and scientific communities. Popular news magazines such as *Time* and *Newsweek* and television shows have devoted ample coverage to the interplay of religion and health. Many spiritual activities aimed at improving or maintaining health, such as yoga and meditation, have become very popular. Moreover, studies have clearly shown that many patients consider religion to be very important and would like their physicians to discuss religious issues with them. We will review the challenges that researchers and health care practitioners may face in designing appropriate studies and translating results to clinical practice. We will also discuss future directions in the roles of religion and spirituality in health care.

A FEW WORDS ABOUT RESEARCH
One of the most important issues related to the measurement of religious and spiritual phenomena has to do with matching up the subjective experience with some kind of objective or scientific measure. For example, if a particular type of meditation reduces blood pressure or is associated with changes in the brain's metabolism, it is critical to know what the

individual actually experienced and how that experience specifically affected that person's physiology. It is also important to keep in mind that almost all of the research studies focus on a particular religious group, a particular disease or problem, or some other very specific health-related factors. Thus, each study often has to be considered by itself rather than extrapolated to the general population. If a study shows that young Jewish women who are more religious have lower levels of unwanted pregnancy, that only means that that is the case for young Jewish women. It may not be the case for other religions, other ethnic backgrounds, or other adolescent problems. That being said, there is such a growing amount of research in this area that we are now able to say much more about religious and spiritual affects on health.

Subjective Measures

The most important measures of religious and spiritual phenomena are those that pertain to the subjective nature of the experience. When any person has a religious or spiritual experience, they can usually try to describe it in terms of various cognitive, behavioral, and emotional parameters. Furthermore, a person will usually define the experience as "spiritual," which distinguishes it from others that are regarded as "nonspiritual." The issue of measuring the subjective nature of these experiences is akin to opening the mysterious "black box" in which something is happening, but is not immediately observable to an outside observer. The problem becomes more difficult when trying to compare experiences across individuals and across cultures. A spiritual experience for a Jew may be vastly different from a spiritual experience for a Hindu. Furthermore, there is likely to be a continuum of experiences ranging from barely perceptible to absolutely mystical. The question for any researcher is how to get some handle on the subjective component of such experiences. Is there a way to quantify and compare the subjective feelings and thoughts that individuals have regarding their spiritual experiences?

There is another interesting problem with the current questions researchers ask in an attempt to measure the subjective nature of spiritual or religious experiences. This arises from the fact that most questions of spirituality and religiousness require the individual to respond in terms of psychological, emotional, or cognitive processes. Thus, questions are phrased: How did it make you feel? What sensory experiences did you have? What did you think about your experience? On one hand, such measures are very valuable to individuals interested in exploring the neural correlates of such experiences because psychological, emotional, and cognitive elements can usually be related to specific brain structures or function. The problem with phrasing questions in this way is that one never actually escapes the neuropsychological perspective to get at something that might be "truly" spiritual. It might be suggested that the only way in which an investigator can reach something that is truly spiritual would be through a process of elimination in which all other factors—i.e., cognitive, emotional, sensory— are eliminated through the analysis, leaving only the spiritual components of the experience. In other words, the most interesting result from a brain scan of someone in prayer would be to find no significant change in the brain during the time that the individual has the most profound spiritual experience. However, as we shall see, it is very difficult to capture such experiences, let alone try to measure them.

Part of the problem with developing adequate measures is ensuring that they measure what they claim to measure. A subjective questionnaire designed to measure the degree of an individual's religiousness needs to focus on the things that make someone religious. However, this first requires a clear definition of religiousness and spirituality. Furthermore, these definitions must be operationalized so that any measure or study can have a firm enough grasp to actually measure something. To that end, it is important to avoid narrow definitions that might impede research and also to avoid broad definitions that cannot be measured. For example, definitions of religion that pertain to a single God would eliminate almost two billion Hindu and Buddhist individuals from analysis. On the other hand, a definition of religiousness that is too broad might end up including many bizarre experiences and practices such as cults or devil worship.

One final issue, which is related to problems with definitions, is that there are so many approaches to religious and spiritual phenomena that it is often difficult to generalize from one study to another. Scholars frequently point out that one type of meditation practice may be very different from other types, or one type of experience might be substantially different from other types. It is certainly critical to ensure that any study clearly states the specific practices, subpractices, and traditions involved. Furthermore, changes in the brain or body associated with one type of meditative practice may not be specifically related to a different type of practice. Of course, the dynamic nature of this body of research may also provide new ways of categorizing certain practices or experiences so that one can address the question regarding whether different types of meditation truly are different, or are only experienced as different.

Given the problems with the subjective measurement of religious and spiritual phenomena, it is also important to try to create some type of objective measure. Objective measures of religious and spiritual phenomena typically include a variety of physiological and neurophysiological measures. Several types of measures that have already been reported in the literature include blood pressure, heart rate, and hormone and immune function. It is also important to link such physiological changes to health-related changes. Thus, if a hypothetical study showed that the practice of meditation results in changes in the immune system, it would be very helpful to know if that translated into a lower risk of getting the flu or maybe even cancer.

Neurophysiological changes associated with religious and spiritual states can be obtained through a number of techniques that each have their own advantages and disadvantages. Early studies of meditation practices made substantial use of electroencephalography (EEG), which measures electrical activity in the brain. Functional neuroimaging studies of religious and spiritual phenomena have utilized positron emission tomography (PET), single photon emission computed tomography (SPECT), and functional magnetic resonance imaging (fMRI). In general, such techniques can measure functional changes in the brain in pathological conditions, in response to pharmacological interventions, and during various activation states.

NEUROPHYSIOLOGICAL FINDINGS
ASSOCIATED WITH SPIRITUAL PRACTICES

Brain imaging studies of spiritual practices have used all of the available techniques. In general, there seems to be an extended network of brain structures that get into the act when people engage in spiritual practices. Several studies have shown that when people perform a practice in which they actively focus their mind on something such as a mantra or image of a sacred object, they activate their frontal lobes. The frontal lobes activate whenever we focus our mind on anything. So focusing on a spiritual object should also result in increased frontal lobe activity.

Once the frontal lobes are activated they interact with a number of other important structures in the brain. The thalamus is deeply connected with the frontal lobes and is a key relay in the brain that enables different parts of the brain to interact with each other as well as for the brain to interact with the rest of the body. As the frontal lobes and thalamus are activated, the parietal lobe also becomes involved. The parietal lobe typically takes our sensory information and creates for us a sense of our self and orients that self in the world. As one deepens the focus on the sacred object, the brain screens out irrelevant sensory information on its way to the parietal lobe. As this continues, more and more information is prevented from reaching the parietal lobe. Even though this part of the brain is trying to create a sense of self, it no longer has the information upon which to do so. We believe that this is associated with the experience of losing the sense of self and also a sense of space and time, which are commonly reported during spiritual practices. Brain imaging studies of practices such as meditation and prayer have typically shown a decrease of activity in the parietal lobes associated with the experience of losing the sense of self.

The above described functional imaging studies of meditation suggest that there is a network associated with such practices that includes changes in the attentional system of the brain including the prefrontal cortex, cingulate gyrus, and superior parietal lobes. There also appear to be changes of activity in the limbic areas, the emotional structures of the brain, such as the amygdala and hippocampus. These key structures are probably associated with the intense emotional responses that can often occur during meditation and related spiritual practices.

A very small but crucial structure called the hypothalamus is also probably associated with a variety of spiritual practices and experiences. This structure controls many body functions such as heart rate, blood pressure, and respiration. The hypothalamus also regulates most of our body's hormone systems. Finally, the hypothalamus helps to control the autonomic nervous system that regulates our arousal (or sympathetic) and quiescent (or parasympathetic) functions in the body. Since a number of studies have shown changes in hormone function as well as changes in autonomic activity, it makes sense that the hypothalamus would play a key role during spiritual experiences. The autonomic nervous system in particular seems to be involved because people typically report either intense feelings of arousal or intense feelings of bliss during such practices. In fact, an intriguing aspect of certain mystical experiences is the simultaneous sense of arousal and quiescence. This might be described as an active bliss.

Several studies have also explored the more chemical nature of spiritual experiences. For example, one brain scan study showed a release of dopamine during meditation practice. Dopamine is a neurotransmitter that is involved with positive emotions, including the reward system of the brain and even intense feelings of euphoria. For example, dopamine is the primary mediator for the effects of cocaine. The release of dopamine during meditation practice certainly may help to explain the frequently described intense positive feelings. Other studies have shown changes in the body's hormone systems. Notably cortisol, the body's main stress hormone, is typically found to be decreased during meditation practices. This reflects a lower stress state of the individual. Since cortisol also suppresses the immune system, lower levels of cortisol during meditation may help to enhance immune system function. This might ultimately have a beneficial effect on how the body handles disease. This leads us to a larger discussion of the overall relationship between religion, spirituality, and health. After all, if there are physiological effects, there should be health effects. Of course health effects begin at the interface between the health care provider and the patient.

INTEGRATING RELIGION AND HEALTH CARE
Studies have confirmed that religion and spirituality play significant roles in many people's lives. Over 90 percent of Americans

believe in God or a higher power, 90 percent pray, 75 percent pray on a daily basis, 69 percent are members of a church or synagogue, 40 percent attend a church or synagogue regularly, 60 percent consider religion to be very important in their lives, and 82 percent acknowledge a personal need for spiritual growth. Studies have also suggested that patients are interested in integrating religion with their health care. Over 75 percent of surveyed patients want physicians to include spiritual issues in their medical care, approximately 40 percent want physicians to discuss their religious faith with them, and nearly 50 percent would like physicians to pray with them. Many physicians seem to agree that spiritual well-being is an important component of health and that it should be addressed with patients, but only a minority (less than 20 percent) do so with any regularity. Surveyed physicians blame this discrepancy on lack of time, inadequate training, discomfort in addressing the topics, and difficulty in identifying patients who want to discuss spiritual issues.

Educators have responded by offering courses, conferences, and curricula in medical schools, post-graduate training, and continuing medical education. However, some question the relevance and appropriateness of discussing religion and spirituality in the health care setting, fearing that it gives health care workers the opportunity to impose personal religious beliefs on others and that necessary medical interventions may be replaced by religious interventions. Sloan and colleagues cautioned that patients may be forced to believe that their illnesses are due solely to poor faith. Moreover, there is considerable debate over how religion should be integrated with health care and who should be responsible, especially when health care providers are agnostic or atheist.

Despite this controversy, there are many signs that the role of religion in health care is increasing. For instance, the *Diagnostic and Statistical Manual of Mental Disorders*, which is the fundamental book on mental disorders, now recognizes religion and spirituality as relevant sources of either emotional distress or support. Also, the guidelines of the Joint Commission on Accreditation of Healthcare Organizations (JCAHO) require hospitals to meet the spiritual needs of patients. The biomedical research literature has reflected this trend as well. The frequency of studies on religion and spirituality and health has dramatically increased over the past decade with a more than 600 percent increase in spirituality and health publications and a 27 percent increase in religion and health publications from 1993 to 2002.

Some have recommended that physicians and other health care providers routinely take religious and spiritual histories of their patients to better understand patients' religious background, determine how they may be using religion to cope with illness, open the door for future discussions about any spiritual or religious issues, and help detect potentially deleterious side effects from religious and spiritual activities. It may also be a way of detecting spiritual distress. There has been greater emphasis in integrating various religious resources and professionals into patient care, especially when the patient is near the end of life. Some effort has been made to train health care providers to listen appropriately to patients' religious concerns, perform clergy-like duties when religious professionals are not available, and better understand spiritual practices.

THE POSITIVE EFFECTS OF RELIGION ON HEALTH
Disease Incidence and Prevalence
Most research has demonstrated that religious involvement correlates with decreased overall health problems and mortality. High levels of religious involvement may be associated with up to seven years of increased life expectancy. In a large analysis of 91,000 people in a Maryland county, those who regularly attended church had a lower prevalence of cirrhosis, emphysema,

suicide, and death from ischemic heart disease. Several studies have implied that religious participation and higher religiousness may have a beneficial effect on blood pressure.

Some results have suggested that health problems and death rates may vary by religion, even when adjusting for major biological, behavioral, and socioeconomic differences. However, the experience of individuals within a given religion can depend significantly on the local environment, so that the results of such comparisons should be viewed carefully. For instance, greater health problems and mortality have been reported among Irish Catholics in Britain, which may be a reflection of their disadvantaged socio-economic status in that country. A study in Holland suggested that smaller religious groups may be less susceptible to infectious disease because of social isolation.

As a whole, the data raise the possibility that something about religion is protective even though it is not clear what might ultimately cause this effect. However, there may be many other related factors, since religious participation can be associated with a number of socioeconomic, lifestyle, ethnic, and geographic differences affecting health.

Disease and Surgical Outcomes

Studies have also suggested that religiousness may correlate with better outcomes after major illnesses and medical procedures. A study of 232 patients following elective open heart surgery showed that a lack of participation in social or community groups and absence of strength and comfort from religion were consistent predictors of death. In elderly women after hip repair, religious belief was associated with lower levels of depressive symptoms and better ability to walk after surgery. And in patients who underwent heart surgery, stronger religious beliefs were associated with shorter hospital stays and fewer complications; interestingly, however, attending religious services predicted longer hospitalizations. Another study did not find spiritual beliefs to significantly affect recovery from spinal surgery.

Studies have looked at whether religiousness improves the survival of patients with different illnesses as well. In a study of African-American women with breast cancer, patients who did not belong to a religion tended to not survive as long as those who did. In a study of women with breast cancer, those individuals who were Seventh Day Adventists had better breast cancer survival than non-Seventh Day Adventists, but this was likely due to earlier diagnosis and treatment. Several other studies of various cancers including colorectal, lung, and breast cancer showed no statistically significant effect of religious involvement on cancer survival. A recent study of patients with heart attacks also revealed no significant association between religiousness and outcome. However, it must be remembered that some diseases have a fairly stable course regardless of treatment or other variables, so it may be less likely that religiousness affects the outcome in such diseases. Furthermore, religious and spiritual beliefs may be more useful in how a person copes with illness rather than whether it actually changes the eventual outcome.

Behavior and Lifestyles

Where there is a benefit between religion and health, lifestyle differences may account for some of the observed effects. Studies in Israel showed that secular residents had diets higher in total fat and saturated fatty acids and higher plasma levels of cholesterol, triglyceride, and low-density lipoprotein than religious subjects. In college students, an inverse correlation between religiousness and behaviors that adversely affect health has been observed. Religious involvement has been shown to be associated with a greater use of seat belts and preventative services. And compared to the general population, Mormons and Seventh Day Adventists have been found to have lower incidence and mortality rates from cancers that are linked to tobacco and alcohol, since they are less likely to use these substances.

Religion can affect alcohol and substance use at several stages. It may affect whether a person initiates use, how significant the use becomes, how the use affects the person's life, and whether the person is able to quit and recover. It is important to remember that the attitudes of religions toward alcohol and substance use vary considerably. Some religious sects strictly prohibit alcohol and substance use, some allow the use of alcohol and have incorporated drinking wine into their rituals, and others use psychoactive substances such as peyote, khat, and hashish to achieve spiritual goals. Most studies have looked at Judeo-Christian religious sects, which may allow the use of alcohol, but are certainly adverse to alcohol abuse and illicit substance use. Therefore, conclusions from these studies may not apply to all religions.

Even among those individuals who use alcohol and drugs, religious involvement is associated with a higher likelihood of using them in moderation rather than of abusing them. In a nationally representative sample of adolescents, personal devotion (defined as a personal relationship with the Divine) and affiliation with more fundamentalist denominations were inversely associated with alcohol and illicit drug use. There are a number of possible reasons for such a finding. Fear of violating religious principles and doctrines can have a powerful effect. Furthermore, religions can play a role in educating people about the dangers of alcohol and drugs. Religious involvement and its accompanying activities may help keep people occupied and prevent idleness and boredom that can lead to substance abuse. There may be peer pressure from other members of the church to remain abstinent, and an absence of peer pressure to try alcohol and other substances.

Moreover, religious involvement could be the effect rather than the cause. Substance abuse may prevent religious involvement. For example, alcoholics compared to nonalcoholics had less involvement in religious practices, less exposure to religious teachings, and fewer religious experiences.

Many feel that spirituality should play a large role in substance abuse cessation programs. Indeed, spirituality already permeates many established programs such as Alcoholics Anonymous. Studies have suggested that religious and spiritual practices may aid recovery. A significant number of recovering intravenous drug abusers seem to use religious healing, relaxation techniques, and meditation. Data suggests that patients often experience spiritual awakenings or religious conversion during recovery. However, not all studies showed that religiously involved patients have better outcomes. Several studies failed to demonstrate sufficient clinical benefit from meditation or intercessory prayer in patients with substance abuse problems.

Religion may play a role in preventing risky sexual behavior. In a study of African-American adolescent females, religiousness correlated with more frank discussions about the risks of sex and avoidance of unsafe sexual situations. In one study of over 3,000 adolescent girls, there was a positive association between personal devotion and fewer sexual partners outside a romantic relationship, religious event attendance and proper birth control use, and religious event attendance and a better understanding of human immunodeficiency virus or pregnancy risks from unprotected intercourse. But these findings are not universal. Some have found no relationship between religiousness and sexual practices. In fact, religious traditions or environments may actually suppress open discussion of sex and contraception, with one study showing that adolescents who discussed safe sex with their mothers tended to be less religious.

General Well-Being

Mental health has been more heavily studied than physical health with regard to spiritual and religious beliefs. Studies have demonstrated religiousness to be positively associated with feelings of well-being in white American, Mexican-American, and African-American populations. Religious service attendance is predictive of higher life satisfaction among elderly Chinese Hong Kong residents and elderly Mexican-American women. Members of religious kibbutzes in Israel reported a higher sense of coherence and less hostility and were more likely to engage in volunteer work than nonmembers. Similar findings occurred in a population of nursing home residents. Hope and optimism seemed to run higher among religious individuals than nonreligious individuals in some study populations. A few studies have compared different religions. For example, one study showed that among elderly women in Hong Kong, Catholics and Buddhists enjoyed better mental health status than Protestants. However, not enough data exist to generate meaningful conclusions.

Depression

A number of investigators have looked at the effects of religion on depression. In general, religiousness and religious activity are associated with less depressive symptoms and a better chance of improvement after treatment for major depression. Prospective studies have also found religious activity to be strongly protective against depression in Protestant and Catholic offspring who share the same religion as their mother.

Studies have also suggested an inverse correlation between religiousness and suicide. Suicide may be less acceptable to people with high religious devotion and orthodox religious beliefs. But again, it is unclear whether suicidal individuals are less likely to hold strong religious beliefs or individuals with strong religious beliefs are less likely to be suicidal.

In terms of treatment itself, there is growing interest in integrating religious and spiritual concepts into psychotherapy for the treatment of depression and anxiety. Several studies have shown that religion-based cognitive therapy has a favorable impact on depression and anxiety, but these studies have not been sufficiently well done and factored out other issues such as medication use, so it is difficult to draw definite conclusions at this time.

Coping with Medical Problems

Religious belief may provide meaning to patients and, in turn, help them better cope with their diseases. Although many major religions have occasionally deemed illness and suffering the result of sin, many believe that pain and suffering can be strengthening, enlightening, and purifying. According to various religious teachings, pain and suffering are inevitable and can be cleansing, test virtue, educate, readjust priorities, stimulate personal growth, and define human life.

Thus, religions may differ in how they confront suffering. While generalizations are difficult to draw, since considerable variability exists within each religion, many Buddhists believe in enduring pain matter-of-factly, many Hindus stress understanding and detachment from pain, many Moslems and Jews favor resisting or fighting pain, and many Christians stress seeking atonement and redemption.

Evidence suggests that religion provides more than just a distraction from suffering. The "diverting attention" and "praying" factors on the Coping Strategies Questionnaire have correlated with pain levels. The social network and support that religions provide may be associated with lower pain levels, and religious belief may improve self-esteem and sense of purpose. Religious attendance appears to buffer people against the effects of stress on mental health. Even in specific diseases such as advanced breast cancer, spirituality appears to improve emotional well-being, self-esteem, feelings of disability, and compliance with medical interventions.

THE NEGATIVE EFFECTS OF RELIGION ON HEALTH

Although most studies have shown positive effects, religion and spirituality also may negatively impact health. For example, religious groups may directly oppose certain health care interventions, such as transfusions or contraception, and convince patients that their ailments are due to noncompliance with religious doctrines rather than organic disease. In a study of North Carolina women, belief in religious intervention was found to sometimes delay African-American women from seeing their physicians for breast lumps. In addition, religions can stigmatize those with certain diseases to the point where they do not seek proper medical care.

On a more societal level, as history has shown, religion can be the source of military conflicts, prejudice, violent behaviors, and other social problems. Religions may ignore or ostracize those who do not belong to their church. Those not belonging to a dominant religion may face obstacles to obtaining resources as well as hardships and stress that deleteriously affect their health. Religious leaders may abuse their own members physically, emotionally, or sexually. Religious laws or dictums may be invoked to justify harmful, oppressive, and injurious behavior.

Additionally, perceived religious transgressions can cause emotional and psychological anguish, manifesting as physical discomfort. This "religious" and "spiritual" pain can be difficult to distinguish from pure physical pain. In extreme cases, spiritual abuse (i.e., convincing people that they are going to suffer eternal punishment) and spiritual terrorism, an extreme form of spiritual abuse, can occur either overtly or insidiously. When a mix of religious, spiritual, and organic sources is causing physical illness, treatment can become complicated. Health care workers must properly balance treating each source.

THE EFFECTS OF SPECIFIC RELIGIOUS AND SPIRITUAL ACTIVITIES ON HEALTH

Religious and spiritual activities and practices have become highly prevalent and may be practiced in either religious or secular manners. Although many of these activities have been correctly or incorrectly linked to specific religions, practicing them does not necessarily connote certain beliefs. In fact, hundreds of variations of each spiritual activity exist, since many have been altered and combined with other activities such as aerobics to develop hybrid techniques. As a result, some forms barely resemble the original versions. Thus, investigators must be very specific in describing the technique or activity that they are examining, and results from one form of meditation or yoga may not apply to other forms.

Prayer

In one of the largest surveys of alternative medicine usage among Americans, one-fourth of respondents used prayer to cope with physical illness. There is evidence that prayer may be associated with less muscle tension, improved cardiovascular and neuroimmunologic parameters, psychological and spiritual peace, a greater sense of purpose, enhanced coping skills, less disability and better physical function in patients with knee pain, and a lower incidence of coronary heart disease. Prayer has also been found to be associated with lower levels of stress, anxiety, and depression.

Intercessory prayer for other individuals suffering from various problems has been much more controversial. In one of the first studies of intercessory prayer, Dr. Randolph Byrd and colleagues showed that patients admitted to a coronary care unit had slightly better outcomes when prayed for compared to those who were not prayed for. Other studies have replicated these initial results with varying degrees of success. Intercessory prayer has not been as successful in the context of substance abuse. And more recently a large trial of intercessory prayer did not show any significant benefit. Proponents of intercessory prayer typically cite that there is little down side, and even if there is some modest benefit, it might be worth it. Future and better studies will be needed to understand whether intercessory prayer really has a medical effect or not.

Meditation

Meditation and meditation-related practices are widely used as alternative therapy for physical ailments. Many physicians routinely recommend meditation techniques to their patients and include them as part of integrated health programs: examples are Dean Ornish's popular heart disease programs and a Stanford arthritis self-care course. Meditative and relaxation techniques are often part of childbirth preparation classes.

Many preliminary studies suggest that meditation may have a number of health benefits, helping people achieve a state of restful alertness with improved reaction time, creativity, and comprehension; decreasing anxiety, depression, irritability, and moodiness; and improving learning ability, memory, self-actualization, feelings of vitality and rejuvenation, and emotional stability. Preliminary studies suggest that meditative practices may benefit and provide acute and chronic support for patients with hypertension, psoriasis, irritable bowel disease, anxiety, and depression. There is also evidence that meditation can improve chronic pain, such as helping patients with fibromyalgia. Moreover, in several studies meditators had better lung and heart function than nonmeditators. There is even some evidence that it might help with cholesterol levels.

Unfortunately, many studies do not specify or describe the type of meditation used, the frequency of use, and how compliant patients actually were. A wide variety of methods may be used, including some in which the body is immobile (e.g., Zazen, Vipassana), others in which the body is let free (e.g., Siddha Yoga, the Latihan, the chaotic meditation of Rajneesh), and still others in which the person participates in daily activities while meditating (e.g., Mahamudra, Shikantaza, Gurdjieff's "self-remembering"). So it is not clear which forms may be beneficial and what aspects of meditation are providing the benefits.

Although physically noninvasive, meditation can be harmful in patients with psychiatric illness, potentially aggravating and precipitating psychotic episodes in delusional or strongly paranoid patients and heightening anxiety in patients with overwhelming anxiety. Moreover, it can trigger the release of repressed memories. Therefore, all patients using meditative techniques should be monitored, especially when a patient first starts using meditation.

Yoga

Yoga is also widely used, often for regular exercise. Contrary to popular misconception, yoga predated Hinduism by several centuries, and as the American Yoga Association emphasizes, since yoga practice does not specify particular higher powers or religious doctrines, it can be compatible with all major religions. In fact, many religions, including many Christian denominations, have adopted yoga techniques.

Yoga is based on a set of theories that have not yet been scientifically proven. Yoga practitioners believe that blockages or shortages of life force can cause disease or decreased resistance to disease and that yoga can restore the flow of life force to different parts of the body. They use a series of stretching, breathing, and relaxation techniques to prepare for meditation and use stretching movements or postures (*asanas*) that aim to increase blood supply and *prana* (vital force) as well as increase the flexibility of the spine, which is thought to improve the nerve supply. They also use breathing techniques (*pranayamas*) to try to improve brain function, eliminate toxins, and store reserve energy in the solar plexus region.

The few limited clinical studies on yoga have been encouraging, showing reduced serum total cholesterol, LDL cholesterol, and triglyceride levels, and improved pulmonary function tests in yoga practitioners. They also suggest that yoga may be associated with acute and long-term decreases in blood pressure and may benefit patients with asthma, hypertension, heart failure, mood disorders, and diabetes. Two small controlled but non-double-blinded studies showed Hatha yoga to significantly alleviate pain in osteoarthritis of the fingers and carpal tunnel syndrome. However, yoga is not completely benign, as certain asanas may be strenuous and cause injury. In fact, yoga practitioners believe some asanas cause disease.

More studies are needed to determine the benefits (and potential dangers) of yoga. Like meditation, many forms of yoga have emerged. Some involve significant aerobic exercise. Others involve significant strength and conditioning work. Many yoga practices include changes in diet and lifestyles. It may be difficult to draw the line between yoga and other practices that have established health benefits such as exercise. Therefore, future studies should focus on specific yoga forms and movements and avoid making general conclusions about all yoga practices.

Faith Healing

Faith healers use prayer or other religious practices to combat disease. Surveys have found that a fair number of patients in rural (21 percent) and inner city (10 percent) populations have used faith healers, and many physicians (23 percent) believe that faith healers can heal patients. Despite numerous anecdotes of healing miracles, there has been no consistent and convincing scientific proof that faith healers are effective. Additionally, it has not been determined whether faith healers affect patients psychologically or physiologically, and what factors may make them effective. Conclusions cannot be drawn until further research is performed.

CONCLUSION: ARE WE HEADING TOWARD PARADIGM SHIFT? While the biological and health evaluation of religious and spiritual phenomena has advanced considerably since some of the initial studies that were performed over thirty years ago, this field of research is still in its early stages. There are many unique methodological issues that face this field in addition to the potentially more problematic barriers of funding and academic stature. However, pursuit of such projects may ultimately pay large dividends both for science and religion. From the religious perspective, the results of such studies may help toward a better understanding of the human experience of religion. These studies enhance human knowledge of how spiritual and religious pursuits affect the mind, brain, body, and behavior. From the scientific perspective, such research may shed new light on the complex workings of the human brain as well as the relationship between brain states and body physiology. Addressing methodological and statistical issues can enhance both fields, since such issues may result in improved scientific and statistical techniques and also contribute to theological and philosophical dialogue.

All of this information leads to a potentially fascinating and powerful possibility. Do we need to change our most fundamental way of understanding human health and well-being?

For the past century, the biomedical world has focused almost exclusively on the biological models of health and disease. However, today, we are revolutionizing the way in which we think about the entire person. We have come to realize that people are composed of a biological, psychological, social, and spiritual domain. In order to fully care for an individual, we really need to be able to take care of the person along all of those domains. The research further suggests a very complex linkage between spirituality and health. And if there is energy, spirit, or some other aspect of the human person that is responsible in some way for health and disease, this could dramatically change the existing paradigm of medicine and lead to a new, highly integrated way of healing.

How do different types of meditation practices match up—and how do they serve different goals, from relaxation to spiritual enhancement? In the wealth of research on meditation, what kinds of negative effects have been uncovered? What is lost when meditation is extracted from its spiritual context? Dr. Joan H. Hagemen provides an informed guide to different meditation techniques and the large body of research that reveals the great variety of pros and cons to regular practice. From awareness and enhanced concentration to reduced anxiety and better attitudes, the shared goals remain the same—to achieve an enhanced state of balance and change one's consciousness.

Not All Meditation Is the Same

A Brief Overview of Perspectives, Techniques, and Outcomes

JOAN H. HAGEMAN, PH.D.

A common misconception is that all meditation practices are the same. I have found through my research that they are not, even though the end result may be similar in the sense of achieving a more subjective sense of well-being. In terms of describing what meditation is and what it does, there are many different perspectives that range along a continuum from the sacred to the secular in the scientific literature. This chapter will briefly capture the most prominent perspectives, techniques, and outcomes. There are many others, but there is not space to include them here.

WHAT IS MEDITATION?

From a strict psychophysiological lens, meditation is defined as the intentional self-regulation of attention that is used for self-inquiry, whereas Andrzej Kokoszka (1990) suggests that meditation may also involve self-experience, self-realization, and/or a way to achieve the discovery of ultimate truth according to some religious traditions (as cited by Perez-De-Albeniz and Holmes, 2000). The *Random House Dictionary* (1996, p. 843) defines it as a "devout religious contemplation or spiritual introspection." Among other perspectives, meditation is also defined and described from both operational and philosophical perspectives.

Neuroscience focuses on the brain functions that are involved in meditation, such as the frontal cortex, amygdala, thalamus, parietal lobe, temporal lobe, and other brain functions. It appears that the human is neurologically hard-wired to evoke certain perceptions and sensations during such acts as chanting, dance, meditation, prayer, religious ritual and contemplation, and yoga (Alper, 2001). There is also the tendency to interpret these perceptions and sensations cross-culturally as indicative of a divine, sacred, or transcendental reality. Recent discoveries in neuroscience seem to contradict the notion of such sacredness by suggesting that these experiences are simply the effects of electrochemical impulses interpreted by the brain. Matthew Alper (2001) agrees with this stance. He proposes that spiritual consciousness first emerges in the human child's preoperational development stage, and draws attention to his observations that during meditation: (a) the amygdala, which has the function to alert one when a threat is sensed, becomes deactivated; (b) blood flow is decreased to the parietal lobe of the brain, which has the function of orienting one to space and marking the distinction between self and the external world; (c) the temporal lobe, which has the function of marking the passage of time, is quieted; (d) the frontal lobe becomes activated; and, (e) the interaction of these brain functions collectively serve to focus the individual's attention and thereby convey a sense of absolute reality that is greater than the reality of everyday life. Alper contends that these experiences are strictly the product of human cognition. In contrast, Andrew B. Newberg (2002), from a neurotheology perspective, proposes that neuroscience has its limitations in answering epistemological and ontological questions.

From another perspective, some consider that meditation is related to daydreaming and hypnosis (Fromm, 1975) or autogenic training, cardiovascular and neurovascular feedback, prayer, and relaxation techniques (Kokoszka, 1994). Philip Snaith (1998), in opposition to this idea, argues that meditation is different from these techniques or practices because it emphasizes the maintenance of alertness and the expansion of self-awareness from the respective philosophical cognitions, and increases the sense of integration and cohesiveness. From these brief definitions, one can easily glean that there is a diversity of opinion on what meditation is. Likewise, there is disagreement in terms of categorizing the varied techniques of meditation.

MEDITATION TECHNIQUES

Although there are many different techniques for meditation, Deane H. Shapiro (1982) classifies three primary broad groupings of attentional strategies: (a) *mindfulness,* focuses on the field or background perception and experience, and might be described as a wide-angle lens attention; (b) *concentrative,* focuses on the field or background perception and experience, and might be described as zoom-lens attention; and, (c) *integrated,* which involves a shift between the field and object of attention.

In contrast, Eugene d'Aquili and Andrew B. Newberg (1993) suggest that there are only two basic categories of meditative practice: *passive* and *active*. By their definitions, passive meditation is an attempt to reach a subjective state characterized by a sense of no space, no time, and no thought, whereas active meditation is designed to lead to a subjective experience of absorption with the object of focus (as cited by Newberg and Iversen, 2002).

Furthermore, there may be a profound effect on brain functions via the specific characteristics of a meditative practice in how mediation is performed (i.e., verbal, visual, movement), and how it is experienced. For example, brain neuroplasticity and affective style, in addition to immune responses, are positively effected with mindfulness meditation (Davidson, 2004; Davidson et al., 2003).

In terms of behavioral descriptors in how meditation is experienced, John L. Craven (1989) identifies five components: (a) altered state of awareness, (b) concentration, (c) maintenance of self-observing attitude, (d) relaxation, and (e) suspension of logical thought processes. This author and colleagues (Hageman, 2007a; 2007b) clarify that attentional strategies effect how emotion is presented in the stream of consciousness during meditation. As such, meditation may be practiced while in silence, sitting, reclining, dancing, walking, and/or doing various exercises that aim to break down the habitual automatic mental categories, serving to regain the primary nature of perceptions and events and to focus attention *on the process* rather than the desired outcome. Various meditative practices include breathing techniques, prescribed behaviors, bodily postures, and/or specific exercises that are unique to the practice, which are oriented toward the respective beliefs focused on enhanced awareness, harmony, balance, and/or enlightenment. There is some overlap of these techniques from practice to practice, but typically there are definitive techniques to each practice.

In the Chinese Qigong meditation, for example, the person concentrates on the energy in the body, starting at the lower abdomen, and through visualization circulates the *Qi* energy through various parts of the body until the energy is dispersed. This process is combined with an instructor's suggestions that are repetitive, positive, and reinforcing along with the individual's own suggestions, which usually culminate in an individual's strong belief that their own individual energy can be manipulated at will. Kouksundo (also known as Sundo Taoism), as another example, also focuses on breathing and the dispersion of energy throughout the body, but its breathing technique (*tancheon*) is different in that it begins much lower in the abdomen just above the pelvic bone, and its exercises are similar to some positions in martial arts that are more oriented toward stretching and balance. Other practices focus on the breath via the nostrils combined with mantras and chanting, whereas some practices focus on silence or a form of hyperventilation combined with cognitive strategies (Hageman, Krippner, and Wickramasekera, 2006).

The Eastern Orthodox Church focuses on the Hesychastic Prayer for meditation, which has a superficial resemblance to Buddhism and various Hindu meditations. The Hesychastic Prayer may be done along with the chanting of the Purity of Heart prayer and other mantras. The Jewish meditation's goal is to achieve *Devekut,* which is the attempt to bind oneself to God: the Jewish counterpart to enlightenment. These meditations may be performed at any time for three minutes or more and may be described as moments of mindfulness. The Sufi tradition may use either silent meditation, mantras, or dance. Indic tantra meditation may involve active meditation, sometimes in addition to tantric sexual expression. There are also various forms of yoga meditations (e.g., concentration, mindfulness, raising of kundalini energery, visualization). Buddhism meditation may involve concentration, insight, mindfulness, and visualization. Zen philosophy involves a specific form of meditation called *zazen* (seated meditation) that is basically the study of one's self. The basic goal of zen meditation is to achieve *satori*, which is individual enlightenment, for which concentration, insight, and mindfulness techniques may be used. Clearly, there are many different meditation techniques; moreover, their outcomes are just as diverse.

MEDITATION AND ITS OUTCOMES

Just as there are different forms of meditation, there are differences in the perspectives toward understanding one's self related to the meditative practice. For example, Buddhist ideology views the self as illusory, and asserts that human development proceeds through a series of developmental stages. Buddhist psychology holds that an individual's clinging to personal experience is the deepest psychopathological problem, which propagates the formation and overattachment to the self. In contrast, psychoanalytic object relations theory in Western psychology (Greenberg and Mitchell, 1983) holds that psychopathology is the inability to establish a cohesive integrated self. Both object relations theory and Buddhist thought agree that the human goes through developmental stages. There are also differences in how cultures view the individual's role in society (e.g., collectivism, individualism) that impact the esoteric meanings applied to specific meditation practices.

Traditionally, meditation has been practiced within a religious context; however, especially in the West, many techniques of meditation have been extracted from the context of philosophical and spiritual ideologies and applied to promote individual well-being. In this respect, a preponderance of literature in the scientific journals and research efforts about meditation is based on meditation's personal health enhancing aspects without the esoteric underpinnings (e.g., Epstein, 1990; Shapiro, 1994). From the Western psychological perspective, the process of meditation suspends the habitual logical verbal construction and thus frees individuals of their usual defenses. This allows an individual's consciousness to move in new directions (Bogart, 1991). Nonetheless, there are varying reports across cultures on the benefits and adverse effects of meditation.

Even though much of the following research was not based upon a true experimental research design, some findings suggest that meditation: (a) prompts an integration of subjective experiences, increases acceptance and tolerance of affect, and increases self-awareness (Craven, 1989); (b) optimizes the process of memory (Atwood and Maltin, 1991); (c) increases vigor (Kutz, Leserman, Dorrington, Morrison, Borysenko, and Benson, 1985); (d) increases happiness and joy, positive thinking, self-confidence, effectiveness, and problem solving skills (Shapiro, 1992); (e) enhances acceptance and compassion and tolerance to self and others (Dua and Swinden, 1992); and, (f) increases relaxation, resilience, and the ability to control feelings (Scheler, 1992).

Other research suggests additional benefits to meditation: (a) it helps an individual to understand that there are not necessarily quick solutions to problems or concerns (Atwood and Maltin, 1991); (b) positive effects are created by specific techniques such as physical postures, attentional focus, style, and breathing (Colby, 1991); and, (c) it produces an integrated response with peripheral circulatory and metabolic changes in the central nervous system (Jevning, Wallace, and Beidebach, 1992) that involves such effects as alpha, beta, and theta brain wave coherences (Telles and Desraju, 1993), brain stem evoked responses (Liu, Rong-Quing, Guo-Zhang, and Chi-Mang, 1990), and metabolic effects (Harte, Eifert, and Smith, 1995). The metabolic effects also include the meditator's ability to change metabolic rate at will (Benson, Malhotra, Goldman, Jacobs, and Hopkins, 1990). Measures of cerebral blood flow depict differential activity in associated cortices known to participate in imagery and in meditation (Lou, Kjaer, Friberg, Wildsciodtz, Holm, and Nowak, 1999).

As mentioned above, though not inclusive, much research has addressed the beneficial aspects of meditation; however, not all individuals experience positive side effects. In fact, Shapiro (1992) found that 62.9 percent of the participants in one of his research projects reported adverse effects either during or after meditation. He found additionally that 7.4 percent experienced profound adverse effects, and that the length of practice ranging from sixteen to 105 months did not serve to change the quality and frequency of adverse side effects (e.g., being more judgmental; boredom; confusion and disorientation; decreased motivation in life; depression; feeling addicted to meditation; feeling spaced out and exhibiting impaired reality testing; increased negativity; pain; paradoxical increases in tension; relaxation-induced anxiety and/or panic).

Craven (1989) also found additional side effects (e.g., anxiety-provoking phenomena; destructive behavior; elation; feelings of guilt; grandiosity; mild dissociation; psychosis-like symptoms; suicidal feelings; uncomfortable kinesthetic sensations). Ilan Kutz and colleagues (Kutz, Leserman et al., 1985) found that some participants experienced a sense of defenselessness, which produced unpleasant affective experiences (e.g., anger, apprehension, despair, sobbing, hidden memories) and themes from the past (e.g., abandonment, incest, rejection). It is not uncommon for some meditators, who claim to have "found the answers," to be actively engaged in a subtle maneuver of avoiding the solution to personal issues. From this perspective, Shapiro (1992) recommends some caution when the idea is presented that adverse effects are only part of the path and that it takes years of practice to resolve the adverse effects. He argues that this line of reasoning is reminiscent of the misuse in the classical psychoanalytic dictum that "insight causes cure." Hence, if one is not cured, then one needs more insight.

From personality theory perspectives, it is unclear whether certain personality types are more likely to try meditation or whether the effect of meditation increases the awareness of covert feelings, certain personality traits (e.g., extraversion, introversion, hypnotic susceptibility, neuroticism), and symptomology (Morse, 1984). Most research on meditation and personality has focused on neuroticism (negative affect) and anxiety.

Although different meditation techniques may be associated with different outcomes, the length of regular meditative practice may not be as definitive a critical agent to explain anxiety reduction as some other effects. There may also be a *ceiling effect* regarding the length of practice and anxiety reduction. There are contrasting findings in which some researchers found that a decrease in anxiety was associated with length of practice (Delmonte, 1981a), whereas other research did not confirm it (Zuroff and Schwarta, 1978) or indicated that length of practice was not a consistent measurement for positive change (Peters, Benson, and Porter, 1977).

On a more positive contrast, Jonathan C. Smith (1978) found that individuals who display the greatest reduction in trait anxiety and maintain a meditative practice tend to be: (a) reserved, detached, and aloof (i.e., sizothymic); or, (b) charmed by imagination, completely absorbed, demonstrating a facility to dissociate and/or engage in autonomous self-absorbed relaxation, and imaginatively enthralled by inner action (i.e., autia). This conclusion was presented in terms of Raymond B. Cattell's (1957) personality factors that involve the levels of social withdrawal (sizothymia) and high absorption in idea (autia) dimensions. These findings are consistent with the notion that individuals who regularly practice meditation and are high on hypnotizability would be more likely to show substantial reduction in anxiety (Heide, Wadlington, and Lundy, 1980). Moreover, individuals who are attracted to meditation may be relatively introverted and may become less introverted with length of practice. It is further theorized that extroverts may be less inclined to be involved in a meditative practice, but there does not appear to be any substantiative documenation to give support to the notion that a meditative practice may change the extroversion-introversion personality dimension.

Michael M. Delmonte (1980, 1981b, 1985) pointed out that the attrition from meditation practice could be predicted by negative self-concepts and high levels of symptomology (e.g., high levels of anxiety; neuroticism; psychological malaise); however, individuals who adhere to a meditative practice for intrinsic reasons (e.g., are relatively psychologically healthy; do not use meditation to solve serious problems of living) are likely to experience reduced anxiety, reduced depression, and increased self-actualization. Delmonte (1981b) also suggested that hypnotic responsiveness increases with the length of practice, and that the individual's expectancy of positive benefit is related to the frequency of practice and the reported benefits of meditative practice. Although Irving Kirsch and David Henry (1979) found that expectancy of benefit was significantly related to reduced anxiety, David C. Zuroff and J. Conrad Schwarz (1978) did not confirm this relationship and concluded that the effects of meditation might be more readily apparent in self-report measures than it is in behavioral or physiological measures. This author suggests that "faking good" may be more prominent in the self-report than in other measures, but that there may also be some inherent desynchrony among the measures of anxiety and arousal (e.g., physiological, cognitive, behavioral, biochemical).

Regardless of the conflicting reports of whether anxiety reduction is due to meditation or is the result of a quasi-placebo effect, increased awareness is a common theme in most psychotherapies and in *all* spiritual practices. Meditation also allows practitioners to step out of their own conceptual limitations, which is a process indicative of insight and creativity and the converse of neuroticism (Greguire, 1990). Although some may view meditation as the split between the experiencing ego and the observing ego as described by Sigmund Freud (1930/1961) or as a regression in the service of the ego (Atwood and Maltin, 1991) to explain its effects, meditation may be most helpful to those individuals who have achieved an adequate level of personality organization and who have also addressed certain fundamental ego-based issues (e.g., intimacy, livelihood, self-esteem, sexuality).

Even so, there are different types of meditation that may have short- and long-term benefits including the relaxation response, but meditation is neither free of side effects nor of contraindictations. This author suggests that the removal of meditation techniques from their theoretical and belief contexts of differing epistemologies may serve to dilute their ultimate benefits to the practitioner. Although meditation may bring positive benefits to the individual for multiple reasons, it cannot be ignored that the expectancy benefits are foundational to the epistemologies of the meditative practice. Both the Eastern and the Western practices of meditation, from their religious or their spiritual epistemological stances, tout specific benefits to the individual in terms of adherence to a way of life, enlightenment, happiness and well-being, and ontology. Moreover, psychopathology is a cultural determinant and the use of absorption, dissociative proclivity, or hypnotic responsiveness in a meditative practice also carries cultural guidelines as to what is pathology and what is not.

The practice of meditation from a religio-spiritual lens always includes some concept of divinity and the individual's place in the world. The biomedical, the psychobiomedical, and the neurological view of meditation to some extent strip the meditative practice from its origins, which may add to the dilution and potential adverse effects of the meditative practice. In addition, the misuse of meditation within a religio-spiritual dynamic may serve to inhibit the positive effects and/or increase the negative aftereffects of meditation.

In conclusion, the controversy between the two perspectives of the brain's role in consciousness as either (a) an organ that serves to release, permit, or transmit consciousness or (b) a physical producer of consciousness, is long standing, which has been elaborated by William James (1898/1960). From a cross-cultural lens, this author (Hageman, 2006) agrees that neuroscience has its limitations in fully explaining the purpose and outcomes of meditation. The neurological mechanisms that allow for ritual behaviors, such as those involved in meditation, are very important in the clarification of a body-mind interaction, and the potential for the human to self-heal, among other benefits. Though this controversy will most likely continue for some time, most meditators who practice from a religio-spiritual orientation consider the issue resolved. Nevertheless, it is important for science to distinguish the role of belief in health and well-being in the effort to fully delineate the impact of meditation.

For the layman practitioner, the various meditation techniques offer ways to gain access to higher levels of personal understanding as well as relaxation methods to help calm the mind and the body. In this author's opinion, higher states of consciousness that may be achieved through a meditative practice offer the potential for the individual to open the self to a connection to the divine, no matter how the individual might define his or her own sense of the divine and reality. Meditation is not a "cure-all," but it does offer another way to enhance one's well-being physically, mentally, and spiritually.

The fact that there are so many types of meditations is encouraging because individuals and cultures are different. The person who tends to be highly imaginative might more easily use active meditation techniques, because they can more quickly acclimate to the process of imagery, and achieve a state of consciousness different than their ordinary one. The person who is trained to use a technique to calm the mind might find the process of imagery distracting and thus have a more difficult time calming the mind. The person who is adept at both creative imagery and calming of the mind can more easily benefit from a technique that combines both approaches. One word of caution: any technique (e.g., meditation, hypnosis, prayer, visualization, chanting, drumming, dancing) that is used to achieve a clarity of thought and purpose by *changing* the individual's state of consciousness will tend to uncover the inconsistencies in a person's emotional and mental status. For most, the uncovering of these inconsistencies is temporarily uncomfortable and unsettling. For others, the inconsistencies may be so overwhelming that help from a friend, counselor, medical professional, or spiritual advisor may be warranted. In either event, the primary goal of meditation is to achieve a better balance within the interaction of the body, the mind, and the spirit.

Does prayer heal? Can intention cure? Can one person's thoughts effect another person's physical condition from a great distance? These are questions that have been asked for centuries, and modern science is now looking for answers. In this chapter, an excerpt from *Whole Person Healthcare*, Dr. Marilyn Mandala Schlitz and Dr. Dean Radin, a longtime research team with the Institute of Noetic Sciences, present the science of distant healing. They provide a comprehensive overview and analysis of the many clinical studies that have been done and guidelines for future exploration in this complex and controversial field.

Prayer and Intention in Distant Healing

Assessing the Evidence

MARILYN MANDALA SCHLITZ, PH.D., AND DEAN RADIN, PH.D.

INTRODUCTION

Throughout history and in almost all cultures, people have claimed they were healed by another person's caring intention or will (Whitmont, 1993). From botanicas in Mexico, street markets in Senegal, the desert of the Kalahari, healing shrines in Japan, and suburban neighborhoods in the United States, we find settings in which people attempt to help others by consciously intending their well-being, even at a distance (Schlitz and Braud, 1997a).

Distant healing intention is often associated with the religious practice of prayer, and rituals for fostering such intentions can be found in all the major religions. Some individuals, such as Carmelite nuns, spend their lives in contemplative prayer, and some monks and nuns devote a substantial proportion of their prayers to requests for healing. For example, the Unity Church has offered prayers on behalf of anyone who requests it, twenty-four hours a day and 365 days a year, for over a century. In Jerusalem, an Internet prayer service allows people around the globe to request prayer at the Wailing Wall. During the holy month of Ramadan, millions of Moslems gather at Mecca to engage in group prayer several times each day.

In contemporary U.S. culture, it is difficult to determine the precise prevalence of the use of distant healing intention as a complementary and alternative medicine (CAM) therapy, not because it is rarely used but because it is so popular that surveys have had to focus on finding the exceptions. We do know that distant intention is the most common healing practice used outside of conventional medicine. In a recent survey of adult Americans, conducted by the Centers for Disease Control and Prevention's National Center for Health Statistics, of the top five most popular CAM healing practices, three involved prayer and spirituality (Barnes, Powell-Griner, McFann and Nahin, 2004), the most popular CAM practice was prayer for self, and the third most popular was prayer for others.

An earlier national survey found that 82 percent of Americans believed in the healing power of prayer, and 64 percent felt that physicians should pray with patients who request it (Wallis, 1996b). Another survey found that 19 percent of cancer patients reported that they augmented their conventional medical care with prayer or spiritual healing (Cassileth, 1984). And a survey of American Cancer Society support groups for women with breast cancer showed that 88 percent found spiritual or religious practice to be important in coping with their illness (Johnson and Spilka, 1991), although the extent to which specific prayers or intentions of healing were part of their activities was not clear. In acute illnesses, such as cardiac events, these numbers are higher. For example, Saudia, Kinney, Brown, and Young-Ward (1991) found that 96 percent of patients stated that they prayed for their health before undergoing surgery. Some 33 percent of Hispanic patients with AIDS reportedly sought such prayer assistance (Suarez, 1996). And in the United Kingdom, there are more distant healers (approximately 14,000) than therapists from any other branch of CAM (Astin, Harkness, and Ernst, 2000), indicating the widespread practice and use of distant healing.

Among medical professionals, the concepts of spiritual healing, energy healing, and prayer are slowly gaining acceptance as well. In a 1996 survey of northern California physicians (Wallis, 1996b), 13 percent of practitioners reported using or recommending prayer or religious healing as an adjunct to conventional interventions. Therapeutic touch, which can be performed at a distance, is used by nurses in at least 80 hospitals in the United States (Maxwell, 1996) and has been taught to more than 43,000 health care professionals (Krieger, 1979). Among the lay public, Reiki International, the largest training organization for "subtle-energy healing," reports having certified more than 500,000 practitioners worldwide. While Reiki healing is frequently performed through physical contact, it is also regularly practiced over distances of thousands of miles (Schlitz and Braud, 1985).

Many terms have been used to describe intentional interventions. They include intercessory prayer, spiritual healing, nondirected prayer, intentionality, energy healing, shamanic healing, nonlocal healing, noncontact therapeutic touch, and level III Reiki. Each of these modalities describes a particular theoretical, cultural, and pragmatic approach toward mediating a healing or biological change through mental intention of one person toward another (Schlitz and Braud, 1997a). Those who engage in distant healing often share the conviction that their process involves contact with an ineffable spiritual realm.

While many patients and health care providers regard intention and prayer as vitally important, what support is there that distant intention extends beyond mundane psychological and sociological explanations? From a psychological perspective, all forms of intentional therapy may be thought of as employing a simple coping mechanism in the face of uncertainty or dire need. In addition, the concept that prayer for self promotes healing is no longer considered radical because of the growing literature on the salutary effects of meditation and placebo and, perhaps more importantly, the plausibility of psychoneuroimmunological models of self-regulation (Kiecolt-Glaser, McGuire, Robles, and Glaser, 2002).

Likewise, prayer for others is understandable as a practical coping mechanism, but the idea that it might be efficacious remains controversial. Distant healing effects are considered scientifically doubtful because the term *distant* in this context means shielded from all known causal interactions (Sloan and Ramakrishnan, 2005; Wallis, 1996a). Science is slowly coming to grips with the concept of "spooky action at a distance" in fundamental physics (Walach, 2005), but so far the idea that nonlocal effects might also be important in the behavior of living systems evokes as much scorn as it does interest. Because the mechanisms underlying distant healing are unknown, most experiments studying the hypothesized effects have been concerned with the more straightforward empirical question: Does it work?

THE SCIENCE OF DISTANT HEALING
Distant healing intention (DHI) may be defined as "a compassionate mental act intended to improve the health and well-being of another person at a distance" (Sicher, Targ, Moore, and

Smith, 1998). The fundamental assumption in DHI is that the intentions of one person can affect the physiological state of another person who is distant from the healer.

Over the past half century, researchers have developed techniques for measuring possible distant healing effects on living systems (Benor, 1993; Dossey, 1993; May and Vilenskaya, 1994; Schlitz et al., 2003; Schmidt, Schneider, Utts, and Walach, 2004; Solfvin, 1984). The goal of these experiments has been to see whether an individual's intentions can produce a measurable response in a distant living system. The best experiments have employed rigorously controlled designs that rule out all known conventional sources of influence, including environmental factors, physical manipulations, suggestion, and expectancy (Schlitz et al., 2003).

A relatively small but compelling body of experimental literature supports the DHI effect in organisms ranging from bacteria (Nash, 1982) to laboratory animals (Snel, van der Sijde, and Wiegant, 1995) to randomized clinical trials with human patients (Byrd, 1988; Sicher et al., 1998). As of 1992, at least 131 controlled DHI studies had been published, of which 56 found a statistically significant effect (Benor, 1992). More recent reviews of subsets of these experiments continue to show positive trends (Astin et al., 2000; Schmidt et al., 2004). We will review a few of these experiments to illustrate the research and its relevance to assessing the plausibility of genuine distant healing.

DISTANT HEALING INTENTIONS IN
A BASIC SCIENCE PARADIGM

Numerous studies have addressed the question of whether physiological measures—specifically autonomic nervous system activity in humans—might be susceptible to distant intentions. In the majority of these experiments, electrodermal activity (EDA) was used as the physiological measure. EDA provides a sensitive, noninvasive measure of the degree of activation in the autonomic nervous system.

Beginning in the 1970s, Braud and Schlitz conducted a series of experiments in which skin conductance was measured in the target person (a "receiver"), while a "sender" in an isolated, distant room attempted to interact with him or her by means of calming or activating thoughts, images, or intentions (Braud and Schlitz, 1983; Schlitz and Braud, 1997a; Schlitz and LaBerge, 1997). In these studies, the sender's intentions were not necessarily aimed toward distant *healing*, but the experimental task was consistent with a distant mental influence as proposed by DHI.

In 2004, psychologist Stefan Schmidt and his colleagues from the University of Freiburg Hospital, Germany, published a metaanalysis of these EDA-based experiments in the *British Journal of Psychology* (Schmidt et al., 2004). Schmidt's team found 40 experiments conducted between 1977 and 2000. Overall the results were in favor of replicable DHI-like interactions ($p < 0.001$, Cohen's d weighted effect size $d < 0.11$). The possibility of inflated statistical results due to selective reporting practices was investigated, and no such biases were found. In addition, no significant relationships were found between experimental methods and the resulting outcomes, so the results were not explainable as design flaws. In a second set of EDA-based experiments focusing on an effect conceptually similar to distant intention, namely "the sense of being stared at" (over closed circuit television to avoid sensory interactions), Schmidt's team found 15 experiments conducted between 1989 and 1998. The metaanalysis again found a significant overall effect ($p = 0.01$, Cohen's $d = 0.13$), no evidence of selective reporting biases, and no relationship between study quality and outcome. In discussing their findings, Schmidt's group noted that "because of the unconventional claim of the studies under research, we always chose a more conservative strategy whenever such a decision had to be made." They concluded that, for both classes of experiments, "There is a small, but significant effect. This result corresponds to the recent findings of studies on distant healing and the 'feeling of being stared at.' Therefore, the existence of some anomaly related to distant intentions cannot be ruled out."

With decades of repeatable, statistically significant findings reported from different laboratories, confidence is increasing that DHI effects are real. The absolute magnitude of the effects observed in the laboratory is small, but this is true for many other medically relevant effects. For example, a major clinical study on the use of aspirin to prevent second heart attacks was stopped early because researchers decided it was unethical to withhold the drug from the control group given its observed, positive effects. The effect size for the aspirin effect was 0.03— nearly four times smaller than the equivalent distant intention effect size of 0.11 (Schlitz and Braud, 1997b).

A recent experiment attempted to build a bridge between basic science investigations of distant healing using healthy volunteers and clinical studies on distant healing under conditions of genuine need (Radin et al., in press). The study investigated what would happen when the powerful motivations associated with clinical trials of DHI were combined with the controlled context and objective measures offered by laboratory protocols. It also explored the role of training in potentially modulating DHI effects. In the "trained group," the sender of distant healing (the healthy partner) attended a day-long training program involving discussion and practice of a secular DHI technique based on the Tibetan Buddhism practice of Tonglen meditation, Judeo-Christian forms of meditation, and therapeutic touch.

After attending the training session and practicing the DHI meditation daily for three months, each healthy partner and his or her spouse or friend undergoing treatment for cancer were tested in the laboratory. In a wait group condition, the couple was tested before the healthy partner attended the training. A third control group condition consisted of healthy couples who received no training. The results of this experiment showed that the overall effect size for the motivated condition was 0.74, nearly 7 times larger than the earlier DHI metaanalytic estimate of 0.11, and over 24 times larger than the aspirin study mentioned above. This suggests that distant healing practiced with very high motivation and training may be far more robust than previously observed in laboratory studies.

DHI IN CLINICAL STUDIES: ADDRESSING THE "SO WHAT?" QUESTION

Although there appears to be evidence to support proof of principal for the hypothesis that the intentions of one person have a measurable effect on the biology of another living system, we are still left with the question: Does DHI have clinical relevance? Can focused intention affect the course of healing within real patient populations? To date, only a small number of scientific studies have directly addressed this important question. So far, these clinical studies provide conflicting evidence that DHI can improve medically relevant outcomes in people suffering from conditions including arthritis, cardiac problems, hernia surgery, and AIDS. Interpretation of these clinical studies is complicated by lack of homogeneity in patient populations, lack of control and documentation of current medications, lack of consistency in healer background and intervention (Sicher, Targ, and Smith, 1998), and uncertainty about the role of patient expectancies and belief in DHI outcomes. However, this is not to say that there is no evidence. The majority of randomized, double-blind investigations to date support the clinical efficacy of DHI (Roberts, Ahmed, and Hall, 2000; Schlitz and Lewis, 1996). In a systematic review published in the *Annals of Internal*

Medicine, John Astin and colleagues (2000) found that 57 percent (13 of 23) of the published randomized, controlled clinical
trials (RCTs) on DHI showed a positive treatment effect in a
wide range of human populations, including both genders and
a wide range of ages and ethnicities. As noted by Astin and colleagues (2000, 910):

> *We believe that additional studies of distant healing that*
> *address the methodological issues outlined above are now*
> *called for to help resolve some of the discrepant findings in*
> *the literature and shed further light on the potential efficacy of*
> *these approaches.*

Clinical trials of DHI were initiated in a seminal study by
cardiologist Randolph C. Byrd (1988). In the 1980s, Byrd, then
a cardiologist at San Francisco General Hospital, conducted
an RCT to assess the effects of intercessory prayer on health
outcomes in 393 patients admitted to the coronary care unit.
Patients were randomly assigned to a prayed-for group or a control group; both groups underwent comparable conventional
medical treatment. The healers Byrd chose were people with an
active Christian life manifested by daily devotional prayer and
an active fellowship with a local church. Each person prayed
daily that the cardiac patients would achieve specific outcomes,
including rapid recovery, prevention of complications and death,
and any other areas they believed helpful to the patient.

The study results showed that members of the group receiving
healing prayer were five times less likely to require antibiotics
and three times less likely to develop pulmonary edema compared to the control group. In addition, fewer among them
died compared to the control group, and none of the prayed-
for group required endotracheal intubation, while 12 in the
control group did.

These results were intriguing, but the study was not without problems. Byrd did not assess the psychological health of those entering the study; thus, it is possible that the treated and control groups differed in this regard. Nevertheless, the results of this experiment have been quoted from pulpits to podiums and hailed enthusiastically as proof that prayer really works.

Given the scientific, social, and possible spiritual relevance of Byrd's findings, it is surprising that it took another dozen years for other researchers to conduct a more rigorously controlled replication. Finally, Harris and colleagues (1999), working with 999 patients admitted to a hospital coronary care unit, found that the medical course of his patients was better in those who were prayed for than in the control group. Harris's study, unlike Byrd's, used distant healers from a variety of Christian traditions (35 percent were listed as nondenominational, 27 percent Episcopalian, and the remainder were either Protestant or Roman Catholic). Harris also chose a more global score to assess the outcome of prayer on coronary recovery. Like Byrd, Harris concluded that his patients significantly benefited from the intercessory prayer they received.

Together, these two studies provided preliminary evidence that the intention of people engaged in healing prayer can affect the physical well-being of people at a distance. A few years after the Harris study, another study of DHI was reported in the *Western Journal of Medicine* by Fred Sicher and his colleagues (1998). These observations included a small pilot and a larger confirmation study involving the effects of intercessory (petitionary) prayer on patients with advanced AIDS. Their choice of healers was interesting. Because it is not known whether one form of distant healing is more effective than another, Sicher incorporated a wide range of self-identified healing practitioners, representing many different healing, spiritual, and religious traditions. They reasoned that by combining

DHI efforts they would be more likely to see a positive effect than by relying on a fortuitous choice of one particular practice that might be effective. Healers received a photograph of their patient, his or her last name and first initial, and sometimes the T-cell count (an index of immune system functioning). The healers provided DHI to each patient for seven days, and at six months the prayed-for patients had acquired significantly fewer new AIDS-defining illnesses, had lower illness severity, fewer doctor visits, fewer hospitalizations, fewer days of hospitalizations, and improved mood as compared to the control patients. These were highly significant outcomes, given that AIDS at the time of this study had a grim prognosis and no effective treatments.

After the systematic review by Astin et al. was completed, an additional three DHI RCTs have been published; none found significant evidence for a DHI effect. In the first, an NIH-funded clinical trial initiated by Elisabeth Targ and others at California Pacific Medical Center (later completed by John Astin), distant prayer had no effect on outcomes for AIDS patients. However, there was a surprising outcome: the treated patients correctly guessed that they were assigned to the treatment group to a highly statistically significant degree, unlike the control patients, who guessed at chance. This suggests that the treated patients accurately sensed the healers' distant intentions, but those perceptions did not correlate with medically relevant outcomes. This finding is consistent with laboratory DHI studies, which also indicate that one person's intentions can influence the nervous system of a distant person, without implying a healing effect.

The second DHI study was conducted under the direction of cardiologist Mitchell Krucoff of Duke University Medical Center. Earlier in his career, Dr. Krucoff was a volunteer at a spiritually based hospital in an ashram in rural India. There he observed that, despite sometimes primitive facilities (it was the only place he had ever seen bare feet in an operating room) and poor prognoses, patients appeared relaxed and calm, filled with a sense of well-being. He wondered what created the "healing space" he had experienced? Could the same atmosphere in the ashram's hospital be translated into a state-of-the-art hospital in the United States, and would the combination of modern medical care and attention to spiritual well-being help patients more than standard medical care alone?

To test these questions, Krucoff conducted a pilot project on 150 cardiology patients scheduled for angioplasty at the Durham Veterans Affairs Medical Center from April 1997 to April 1998. Before the procedure, each patient was randomly assigned to either standard care or to an intervention involving guided imagery, stress relaxation, healing touch—all performed at patients' bedsides—or to intercessory prayer, which was distributed among prayer groups including Buddhists, Roman Catholics, Moravians, Jews, Baptists, and the Unity School of Christianity. The results showed that all of the interventions were helpful, and patients in the prayer group did the best (Krucoff, Crater, and Green, 2001). However, a larger and more recent follow-up study involving 748 cardiac patients (Krucoff et al., 2005) found no overall result on the primary study outcome. A surprisingly strong effect was observed in one condition in which a group of people were assigned to pray for the prayers. This potential additive or "booster" effect leaves researchers intrigued despite the failure of the primary outcome to support the DHI hypothesis.

In the third recent clinical study involving cardiac patients, conducted by Herbert Benson and his colleagues (2006) at Harvard Medical School, a group who received intercessory prayer without knowing that they were in the treatment group showed no improvement. But the group who did know that they were the object of distant prayer showed results that were significantly *worse* than the control group. This new experimental condition, which combines expectation plus DHI, had not been studied before, and it implies that, under some conditions, knowledge of receiving prayer may have a detrimental effect. Some researchers speculate that this might have occurred because patients with such knowledge may have feared that they were receiving prayer because their health had a particularly poor prognosis.

Based on all clinical trials conducted so far, we are left with more questions than answers. Should we conclude that DHI does not influence healing based on recent experiments that failed to show an effect? Or should the weight of all published clinical and experimental studies influence our decision in a more positive direction? Should we conclude from the Harvard study that knowing someone is praying for us might cause harm? Does it make sense that DHI can be effective independent of any personal relationship between the person who prays and the person who is prayed for?

Researchers are faced with these and other challenges in designing and establishing scientific protocols to objectively measure whether a particular medical problem may be helped by prayer or intention. Some of the most significant and still unresolved experimental questions include what type of prayer to use, how often to pray, how to describe what healers did so that others may reproduce the results, and how to match the belief systems of the patient with that of the healer. Investigators also face sociological constraints from both scientists and theists, neither of whom wants this research to take place at all. The former assert that prayer is nonscientific, and the latter maintain that testing prayer is blasphemous.

None of the clinical trials conducted so far has made use of what scientists call "ecological validity." This means the trials were not designed to model what happens in real life, where people often know the person for whom they are pray-ing and with whom they have a meaningful relationship. In the Harvard study, for example, prayer groups were instructed for the sake of standardization to use a prescripted prayer that was different from what those who prayed used in their normal practice. So the Harvard experiment did not really test what the healers claimed works for them. In addition, in most of the clinical studies, the investigators were tightly focused on medi-cal outcomes, and hardly any attention was paid to the inner experiences of the healers and the patients.

THEORETICAL CONTEXT FOR DISTANT HEALING

One of the primary reasons that mainstream science and medi-cal researchers doubt that distant healing is effective is that it seems to violate what might be called folklore physics—the physics of everyday experience. Sloan and Ramakrishnan (2005) assert that: "Nothing in our contemporary scientific views of the universe or consciousness can account for how the 'healing intentions' or prayers of distant intercessors could possibly influence the [physiology] of patients even nearby let alone at a great distance" (1769–1770).

But is it true that nothing in science suggests the presence of connections between apparently isolated objects? Quantum entanglement, a far from common-sense effect predicted by quantum theory—described by Einstein as "spooky action at a distance" and later demonstrated as fact in the labora-tory (Walach, 2005)—shows that, under certain conditions, particles that interact remain instantaneously connected after they separate, regardless of distance in space or time. If this property is truly as fundamental as it appears to be, then in principle everything in the universe might be entangled to some degree (Radin, 2006). Everyday objects do not appear to show such entanglements, and there are arguments why quantum entanglement would be diffcult to sustain at the human scale.

But one cannot help wondering, what if this concept *did* apply to humans. In the case of indifferent, unmotivated couple, entanglements between their minds and bodies may be difficult to detect. But in a highly motivated couple, such as a dedicated healer and a patient in great need, the underlying correlations might become more evident. Such a relational model is appealing because it does not require anything (force, energy, or signals) to pass between the healer and the patient. Instead, it postulates a physical correlation that is always present between people (and everything else) due to the "nonlocal threads" from which the fabric of reality is woven (Radin, 2006; Walach, 2005).

COMMON ELEMENTS ACROSS ALL HEALING PRACTICES

Many spiritual practitioners maintain that anyone can be a healer: all that is required is a compassionate heart. At the other end of the spectrum, some traditions believe that only a special few have the gift of healing. Meanwhile, research by Elisabeth Targ and others suggests that most people have inherent healing capacities but that special training, motivation, and practice are required to bring these gifts to fruition. In our studies of healing practices across many traditions, we have found a few common guidelines. These include:

Set an intention: Bring one's awareness, with purpose and a sense of efficacy, toward a healing response in the distant person.
Focus attention: Cultivate a state of concentration on the intention. For healing, this requires a mind focused on the act of intending a healing outcome.
Cultivate love and compassion: Compassion is one

person's selfless love and care for another's suffering. Experience a sense of connection to others.

Suspend disbelief: Confidence and openness to the healing method is associated with the ability to give and receive distant healing.

Take time: Professional healers often set aside at least an hour a day to provide healing intention.

CONCLUSION

Surveys consistently show that distant healing intention (in a secular sense) and prayer (in a religious sense) are very commonly used. The question is whether these practices and beliefs are efficacious beyond acting as psychological coping strategies. We have addressed this question by splitting the relevant evidence into basic science, which seeks a proof-of-principle answer, and clinical research, which seeks to understand possible applications. The answer to the first question appears to be yes. The laboratory studies have been successfully replicated by numerous researchers around the world, and metaanalyses continue to provide significant evidence for these effects.

The answer to the second question—do these influences produce medically efficacious outcomes?—is more complex. Overall, the clinical trials suggest that DHI occasionally improves some patients' health under some circumstances. However, the effects are not easy to reproduce, and they appear to interact strongly with many factors that are difficult to control. These include variables such as who is praying, for what exactly they are praying, how they pray, their usual mode or style of prayer, the relationships among the healers, the patients, and the investigators, and so on. Dozens of such factors make studying the effects of intention on healing exceptionally challenging.

In her book, *Kitchen Table Wisdom*, oncologist Rachel Remen observes, "An unanswered question is a fine traveling companion. It sharpens your eye for the road." DHI researchers have discovered over the last few decades that their collective eyes are becoming increasingly sharpened. What we've learned so far is that there is something interesting about the role of distant intention in healing, and that this something appears to be highly sensitive to the questions being asked about it. Undoubtedly, as new questions are posed, surprising new answers will patiently await us.

TOOL KIT FOR CHANGE

Role and Perspective of the Health Care Professional
1. Prayer and compassionate intention are vital aspects of many patients' practice. As such, it is important for health care professionals to have knowledge and sensitivity about what is known about these modalities.
2. Many patients today want their practitioners to pray with them; an informed opinion on the role of prayer in healing is vital to effective communication and increased compliance.
3. Attending to their own spiritual care is an important part of health professional wellness.

Role and Perspective of the Participant
1. One way in which patients take an active role in their management of pain or suffering is the use of compassionate intention and prayer for self and others.
2. Distant healing is a sought-after form of healing intervention by many patients and has been shown to reduce stress and anxiety.
3. Data from laboratory studies support the usefulness of

distant healing as a component of an integral program—
one with which patients can be actively involved.

Interconnection: The Global Perspective

1. Prayer and healing are part of a worldview that
includes dimensions that are not included in standard
medical education.
2. Gaining knowledge of other worldviews is useful
for enhanced communication between patients, health
professionals, and the family and society in which they live.

Can distant intentionality (DI), defined as sending thoughts at a distance, actually change the brain function of the person who is said to be receiving the thoughts? In the following study, internationally recognized researcher of medicine and psychology Dr. Jeanne Achterberg and other researchers used functional magnetic resonance imaging (fMRI) to recorded the effects of DI by a group of healers from various spiritual traditions on a group of test subjects with whom they had close personal bonds. The results are provocative.

Evidence for Correlations Between Distant Intentionality and Brain Function in Recipients

A *Functional Magnetic Resonance Imaging Analysis*

JEANNE ACHTERBERG, PH.D., KARIN COOKE, TODD RICHARDS, LEANNA J. STANDISH, LEILA KOZAK, JAMES LAKE

INTRODUCTION

From the beginnings of medical history, humans have held a belief in a spiritual connection to others separated from them at a distance. These beliefs have been held as the basis for the efficacy of prayer, so-called energy healing, and the ability to heal others at a distance ("nonlocal healing"). Despite the longevity of the concept, these phenomena are largely dismissed by the advocates of the biomedical model because they do not fit the current scientific paradigm. The purpose of this study was to determine whether brain changes may be measured using fMRI in the recipients of distant intentionality. In this paper, distant intentionality (DI) is used as a phrase that subsumes prayer, energy healing, healing at a distance, spiritual healing, Therapeutic or Healing Touch, transpersonal imagery, remote mental healing, and other practices based on putative connection in the absence of mechanisms of sensory contact.[1]

There is a growing interest in the scientific community to study different forms of DI. In a recent publication summarizing the current research on healing, at least 2,200 published reports on spiritual healing, prayer, energy medicine, and mental intention effects were noted, as well as other examples of distant healing intentionality (DHI) or DI.[2] The researchers noted the weak designs of many of the studies reviewed, concluding generally that the results merit further study using sound methodology.

The neurophysiologic aspects of mystical, meditative, or spiritual states have been studied with imaging technologies. Numerous studies of mystical or religious experiences using single photon emission computed tomographic (SPECT) scans to capture brain function have been reported.[3,4] Several of the studies showed reduced regional brain metabolic activity in the posterior superior parietal lobe during intense or peak religious moments. Among the groups they studied were Tibetan meditators and Franciscan nuns at prayer.

In a study of five individuals who had practiced Kundalini yoga for at least four years, changes were found that occurred in many areas associated with attention and control of the autonomic nervous system (dorsolateral, prefrontal, and parietal cortices, hippocampus, temporal lobe, and the anterior cingulate cortex).[5] Still more relevant to the current study is the evidence of correlative activity between the brain function of two individuals separated by distance, and in the absence of sensory mechanisms of contact. What has been referred to as "extrasensory induction" has been reported in 15 pairs of monozygotic twins who were sensory-isolated from each other and in separate rooms. In two of the 15 pairs, changes in EEG alpha rhythms in one twin were observed simultaneously in the other.[6]

A series of papers[7-9] reports several EEG studies showing that a visually evoked potential in one member of a pair of individuals who felt a close personal connection occurred at above chance rates in the nonstimulated brain of the other who was at a distance in an electromagnetically shielded room. Although these studies were highly criticized because of serious methodological issues, findings were later replicated using appropriate statistical detection methods and improved control conditions by two other independent laboratories using EEG technology.[10,11] An additional study that employed a similar paradigm reported significantly correlated fMRI signals between distant human brains.[12]

Nineteen studies replicating an apparent effect of interconnectivity at a distance have been reported.[13] These studies show above-chance correlations in electrodermal activity (EDA), a measure of stress and arousal, between isolated subjects. In their protocol, one subject was instructed to randomly send anxiety-provoking or relaxing images to the other subject, who was located in a distant room. EDA in the receiver subject was correlated above chance, suggesting that the mental images of senders influenced the state of arousal of receivers.

In summary, existing findings seem to suggest the positive effects of DI, the localization of brain areas activated during prayerful or meditative states, and the correlation of brain function between pairs of individuals. These data point to the next logical step, which is to investigate the effect of DI on the brain function of the recipient. The research question investigated by this study is: "Is there evidence for correlations between distant intentionality and brain function in recipients of distant intentionality who are tested using fMRI?"

METHODS
Subjects
Twenty-two participants (11 pairs of healers and recipients of DI) were recruited on the Island of Hawaii. Healers were chosen who claimed to have the skills to communicate in some "non-local" form. In this first effort to document the effect of DI, it was important to use participants who already had training and experience in DI within their traditions. There was no attempt to document their ability to heal within the confines of this study. Often healers attempt to heal illness of a psychological and spiritual nature, and the typical medical records are of little use. To reiterate, though, the study is not about healing per se, but whether there is some correlation in the intention to connect at a distance with a person. The authors asked each healer to name someone with whom they felt a bonded or close connection.

This decision was based on research cited earlier that indicates close or bonded individuals may be more likely to show correlated physiologic effects.

Inclusion criteria for the healers included:

1. Acknowledgment within their communities for their healing abilities
2. Fulfilling cultural requirements for training, apprenticeship, and practice
3. Ability to name an individual with whom they claim a special connection, who understands the goals of the experiment and is willing to undergo an fMRI scan

4. A stated belief in their ability to turn on and off their intentions within a time frame of approximately 2 to 4 minutes

The inclusion criteria for the receivers of DI included:

1. Being selected by the healer as someone with whom they feel a close or empathic connection
2. Having the standard requirements for receiving an MRI (no implanted devices or metal objects such as pacemakers, joint pins) and no history of claustrophobia
3. Willingness to undergo an MRI scan of 34 minutes' duration and a postscan interview

Three men and eight women with an age range of 46 to 71 participated as healers. The recipients of the healing ranged in age from 44 to 61 and included three men and eight women. On average, healers had been practicing their healing traditions for 23 years.

The healers represented a variety of practices, including Healing Touch (a practice of distant healing and laying on of hands, conducted primarily by nurses trained in the method); *pule,* a traditional Hawaiian healing form that consists of prayer, chant, and song by a spiritual elder or Kahuna; Peruvian shamanic healing; Reiki (a form of energy healing that may have ancient origins and was purportedly rediscovered in the nineteenth century in Japan); vibration or sound healing; and three eclectic forms of DI that did not fit into established traditions. Additionally, three of the pairs represented a Chinese method of healing called Qigong, and all three trials were conducted by the same Qigong master.

Procedures
The study protocol was approved by the Institutional Review Board, University of Hawaii, John Burns School of Medicine.

The study was conducted in the Department of Radiology, North Hawaii Community Hospital in Waimea from August 2003 through July 2004.

Prescan. Both members of each pair signed an informed consent form and filled out a demographic questionnaire. A semistructured interview was conducted with each healer within four days before the scan to elicit information on his or her DI practices. Then the healers were given information about their role, and the On (Send) and Off (No Send) procedures were described. Standardized instructions included the information that they should try to connect with the receiver during the On condition in ways that were prescribed by their own DI practice. This was most frequently described as sending energy, prayer, or good intentions, or as thinking of the individual in the scanner and wishing for them the highest good. All of the healers claimed that they were not the cause of any healing effect, but rather were a conduit for a spiritual or cosmic source. During the Off conditions, they were instructed to take their attention away from the person in the scanner.

The recipients of DI were instructed to relax as much as possible in the scanner environment. They were provided with a call button and given instructions on using it if they were distressed, had questions, or needed to stop the procedure. However, no one used it for contact during the study trials. They were made aware that the healers would be performing DI. They were not provided with any information about the timing of the On/Off conditions. Because the healers were not informed about the timing of the On/Off signals before the trials, they could not have coached their receivers before the scan.

Experimental conditions. The healer was in the electromagnetically shielded control room and physically and optically isolated from the receiver in the scanner. The radiology technician, research nurse, and principal investigator were also in the control room. During the course of the experiment, the healer was verbally instructed by one of the researchers with cues to start and stop the DI. The random pattern of the twelve 2-minute intervals was determined prior to the onset of the study using a coin toss. A single randomized sequence that had an equal number of on and off sessions was used for each session. The pattern was off, on, on, off, on, off, off, on, on, off, on, off, for a total of six 2-minute On periods and six 2-minute Off periods. In three instances, it should be noted that the length of the interval was 4 minutes because two of the On or Off conditions occurred back to back. This pattern remained the same for each healer. The total time the recipients of DI were in the scanner was 34 minutes, which included a 10-minute structural baseline of sagittal and transverse images. During the time in the scanner, no physical or sensory contact was made with the recipient by any member of the research team.

RESULTS

The FSL software produces a quantitative table of cluster results that includes: cluster size, probability for each cluster, z scores, x y z coordinates of the cluster in Talaraich space and contrast of parameter estimates. If a cluster is significant in a group analysis it means that there were specific brain regions in which the combined subjects had enough activation to raise the z score above the noise level threshold.

In other words, if all of the subjects had random activation at different places in the brain, then there would be no group activation. One of the two clusters was highly statistically significant ($p = 0.000127$).

DISCUSSION AND CONCLUSIONS

Group analysis revealed significant activation in several areas of the brain, especially the anterior cingulate cortex, frontal superior areas, and the precuneus. The authors' anatomic definitions are correct if the Tzourio-Mazoyer atlas is used.[14] It was produced as a segmentation of the MNI atlas. This is available in MRIcro as ANALYZE files. The conventionally ascribed functions of the cingulate cortex are considered executive control, and decision making at this level determines both verbal and motor responses.

The rostral anterior cingulate cortex area has been shown to be activated during the height of opioid and placebo analgesia response.[15] The frontal lobes are generally regarded as modulating information processing, judgment, and decision making. Little is known about the function of the precuneus; however, it has been recently argued that it, along with the anterior cingulate gyrus, may be a part of a neural network that is involved in resting consciousness and self-reflection.[16]

Overall, the results show significant activation of brain regions coincident with DI intervals. Even though the results of individual analyses and group analysis were statistically significant, the internal validity of these findings is challenged on several fronts. First, from the data accumulated it is not possible to establish causal factors for the demonstrated effects. For example, three people (the radiology technician, research nurse, and principal investigator) were in the control booth and aware of the timing of the On and Off conditions. Given these facts, it is not possible to know to what extent they influenced the findings, even though they were not deliberately sending distant intentions. Second, because the study design used a variety of healing traditions, one cannot know whether the particular modality caused the effect or it was a function of some unique and idiosyncratic interaction between members of the pair. Finally, no independent measure of the healer's abilities is available. The healing traditions represented are poorly researched, and the empiric evidence for the prowess of any given practitioner is a matter of conjecture.

Given that there are no known biological processes that can account for the significant effect of the DI protocol, the results of this study may be interpreted as consistent with the idea of entanglement in quantum mechanics theory.[17] Entanglement has been confirmed to occur between photons, and many have speculated that certain highly organized macroscopic systems, including the brain, exhibit the property of entanglement with other complex systems. In a recent study, evidence was found for nonlocal connections between separated preparations of human neurons.[18] These findings, plus the current study correlating brain activity in two sensory-isolated humans, do not fit the classic model of physics and can be interpreted as consistent with entanglement at the macroscopic level.

Several future research directions are suggested, such as replicating the present study using the same healers and recipients; examining the importance of empathy or close relationship by pairing healers with subjects who are unknown to them; using a similar protocol to study possible relationships between DI and healing in a sample of patients with a particular medical diagnosis; studying possible group effects of several DI practitioners on a subject in the scanner, and scanning healers during the DI protocol with the goals of identifying brain structures and functional brain changes during the DI state.

In summary, these findings support previous research on distant healing suggesting that human intentions may directly affect others in ways that are not entirely understood.

The authors express deep appreciation to the Earl and Doris Bakken Foundation, Kailua Kona, Hawaii, for the generous support of this research, and thank Steve Bauman, PhD, and Greg Hickok, PhD, for their consultations. The authors are grateful for the cooperation and facilities of North Hawaii Community Hospital and Roy Young's technical assistance.

Healing practices like Qigong, Johrei, Reiki, and Therapeutic Touch
are being actively studied to discover if there is a way to scientifically
measure the efficacy of biofield therapies. Based on focused energy
or mental intention, many of these biofield methods claim to combat
disease. Dr. Garret Yount and his research team tested these claims
in the following study, asking the question: Can biofield treatments
like Qigong and Therapeutic Touch keep brain cells alive?

Evaluating Biofield Treatments in the Laboratory

GARRET YOUNT, PH.D., JUSTIN MAGER, DAN MOORE,
DENISE BENDL, KENNETH RACHLIN

INTRODUCTION

Can biofield therapies, based on mental or spiritual interactions with patients at an energetic level, be studied in the
laboratory in a manner similar to other biomedical interventions? Published scientific reports indicating that isolated cells
growing in culture can register the effects of biofield treatments
constitute some of the most objective evidence for the efficacy of
these therapies. The far-reaching implications of this possibility
inspired our research group at the California Pacific Medical
Center to apply a stricter standard than is generally applied in

the field when approaching this topic.[1] Our approach was to include an equal number of independent experiments involving no healing intervention to measure the intrinsic variability in the experimental systems throughout the project. This report summarizes the results of the fifth[2] in a series of biofield studies conducted by our group incorporating such systematic negative controls.[3] This study tested whether healing treatments by experienced biofield practitioners can protect human brain cells against oxidative stress.

Background

Healing involving the manipulation of some form of superphysical energy has been described and practiced throughout history in virtually every known culture.[4] Many of these healing traditions involve rituals and practices in which a healer mediates the healing, placing their hands on or near the recipient. This form of healing has come to be termed biofield therapy and includes external Qigong, Johrei, Reiki, and Therapeutic Touch, among others. Practitioners of biofield therapies purport that during this healing relationship, the healer draws or channels superphysical energy and directs this *bioenergy* toward a biofield target. Some hypothesize that these interventions may work by impacting the global regulatory processes of life rather than the physical structures of the body.[5] Others hypothesize that the strong interpersonal component inherent in biofield treatments may mediate the effects on patients, for example by triggering neural circuits promoting calm physiological states contributing to health.[6] If there is scientific validity to these therapies, it is likely that more than one mechanism contributes to the overall healing process.

A small number of randomized, peer-reviewed clinical studies indicate that healing effects can be measured following biofield therapies but it is difficult to distinguish whether these effects are due to energetic emissions or to activation of innate healing abilities (e.g., the power of suggestion). The majority of the clinical studies of biofield therapies that have been conducted involve Therapeutic Touch, a semiformalized process used by nurses and others.[7] Fifty-eight percent of these studies showed a statistically significant result but the quality of these studies was judged poor to fair.[8] A large body of Chinese literature on clinical studies of Qigong therapy exists, but again, the quality of these studies has been questioned.[9]

In vitro studies of biofield therapies involving cells growing in culture are able to be performed in tightly controlled environments, which minimize confounding variables such as the power of suggestion. More than one hundred *in vitro* studies are reported in the Chinese literature indicating a robust responsiveness of cultured cells to Qigong but these were judged as being of poor quality.[8] The *in vitro* investigations reported in peer-reviewed journals show mixed results. Studies using cancer cells as the target of biofield treatments have shown both a growth inhibition[10] and no effect.[11, 12] Studies using normal cells as the target of biofield treatments have shown associated changes in intracellular calcium concentrations[13, 14] and another study showed an influence on the growth of bacteria.[15] Evaluating the balance of these and other *in vitro* studies is made difficult because, almost universally, reported effects of biofield therapies on cultured cells are small in magnitude and highly variable.

An *in vitro* study reported by investigators at the University of Oklahoma with co-authors from the University of Sherbrooke, Harvard Medical School, and the National Institutes of Health stands out in that it claims dramatic and reproducible effects.[16] This group tested whether treatments by a well-known Qigong practitioner can protect rat brain cells from cell death induced by oxidative stress in the form of exposure to hydrogen peroxide

(H_2O_2). Their findings suggest that Qigong treatments can reproducibly block the damaging effects of H_2O_2 to such a degree that they outperform pharmaceutical compounds currently in use as protective agents against oxidative stress. Considering the general importance of oxidative stress as a causative factor in many human diseases,[17] the need to determine the validity of these results in independent laboratories is urgent. Thus, we recruited a group of highly experienced and well-known biofield therapy practitioners to participate in a series of experiments treating cells exposed to H_2O_2. Importantly, all of the practitioners were agreeable to participation in studies at multiple institutions to enable future attempts to replicate the experiments reported here.

METHODS
Cell Culture
A large population of normal human astrocytes was divided into aliquots and frozen cryogenically for storage. Fresh aliquots were thawed at the start of each experiment and cultured within a Plexiglas incubation chamber attached to a computerized time-lapse microscope equipped with a heated stage. The chamber maintained optimum environmental conditions (37°C, 5 percent CO^2) by independent digital control units. Cells were seeded into four individual wells of a six-well plate at a density of 30,000 cells per well. H_2O_2 was added to independent cultures while still in the microscope incubation chamber at final concentrations of 600, 700, 800, and 900 µM.

Computerized Time-lapse Microscopy
Two sets of phase contrast images from each well were acquired at 300-second intervals. Every cell in the initial microscopic field was identified and numbered. All identified cells and their progeny were tracked as long as they remained within the

microscopic field. Cells that entered the microscopic field after the initial frame were not included, nor were cells identified as dead at the start of the experiment. Cell death was defined by morphological behaviors characteristic of programmed cell death including retraction of lamellipodia, rounding up, membrane blebbing, and loss of membrane integrity.[18] Cell deaths were counted for varying numbers of cells over a 5-hour period, with counts being made every half hour.

Healing Intervention

Six highly experienced biofield practitioners participated; all were internationally revered within their respective disciplines and had more than seventeen years experience treating patients. This elite team included two Qigong practitioners, two Johrei practitioners, and two internationally known healers who have developed teachable methods of biofield therapy based on innate healing abilities. To avoid implicit endorsement, practitioners were compensated for their participation through honoraria and their identities and the details of the individual techniques remain confidential. Over a period of five months, practitioners visited the laboratory individually. Healing treatments were delivered by a single practitioner 15 minutes before the cells were exposed to H_2O_2 and then 15 minutes immediately following H_2O_2 exposure. The Plexiglas wall of the incubation chamber insured that the practitioners' hands remained at least 20 cm away from the cultures at all times. For control experiments, nobody entered the microscope room during the treatment period.

The nature of the target cells was discussed with each of the practitioners prior to initiating the experiments, including the possibility that healing treatments might hasten the death of cells injured by oxidative stress because of some innate need of the cells. In light of the many potential outcomes, it was made explicit that our intention was to assess the ability of biofield treatments to protect the cells from H_2O_2-induced cell death. In general, the techniques employed by both Qigong practitioners involved first assessing the Qi of the cells through a specialized mode of perception. Secondly, the Qigong practitioners delivered external Qi toward the cells in accordance with the perceived needs of the cells. Lastly, the Qigong practitioners released any unhealthy Qi from the system. One of the two biofield healers followed procedures that were very similar to those of the Qigong practitioners, in that a form of bioenergy of the cells was first assessed and then affected by the emission of bioenergy from the healer. The approach of the Johrei practitioners was to channel divine light to the cells. Both of the Johrei practitioners followed a series of five mental procedures as follows: (1) establishing a connection to the divine, (2) consciously relaxing the body and mind, (3) visualizing healing energy traveling through the upraised hand and penetrating the cellular target, (4) taking enjoyment in participating in the experiment, (5) maintaining a feeling of gratitude. The technique of the second biofield healer resembled that of the Johrei practitioners because it involved a series of routine mental tasks that were not directly intended to produce healing. These mental tasks were practiced simultaneously with a physical technique intended to direct energy.

Blinding and Randomization

Experiments were conducted with blinding applied to each of the scientists based on previously reported methods.[19] Briefly, the experimental protocol was divided among scientists such that those responsible for handling of the cell cultures, escorting the practitioners, and gathering the raw data were all blind to each other's activities until data analyses were complete. The blinding procedures insured that the scientists handling the cells and analyzing the data were not aware of whether the cells had received biofield treatments. The location of each culture was randomly assigned to wells in the six-well plate using an online pseudo-random number generator so that each plate had equal likelihood of assignment to any incubator position. This allowed testing of whether placement in the incubator had any effect.

RESULTS
Time-lapse microscopy allowed us to observe the rate of cell death in cultures before and after treatment periods. A series of 48 independent experiments were conducted; half involved healing treatments by a biofield practitioner and half were separate control experiments involving no intervention during the treatment periods.

Each practitioner participated in four independent experiments over a two-day visit to the laboratory. Four control experiments were conducted in the days immediately following each practitioner visit. The cell cultures became contaminated during the visit by one practitioner, resulting in the eight experiments from this set (four control and four treated) being dropped from the analysis. In the remaining 40 experiments, a total of 3,755 cells were followed in control samples and 4,087 cells were followed in samples exposed to biofield treatments. The average number of cells observed in independent wells was 47 for control samples and 51 for treated samples.

We used a generalized linear model to determine whether the numbers of cell deaths over the five-hour observation period beginning at the start of treatment was significantly related to concentration of H_2O_2, date of experiment (considered as an ordinal variable with value 1 for the first date and 5 for the last date), and treatment type (biofield treatment vs. control), adjusting for number of cells at the start (i.e., before treatment). The model stipulated a binomial distribution with logit link function. Examination of residuals (observed deaths minus model-predicted deaths) revealed that, after fitting, observed counts were more variable than predicted by a binomial distribution. The analysis was repeated using deviance divided by residual degrees of freedom as a scaling parameter to adjust the standard errors for the model parameters and p-values for statistical significance. Testing was carried out hierarchically: first we tested for overall dose, date, and treatment type effects; then we tested for dose and treatment effects within each practitioner. Testing was carried out hierarchically to minimize false positives due to multiple testing, with tests at lower levels only being carried out after establishing that the higher-level factor was statistically significant.

No effect of biofield treatment was apparent when considering all of the experiments together as a whole. The dose response to increasing concentrations of H_2O_2 was clear and consistent, verifying that the target cells were in a dynamic, functional state that could be influenced by external stimuli. Initial analysis of cell deaths showed significant differences between H_2O_2 doses and between groups of experiments involving different practitioners, but no significant differences between control and treatment conditions. In post hoc analyses, the data were broken down by sets associated with individual practitioners and two were associated with only borderline significant reduction in cell death.

DISCUSSION
The lack of cellular responsiveness we observed in this study may be an indication that biofield therapies do not operate through the emission of an energy that can directly impact a person's body. Yet the possibility remains that cultured cells are not an appropriate target for biofield treatments because of their isolation from the human body. Biofield treatments might include an informational component that requires organized

cellular networks for detection, for example. Alternatively, biofield therapies might also require the presence of an *organized* biofield that could dissipate from cells kept alive after the donor is deceased. These and other reasons might explain the lack of cellular responsiveness to biofield treatments, but the results reported from the University of Oklahoma, using a similar model, suggest otherwise.[16] Resolving this apparent discrepancy would help to direct future research in this area because the issue of whether or not purely mental or spiritual activities can directly impact a person's body is pivotal in the field.

The divergence of the results reported here with those reported from the University of Oklahoma may be due to one or more differences in the experimental protocols. One difference in the protocols is the use of different cell types. We used human glial cells and the Oklahoma group used rat neuronal cells. We used human glial cells in this study for two reasons: (1) human cells more closely approximate clinical treatment settings, and (2) glial cells proliferate indefinitely and thus would allow the use of cells with an identical genetic makeup in future replication attempts in independent laboratories. Although both neuronal and glial cells originate from the brain, further specialization in information processing may have better equipped the rat neuronal cells to sense signals sent by biofield practitioners.

Another unique aspect of the protocol followed in the study reported here is the inclusion of an equal number of control experiments without any involvement of biofield practitioners. These systematic negative controls provided a measure of intrinsic variability of the experimental system throughout the entire study. Indeed, results from a series of studies in our laboratory incorporating systematic negative controls are consistent with those reported here; all found no evidence that biofield treatments were associated with cellular responses outside what could be explained by experimental variability.[20-23]

The credentials of the practitioners in both the University of Oklahoma study and this study are exceptional, yet one individual performed all of the biofield treatments in the University of Oklahoma study. It is possible that this individual has unique abilities over and above those of even the most highly experienced biofield practitioners. Thus, we argue that a research priority in the field should be to assess the reproducibility of the experiments reported by the University of Oklahoma in independent laboratories with the same practitioner and students of that practitioner. We would also urge that future studies of biofield therapies include systematic negative controls to bolster the validity of outcomes.

The authors wish to thank Brian Wong, Tri Luu, and Chester Huber for technical assistance. This work was funded by the Rockefeller-Samueli Center for Research in Mind-Body Energy and the Samueli Institute for Information Biology. The contents of the manuscript are solely the responsibility of the authors and do not necessarily represent the official views of the funders.

The tradition of African and Brazilian spiritual mediums and practitioners, otherwise known as medicine men and shamans, is a long one. Dr. Stanley Krippner and Dr. Ian Wickramasekera decided to investigate the practice from a variety of angles, including how the brain activity and physical condition of these mediums change when they are in a "trance" or altered state of consciousness while receiving messages from spirits. They address several questions: Are such practitioners more vulnerable to pathological health issues? How do dissociative trances manifest themselves in the brain?

Absorption and Dissociation in Spiritistic Brazilian Mediums

STANLEY KRIPPNER, PH.D., AND IAN WICKRAMASEKERA

INTRODUCTION

In 2000, we accepted an invitation to initiate a research study with two Brazilian spiritistic practitioners, the first a leader of rituals in both the Candomblé and the Umbanda religions, and the second a practitioner of Kardecismo spiritism. Both were regarded as "mediums" by their communities; i.e., they were thought to be able to convey messages from the dead and from other noncorporeal entities to the living.

The purpose of our study was not to evaluate the purported mediumistic abilities of these two practitioners, but to initiate psychological and psychophysiological studies that could be carried out with other practitioners from similar cultural backgrounds.

Our theoretical framework was the "high risk model" of psychosomatic and psychogenic illness. In other words, people whose mind/body relationships are incongruent and inconsistent are at "risk" for coming down with such conditions as chronic fatigue syndrome, gastrointestinal problems, lower back pains, and the like.

CULTURAL BACKGROUND

In Brazil, mediumship is a central component within the ritual practice of spiritistic religions. Mediumship involves the belief in the bodily incorporation of spiritual agents and/or the channeling of information from the divine world to the material world, often for therapeutic purposes. In the United States, "mediums" are conceptualized somewhat differently from "channelers," the former focusing on communication with the dead and the latter with a broader scope of "entities."

Mediumship is typically induced during so-called altered states of consciousness that play an important role in the rituals of "spiritistic religions," in other words, those Brazilian religions in which "spirits" occupy a central role: for example, Candomblé, Kardecismo, and Umbanda. Prevalent in their mythologies were stories about a "Sky God" and the *orixás* (also spelled *orishas*), who symbolized the primordial forces of nature. The *orixás* were believed to be powerful and terrifying, but also human in that they could be talked to and pleaded with, as well as influenced through special offerings. They could also take hold of the human mind and body through acts of spirit "incorporation," which were central features in African ritual practice.

African religious practitioners gained access to supernatural power in three ways: by making offerings to the *orixás*; by "divining," or foretelling the future with the help of an *orixá*;

and by being taken over by an *orixá*, ancestral spirit, or other entity who—when benevolent—would warn the community about possible calamities, diagnose illnesses, and prescribe cures. The "medium" or person through whom these spirits spoke and moved typically performed this task voluntarily, usually claiming not to remember the experience once it ended. The "trance," or altered state of consciousness required for the voluntary gift of the medium's mind and body to the *orixá* or spirit, was typically brought about by dancing, singing, and drumming. Of these practices, letting the *orixá* "inhabit" one's body temporarily best survived the transition from Africa to Brazil, and occasionally integrated indigenous New World techniques of mind alteration, such as using strong tobacco.

Of all the Brazilian spiritist movements, Candomblé is the one that most closely resembles the original religions of Africa, retaining the original names and worship of many West African *orixás* (Bastide, 1960). In Candomblé, devotion is typically reserved for only the *orixás* and *exús* (the messengers of the deities), which reflects its African heritage. The name "Candomblé" seems to have derived from *candombe* or *gandombe*, a community dance performed by slaves who worked on coffee plantations.

The other two most prominent spiritist movements are Kardecismo (also called Spiritism, but not to be confused with the general reference to Afro-Brazilian "spiritistic" traditions) and Umbanda. The former drew heavily upon the teachings of Allen Kardec, a French pedagogue and spiritualist (or "spiritist," as he preferred to be called), while the latter gave a greater emphasis to Brazil's Christian heritage than to the African *orixás*.

Candomblé, Kardecismo, and Umbanda, as the three major spiritistic groupings, can be differentiated along an *ethnic/class*-oriented continuum. Umbanda is situated at the center of this continuum—with *cultos de nação* (cults of African nations, like

Candomblé) at one extreme and the "more European" Kardecism on the other. Umbandistas typically draw from a broad range of beliefs and practices associated with either the "magical" Afro-Brazilian pole or the "pseudo-scientific" European-Brazilian pole. The ethnic makeups of these religious groups have historically reflected this continuum with Candomblé appealing mainly to Afro-Brazilians of poorer segments of society, Kardecismo appealing to middle-class European-Brazilians, and Umbanda appealing to a more varied mixture of ethnicities, primarily of lower classes. However, descriptions of recent changes in ethnic and class demography in each religious group defy any rigid categorization along these lines and testify to the changing religious landscape in Brazil. Along a spiritual continuum, however, the three groupings represent a commonality of belief in the spirit realm, the power and efficacy of spirit agents, and the ability of humans to interact with and embody these agents through the ritualized methods of dissociative trance such as possession.

In the late nineteenth century, and well into the twentieth, the practice of mediumship by members of these three groups and several smaller sects was identified with psychopathology by the psychiatric establishment in Brazil. In the 1920s, Nina Rodrigues considered mediumistic activity the outcome of "hysterical phenomena" allowed by the "extreme neuropathic or hysterical" and "profoundly superstitious" personality of the Negro. In 1931, Xavier de Oliveira claimed that in a period of twelve years, 9.4 percent of a total of 18,281 patients hospitalized in the Psychiatric Clinic of the University of Rio de Janeiro "suffered psychosis caused only and exclusively by Spiritism." Pacheco e Silva maintained that Kardec Spiritism and African-Brazilian mediumship act "predominantly from proneness, aggravating an already existing psychosis or stimulating latent mental disturbances in an individual of psychopathic constitution." However, these negative clinical assessments of Kardec

Spiritism and the African-Brazilian mediumistic practices were likely the result of the period's preoccupation with European scientific models as well as an unusual alliance between people from Roman Catholic and materialist backgrounds.

Within the rubric established by Roger Bastide (in the 1970s) and Lewis-Fernandez and Arthur Kleinman (in the 1990s), research data have been collected that support the position that mediumship is a skill, one that can empower its practitioners (especially if they are women in a patriarchal culture) and provide support for members of the community who are suffering from anxiety, depression, and other afflictions.

POSSESSION AND DISSOCIATION

The term "incorporation" is used by spiritistic groups in Brazil to describe situations in which practitioners allow themselves to be "taken over" by a "spirit entity" and is exemplified by mediums who volunteer their mind or body to the *orixás*. On the other hand, the term "possession" is used to define the experience of an involuntary takeover, one that is usually distressing, unwelcome, and sometimes long lasting.

However, there have been difficulties disambiguating the relationship between "possession" and concepts like "trance," "altered states," and "dissociation." In their 1972 study of the Batuque, an Afro-Brazilian possession tradition, Leacock and Leacock conceive of "possession" as "the presence in the human body of a supernatural being" and trance as "an altered psychological state." Although they also employ the expression "trance-possession," it would be a mistake to assume that the terms are synonymous. Distinctions must be made that regard "possession" as belief and "possession" as experience. That is, "possession" can refer to the *belief* in the potential for voluntary or spontaneous interaction with, or incorporation of, a benevolent or malevolent spirit.

Possession can occur without physiological alterations of consciousness (as with members of the Ethiopian *zâr* cult) or it can occur when the incorporation of a spirit is experienced concurrently with psychophysiological changes. The anthropologist Erika Bourguignon differentiated between "possession" (in which a "spirit" has produced changes in someone's behavior, health, or disposition without an accompanying shift in awareness), "possession trance" (in which someone loses conscious awareness, while the invading spirit's own behavior, speech patterns, and body movements "take over" and can be observed by outsiders), and "trance" (a so-called "altered state of consciousness" including the loss of conscious awareness without the presence of a spirit or other outside entity).

In "possession trance," the intrusive spirit may be quite benevolent, bringing new insights to the "possessed" individual by means of "automatic writing," "channeling," or "mediumship." Such instances are quite different from cases in which a malevolent sorcerer's curse or spirit entity's "earthbound" impulses and desires cause an invading entity to take over a victim's body. These types of "trance" are extremely dissociative; in other words, a person manifests experiences and behaviors that seem to exist apart from, or appear to have been disconnected from, the mainstream (or flow) of his or her conscious awareness, behavioral repertoire, and/or self-identity.

From a psychophysiological perspective, "dissociation" involves the disengagement of cognitive processes from their executive, higher-order, volitional faculties. Winkelman suggests that a wide range of culturally patterned induction techniques lead to generalized *parasympathetic dominance* in which the brain's frontal cortex exhibits high-voltage, slow-wave, synchronous EEG patterns (e.g., theta rhythms) that originate in the limbic system (hippocampal-septal region and the amygdala) and proceed to frontal regions via limbic-frontal innervations.

Winkelman also indicates that the involvement of the limbic system is an important part of the neural architecture of dissociative trance. Evidence shows that parasympathetic dominance can be induced through drumming, dancing, and chanting, all of which are common features of ritual practice. The results of a field study conducted by Don and Moura suggest the presence of a hyper-aroused brain state associated with the possession-trance behaviors of mediums. Don and Moura brought a portable electroencephalograph to remote areas of Brazil to conduct this pioneering research study.

RESEARCH PARTICIPANTS
We enlisted the cooperation of two mediums who were believed by their communities to be capable of incorporating discarnate entities. Both practitioners signed informed consent forms (designed by the Saybrook Institutional Review Board), and both encouraged us to use their actual names. A local tour guide (Eraldo), who was not associated with any of the local spiritistic movements, served as a comparison "control participant" because when working with individuals with special abilities, it is useful to make intracultural comparisons.

One of the practitioners we tested was Pai Ely (born in 1932 as Manoel Rabelo Pereira), a *pai-de-santo* ("father of the spirits") in Recife, Brazil. He conducts both Candomblé and Umbanda services at a *terreiro* or temple called the Lar de Ita Center. Earlier in his life, Pai Ely was a bank executive before he began to see and hear spirits and *orixás* when he was in his forties.

Master Oascati, Pai Ely's teacher from Benin, Africa, explained to him that it is extremely easy for one's own biases, experiences, and fantasies to contaminate the spiritual message. In Pai Ely's words, "The *orixá* paints only one small part of the picture; the medium must paint the rest." As a result, the client receives no "pure" information; according to Pai Ely it is unusual for more than 25 percent of the *orixá's* message to get through. Furthermore, many of the messages are from *exús* or from the "lower" ancestral spirits.

The other medium we tested, José Jacques Andrade, born in 1945, is active in the Kardec Spiritism movement. During a visit to his center (the Leonardo da Vinci Salon of Mediumistic Art) in 1998, Krippner observed a ceremony, which culminated with Andrade "incorporating" several famous artists (e.g., Monet, da Vinci, Cezanne). In preparation for this occurrence, Andrade and his group sang several hymns and prayed. Once the spirits had been "called," Andrade dipped both of his hands into jars of paint and, with two canvasses in front of him, swiftly began painting landscapes, still lifes, and portraits, two at a time.

Our third research participant was Eraldo, a schoolteacher and tour guide (born in 1945). He had assisted Krippner as a translator in 1993 and 1995, and was familiar with the spiritist religions of the area. All research participants denied being on any form of medication before or during the testing.

MEASURES
Dissociation
The revised version of the Dissociative Experiences Scale (DES) used in this study consists of 28 items that ask what percentage of the time (i.e., zero to 100 percent in intervals of 10) an individual experiences certain dissociative events or perceptions. The higher the DES score, the more likely it is that the respondent has a dissociative identity disorder; however, only 17 percent of those who score above 30 on the DES are diagnosed with the disorder.

Absorption
The Tellegen Absorption Scale (TAS) is intended to measure an individual's capacity for experiences that involve both the

narrowing and broadening of attentional focus. These attentional states are characterized by a significant restructuring of one's phenomenal self and worldview. Roche and McConkey call absorption a capacity to experience alterations of cognition and emotion over a broad range of situational experiences. The TAS consists of 34 true or false response items; administration time is approximately 10 minutes. A Portuguese translation of the TAS was employed in this study.

Psychophysiological Measures
Krippner and his associates obtained psychophysiological data from all three research participants with a portable computerized polygraph when they attended a parapsychological conference in Recife in 1999. They collected the polygraph data in a Recife hotel room.

The psychophysiological equipment that was used in this study measures hand temperature, heart rate, bilateral skin conductance, muscle tension (electromyography or EMG), and electrical brain activity (electroencephalography or EEG). It records responses from both the peripheral nervous system (PNS) and the central nervous system (CNS).

Each participant's psychophysiology was measured under two baseline resting conditions (eyes open; eyes closed). Each person's psychophysiology was then measured while performing intense imaginative work (e.g., "incorporating" a celebrated artist from the "spirit world" in the case of Andrade, or a discarnate entity in the case of Pai Ely) and again during the return to baseline conditions (eyes open; eyes closed). Each condition lasted for four minutes.

RESULTS: DISSOCIATIVE EXPERIENCES SCALE
Andrade obtained a score of 72, and Pai Ely obtained a score of 87, both of which fall in the "highly dissociative" category;

Eraldo received a score of 54, which also places him in the "highly dissociative" category. Accordingly, all three respondents reported that they often "have the experience of sometimes remembering a past event so vividly that [it feels] as if they were reliving that event," but only the mediums reported that they often "have the experience of feeling that their body does not seem to belong to them."

RESULTS: TELLEGEN ABSORPTION SCALE

Pai Ely obtained a score of 28, which places him in the "high absorption" category. Both Andrade and Eraldo received scores of 21, which place them in the "medium absorption" category. All three research participants claimed they were moved by songs that they enjoyed, were caught up in the action while watching a movie, and liked to watch clouds take various shapes in the sky. However, only Pai Ely claimed to anticipate statements from other people when discussing allegedly supernatural experiences, to feel imaginary matters with such intensity that they seemed real, and for music to produce colorful pictures. Pai Ely also claimed to think in visual images, to imagine his body becoming so heavy it would not move, and to occasionally feel "suspended in air" while listening to a band or orchestra.

PSYCHOPHYSIOLOGICAL RESULTS: ANDRADE

In general, the psychophysiological data obtained from Andrade reveals several incongruent findings: (1) there was a general reduction in skin conduction level across conditions. Since skin conduction is a measure of sympathetic activation or withdrawal, it is unusual to find it associated with constriction of the blood vessels and increased muscle tension during the imagination task, typically considered a relaxing condition— both sets of data suggest increased sympathetic activation in these response systems. (2) The increase in muscle tension during the eyes-closed imagination condition and the associated increase in the percentage of alpha brain wave activity during imagination are also paradoxical: these two measures (muscle tension and alpha brain waves) are typically negatively associated, not positively associated. The former indicates tension and the latter indicates relaxation.

We concluded that there were specific incongruences in the peripheral (or outer) and central (or inner) physiological response systems. These include deviations during Andrade's imagination condition that were discrepant from what is typically seen during an eyes-closed imagination condition. This supports a previous finding that physiological incongruences and differences are frequent outcomes of testing sessions with people claiming "mediumistic" abilities. Not only are there incongruences between the medium's verbal reports and behavioral observations, but also between their psychophysiological response systems.

PSYCHOPHYSIOLOGICAL RESULTS: PAI ELY

Pai Ely displayed incongruences between major physiological response systems, particularly during the imagination condition. Significant sympathetic activation was observed in the autonomic nervous system (ANS), but relaxation was noted in the central nervous system (CNS). The ANS and CNS typically function in a more integrated manner.

PSYCHOPHYSIOLOGICAL RESULTS: ERALDO

In the case of Eraldo, there were fewer discrepancies between CNS (e.g., brain wave activity) and ANS (muscle tension, blood vessel constriction, heart rate) response systems. All scores were in the normal range and were essentially congruent. However, there was a large increase in EEG alpha wave percentage in both eyes-closed conditions. This finding is consistent with Eraldo's score of 21 on the absorption scale. Despite falling in the "medium absorption" category, it was exactly the same as that of Andrade.

DISCUSSION: ABSORPTION AND DISSOCIATION

Individuals with high scores on the Tellegen Absorption Scale tend to have a strong empathic capacity. This is especially relevant in the case of Pai Ely, who deals daily with people under stress. There are members of his congregation, as well as many outsiders, who come to him for relief from some real or imagined misfortune, interpersonal conflict, or health problem.

While Andrade's score on the absorption scale was not as high as Pai Ely's, he does not have to deal as extensively or intimately with clients. When Andrade "incorporates" his artistic predecessors from the "spirit world," he often becomes so absorbed with the task that he claims not to recall the details when the discarnate entities leave the scene. This provides an important contrast to Pai Ely's perpetual involvement in the problems of his congregation and clients.

DISCUSSION: PHYSIOLOGICAL MEASURES

People with incongruences between CNS and ANS responses can be described as periodically inhabiting two worlds, one in which they are critical, rational, and practical, and another into which their fantasy and emotional reactivity expand and deepen. As such, they are often "at risk" for somaticization, i.e., psychosomatic illnesses. Both sets of descriptors apply to Pai Ely, who "incorporates" discarnate entities while also managing a large and successful temple.

The other medium, Jacques Andrade, also displayed CNS/ANS incongruences, despite receiving a score in the "medium absorption" category. His duties at the Kardec temple are not as demanding as those of Pai Ely, nor does he spend the amount of time "incorporating" entities, as does the *pai-de-santo*.

Incongruences between CNS and ANS response systems are not unusual among spiritual practitioners. It is taken for granted that some practitioners, especially self-styled "mediums" and "channelers," will demonstrate incongruences between their behavioral observations and verbal reports. For example, they might appear calm and composed, but speak of calamitous events from their clients' "past lives" or terrifying episodes from the lives of their clients' deceased relatives.

It would be useful to administer the Creative Imagination Scale to test for fantasy-proneness, and the Hartmann Boundaries Questionnaire to evaluate thinness and thickness of psychological "boundaries." In other words, there are many aspects of the mind/body relationships of these two remarkable practitioners that we did not study.

CONCLUSION

Spiritual practitioners often are "at risk" for stress-related symptoms because of these incongruences. Among the most common incongruences are verbal reports of low negative affect while psychophysiological test data indicate otherwise.

The practical implications of these data involve the health status of mediumistic practitioners. Given the incongruences that often characterize their physiological response systems, they need to voluntarily create "buffers" that will help them maintain their physical and emotional well-being. In their 2002 study of Kardec mediums, Negro, Palladino-Negro, and Louza found that those research participants characterized by extensive training attained favorable scores on measures of socialization and adaptation. However, pathological signs were detected among the group of younger mediums with less training and diminished social support.

The stress that accompanies mediumship can be modified by social support systems, by programs that involve voluntarily control of internal states (e.g., biofeedback, meditation), and by regimens for healthy living. There is some evidence that, at least in the United States, self-styled "mediums" and "channelers" are at greater risk than are other spiritual practitioners such as "healers" and "intuitives." If this is correct, self-care and healthy lifestyles need to accompany the concern that these practitioners frequently demonstrate toward their students and clients.

The authors express their gratitude to the Institute of Noetic Sciences, the Saybrook Graduate School Chair for the Study of Consciousness, the Society for Scientific Exploration, the Tinker Foundation, and to Dr. Lonnie Barbach for their financial support for this investigation.

Transformations of consciousness—those moments that change one's life forever—are experienced by people from all different spiritual and cultural backgrounds, and can arrive by many different means, from meditation or prayer to a personal tragedy or a life-threatening illness. Marilyn Mandala Schlitz, Ph.D., Cassandra Vieten, Ph.D., and Tina Amorok, Psy.D., leading scientists from the Institute of Noetic Sciences, set out to explore what facilitates such transformations, regardless of the practice or belief or circumstances they sprang from. In the following adapted excerpt from their book *Living Deeply: The Art and Science of Transformation in Everyday Life,* they share data gathered from individuals of every background imaginable, all of whom have experienced profound moments of transformation. Among the many things they uncovered were some basic principles for opening to and deepening the transformative process in our lives.

Living Deeply

The Art and Science of Transformation in Everyday Life

MARILYN MANDALA SCHLITZ, PH.D., CASSANDRA VIETEN, PH.D., AND TINA AMOROK, PSY.D.

We are at a unique moment in human history. Never before have so many worldviews, belief systems, and ways of understanding reality come into contact. Buddhist monks are sitting down with Harvard scientists to talk about the neuroscience of mindfulness. Indigenous healers are working side by side with physicians to treat patients in major hospitals. Quantum physicists and living-systems biologists are confirming traditionally held spiritual views of consciousness.

This engagement of different ways of understanding what's real and true is leading to the discovery of new tools for living in the midst of complexity. As ancient spiritual wisdom converges with the latest scientific understandings of the world and our place in it, we are finding new answers to the age-old questions of "Who am I?" and "What am I capable of becoming?"

In this essay, we share some of what we've learned about transformations in consciousness, through a decade-long program of research at the Institute of Noetic Sciences (IONS). Edgar Mitchell, an Apollo 14 astronaut, founded IONS in 1973. Having had the remarkable opportunity to walk on the moon, Mitchell then had the window seat on the way home. During the flight back, a moment of epiphany occurred in which his entire sense of meaning and purpose shifted. In that moment he understood that the major crises of our times are due not to aspects inherent to the external world, but to flawed and inadequate worldviews. The mission of IONS is to explore consciousness through both science and human experience in order to advance individual and collective transformation.

Noetic refers to knowledge that comes to us directly through our subjective experiences or inner authority. This type of knowledge might take the form of an intuition that helps guide one's decisions, or an epiphany that leads one to a creative breakthrough. Moreover, noetic experiences often carry an unusual level of authority that can help guide one to new understandings and new ways of being. Noetic experiences thus differ from the kind of knowledge that comes through reason or the objective study of the external world. However, we argue that it is both possible and necessary to bring to this realm of intuitive knowledge a scientific perspective and method. Bringing a scientific approach to noetic phenomena has allowed IONS to delve deeply into the nature of human consciousness and its vast potentials.

MARILYN MANDALA SCHLITZ, PH.D., CASSANDRA VIETEN, PH.D., AND TINA AMOROK, PSY.D.

Transformative experiences such as the one Edgar Mitchell describes are not uncommon. The General Social Survey in 2004 found that about 50 percent of Americans report having had a religious or spiritual experience that changed their lives. Miller and C'de Baca (1994, 2001) have described a phenomenon they term quantum change, defined as "sudden, dramatic, and enduring transformations that affect a broad range of personal emotion, cognition, and behavior." Noting that behavioral science had yet to develop even a name for these commonly reported experiences, Miller and C'de Baca use the metaphor of quantum physics to discuss these kinds of sudden transformations. One of the hallmarks of a *quantum change*, the researchers found, is the recognition that something unusual is occurring, something that means your life will never be the same again. Such changes are rarely remembered as willful or voluntary events; rather, the majority of people whom the authors interviewed reported that the experience took them completely by surprise; it was both unannounced and uninvited. Another hallmark of quantum change is the sense that what has happened to you is profoundly beneficial and positive. Finally, the authors argue that the sudden change they have studied is permanent. In Miller and C'de Baca's own words, "quantum changes convey the sense of having passed through a one-way door. There is no going back."

All science, and all spirituality, begin with the quest to explore and then describe in detail a phenomenon—what causes it, what factors facilitate it, what factors inhibit it, what its outcomes are, and what mechanisms explain its occurrence—often to discover how the process can be facilitated intentionally. A good example is cancer remission. It is as natural for scientists as it is for mystics to delve as deeply as possible into healing events and positive outcomes in hopes that a deeper understanding of the phenomena will yield clues to facilitating or supporting the positive process in others. For the mystic, this exploration might lead to a deep inward journey, initiation into the mysteries of traditions that seem to hold some keys to the experience, or many years of painstaking spiritual practices that shed light on the phenomenon. For the scientist, it may involve years of data collection and analysis, whether this takes the form of detailed interviews, reams of EEG printouts, hundred-megabyte data-bases of brain scans, or step-by-step clinical trials that test and retest potential biological targets or pharmacologic agents, also to shed greater light on the phenomenon of interest. In our case, our single-minded focus was on the phenomenon of experiences people have, and practices they engage in, that stimulate and sustain a new worldview that may best be described as positive consciousness transformation (a term we will unpack later in more detail).

In the fall of 1997, our team of researchers initiated a study focused on the process of transformation. We collected hundreds of narrative descriptions of transformations experienced by people representing many walks of life. From mundane to life-threatening, these experiences led our respondents to fundamental shifts in their sense of self and their way of being in the world. For one man it came during his time as a conscientious objector in Vietnam. Through a specific prayer, in an extraordinary moment, he found inner peace even as he saw his colleagues being shot down. For a mother and daughter, it came when the mother used energy healing to help her distraught daughter find balance during a life transition, leading to profound transformative shifts for both.

We were intrigued by the fact that while the experiences people shared with us differed widely, a golden thread of com-monality shone through them all. Some experiences occurred in exceptional situations; others in ordinary, everyday situa-tions. Some were initiated by experiences of great suffering; others by experiences of awe and wonder. But in each, a radical broadening of worldview and redefinition of identity, meaning, and purpose took place.

Despite differences in content and context, the process of transformation was described very similarly—often even with the very same words. Whether told by a seasoned meditator or a mother of three who had never meditated at all, these stories hinted at a jewel-like tapestry of human experience that transcends cultural differences. As we analyzed the stories for patterns that would shed light on the inner workings of transformation, we found ourselves filled with more questions: What constitutes a transformation of consciousness? What triggers transformation? How can we sustain the moments that move us beyond ourselves? And what impact do transformational experiences have on how we live our lives?

Seeking answers, we took advantage of the wide range of teachers and leaders in the human potential movement living and working in the San Francisco Bay Area and convened three focus groups between September 1998 and May 1999. To our surprise and delight, teachers from different transformational programs came eagerly. They, too, were seeking answers to questions about the mystery of transformation. The discussions were poignant, honest, and often profoundly moving. Together we began to map deep inventories of life experience that led the participants to express gratitude, feelings of connectedness, and a strong sense of community. Often, the transformational journey is lonely, even for the masters themselves.

Inspired—and still filled with more questions than answers—we decided to probe the topic of transformation more deeply, and with greater scientific rigor. Beginning in 2002, we invited fifty world-renowned scholars, teachers, and practitioners to participate in detailed research interviews; an additional ten teachers were selected to help round out our research sample. These teachers were selected specifically to represent a diverse range of transformative practices and philosophies. They represent traditional religions, spiritual philosophies, and modern transformative movements with roots in Eastern, Western, and indigenous traditions, as well as forms that blend many paths—sometimes referred to as integral. Our overarching goals were to explore the phenomenon of consciousness transformation and learn more about the various transformative paths that lead to beneficial outcomes for self and community. From these hundred hours of videotaped interview data, we engaged in a rigorous process of qualitative analysis, systematically coding each interview line by line, and distilling from the resulting nearly 20,000 lines of data a set of common themes relevant to many different aspects of transformation. How does it begin? What qualities can each individual bring to the process? What practices are helpful to support the transformative process? What are the most relevant qualities one cultivates through transforming their worldview?

In addition, we launched an online survey, both to begin to answer some of the questions that remained and to test some of our hypotheses (Vieten, Cohen, and Schlitz, 2008). Do contemplative practices really foster the transformative process? Is a teacher or a community of like-minded practitioners useful? What kinds of practices are most helpful to what kinds of people? We heard from a schoolteacher in Illinois, a nurse in New York, a businessman in Los Angeles, and many others. Answering dozens of specific and open-ended questions, over a thousand respondents helped us learn more about similarities and differences in the transformative process across people and practices. While this sample is self-selected, and as such isn't representative of the general public in the way a random selection of all American households would be, it has offered a valuable opportunity for studying transformation in a large number of people who have lived through the process. Over

80 percent of those sampled reported having had at least one profoundly transformative experience, and 90 percent engage regularly in some form of transformative practice. The lives of these nine hundred people have become natural laboratories for studying the transformative process.

Throughout our research, we were guided by both perennialism and pluralism. The "perennial philosophy" was a term first used by sixteenth-century Italian philosopher Agostino Steuco in his book *De perenni philosophia libri X* of 1540. In the eighteenth century, German mathematician and philosopher Gottfried Leibniz used this term to designate a universal or shared set of truths that underlie all philosophies and religions, and Aldous Huxley later popularized it in his classic book *The Perennial Philosophy* (1945). Similarly, in our research we sought to find commonalities in the transformative process, across individuals, cultures, religions, and philosophies—a common map of the transformative terrain that would apply to people from all walks of life. As much as there are things that distinguish each of the perspectives, practices, or approaches we studied, our goal has been to find points of intersection.

On the other hand, as we engaged in our comparative analysis, we were informed by the work of cultural pluralism. Diana Eck of the Pluralism Project at Harvard University makes the distinction between diversity, which is a demographic fact, and pluralism, which is the celebration of difference (2006). Pluralism is an active engagement with diversity. It requires participation with "the other." Pluralism recognizes that while there is common and enduring wisdom that can be found in edicts such as the Golden Rule—wisdom that is likely to be equally applicable to all traditions—it's a serious oversimplification to view disparate religious, spiritual, and transformative frameworks as homogeneous. Our experience thus far is that while commonalities among traditions point to a robust model of transformation that goes beyond sects and cultures, each individual tradition—and each individual person—provides a unique perspective that the others may not have. Forest-dwelling Buddhist monks who have explored the nature of their own minds for hours and years on end in silent solitude are likely to have something different to tell us about transformation than do nuns who have dedicated their lives to serving in urban-jungle soup kitchens.

Ultimately, our research represents a kind of map of the transformative terrain. While we aren't able to traverse the entire terrain by ourselves, we have been able to talk to the explorers who have been there, some of whom have traversed common pathways and some of whom have taken exotic journeys and are bringing back their travel journals to share what they found. We explored the mystery of consciousness with a Christian monk, a Lakota elder, a rabbi, and a Zen Buddhist roshi. We identified the common elements of transformation in the experiences of a Himalayan yoga swami, a transpersonal psychologist, a seasoned oncologist, and a Methodist minister. We found, amazingly, that an evangelical Christian, a successful businessman, a devout Sufi, a skilled athlete, a dedicated physician, a reluctant soldier, a Jewish mother, and an agnostic musician are all walking surprisingly similar paths. We share some of these overlapping cartographies with you in hopes that you will recognize some of the terrain yourself and begin to more consciously create your own path to transformation.

In each phase of our research program, what has touched us most—what was emphasized again and again, and what we want to share with you—is the fact that transformation is an ongoing, natural process that's available to you right now. It's something that you can cooperate with in ways large and small, every day of your life. This excerpt from our new book, *Living Deeply: The Art and Science of Transformation in Everyday Life*, will highlight resources to help you maintain your balance, while recruiting you to actively collaborate with the forces—both internal and external—that conspire to move you toward wholeness.

LIVING DEEPLY

Our decade of research on transformation has found that dramatic and lasting change for the better springs from radically shifting your perspective of who you are. The most essential change, the one from which all other changes spring, is a change in your worldview and your perception of what's possible. Great external changes often come out of this shift in perspective. You may well find that as meaning and purpose become more clear to you, things that are out of alignment in your life gradually (and sometimes quickly) fall away. But the most fundamental change is within you; it is a profound shift in your perspective, where you direct your attention and your intention.

Seeing with New Eyes

What is it that actually shifts in a transformational experience? Before we begin to delve more deeply into the terrain of consciousness transformation, let's define what we mean by consciousness. Consciousness is the quality of mind that includes your own internal reality.

Most of our teachers told us that consciousness extends beyond our personal awareness and perceptions, and that ultimately, consciousness is the ground of Being. Integral scholar, Haridas Chaudhuri (1977) notes that Heidegger's concept of "Being" is similar to the Upanishad concept of the ultimate ground of Being or "Bahman." He writes, "It is that from which all beings are born, that which when born they live, and that which when departing, they enter" (25). In the ontological sense, consciousness is the life force behind, within and beyond the phenomenal world. In this way our research findings affirm that all things have consciousness and what we are exploring is how the human experience of this abiding consciousness transforms. The human experience of consciousness is the quality of mind.

It includes self-awareness, your relationships to your environment, the people in your life, and your worldview or model of reality. Simply put, your consciousness determines how you experience the world. Your consciousness, or your perception of reality, is created by the interactions of your subjective and objective lives. Your subjective life is what exists in your inner experience; your objective life is what's "out there" in the world. The convergence of your self-identity and your perceptions of the world gives rise to your worldview—and thus how you relate to, mediate, and ascribe meaning to both these inner and outer worlds.

States of consciousness occur on a continuum from being awake and aware of yourself and your environment to being in an unaware, not-wakeful state of dreamless sleep or coma. While we're most aware of two particular levels of consciousness— being awake and asleep—there are, in fact, many levels of consciousness, including nonordinary states of consciousness. In the course of an average day, you may experience a range of these states, such as: intense alertness, daydreaming, grogginess, sleeping and dreaming, heightened emotional states, or intoxication from alcohol or drugs. If you've ever experienced general anesthesia, you've traveled through many states of consciousness in a very short period of time.

However, consciousness not only refers to these transient, ever-changing states; it also refers to the way that we perceive things in general and across situations. When used this way, consciousness designates the overall way that you perceive the world and your place in it. In other words, your consciousness is every aspect of how you experience and understand reality. If all of your experiences, your various states of consciousness, were weather patterns—clouds, rain, rainbows, tornados, hurricanes, or summer breezes—your consciousness would be the sky in which they take place. Your consciousness is the context in which all of your experiences, perceptions, thoughts, or feelings converge.

It is this abiding aspect of consciousness that we're most interested in when we talk about consciousness transformation. The general consciousness you possess profoundly influences the states of consciousness you experience on a day-to-day basis. For example, if you're a person who tends to be generally optimistic, your general consciousness probably includes the assumptions that, overall, people are good and finding a solution to a problem is almost always possible. Thus, in your daily life, you'll react to situations in a generally trusting and open manner. In contrast, if you're a person who tends to react aggressively to difficult situations, your general consciousness probably includes the assumptions that the world isn't safe and you must defend yourself against even the smallest perceived threat. In other words, our various states of consciousness emerge out of our general pattern—personality traits, attitudes, beliefs, behaviors, etc.—of relating to the world. You can see, therefore, how transforming your general consciousness can have profound implications for the way you think, behave, and feel in your everyday life.

Ultimately, we define consciousness transformation as a profound shift in your experience of consciousness, resulting in long-lasting changes in the way you understand and relate to yourself, others, and the world. We use the term "transformative experience" to refer to an experience that results in a lasting change in worldview, as opposed to an extreme, extraordinary, peak, or spiritual experience that doesn't necessarily translate into long-term changes in your way of being.

Although transformation results in changes in thoughts, feelings, and behaviors, the actual process doesn't require changing these things directly. In fact, most experts we interviewed told us that consciousness itself doesn't change. Instead, it is your perception of consciousness that changes. Said in another way, who you are "authentically" doesn't change—rather, as false selves are shed and buried elements of yourself are retrieved and integrated, your expression of your self aligns with who you truly are. Thought patterns, attitudes, behaviors, and ways of being in the world that are incongruent with your core self may drop away. While there are no magic formulas for how consciousness transformations come about, our research across different traditions and practices reveals informative patterns.

Is this shift in perspective purely subjective, something that we can only experience firsthand, or can science offer us a more objective understanding of how people come to see the world in a completely new way? Daniel Simons, an associate professor at the University of Illinois at Urbana-Champaign, conducts research on visual cognition, perception, attention, and memory. Particularly fascinating is his research on inattentional blindness, which he defines as people's "failure to notice unusual and salient events in their visual world when attention is otherwise engaged and the events are unexpected" (Simons and Chabris, 1999, 1062).

Simons's studies build on the work of psychologists Arien Mack of the New School for Social Research and Irvin Rock, formerly at the University of California, Berkeley (Mack and Rock, 1998). All of these scientists explore the nature of perception when attention is directed away from a target object. In a series of fascinating studies, these researchers have shown that we can literally miss the proverbial elephant (or in this case, gorilla) in the room if we are not expecting to see it or our attention is fixated on other things.

In one classic experiment, participants are asked to pay attention to a video in which three people in black shirts and three people in white shirts pass a basketball to one another. Participants are asked to count the number of times the team with the white shirts passes the ball to one another. In most instances, participants are quite close to one another in their final figures, some saying sixteen times, a few reporting fifteen times, others saying seventeen times (Simons and Chabris, 1999). This discrepancy alone speaks to how people can perceive the exact same situation slightly differently. (If you'd like to try this experiment for yourself before the spoiler in the next paragraph, stop reading right now and visit the Visual Cognition Laboratories website at http://viscog.beckman.uiuc. edu/djs_lab/demos.html. You won't be disappointed!)

Vastly more interesting is what happens next, when researchers instruct the participants to watch the exact same video, this time without focusing on anything in particular. Almost all participants now see a life-size person in a gorilla suit walk directly into the center of the basketball game, stop, pound on his chest several times, and saunter out. People who participate in this exercise frequently don't believe that this is the same video. It is.

Studies like this one suggest that our brains are wired so that we don't consciously perceive even major aspects of our experience when our focus is fixed on something else. Other types of perceptual blindness, such as change blindness, occur when we fail to perceive significant changes in what we're seeing because the change happens very gradually—very much like the frog in the pot who doesn't notice that the water is boiling if it happens slowly enough. In Mack and Rock's book, *Inattentional Blindness* (1998), the researchers emphasize that perception doesn't just depend on having open, functional eyes. Rather, perception depends on attention, and attention depends on underlying cognitive processes. They've concluded from their research that without attention, nothing is consciously perceived. People inhibit their attention from unexpected stimuli, thus preventing conscious perception. This, in turn, leads to significant increases in inattentional blindness.

How does this relate to the role that perspective shifts play in transformations? These findings tell us that when we're focused on something and encounter an experience that isn't expected, we may not consciously perceive its existence. It's possible, particularly in relation to sudden transformations, that when your attention broadens from what has been preoccupying it and is brought into a more open field of awareness, your inattentional blindness is "cured"—what you couldn't consciously perceive previously is now revealed. This fits very well with what many teachers from various traditions told us. There may be much more to your life than you're allowing yourself to be aware of.

DOORWAYS TO TRANSFORMATION

How do consciousness transformations—the kind that make a long-term difference in your life—begin? You can probably identify in retrospect some turning points in your life, times about which you can honestly say, "After that I was never the same." For example, you may have experienced a shift in perspective after a serious illness, or the loss of a loved one, or a particularly awe-inspiring moment like giving birth to a child or visiting the Great Pyramids. But these moments are unpredictable. They can seem so random, and so particular to each unique situation, that you may wonder, "Do I just have to wait until I get blown away by some big moment to make a real change?"

MARILYN MANDALA SCHLITZ, PH.D., CASSANDRA VIETEN, PH.D., AND TINA AMOROK, PSY.D.

Perhaps the most robust finding of our research is common knowledge—profound transformations are frequently triggered by intense suffering or crisis. Difficult or painful life events often create new levels of openness or vulnerability, thus setting the stage for a shift in worldview. A brush with death, the loss of a loved one, a mental or emotional breakdown, an injury, loss of a job—such painful challenges can shatter defenses that have taken us a lifetime to build. Whether it's the difficulty of realizing that something isn't working in your life, or the suffering you experience when painful challenges cross your path, our research participants identified pain as far and away the most common catalyst for change.

Of course, not all doorways to or catalysts of transformation are filled with pain. Of our survey respondents, exactly equal numbers became interested in transformation after a difficult life event as due to some other process or event. And although 23 percent said the transformative experience was very unpleasant, 51 percent described it as very pleasant. In fact, the emotions most commonly cited as accompanying transformative experiences included feeling "interested, alert, attentive, and inspired" (Vieten, Cohen, and Schlitz, 2008). Moments of profound awe, wonder, or transcendent bliss can provide a glimpse of something that is so compelling, so completely beyond what you've previously realized is possible, that they can instill in you a strong intention to find out more about what happened—no matter what it takes.

For many people, noetic experiences occur in the context of a nonordinary state of consciousness. Charles Tart describes nonordinary states of consciousness as denoting "alterations in both the content and pattern of the functioning of consciousness" (1975, 16). Stan Grof, one of our research participants, a founder of the field of transpersonal psychology and a pioneer in the study of nonordinary states of consciousness, argues that transformation comes about when you're forced to reconcile your ordinary worldview with insights gained from extraordinary or nonordinary experiences.

There is a transformational relationship between the experience of everyday life and the experience of the other dimensions from which we are normally cut off. When you open to these normally hidden dimensions, it transforms you, because you have to take that experience into consideration. Like when people discovered that the world was round, when up to that point they believed it was flat. The experiences that you can have in nonordinary states are equally radical. You realize that your perception of the world and yourself was not accurate before. You have new experiences that you cannot ignore. You have to integrate them into your everyday experience of the world. This changes both who you think you are and your understanding of the nature of reality. (Grof, 2003)

PATHS AND PRACTICES

Now that we're aware of our tendency both to disregard new information and, when we do notice it, to try to fit it into our expectations (as described in the inattentional blindness section above), what qualities can you cultivate to help you attend to and get the most out of potentially transformative experiences? How do you translate extraordinary—or even ordinary—life experiences into transformations that result in significant, long-lasting changes in your consciousness?

Even when a transformative experience is deeply profound, new realizations can be fragile. To take hold, transformations must be reinforced. As one of our research participants Reverend Lauren Artress told us, "Transformation disappears if you don't honor it" (2003). Changes in your worldview can happen in an instant, but mastery of new kinds of thought or behavior often requires the cultivation of new ways of being.

Most of our interviewees and survey respondents emphasized the importance of a regular transformative practice. Of our self-selected survey sample, 68 percent reported engaging in a formal practice, with the most common practices being meditation and devotional practices such as prayer. A full 73 percent reported engaging in informal practices, including writing, reading, visualization, studying spiritual or consciousness-oriented topics, walking in nature, personal prayer, music, art, and affirmations (Vieten, Cohen, and Schlitz, 2008).

Of course, there are literally thousands of different ways to engage in transformative practice. Moreover, transformative practices themselves can take many different forms, ranging from contemplative prayer to mindfulness meditation, from the Twelve Steps of Alcoholics Anonymous to Holotropic Breathwork, from walking a labyrinth to growing a garden—and many more. With all this diversity, it's fair to ask, what exactly makes something a transformative practice? While we don't want to gloss over this rich diversity of forms, our research suggests that there are four essential elements of transformative practice that appear across widely varying traditions. These include: intention, attention, repetition, and a generous dose of guidance to round out the practice equation. We've also seen that practice on its own isn't enough: if practice becomes an end rather than a means, it can become an obstacle to the transformative process.

WHY PRACTICE?

We've shared some of the ways that transformative practice works to affect profound and lasting life changes. But questions still remain: What does practice do? How exactly does it work? How can sitting in silence for a brief period every day have far-reaching and profound effects on your life? Why would moving your body in particular ways every day affect your mental and emotional health to a large extent? Indeed, how do contemplative practices, such as meditation, prayer, or walking in nature, actually move us through the process of transformation?

Our research suggests five ways in which practices inform the transformative process. First, they can help you cultivate insight into your situation and the true nature of things. Second, they can help return the ego to its appropriate role: a useful tool for navigating the ins and outs of the material world, but only one of many aspects of your internal life. Practice can make room for other aspects of your being—creativity, intuition, surprise, emotion, physicality, etc.—to emerge and take their rightful places as sources of inspiration, information, and motivation. And as you build a more complete self-structure, you can transcend the limited, self-centered, egoic sense of self. You learn to ride the ego; it serves you rather than you serving it. Third, as you become more in touch with your authentic self, you begin to clear away whatever is out of alignment with that self. Many transformative practices include elements of purification that can help you rid yourself of outdated beliefs and habits that no longer serve you. Fourth, as these blocks are cleared away, you become better able to move out of the past and into the present, into a place of power and acceptance. Living in the moment becomes a way of finding the beauty in all your thoughts and deeds. And finally, our research suggests that transformation requires a balance between courage, determination, discipline, and choice on the one hand, and letting go, acceptance, and surrendering to the mystery of transformation on the other. Releasing control and learning to embrace the unknown are as important to transformation as is sustaining a strong intention and motivation to live deeply in each moment, for the transformative journey can take you to places that you would never have dreamed, through circuitous routes that you could never have predicted.

456   MARILYN MANDALA SCHLITZ, PH.D., CASSANDRA VIETEN, PH.D., AND TINA AMOROK, PSY.D.

MILESTONES OF CONSCIOUSNESS TRANSFORMATION

Embodying transformation is a process of continual exploration. It can be a simple act of compassion, or a moment when you stopped and felt gratitude. By finding ways to remind yourself to be aware, you can begin to live transformation in every thought and deed. As life and practice become a seamless whole, you may experience core shifts in your personal identity that translate into lasting changes in worldview. Through this shift in worldview, our research suggests that over time, you begin to see glimmers of the sacred shining through even the most mundane and sorrowful of experiences in everyday life. Our emerging model of transformation recognizes the dynamic and nonlinear nature of the transformative process. This idea is as revolutionary as it is ancient. Living deeply doesn't require retreating to a mountaintop or embarking on a hero's journey; rather, the convergence of life and practice is about the hero's return—in which you bring the fruits of your journey of self-discovery back home, into your life, your family, and your community.

The goal of our work has been to weave together the rigors of the scientific perspective with the deep wisdom of the world's traditions to create a nondenominational, multicultural map to help guide you on your way through the transformations—whether large or small—that impact your life, your relationships, and your community. We seek to unearth the commonalities of diverse practices, to decipher pathways to transformation that you can use regardless of whether you're religious or spiritual; involved in business, the military, or the PTA; or get your peace of mind from meditation or the golf course. Ultimately, our findings encourage you to become the scientist of your own experience and the cartographer of your own transformative journey. The opportunity is yours. Welcome to the adventure.

Notes

Candace Pert with Nancy Marriott: The Science of Emotions and Consciousness

Sources for this chapter include:

Healy, David. 1997. *The antidepressant era*. Cambridge, MA: Harvard University Press. This historical and neurochemical analysis leads to a clear look at what antidepressants reveal about both the workings of the brain and the sociology of drug marketing.

Kandel, Eric R. 2006. *In search of memory: The emergence of a new science of mind*. New York: W.W. Norton.

Mezey, Eva. 2003. Transplanted bone marrow generates new neurons in human brains. *Proceedings of National Academy of Science USA*, February 4.

Pert, A., C. Pert, and M. Mishkin. 1981. Opiate receptor gradients in monkey cerebral cortex: Correspondence with sensory processing hierarchies. *Science* 211 (March 13).

Overton, Donald (Professor of Psychology, McGill University; Director, Social Neuroscience Laboratory).

See the Swedish study by Reckner-Olsson, A. et al. 2001. Comorbidity and lifestyle, reproductive factors, and environmental exposures associated with rheumatoid arthritis. *Annals of the Rheumatic Diseases* 60 (October): 934-939.

The primary scientific studies that discuss the stem-cell origins of small-cell lung cancer and the ability of emotional neuropeptides to direct tumor cell metastases are Ruff, M. R., and C. B. Pert. 1985. Origin of small cell lung cancer. *Science* 229: 679–680; and Ruff, M. R., E. Schiffmann, V. Terranova, and C. B. Pert. 1985. Neuropeptides are chemoattractants for human macrophages and tumor cells: a mechanism for metastasis. *Clinical Immunology Immunopathology* 37: 387–396.

Stone, Hal, and Sidra Stone. Materials (books, tapes, CDs) available through their website: http://delos-inc.com.

Gary Small: Effects of a Fourteen-Day Healthy Longevity Lifestyle Program on Cognition and Brain Function

1. T. Crook, R. T. Bartus, S. H. Ferris et al., Age-associated memory impairment: proposed diagnostic criteria and measures of clinical change: Report of a National Institute of Mental Health work group, *Developmental Neuropsychology* 2 (1986): 261–276.

2. G. J. Larrabee and T. H. Crook, Estimated prevalence of age-associated memory impairment derived from standardized tests of memory function, *International Psychogeriatrics* 6 (1994): 95–104.

3. R. C. Petersen, J. C. Stevens, M. Ganguli et al., Practice parameter: Early detection of dementia: Mild cognitive impairment (an evidence-based review); Report of the quality standards subcommittee of the American Academy of Neurology, *Neurology* 56 (2001): 1133–1142.

4. R. L. Kahn and J. W. Rowe, *Successful aging* (New York: Pantheon, 1998).

5. M. P. Mattson, Existing data suggest that Alzheimer's disease is preventable, *Annals of the New York Academy of Sciences* 924 (2004): 153–159.

6. H. M. Fillit, R. N. Butler, A. W. O'Connell et al., Achieving and maintaining cognitive vitality with aging, *Mayo Clinic Proceedings* 77 (2002): 681–696.

7. G. W. Small, What we need to know about age related memory loss, *BMJ* 324 (2002): 1502–1505.

8. G. Small and G. Vorgan, *The longevity bible* (New York: Hyperion, 2006).

9. H. Van Praag, G. Kempermann, and F. H. Gage, Neural consequences of environmental enrichment, *Nature Reviews Neuroscience* 1 (2000): 191–198.

10. T. Fritsch, K. A. Smyth, S. M. Debanne et al., Participation in novelty-seeking leisure activities and Alzheimer's disease, *Journal of Geriatric Psychiatry and Neurology* 18 (2005): 134–141.

11. T. Del Ser, V. Hachinski, H. Merskey et al., An autopsy-verified study of the effect of education on degenerative dementia, *Brain* 122 (1999): 2309–2319.

12. K. Ball, D. B. Berch, K. F. Helmers et al., Effects of cognitive training interventions with older adults: A randomized controlled trial, *JAMA: Journal of the American Medical Association* 288 (2002): 2271–2281.

13. F. H. Gage, Neurogenesis in the adult brain, *Journal of Neuroscience* 22 (2002): 612–613.

14. R. P. Friedland, T. Fritsch, K. A. Smyth et al., Patients with Alzheimer's disease have reduced activities in midlife compared with healthy control-group members, *Proceedings of the National Academy of Sciences USA* 98 (2001): 3440–3445.

15. A. F. Kramer, S. Hahn, E. McAuley et al., Exercise, aging and cognition: Healthy body, healthy mind? in *Human factors interventions for the health care of older adults*, ed. A. D. Fisk and W. Rogers (Hillsdale, NJ: Erlbaum, 2001).

16. J. A. Luchsinger, M. X. Tang, S. Shea et al., Caloric intake and the risk of Alzheimer disease, *Archives of Neurology* 549 (2002): 1258–1263.

17. H. C. Hendrie, A. Ogunniyi, K. S. Hall et al., Incidence of dementia and Alzheimer disease in 2 communities: Yoruba residing in Ibadan, Nigeria, and African Americans residing in Indianapolis, Indiana, *JAMA: Journal of the American Medical Association* 285 (2001): 739–747.

18. V. Solfrizzi, F. Panza, F. Torres et al., High monounsaturated fatty acids intake protects against age-related cognitive decline, *Neurology* 52 (1999): 1563–1569.

19. M. J. Engelhart, M. I. Geerlings, A. Ruitenberg et al., Dietary intake of antioxidants and risk of Alzheimer disease, *JAMA: Journal of the American Medical Association* 287 (2002): 3223–3229.

20. W. Willett, J. Manson, and S. Liu, Glycemic index, glycemic load, and risk of type 2 diabetes, *American Journal of Clinical Nutrition* 76 (2002): 274S–278S.

21. K. Oh, F. B. Hu, E. Cho et al., Carbohydrate intake, glycemic index, glycemic load, and dietary fiber in relation to risk of stroke in women, *American Journal Epidemiology* 161 (2005): 161–169.

22. R. M. Sapolsky, Glucocorticoids, stress, and their adverse neurological effects: relevance to aging, *Experimental Gerontology* 34 (1999): 721–732.

23. J. W. Newcomer, G. Selke, A. K. Melson et al., Decreased memory performance in healthy humans induced by stress-level cortisol treatment, *Archives of General Psychiatry* 56 (1999): 527–533.

24. R. S. Wilson, D. A. Evans, J. L. Bienas et al., Proneness to psychological distress is associated with risk of Alzheimer's disease, *Neurology* 61 (2003): 1479–1485.

25. G. W. Small, P. V. Rabins, P. P. Barry et al., Diagnosis and treatment of Alzheimer disease and related disorders: Consensus statement of the American Association for Geriatric Psychiatry, the Alzheimer's Association, and the American Geriatrics Society, *JAMA: Journal of the American Medical Association* 278 (1997): 1363–1371.

26. *Diagnostic and statistical manual of mental disorders DSM-IV-TR* (text revision) (Washington, DC: American Psychiatric Association, 2000).

27. M. Folstein, S. Folstein, and P. McHugh, "Mini-mental state": A practical method for grading the cognitive state of patients for the clinician, *Journal of Psychiatric Research* 12 (1975): 189–198.

28. M. Hamilton, A rating scale for depression, *Journal of Neurology, Neurosurgery and Psychiatry* 23 (1960): 56–62.

29. H. Buschke and P. A. Fuld, Evaluating storage, retention and retrieval in disordered memory and learning, *Neurology* 24 (1974): 1019–1025.

30. A. L. Benton and K. Hamsher, *Multilingual aphasia examination* (Iowa City, IA: University of Iowa, 1976/1978).

31. M. R. Gilewski and E. M. Zelinski, Memory functioning questionnaire (MFQ), *Psychopharmacology Bulletin* 24 (1988): 665–670.

32. M. J. Gilewski and E. M. Zelinski, Questionnaire assessment of memory complaints, in *Handbook for clinical memory assessment of older adults*, ed. L. W. Poon (Washington, DC: American Psychological Association, 1986), 93–107.

33. G. Small and G. Vorgan, *The memory prescription* (New York: Hyperion, 2004).

34. S. Funahashi, K. Takeda, and Y. Watanabe, Neural mechanisms of spatial working memory: Contributions of the dorsolateral prefrontal cortex and the thalamic mediodorsal nucleus, *Cognitive, Affective, and Behavioral Neuroscience* 4 (2004): 409–420.

35. E. C. Miotto, C. R. Savage, J. J. Evans et al., Bilateral activation of the prefrontal cortex after strategic semantic cognitive training, *Human Brain Mapping* 27, no. 4 (2006): 288-295.

36. S. J. Mathew, X. Mao, J. D. Coplan et al., Dorsolateral prefrontal cortical pathology in generalized anxiety disorder: A proton magnetic resonance spectroscopic imaging study, *American Journal of Psychiatry* 161 (2004): 1119–1121.

37. B. Ravnkilde, P. Videbech, R. Rosenberg et al., Putative tests of frontal lobe function: A PET-study of brain activation during Stroop's Test and verbal fluency, *Journal of Clinical and Experimental Neuropsychology* 24 (2002): 534–547.

38. R. J. Haier, B. V. Siegel, A. MacLachlan et al., Regional glucose metabolic changes after learning a complex visuospatial/motor task: A positron emission tomographic study, *Brain Research* 570 (1992): 134–143.

39. S. Y. Bookheimer, M. H. Strojwas, M. S. Cohen et al., Brain activation in people at genetic risk for Alzheimer's disease, *New England Journal of Medicine* 343 (2000): 450–456.

40. L. J. Podewils, R. N. McLay, G. W. Rebok et al., Relationship of self-perceptions of memory and worry to objective measures of memory and cognition in the general population, *Psychosomatics* 44 (2003): 461–470.

41. W. C. Knowler, E. Barrett-Connor, S. E. Fowler et al., Reduction in the incidence of type 2 diabetes with lifestyle intervention or metformin, *New England Journal of Medicine* 346 (2002): 393–403.

42. J. A. Blumenthal, M. Babyak, J. Wei et al., Usefulness of psychosocial treatment of mental stress-induced myocardial ischemia in men, *American Journal of Cardiology* 89 (2002): 164–168.

Larry Dossey: Compassion and Healing

1. K. Armstrong, Compassion is the key, *Resurgence* 235 (March/April 2006): 33–34.

2. Ontario Consultants on Religious Tolerance/Religious Tolerance.org, Shared belief in the 'golden rule': Ethics of reciprocity, http://www.religioustolerance.org/reciproc.htm (accessed July 13, 2006).

3. American Humanist Association, Humanist manifestos I and II, Ethics section, http://www.jcn.com/manifestos.html (accessed July 13, 2006).

4. J. Achterberg, K. Cooke, R. Richards, L. Standish, L. Kozak, and J. Lake, Evidence for correlations between distant intentionality and brain function in recipients: A functional magnetic resonance imaging analysis, *Journal of Alternative and Complementary Medicine* 11, no. 6, (2005): 965–971.

5. J. Wadkerman, C. Seiter, H. Keibel, and H. Walach, Correlations between brain electrical activities of two spatially separated human subjects, *Neuroscience Letters* 336 (2003): 60–64.

6. L. Standish, L. Kozak, L. Johnson, L. C. Johnson, and T. Richards, Electroencephalographic evidence of correlated event-related signals between the brains of spatially and sensory isolated human subjects, *Journal of Alternative and Complementary Medicine* 10, no. 2 (2004): 307–314.

7. T. D. Duane and T. Behrendt, Extrasensory electroencephalographic induction between identical twins, *Science* 1965, 150-367.

8. D. Radin, Event-related electroencephalographic correlations between isolated human subjects, *Journal of Alternative and Complementary Medicine* 10, no. 2 (2004): 315-323.

9. F. Sicher, E. Targ, D. Moore, and H. S. Smith, A randomized double-blind study of the effect of distant healing in a population with advanced AIDS—Report of a small-scale study, *Western Journal of Medicine* 169, no. 6 (1998): 356–363.

10. W. B. Jonas and C. C. Crawford, *Healing, intention and energy medicine* (New York: Churchill Livingstone, 2003), xv–xix.

11. J. T. Chibnall, J. M. Jeral, and M. A. Cerullo, Experiments in distant intercessory prayer: God, science, and the lesson of Massah, *Archives of Internal Medicine* 161 (2001): 2529–2536.

12. K. S. Thomson, The revival of experiments in prayer, *American Scientist* 84 (1996): 532–534.

13. L. Dossey and D. B. Hufford, Are prayer experiments legitimate? Twenty criticisms, *Explore* 1 (2005): 109–117.

14. L. Dossey, *Reinventing medicine* (San Francisco: HarperSanFrancisco, 1999).

15. D. Radin, *Entangled minds* (New York: Paraview, 2006), 235.

16. H. Ishii, M. Nagashima, M. Tanno, A. Nakajima, and S. Yoshino, Does being easily moved to tears as a response to psychological stress reflect response to treatment and the general prognosis in patients with rheumatoid arthritis? *Clinical and Experimental Rheumatology* 21, no. 5 (2003): 611–616.

17. H. Benson et al., Study of the Therapeutic Effects of Intercessory Prayer (STEP) in cardiac bypass patients: A multicenter randomized trial of uncertainty and certainty of receiving intercessory prayer, *American Heart Journal* 151 (2006): 934–42.

18. C. Kalb, Spirituality: Don't pray for me! Please! *Newsweek*, Periscope, www.msnbc.msn.com/id/12112810/site/newsweek/.

19. L. A. Fogarty, B. A. Curbow, J. R. Wingard, K. McDonnell, and M. R. Somerfield, Can 40 seconds of compassion reduce patient anxiety? *Journal of Clinical Oncology* 17, no. 1 (1999): 371–379.

20. D. A. Redelmeier, J. P. Molin, and R. Tibshirani, A randomized trial of compassionate care for the homeless in an emergency department, *Lancet* 345, no. 8958 (1995): 1131–34.

21. M. Mittelman, quoted in T. Traubman, Wanted: Medical student, compassionate and personable, *Haaretz*, www.haaretz.com/hasen/pages/RegisterSiteEng.jhtml?contrassI=null&requestid=233637 (accessed April 15, 2006).

22. E. Mumford, H. J. Schlesinger, and G. V. Glass, The effects of psychological intervention on recovery from surgery and heart attacks: An analysis of the literature, *American Journal of Public Health* 72 (1982): 141–151.

23. A. Einstein, quoted in The Quotations Page, www.quotationspage.com/search.php3?homesearch=compassion&startsearch=Search (accessed July 17, 2006).

Daniel J. Siegel: Reflections on the Mindful Brain

Ackerman, D., J. Kabat-Zinn, J. O'Donohue, and D. J. Siegel. 2006. Mind and moment: Mindfulness, neuroscience, and the poetry of transformation in everyday life. February. Conference recordings (available through MindsightInstitute.com).

Ackerman, D., J. Kabat-Zinn, and D. J. Siegel. 2005. Presented at the panel discussion at the 28th Annual Psychotherapy Networker Symposium, Washington DC, March. Audio recordings (available at PsychotherapyNetworker.org).

Anderson, N. B. (with P. E. Anderson). 2003. *Emotional longevity: What really determines how long you live.* New York: Viking.

Armstrong, K. 1993. *History of God.* New York: Ballantine Books.

Baer, R. A., G. T. Smith, J. Hopkins, J. Krietemeyer, and L. Toney. 2006. Using self-report assessment methods to explore facets of mindfulness. *Assessment* 13, no. 1: 27–45.

Baxter, L. R., J. M. Schwartz, K. S. Bergman, M. P. Szuba, B. H. Guze, J. C. Mazziotta, A. Alazraki, C. E. Selin, H. K. Ferng, P. Munford et al. 1992. Caudate glucose metabolic rate changes with both drug and behavior therapy for obsessive-compulsive disorder. *Archives of General Psychiatry* 49, no. 9: 681–689.

Bishop, S. R., M. Lau, S. Shapiro, L. Carlson, N. D. Anderson, and J. Carmody et al. 2004. Mindfulness: A proposed operational definition. *Clinical Psychology: Science and Practice* 11, no. 3: 230–241.

Cozolino, L. J. 2002. *The neuroscience of psychotherapy: Building and rebuilding the human brain.* New York: W. W. Norton.

Cozolino, L. J. 2006. *The neuroscience of human relationships: Attachment and the development of the social brain.* New York: W. W. Norton.

Davidson, R. J., J. Kabat-Zinn, J. Schumacher, M. Rosenkranz, D. Muller, S. F. Santorelli, F. Urbanowski, A. Harrington, K. Bonus, and J. F. Sheridan. 2003. Alterations in brain and immune function produced by mindfulness meditation. *Psychosomatic Medicine* 65, no. 4: 564–570.

Dimidjian, S., and M. M. Linehan. 2003a. Defining an agenda for future research on the clinical application of mindfulness practice. *Clinical Psychology: Science and Practice* 10, no. 2: 166–171.

Dimidjian, S. D., and M. M. Linehan. 2003b. Mindful practice. In *Cognitive behavior therapy: Applying empirically supported techniques in your practice*, ed. W. O'Donohue, J. Fisher, and S. Hayes, 229–237. New York: Wiley.

Epstein, M. 1995. *Thoughts without a thinker: Psychotherapy from a Buddhist perspective.* New York: Basic Books.

Epstein, R. M. 1999. Mindful practice. *JAMA: Journal of the American Medical Association* 282, no. 9: 833–839.

Fitzpatrick-Hopler, G. June 2006. Christian contemplative practice: Centering prayer. Presented at the Mind, Life Summer Research Institute, Garrison, NY.

Fletcher, L., and S. C. Hayes. 2006. Relational Frame Theory, Acceptance and Commitment Therapy, and a functional analytic definition of mindfulness. *Journal of Rational Emotive and Cognitive Behavioral Therapy* 23, no. 4: 315–336.

Germer, C. K., R. D. Siegel, and P. R. Fulton, eds. 2005. *Mindfulness and psychotherapy.* New York: Guilford Press.

Goleman, D. 1988. *The meditative mind: The varieties of meditative experience.* Los Angeles: J. P. Tarcher.

Goleman, D. 2007. *Social intelligence: The new science of human relationships.* New York: Bantam Books.

Grossman, P., L. Niemann, S. Schmidt, and H. Walach. 2004. Mindfulness-based stress reduction and health benefits: A meta-analysis. *Journal of psychosomatic research* 57, no. 1: 35–43.

Hayes, S. C. 2004. Acceptance and Commitment Therapy, Relational Frame Theory, and the third wave of behavioral and cognitive therapies. *Behavior Therapy* 35, no. 4: 639–665.

Hayes, S. C., V. M. Follette, and M. M. Linehan, eds. 2004. *Mindfulness and acceptance: Expanding the cognitive-behavioral tradition.* New York: Guilford Press.

Hayes, S. C., K. D. Strosahl, and K. G. Wilson. 1999. *Acceptance and commitment therapy: An experiential approach to behavior change.* New York: Guilford Press.

Jones, B. 2001. Changes in cytokine production in healthy subjects practicing Guolin Qigong: a pilot study. *BMC Complementary and Alternative Medicine* 1: 1–8.

Kabat-Zinn, J. 1990. *Full catastrophe living: Using the wisdom of your body and mind to face stress, pain, and illness.* New York: Delacorte Press.

Kabat-Zinn, J. 1995. *Wherever you go, there you are.* New York: Hyperion Press.

Kabat-Zinn, J. 2003. Mindfulness-based interventions in context: Past, present, and future. *Clinical Psychology: Science and Practice* 10, no. 2: 144–156.

Kaiser-Greenland, S. 2006. Information from Inner Kids Organizational Website. www.innerkids.com.

Keating, T. 2005. The orthodoxy of centering prayer. Presented at the 13th Annual Investigating the Mind: The Science and Clinical Applications in Mediation Meeting, Washington DC.

Kornfield, J. 1993. *A path with heart.* New York: Bantam Books.

Kornfield, J. In press. *The wise heart.* New York: Bantam Books.

Langer, E. J. 1989. *Mindfulness.* Cambridge, MA: De Capo Press.

Langer, E. J. 1997. *The power of mindful learning.* Cambridge: MA, De Capo Press.

Langer, E. J. 2000. Mindful learning. *Current directions in psychological science* 9, no. 6: 220–223.

Linehan, M. M. 1993a. *Cognitive-behavioral treatment of borderline personality disorder.* New York: Guilford Press.

Linehan, M. M. 1993b. *Skills training manual for treating borderline personality disorder.* New York: Guilford Press.

Lutz, A., J. D. Dunne, and R. J. Davidson. 2007. Meditation and the neuroscience of consciousness. In *The Cambridge handbook of consciousness,* ed. P. D. Zelazo, M. Moscovitch, and E. Thompson. New York: Cambridge University Press.

Marlatt, G. A., and J. R. Gordon. 1985. *Relapse prevention: Maintenance strategy in the treatment of addictive behavior.* New York: Guilford Press.

Mayberg, H. 2005. Paths to recovery: Neural substrates of cognitive mindfulness-based interventions for the treatment of depression. Presented at the 13th Annual Investigating the Mind: The Science and Clinical Applications in Mediation Meeting, Washington D.C.

Pargament, K. I. 1997. *The psychology of religion and coping: Theory, research, and practice*. New York: Guilford Press.

Parks, G. A., B. K. Anderson, and G. A. Marlatt. 2001. Relapse prevention therapy. In *Interpersonal handbook of alcohol dependence and problems*, ed. N. Heather, T. J. Peters, and T. Stackwell, 575–592. New York: John Wiley.

Schore, A. N. 1994 *Affect regulation and the origin of the self. The neurobiology of emotional development*. New Jersey: Lawrence Erlbaum Associates.

Schore A. N. 2003a. *Affect dysregulation and the disorders of the self*. New York: Guilford Press.

Schore, A. N. 2003b. *Affect regulation and the repair of the self*. New York: Guilford Press.

Segal, Z. V., J. M. G. Williams, and J. D. Teasdale. 2002. *Mindfulness-based cognitive therapy for depression: A new approach to preventing relapse*. New York: Guilford Press.

Segal, Z. V., J. M. G. Williams, J. D. Teasdale, and J. Kabat-Zinn. 2007. *The mindful way through depression*. New York: Guilford Press.

Siegel, D. J. 1999. *The developing mind*. New York: Guilford Press.

Siegel, D. J. 2001. Toward an interpersonal neurobiology of the developing mind: Attachment, "mindsight," and neural integration. *Infant Mental Health Journal* 22: 67–94.

Siegel, D. J. 2006. An interpersonal neurobiology approach to psychotherapy. *Psychiatric Annals* 36, no. 4: 248–256.

Siegel, D. J. 2008. *The mindful brain: A new audio book*. Boulder, CO: Sounds True.

Siegel, D. J. In press. *Mindsight: Our seventh sense*. New York: Bantam.

Siegel, D. J., and M. Hartzell. 2003. *Parenting from the inside out: How a deeper self-understanding can help you raise children who thrive.*New York: Penguin Putnam.

Solomon, M. F., and D. J. Siegel, eds. (2003). *Healing trauma: Attachment, mind, body and brain*. New York: W.W. Norton.

Hanh, Thich Nhat. 1991. *Peace is every step: The path of mindfulness in everyday life*. New York: Bantam Books.

Wallace, B.A. 2006. *The attention revolution: Unlocking the power of the focused mind*. Boston: Wisdom Publications.

Peter Levine: Trauma and Spirituality

1. Appreciation to Laura Regalbuto and Justin Snavely for their generous time, feedback and editorial assistance.

2. Founder and Senior Advisor, The Foundation for Human Enrichment, Boulder, Colorado, and Distinguished Faculty, Santa Barbara Graduate Institute.

3. P. A. Levine, *Waking the tiger, healing trauma* (Berkeley, CA: North Atlantic Press, 1996).

4. A condition, which today probably would have been diagnosed as fibromyalgia and chronic fatigue syndrome.

5. P. A. Levine, Revisioning anxiety and trauma, in *Giving the body its due,* ed. Maxine Sheets Johnstone (New York: S.U.N.Y. Press, 1991).

6. More about that (and the extremes in heart rate exhibited by Nancy) will be revisited later.

7. This transcript was published in the *Journal, Science* in 1974.

8. In particular, I was fortunate to have several encouraging telephone discussions with Professor Tinbergen himself.

9. *Science* 174, no. 4012 (November 1971): 26.

10. Lower Lake, CA: Integral Publishing, 1976, 1987, 1992.

11. *Kundalini: The evolutionary energy in man* (Boston: Shambhala, 1997).

12. Princeton, NJ: Princeton University Press, 1996.

13. www.traumahealing.com

14. P. A. Levine *Waking the tiger, healing trauma.*

15. Robert Heath, (1978), personal communication, conference on the Biology of the Affectionate Bond, Esalen Institute, Big Sur, CA.

16. Andrew Newberg, Eugene D'Aquili, and Vince Rause, *Why God won't go away: Brain science and the biology of belief* (New York: Ballantine Books, 2002).

17. In reality, it is organized and integrated within the more involuntary aspects of the visceral system (guts) and somatic system (muscles), as well as the central nervous system—CNS (the reptilian brainstem, the limbic system—the paleo-mammalian i.e. old mammal or emotional brain, as well as many other specific areas of the neocortex—the new brain).

18. Actually the parasympathetic branch is additionally divided into a primitive (non-mylenated) and an evolutionarily recent (mylenated) branch.

19. P. A. Levine, Stress, in *Psychophysiology: Systems, processes, and application; A handbook,* ed. M. Coles, E. Donchin, and S. Porges (New York: Guilford Press, 1986).

20. Stress and vegetotherapy, *Journal of Energy and Character,* Fall.

21. Alan N. Schore, *Affect regulation and the origin of the self: The neurobiology of emotional development* (Hillsdale, NJ: Lawrence Erlbaum, 1994).

22. Antonio Damasio, *The feeling of what happens: Body and emotion in the making of consciousness* (Fort Washington, PA: Harvest Books, 2000).

23. Prof. P.L. Dhar, Holistic education and Vipassana, *Buddhism Today*, 2005.

24. P. A. Levine, *Healing trauma: A pioneering program for restoring the wisdom of your body* (Boulder, CO: Sounds True, 2005).

Suzanne Segerstrom: Doing Optimism, Optimists, Pessimists, and Their Potential for Change

1. G. Oettingen, H. Pak, and K. Schnetter, Self-regulation of goal setting: Turning free fantasies about the future into binding goals, *Journal of Personality and Social Psychology* 80 (2001): 736–753.

2. J. H. Riskind, C. S. Sarampote, and M. A. Mercier, For every malady a sovereign cure: Optimism training, *Journal of Cognitive Psychotherapy: An International Quarterly* 10 (1996): 105–117.

3. M. E. P. Seligman, T. A. Steen, N. Park, and C. Peterson, Positive psychology progress: Empirical validation of interventions, *American Psychologist* 60 (2005): 410–421.

4. J. W. Pennebaker, *Opening up: The healing power of expressing emotions* (New York: Guilford, 1997).

5. T. Mann, Effects of future writing and optimism on health behaviors in HIV-infected women, *Annals of Behavioral Medicine* 23: 26–33.

6. S. E. Taylor, L. B. Pham, I. D. Rivkin, and D. A. Armor, Harnessing the imagination: Mental simulation, self-regulation, and coping, *American Psychologist* 53 (1998): 429–439.

7. L. D. Cameron and G. Nicholls, Expression of stressful experiences through writing: Effects of a self-regulation manipulation for pessimists and optimists, *Health Psychology* 17 (1998): 84–92.

8. E. L. Deci and R. M. Ryan, The "what" and "why" of goal pursuits: Human needs and the self-determination of behavior, *Psychological Inquiry* 11 (2000): 227–268.

9. M. R. Lepper, D. Greene, and R. E. Nisbett, Undermining children's intrinsic interest with extrinsic rewards: A test of the overjustification hypothesis, *Journal of Personality and Social Psychology* 28 (1973): 129–137.

10. K. M. Sheldon and L. S. Krieger, Does legal education have undermining effects on law students? Evaluating changes in motivation, values, and well-being, *Behavioral Sciences and the Law* 22 (2004): 261–286.

11. E. T. Higgins, Self-discrepancy: A theory related self and affect, *Psychological Review* 94 (1987): 319–340.

12. K. M. Sheldon, T. Kasser, K. Smith, and T. Share, Personal goals and psychological growth: Testing an intervention to enhance goal attainment and personality integration, *Journal of Personality* 70 (2002): 5–31.

Robert A. Emmons: Gratitude: The Science and Spirit of Thankfulness

Breathnach, S. B. 1996. *The simple abundance journal of gratitude.* New York: Warner.

Diener, E., and R. Biswas-Diener. In press. *Mona Lisa's smile: The science of optimal well-being.* New York: Blackwell.

Emmons, R. A. 2007. *Thanks!: How the new science of gratitude can make you happier.* Boston: Houghton Mifflin.

Emmons, R. A., and J. Hill. 2001. *Words of gratitude for mind, body, and soul.* Radnor, PA: Templeton Foundation Press.

Emmons, R.A., and M. E. McCullough. 2003. Counting blessings versus burdens: Experimental studies of gratitude and subjective well-being in daily life. *Journal of Personality and Social Psychology* 84: 377–389.

Emmons, R. A., and M. E. McCullough, eds. 2004. *The psychology of gratitude.* New York: Oxford University Press.

Fredrickson, B. L. 2004. Gratitude, like other positive emotions, broadens and builds. In *The psychology of gratitude*, ed. R. A. Emmons and M. E. McCullough, 145–166. New York: Oxford University Press.

Fredrickson, B. L., and M. M. Tugade. 2003. What good are positive emotions in crises? A prospective study of resilience and emotional responding following the terrorist attacks on the United States on September 11th, 2001. *Journal of Personality and Social Psychology* 84: 365–376.

Gillani, N. B., and J. C. Mith. 2001. Zen meditation and ABC relaxation theory: An exploration of relaxation states, beliefs, dispositions, and motivations. *Journal of Clinical Psychology* 57: 839–846.

Hay, L. L et al., eds. 1996. *Gratitude: A way of life.* Carlsbad, CA: Hay House.

McCullough, M. E., R. A. Emmons, and J. Tsang. 2002. The grateful disposition: A conceptual and empirical topography. *Journal of Personality and Social Psychology* 82: 112–127.

McCullough, M. E., S. D. Kilpatrick, R. A. Emmons, and D. B. Larson. 2001. Is gratitude a moral affect? *Psychological Bulletin* 127: 249–266.

McCraty, R., and D. Childre. 2004. Gratitude and the heart: The psychophysiology of appreciation. In *The psychology of gratitude*, ed. R. A. Emmons and M. E. McCullough, 230–255. New York: Oxford University Press.

Richelieu, F. 1996. Gratitude: Its healing properties. In *Gratitude: A way of life*, ed. L.L. Hay. Carlsbad, CA: Hay House.

Schwarz, S. 1999. *Values and human experience: essays in honor of the memory of Balduin Schwarz*. New York: P. Lang.

Seligman, M. E. P., T. A. Steen, N. Park, N., and C. Peterson. 2005. Positive psychology progress: Empirical validation of interventions. *American Psychologist* 60: 410–421.

Streng, F. J. 1989. Introduction: Thanksgiving as a worldwide response to life. In *Spoken and unspoken thanks: Some comparative soundings*, ed. J. B. Carman and F. J. Streng, 1–9. Dallas, TX: Center for World Thanksgiving.

Sara L. Warber and Katherine N. Irvine: Nature and Spirit

Aldridge, J., and J. Sempik. 2002. Social and therapeutic horticulture: evidence and messages from research. *Center for Child and Family Research: Evidence* 6.

Appleton, J. 1996. *The Experience of Landscape* New York: John Wiley and Sons.

Australian Research Centre for Water in Society. 2002. Perth domestic water-use study: Household appliance ownership and community attitudinal analysis 1999-2000. CSIRO Land and Water, CSIRO Urban Water Program. Cited in Brown and Grant, 2005.

Backster, C. 2003. *Primary perception: Biocommunication with plants, living foods, and human cells*. Anza, CA: White Rose Millennium Press.

Balling, J. D, and J. H. Falk. 1982. Development of visual preference for natural environments. *Environment and Behavior* 14, no. 1: 5–28.

Bose, J. C. 1906. *Plant response as a means of physiological investigation*. London: Longmans, Green and Company.

Bose, J. C. 1913. *Researches on irritability of plants*. London: Longmans, Green and Company.

Braam, L. 2005. In Touch: plant responses to mechanical stimuli. *New Phytologist* 165: 373–389.

Breslau, N., H. D. Chilcoat, R. C. Kessler, and G. C. Davis. 1999. Previous exposure to trauma and PTSD effects of subsequent trauma: results from the Detroit area survey of trauma. *American Journal of Psychiatry* 156: 902–907.

Brown, C., and M. Grant. 2005. Biodiversity and human health: What role for nature in healthy urban planning? *Built Environment* 31: 326–338.

Cannon, W. B. 1932. *The wisdom of the body.* New York: W. W. Norton.

Cimprich, B. 1992. Attentional fatigue following breast cancer surgery. *Research in Nursing and Health* 15: 192–207.

Cimprich, B. 1993. Development of an intervention to restore attention in cancer patients. *Cancer Nursing* 16, no. 2:83–92.

Cohen, S., D. A. Tyrrell, and A. P. Smith. 1991. Psychological stress and susceptibility to the common cold. *New England Journal of Medicine* 325, no. 9: 606–612.

Coley, R. L., F. E. Kuo, and W.C. Sullivan. 1997. Where does community grow: the social context created by nature in urban public housing. *Behavior and Environment* 29, no. 4: 468–494.

Cooper Marcus, C., and M. Barnes. 1999. *Healing gardens: Therapeutic benefits and design recommendations.* New York: John Wiley and Sons.

Cumes, D. 1998. Nature as medicine: the healing power of the wilderness. *Alternative Therapies* 4, no. 2: 79–86.

Detweiler, M. B., and C. Warf. 2005. Dementia wander garden aids post cerebrovascular strike restorative therapy: A case study. *Alternative Therapies in Health and Medicine* 11, no. 4: 54–8.

Dohrenwend, B. S., B. P. Dohrenwend, M. Dodson, and P.E. Shrout. 1984. Symptoms, hassles, social supports, and life events: problem of confounded measures. *Journal of Abnormal Psychology* 93, no. 2: 222–230.

Driver, B. L., D. Dustin, T. Baltic, G. Elsner, and G. Peterson, eds. 1996. *Nature and the human Spirit: Toward an expanded land management ethic.* State College, PA: Venture Press.

Dustin, D. L. 1994. Spirit and leisure. *Parks and Recreation.* 29, no. 9: 92–96.

Emoto, M. 2004. *The hidden messages in water.* Trans. D. A. Thayne. Hillsboro, OR: Beyond Words Publishing.

Fredrickson, L. M., and D.H. Anderson. 1999. A qualitative exploration of the wilderness experience as a source of spiritual inspiration. *Journal of Environmental Psychology* 19: 21–39.

Frumkin, H. 2001. Beyond toxicity: Human health and the natural environment. *American Journal for Preventive Medicine* 20, no. 3: 234–240.

Fuller, R. A., K. N. Irvine, P. Devine-Wright, P. H. Warren, and K. J. Gaston. 2007. Psychological benefits of greenspace increase with biodiversity. *Biology Letters* 3: 390–394.

Gerlach-Spriggs, N., R. E. Kaufman, and S. B. Warner, Jr. 1998. *Restorative gardens: The healing landscape*. New Haven, CT: Yale University Press.

Grad, B. 1963. A telekinetic effect on plant growth. *International Journal of Parapsychology* 5: 117–133.

Grad, B. 1964. A telekinetic effect on plant growth: II experiments involving treatment of saline in stoppered bottles. *International Journal of Parapsychology* 6: 473–498.

Grahn, P., I.-L. Bengtsson, L. Welen-Andersson, L. Lavesson, L. Lindfors, F. Tauchnitz, and C. Tenngart. 2007. Alnarp rehabilitation garden: possible health effects from the design, from the activities and from the therapeutic team. Paper presented at An International Conference on Innovative Approaches to Research Excellence in Landscape and Health, Edinburgh, Scotland, September 20–23.

Grauds, C. 2001. *Jungle medicine* Marin County, CA: Citron Bay Press.

Griswold, M. 1996. A history of the sanctuary garden. *Design Quarterly* 169: 2–10.

Hawks, S. R., M. L. Hull, R. L. Thalman, and P. M. Richins. 1995. Review of spiritual health: definition, role, and intervention strategies in health promotion. *American Journal of Health Promotion* 9, no. 5: 371–378.

Heintzman, P. 2000. Leisure and spiritual well-being relationships: a qualitative study. *Society and Leisure* 23, no. 1: 41–69.

Herzog, T. R., A. M. Black, K. A. Fountaine, and D. J. Knotts. 1997. Reflection and attentional recovery as distinctive benefits of restorative environments. *Journal of Environmental Psychology* 17: 165–170.

Irvine, K. N. 1997. *Stewardship in the management of private Forests: Some psychological dimensions*. Master's thesis, University of Michigan, Ann Arbor.

Irvine, K. N. 2004. *Work breaks and well-being: The effect of nature on hospital nurses*. PhD dissertation, University of Michigan, Ann Arbor.

James, W. 1892/1985. *Psychology: The Briefer Course*. Ed. G. Allport. Notre Dame, IN: University of Notre Dame Press.

Kamp, D. 1995. Brochure. New York: Dirtworks, Inc.

Kaplan, R. 1983. The role of nature in the urban context. In *Behavior and the natural environment*, ed. I. Altman and J. F. Wohlwill. New York: Plenum Press.

Kaplan, R., L. V. Bardwell, H. A. Ford, and S. Kaplan. 1996. The corporate back-40: employee benefits of wildlife enhancement efforts on corporate land. *Human Dimensions of Wildlife* 1, no. 2: 1–13.

Kaplan, R., and E. J. Herbert. 1987. Cultural and sub-cultural comparisons in preference for natural settings. *Landscape and Urban Planning* 14: 281–293.

Kaplan, R., and S. Kaplan. 1989. *The experience of nature: A psychological perspective*. New York: Cambridge University Press.

Kaplan, S. 1987. Aesthetics, affect, and cognition: environmental preferences from an evolutionary perspective. *Environment and Behavior* 19 (January):3–32.

Kaplan, S. 1995a. Restorative benefits of nature: toward an integrative framework. *Journal of Environmental Psychology* 15: 159–182.

Kaplan, S. 1995b. The urban forest as a source of psychological well-being. In *Urban forest landscapes: Integrating multi-disciplinary perspectives*, ed. G. A. Bradley, 101–108. Seattle, WA: University of Washington Press.

Kaplan, S., J. F. Talbot, and R. Kaplan. 1988. Coping with daily hassles: The impact of nearby nature on the work environment. Project Report. USDA Forest Service, North Central Forest Experiment Station, Urban Forestry Unit Cooperative Agreement 23-85-08.

Katz, R. 1993. *The straight path: A story of healing and transformation in Fiji*. Reading, MA: Addison-Wesley.

Kellert, S. R., and E. O. Wilson, eds. 1993. *The biophilia hypothesis*. Washington, DC: Island Press.

Kiecolt-Glaser, J. I., and R. Glaser. 1995. Psychoneuroimmunology and health consequences: Data and shared mechanisms. *Psychosomatic Medicine* 57: 269–275.

Lazarus, R. S. 1966. *Psychological stress and the coping process*. New York: McGraw-Hill.

Lindburgh, A. M. 1977. *Gift from the sea*. New York: Pantheon Books.

Macintyre, S., A. Ellaway, R. Hiscock, A. Kearns, G. Der, and L. McKay. 2003. What features of the home and the area might help to explain observed relationships between housing tenure and health? Evidence from the west of Scotland. *Health and Place* 9: 207–218.

McEwen, B. S. 1998. Protective and damaging effects of stress mediators. *New England Journal of Medicine* 338, no. 3: 172–179.

McIntyre, N., and J. W. Roggenbuck. 1998. Nature/person transactions during an outdoor adventure experiences: a multi-phasic analysis. *National Recreation and Park Association* 39, no. 4: 401–422.

Merriam-Webster's new collegiate dictionary, 7th ed. 1967. Springfield, MA: G. and C. Merriam Company.

Mooney P., and P. L. Nicell. 1992. The importance of exterior environment for Alzheimer residents: effective care and risk management. *Healthcare FORUM 5.* no. 2: 23–29. Cited in Stevens, 1995.

Morgan, M. 1999. *Mutant message from forever.* New York: Perennial/ HarperCollins.

Orland, B. 1988. Aesthetic preference for rural landscapes: Some resident and visitor differences. In *Environmental aesthetics: Theory, research and applications,* ed. J. L. Nasar, 364–378. New York: Cambridge University Press.

Parsons, R., L. G. Tassinary, R. S. Ulrich, M. R. Hebl,, and M. Grossman-Alexander. 1998. The view from the road: implications for stress recovery and immunization. *Journal of Environmental Psychology* 18: 113–139.

Peat, F. D. 1994. *Lighting the seventh fire: The spiritual ways, healing and science of the Native American.* New York: Birch Lane Press.

Perlin, L. I., L. G. Menaghan, R. S. Ulrich, M. R. Hebl, and J. T. Mullin. 1981. The stress process. *Journal of Health & Social Behavior* 22 (December): 337–356.

Ravuvu, A. D. 1987. *The Fijian ethos.* Suva, Fiji: Institute of Pacific Studies, University of the South Pacific.

Seaward, B. L. 1995. Reflections on human spirituality for the worksite. *American Journal of Health Promotion* 9, no. 3: 165–168.

Selye, H. 1946. The general adaptation syndrome and diseases of adaptation. *Journal of Clinical Endocrinology* 6: 217–230.

Selye, H. 1956. *The stress of life.* New York: McGraw-Hill.

Sheets, V. L., and C. D. Manzer. 1991. Affect, cognition, and urban vegetation: some effects of adding trees along city streets. *Environment and Behavior* 23, no. 3: 285–304.

Shepherd, V. A. 1999. Bioelectricity and the rhythms of sensitive plants: The biophysical research of Jagadis Chandra Bose. *Current Science* 77, no. 1: 189-195.

Sherman, S. A., J. W. Varni, R. S. Ulrich and V. L. Malcarne. 2004. Post-occupancy evaluation of healing gardens in a pediatric cancer center. *Landscape and Urban Planning* 73, nos. 2–3:167–183.

Simson, S. P., and M. C. Straus, ed. 1998. *Horticulture as therapy: Principles and practice.* New York: Haworth Press.

Somé, M. P. 1998. *The healing wisdom of Africa: Finding life purpose through nature, ritual, and community.* New York: Jeremy P. Tarcher/ Putnam.

Stevens, M. 1995. Life in fast-forward reverse. *Landscape Architecture 85*, no. 1: 77–79.

Stigsdotter, U. A., and P. Grahn. 2004. A garden at your doorstep may reduce stress—Private gardens as restorative environments in the city. Paper 00015. Proceedings of the Open Space-People Space Conference, October 27–29, Edinburgh, Scotland.

Sullivan, W. C. 1994. Perceptions of rural-urban fringe: citizen preference for natural and developed settings. *Landscape and Urban Planning 26:* 85–101.

Sullivan, W. C., and F. E. Kuo. 1996. Do trees strengthen urban communities, reduce domestic violence? *Technology Bulletin 4.* USDA Forest Service, Southern Region, Forestry Report R8-FR 56.

Taylor, A. F., A. Wiley, F. E. Kuo, and W. C. Sullivan. 1998. Growing up in the inner city: green spaces as places to grow. *Environment and Behavior 30*, no. 1: 3–27.

Tennessen, C. M., and B. Cimbrich. 1995. Views to nature: effects on attention. *Journal of Environmental Psychology 15:* 77–85.

Thoreau, H. D. 1892/2000. *Walden and Civil disobedience.* Boston, MA: Houghton Mifflin.

Todd, J. E. 1982. *Frederick Law Olmsted: A biography.* Boston, MA: Twayne Publishers.

Turner, R. J., and B. Wheaton. 1995. Checklist measurement of stressful life events. In *Measuring stress: A guide for health and social scientists,* eds. S. Cohen, R. C. Kessler, and L. U. Gordon, 29–53. New York: Oxford University Press.

Ulrich, R. S. 1984. View from a window may influence recovery from surgery. *Science 224:* 420–421.

Ulrich, R. S., R. F. Simons, B. D. Losito, E. Fiorito, M. A. Miles, and M. Zelson. 1991. Stress recovery during exposure to natural and urban environments. *Journal of Environmental Psychology 11:* 201–230.

Warber, S. L., M. D. Fetters, and P. B. Kaufman. 2003. Environmental ethics: finding a moral compass for human-plant interaction. *Alternative Therapies in Health and Medicine 9:* 100–105.

Warber S. L., S. Ingerman, J. Wunder, A. Schreiber, B. W. Gillespie, K. Durda, V. L. Moura, K. Smith, K. Rhodes, and M. Rubenfire. 2007. Healing the heart: a randomized pilot study of a spiritual retreat for acute coronary syndrome patients. *Forschende Komplementarmedizin (Research in Complementary Medicine)* 14, supplement 1: 45–6.

Warner, Jr., S. B. 1995. Restorative landscapes. *Landscape Architecture* 85, no. 1: 128.

Whitehouse, S., J. W. Varni, M. Seid, M. C. Cooper, M. J. Ensberg, J. R. Jacobs, and R. S. Mehlenbeck. 2001. Evaluating a children's hospital garden environment: Utilization and consumer satisfaction. *Journal of Environmental Psychology* 21, no. 3: 301–314.

Williams, T. T. 1992. *Refuge: An unnatural history of family and place.* New York: Vintage Books.

Wilson, E. O. 1984. *Biophilia.* Cambridge, MA: Harvard University Press.

Zuefle, D. M. 1999. The spirituality of recreation. *Parks and Recreation* 34, no. 9: 28, 30–31, 41, 44, 47–8, 197.

Gregg Braden: The Power and Promise of a Spiritually Based Science

1. Jallaludin Rumi, *Love poems from God: Twelve sacred Voices from the East and West,* trans. Daniel Ladinsky (New York: Penguin, 2002), 65.

2. In 325 C.E., Emperor Constantine of the Holy Roman Empire convened a council of the early Christian Church and asked for advice as to which books should be included, or canonized, into the form of the Bible that is still used today. The recommendation of the council was to remove twenty-five books, while editing and condensing another twenty. Archaeological discoveries in the twentieth century, such as those of the Dead Sea Scrolls and Egypt's Nag Hammadi and Coptic Libraries, have given us insight into the contents of a number of these "lost" biblical books, some that had not been seen since the time of the edits. Additionally, the discovery of these libraries has also revealed the original versions of at least another nineteen books that were not included in the final version of the Bible, but which have been available in a modified form.

3. The Gospel of Thomas, trans. and introduced by members of the Coptic Gnostic Library Project of the Institute for Antiquity and Christianity (Claremont, CA), in *The Nag Hammadi library,* ed. James M. Robinson (San Francisco: HarperSanFrancisco, 1990), 131.

4. The Institute of HeartMath Research Center conducts basic research on emotional physiology and heart-brain interactions, clinical and organizational studies, and research on the physiology of learning and optimal performance. These statistics are drawn from an online summary of the communication between the brain and the heart, Head-heart interactions, Website: www.heartmath.org/research/science-of-the-heart/soh_20.html.

5. Michael Wise, Martin Abegg, Jr., and Edward Cook, *The Dead Sea Scrolls: A new translation* (San Francisco: HarperSanFrancisco, 1996), 365.

6. A beautiful example of applying what we know about inner peace to a wartime situation is found in the pioneering study done by David W. Orme-Johnson, Charles N. Alexander, John L. Davies, Howard M. Chandler, and Wallace E. Larimore, International peace project in the Middle East, *The Journal of Conflict Resolution* 32, no. 4 (December 1988): 778.

Bruce H. Lipton: Revealing the Wizard Behind the Curtain: The "New" Biology and Epigenetics

Fraga, M. F. et al. 2006. Epigenetic differences arise during the lifetime of monozygotic twins. *Proceedings of the National Academy of Sciences USA* 102: 10604–10609.

Henry, R. C. 2006. The mental universe. *Nature* 436: 29.

Kling, J. 2003. Put the Blame on Methylation. *The Scientist* 16, no. 12: 27–28.

Lipton, B. H. 1998. Nature, nurture and the power of love. *Journal of Prenatal and Perinatal Psychology and Health* 13: 3–10.

Lipton, B. H. 2001. Nature, nurture and human development. *Journal of Prenatal and Perinatal Psychology and Health* 16:167–180.

Lipton, B. H. 2005. *The biology of belief: Unleashing the power of consciousness, matter and miracles.* Santa Rosa, CA: Elite Books.

Nijhout, H. F. 1990. Metaphors and the role of genes in development. *Bioessays* 12, no. 9: 441–446.

Nørretranders, T. 1998. *The user illusion: Cutting consciousness down to size.* New York: Penguin Books.

Silverman, P. H. 2004. Rethinking genetic determinism. *The Scientist* 18, no. 10: 32.

Szegedy-Maszak, M. 2005. Mysteries of the mind: Your unconscious is making your everyday decisions *U.S. News & World Report*, February 28.

Waters, R. A., and R. L. Jirtle. 2003. Transposable elements: Targets for early Nutritional effects on epigenetic gene regulation. *Molecular and Cell Biology* 23, no. 15: 5293-5300.

Watters, E. 2006. DNA is not destiny. *Discover*, November, 32.

Daniel Goleman: The Brain's Melody

1. F. Varela, J.-P. Lachaux, E. Rodriguez, and J. Martinerie, The Brainweb: Phase synchronization and large-Scale integration, *Nature Reviews: Neuroscience* 2 (2001): 229–39.

2. E. Rodriguez, N. George, J.-P. Lachaux, J. Martinerie, B. Renault, and F. J. Varela, Perception's shadow: Long-Distance synchronization of human brain activity, *Nature* 397 (1999): 430–33.

James H. Austin: Selfless Insight-Wisdom: A Thalamic Gateway

1. Cf. J. Blofeld, *The Zen teachings of Huang-po: On the transmission of mind* (New York. Grove Press). Master Huang-po was a teacher of Master Lin-chi (J. Rinzai).

2. J. Austin, *Zen and the brain: Toward an understanding of meditation and consciousness* (Cambridge, MA: MIT Press, 1998).

3. J. Austin, Consciousness evolves when the self dissolves, *Journal of Consciousness Studies* 7, nos. 11–12 (2000): 209–230

4. J. Austin, *Zen-brain reflections: Reviewing recent developments in meditation and states of consciousness* (Cambridge, MA: MIT Press, 2006).

5. A. Lutz, J. Dunne, and R. Davidson, Meditation and the neuroscience of consciousness: An introduction, in *Cambridge handbook of consciousness*, ed. P. Zelazo, M. Moscovitch, and E. Thompson (New York: Cambridge University Press, 2007).

6. J. Austin, *Zen brain: Selfless insight; The meditative transformations of consciousness* (Cambridge, MA: MIT Press, in press, 2008).

7. M. Fox, M. Corbetta, A. Snyder, et al., Spontaneous neuronal activity distinguishes human dorsal and ventral attention systems, *Proceedings of the National Academy of Sciences USA* 103 (2006): 10046–10051.

8. J. Austin, *Zen Brain: Selfless Insight.*

9. J. Austin, *Zen and The Brain,* 367–370.

10. In contrast, during the state of internal absorption, it is plausible to consider that the reticular nucleus is the gate that shuts off the messages entering through the two geniculate nuclei and the other sensory nuclei in the back of the thalamus. This selective inhibition could explain the way internal absorption dissolves the elementary sense of one's physical Self (along with vision and hearing) yet does not cut the roots of the psychic self.

11. J. Austin, *Selfless insight*, chapter 22.

12. J. Austin. *Zen and the brain*, 452–457; 591–592; 615–617; *Zen- brain reflections*, 303–306.

13. M. Ricard, *Tibet: An inner journey* (New York: Thames and Hudson, 2006), 195. Shabkar was an ordained itinerant sage in the Dzogchen tradition, renowned for his composing and singing "The Flight of the Garuda." Reference 5 discusses the semantic issues related to the subtle Tibetan practice of "open presence." Cultivating a stable, receptive form of awareness, it is conducted with the meditator's eyes open and directed somewhat upward. This elevated gaze is reminiscent of the kind of position that might prove optimal to respond to the natural outdoor sights and sounds known to precipitate kensho.

Les Fehmi and Jim Robbins: Sweet Surrender: Discovering the Benefits of Synchronous Alpha Brain Waves

1. Lester G. Fehmi, J. W. Adkins, and Donald B. Lindsley, Electrophysiological correlates of visual perceptual masking in monkeys, *Experimental Brain Research* 7 (1969): 299–316.

2. See L. Gannon and R. Sternbach, Alpha enhancement as a treatment for pain: A case study, *Behavior Therapy and Experimental Psychiatry* 2 (1971): 209–13; K. Pelletier and E. Peper, Developing a biofeedback model: Alpha EEG feedback as a means for pain control, *International Journal of Clinical and Experimental Hypnosis* 25, no. 4 (1977): 361–71; E. G. Peniston and P. J. Kulkosky, Alpha theta brainwave training for Vietnam veterans with combat-related post traumatic stress disorder, *Medical Psychotherapy* 4 (1991): 47–60; Peniston and Kulkosky, Alcoholic personality and alpha theta brain wave training, *Medical Psychotherapy* 3 (1990): 37–55; J. T. McKnight and Les Fehmi, Attention and neurofeedback synchrony training: Clinical results and their significance, *Journal of Neurotherapy* 5, nos. 1–21 (2001): 45–62; D. Lehmann, W. Lang, and P. Debruyne, Controlled EEG alpha feedback training in normals and headache patients, *Archives of Psychiatry* 221 (1976): 331–43; A. Matthew, H. Mishm, and V. Kumamiah, Alpha feedback in the treatment of tension headache, *Journal of Personality and Clinical Studies* 3, no. 1 (1987): 17–22; Hanslmayr, Sausing, Doppelmayr, Schabus, and Klimerer, Increasing individual upper alpha power by neurofeedback improves cognitive performance in human subjects, *Applied Psychophysiology and Biofeedback* 30, no. 1 (2005).

3. See Ernst Niebur, Steven S. Hsiao, and Kenneth O. Johnson, Synchrony: A neuronal mechanism for attentional selection? *Current Opinion in Neurobiology* 12, no. 2 (2002): 190–95. Also of interest is Pascal Fries, John H. Reynolds, Alan E. Rorie, and Robert Desimone, Modulation of oscillatory neuronal synchronization by selective visual attention, *Science* 291, no. 5508 (2001): 1560–63. Desimone, Fries, and their colleagues believe that synchronous neuronal firing may be a fundamental mechanism for boosting the volume of brain signals representing behaviorally relevant stimuli and that many mental disorders are due to the brain's inability to fire synchronously.

4. William Tiller, *Science and human transformation: Subtle energies, intentionality and consciousness* (Walnut Creek, CA: Pavior Publishing, 1997). Also, "The tendency to synchronize," writes Steven Strogatz, a professor of applied mathematics at Cornell University, in his book *Sync: How order emerges from chaos in the universe, nature and daily life*, "may be the most mysterious and pervasive drive in all of nature."

5. Numerous EEG studies have shown increased synchrony in meditators. See Michael Murphy and Steven Donovan, *The physical and psychological effects of meditation: A review of contemporary research with a comprehensive bibliography, 1931–1996*, 2nd ed. (Petaluma, CA: Institute of Noetic Sciences, 1997). According to that book's editors, "EEG synchronization/coherence with respect to the distribution of alpha activity between the four anatomically distinct regions of the brain— left, right, anterior and posterior—may indicate the effectiveness of meditation."

6. James V. Hardt and Joseph Kamiya, Anxiety change through EEG alpha feedback: Seen only in high-anxiety subjects, *Science* 201 (1978): 79–81.

7. For research indicating that phase coherence is associated with clear or "pure" thinking, see K. Badawi, R. K. Wallace, A. M. Rouzere, and D. Orme-Johnson, Electrophysical changes during periods of respiratory suspension in the transcendental meditation technique, *Psychosomatic Medicine* 46 (1984): 267–76. An earlier study that arrived at similar findings is J. T. Farrow and J. R. Herbert, Breath suspension during the transcendental meditation technique, *Psychosomatic Medicine* 44, no. 2 (1982): 133–53. These same studies also found that alpha synchrony increases in long-term meditators.

Dawson Church: Psychological Clearing as Prelude to Soul Emergence

1. L. Plante, Spirituality soars among scientists, study says, *Spirituality & Health*, November 2, 2005.

2. Jewish Theological Seminary, Survey of physicians' views on miracles, 2004, www.jtsa.edu/research/finkelstein/surveys.

3. G. Ironson, et al., The Ironson-Woods Spirituality/Religiousness Index is associated with long survival, health behaviors, less distress and low cortisol in people with HIV/AIDS, *Annals of Behavioral Medicine* 24, no. 1 (2002): 34.

4. G. Ironson, et al., View of God is associated with disease progression in HIV, paper presented at the annual meeting of the Society of Behavioral Medicine, San Francisco, abstract published in *Annals of Behavioral Medicine* 31 (supplement, March 2006): S074.

5. G. Ironson, H. Kremer, and D. Ironson, Spirituality, spiritual experiences, and spiritual transformations in the face of HIV, in *Spiritual transformation and healing*, ed. J. Koss-Chiono and P. Hefner (Walnut Creek, CA: Altamira Press, 2007).

6. Personal communication with author, 12/12/2007.

7. V. J. Felliti, et al., Relationship of childhood abuse and household dysfunction to many of the leading causes of death in adults: The Adverse Childhood Experiences (ACE) study, *American Journal of Preventive Medicine* 4 (May 14,1998): 245.

8. D. Feinstein, et al., *The promise of energy psychology* (New York: Tarcher, 2005), 108.

9. L. Geronilla and D. Church, Effect of emotional freedom technique and diaphragmatic breathing on post traumatic stress disorder (PTSD), Clinical Trial Registration NCT00514956, 2008.

10. D. Church, The effect of energy psychology on athletic performance: A randomized, controlled, double-Blind study, reported at Meridian Seminar, Toronto, Canada, Oct 15, 2007.

William A. Tiller: Toward a Reliable Bridge of Understanding Between Traditional Science and Spiritual Science

1. W. A. Tiller and W. E. Dibble, Jr., New experimental data revealing an unexpected dimension to materials science and engineering, *Materials Research Innovations* 5 (2001): 21–34.

2. W. A. Tiller, *Science and human transformation: Subtle energies, intentionality and consciousness* (Walnut Creek, CA: Pavior Publishing, 1997).

3. W. A. Tiller, W. E. Dibble, Jr., and M. J. Kohane, *Conscious acts of creation: The emergence of a new physics* (Walnut Creek, CA: Pavior Publishing, 2001).

4. W. A. Tiller, W. E. Dibble, Jr., and J. G. Fandel, *Some science adventures with real magic* (Walnut Creek, CA: Pavior Publishing, 2005).

5. W. A. Tiller, *Psychoenergertic science: A second Copernican-scale revolution* (Walnut Creek, CA: Pavior Publishing, 2007).

6. W. A. Harrison, *Applied quantum mechanics* (Singapore: World Scientific Publishing, 2000).

7. P. Werbos, What do neural nets and quantum theory tell us about mind and reality? in *No matter, never mind*, ed. K. Yasue, M. Jiba, and T.D. Senta (Philadelphia, PA: John Benjamins Publishing Co., 2001).

8. R. M. Eisberg, *Fundamentals of modern physics* (New York: John Wiley and Sons, Inc., 1961), 140–146.

Lynne McTaggart: Entering Hyperspace

1. W. Singer, Neuronal synchrony: A versatile code for the definition of relations? *Neuron* 24 (1999): 49–65; F. Varela et al., The Brainweb: Phase synchronization and large-scale integration, *Nature Reviews: Neuroscience* 2 (2001): 229–39, as reported in A. Lutz et al., Long-term meditators self-induce high-amplitude gamma synchrony during mental practice, *Proceedings of the National Academy of Science* 101, no. 46 (2004): 16369–73.

2. O. Paulsen and T. J. Sejnowski, Natural patterns of activity and long-term synaptic plasticity, *Current Opinion in Neurobiology* 10 (2000): 172–9, as reported in Lutz, Long-term meditators.

3. Although the majority of studies carried out on meditation demonstrate that meditation leads to an increase in alpha rhythms (see Murphy, Meditation), the following are just a few that show that during meditation, subjects evidence spurts of high-frequency beta waves of twenty to forty cycles per second, usually during moments of intense concentration or ecstasy: J. P. Banquet, Spectral analysis of the EEG in meditation, *Electroencephalography and Clinical Neurophysiology* 35 (1973): 143–51; P. Fenwick et al., Metabolic and EEG changes during Transcendental Meditation: An explanation, *Biological Psychology* 5, no. 2 (1977): 101–18; M. A. West, Meditation and the EEG, *Psychological Medicine* 10, no. 2 (1980): 369–75; J. C. Corby et al., Psychophysiological correlates of the practice of tantric yoga meditation, *Postgraduate Medical Journal* 61 (1985): 301–4.

4. N. Das and H. Gastaut, Variations in the electrical activity of the brain, heart and skeletal muscles during yogic meditation and trance, *Electroencephalography and Clinical Neurophysiology*, supplement no. 6 (1955): 211–9.

5. Murphy, Meditation, cites 10 studies showing that heart rate accelerates during these peak moments of meditation.

6. W. W. Surwillo and D. P. Hobson, Brain electrical activity during prayer, *Psychological Reports* 43, no. 1 (1978): 135–43.

7. Murphy, Meditation.

8. Lutz, Long-term meditators.

9. Richard J. Davidson et al., Alterations in brain and immune function produced by mindfulness meditation, *Psychosomatic Medicine* 65 (2003): 564–70.

10. S. Krippner, The technologies of shamanic states of consciousness, in *Consciousness and healing: Integral approaches to mind-body medicine* ed. M. Schlitz and T. Amorok with M. S. Micozzi (St. Louis, MO: Elsevier/ Churchill Livingstone, 2005).

11. Murphy, Meditation.

12.. L. Bernardi et al., Effect of rosary prayer and yoga mantras on autonomic cardiovascular rhythms: Comparative study, *British Medical Journal* 323 (2001): 1446–9.

13. P. Fenwick et al., Metabolic and EEG changes during Transcendental Meditation: An explanation, *Biological Psychology* 5, no. 2 (1977): 101–18.

14. D. Goleman, *Emotional intelligence* (London: Bloomsbury Press, 1996).

15. D. Goleman, Meditation and consciousness: An Asian approach to mental health,

American Journal of Psychotherapy 30, no. 1 (1976): 41–54; G. Schwartz, Biofeedback, self-regulation, and the patterning of physiological processes, *American Scientist* 63, no. 3 (1975): 314–24; D. Goleman, Why the brain blocks daytime dreams, *Psychology Today*, March, 1976, 69–71.

16. P. Williams and M. West, EEG responses to photic stimulation in persons experienced at meditation, *Electroencephalography and Clinical Neurophysiology* 39, no. 5 (1975): 519–22; B. K. Bagchi and M. A. Wenger, Electrophysiological correlates of somenyogi exercises, *Electroencephalography and Clinical Neurophysiology* 7 (1957): 132–49.

17. D. Brown, M. Forte, and M. Dysart, Visual sensitivity and mindfulness meditation, *Perceptual and Motor Skills*58, no. 3 (1984): 775–84; and Differences in visual sensitivity among mindfulness meditators and non-meditators, *Perceptual and Motor Skills* 58, no. 3 (1984): 727–33.

Andrew Newberg: Spirituality, the Brain, and Health

Azari, N. P., J. Nickel, G. Wunderlich, M. Niedeggen, H. Hefter, L. Tellmann, H. Herzog, P. Stoerig, D. Birnbacher, and R. J. Seitz. 2001. Neural correlates of religious experience. *European Journal of Neuroscience* 13, no 8 (April): 1649–52.

D'Aquili, E. G., and A. B. Newberg. 1993. Religious and mystical states: A neuropsychological model. *Zygon* 28: 177–99.

Fowler, J. W. 1981. *Stages of faith*. San Francisco: HarperCollins.

Gellhorn, E., W. F. Kiely. 1972. Mystical states of consciousness: Neurophysiological and clinical aspects. *Journal of Nervous and Mental Disease* 154: 399–405.

Kabat-Zinn, J.. A. O. Massion, J. Kristeller, L. G. Peterson, K. E. Fletcher, L. Pbert, W. R. Lenderking, and S. F Santorelli. 1992. Effectiveness of a meditation-based stress reduction program in the treatment of anxiety disorders. *American Journal of Psychiatry* 149: 936–43.

Kjaer, T. W., C. Bertelsen, P. Piccini, D. Brooks, J. Alving, and H. C. Lou. 2002. Increased dopamine tone during meditation-induced change of consciousness. *Cognition and Brain Research* 13, no. 2 (April): 255–9.

Koenig, H.G., ed. 1998. *Handbook of religion and mental health*. San Diego: Academic Press.

Koenig, H.G., M. E. McCullough, and D. B. Larson, eds. 2001. *Handbook of religion and health*. New York: Oxford University Press.

Larson, D. B., J. P Swyers, and M. E. McCullough, eds. 1998. *Scientific research On spirituality and health: A consensus report*. Washington DC: National Insitute for Healthcare Research.

Lazar, S. W., G. Bush, R. L. Gollub, G. L. Fricchione, G. Khalsa, and H. Benson. 2000. Functional brain mapping of the relaxation response and meditation. *Neuroreport* 11, no. 7 (May 15): 1581–5.

Lou, H. C., T. W. Kjaer, L. Friberg, G. Wildschiodtz, S. Holm, and M. Nowak. 1999. A 15O-H2O PET study of meditation and the resting state of normal consciousness. *Human Brain Mapping* 7, no. 2: 98–105.

McNamara, P., ed. 2006. *Where God and science meet*. Westport, CT: Praeger.

Newberg, A. B., A. Alavi, M. Baime, M. Pourdehnad, J. Santanna, and E. G. D'Aquili. 2001. The measurement of regional cerebral blood flow during the complex cognitive task of meditation: A preliminary SPECT study. *Psychiatry Research: Neuroimaging* 106: 113–122.

Newberg, A. B., E. G. D'Aquili, and V. P. Rause. 2001. *Why God won't go away: Brain science and the biology of belief*. New York: Ballantine Publishing Group.

Newberg, A. B., and J. Iversen. 2003. The neural basis of the complex mental task of meditation: Neurotransmitter and neurochemical considerations. *Medical Hypothesis* 61, no. 2: 282–291.

Sudsuang, R., V. Chentanez, and K. Veluvan. 1991. Effects of Buddhist meditation on serum cortisol and total protein levels, blood pressure, pulse rate, lung volume and reaction time. *Physiology and Behavior* 50: 543–548.

Joan H. Hageman: Not all Meditation Is the Same: A Brief Overview of Perspectives, Techniques, and Outcomes

Alper, M. 2001. *The "God" part of the brain: A scientific interpretation of human spirituality and God.* New York: Rogue Press.

Atwood, J. D., and L. Maltin. 1991. Putting eastern philosophies into western psychotherapies. *American Journal of Psychotherapy* 45: 368–382.

Benson, H., M. S. Malhotra, R. F. Goldman, G. D. Jacobs, and P. J. Hopkins. 1990. Three case reports of the metabolic and electroencephalographic changes during advanced Buddhist meditation techniques. *Behavioral Medicine* 16 (Summer): 90–95.

Bogart, G. 1991. The use of meditation in psychotherapy: A review of the literature. *American Journal of Psychotherapy* 45: 383–412.

Cattell, R. B. 1957. *Personality and motivation, structure and measurement.* Yonkers, NY: World Book.

Colby, F. 1991. An analogue study of the initial carryover effects of meditation, hypnosis and relaxation using native college students. *Biofeedback Self-Regulation* 16, no. 2: 157–165.

Craven, J. L. 1989. Meditation and psychotherapy. *Canadian Journal of Psychiatry* 34: 648–653.

D'Aquili, E. G., and A. B. Newberg. 1993. Religious and mystical states: A neuropsychological model. *Zygon* 28: 177–200.

Davidson, R. J. 2004. Well-being and affective style: Neural substrates and biobehavioural correlates. *American Psychologist* 55: 1196–1214.

Davidson, R. J., J. Kabat-Zinn, J. Schumacher, M. Rosenkranz, D. Muller, S. F. Santorelli et al. 2003. Alterations in brain and immune function produced by mindfulness meditation. *Psychosomatic Medicine* 65: 564–570.

Delmonte, M. M. 1980. Personality characteristics and regularity of meditation. *Psychological Reports* 46, no. 3: 703–712.

Delmonte, M. M. 1981a. Suggestibility and meditation. *Psychological Reports* 48, no. 3: 727–737.

Delmonte, M. M. 1981b. Expectation and meditation. *Psychological Reports* 49, no. 3: 699–709.

Delmonte, M. M. 1985. Biochemical indices associated with meditation practice: A literature review. *Neuroscience Behavioral Reviews* 9, no. 4: 557–561.

Dua, J. K., and M. L. Swinden. 1992. Effectiveness of negative-thoughts-reduction, meditation and placebo training treatment in reducing anger. *Scandinavian Journal of Psychology* 33, no. 2: 135–146.

Epstein, M. 1990. Psychodynamics of meditation: Pitfalls of the spiritual path. *Journal of Transpersonal Psychology* 22: 17–34.

Freud, S. 1961. *Civilization and its discontents* Trans. and ed. J. Strachey. New York: W. W. Norton. (Original work published 1930.)

Fromm, E. 1975. Self-hypnosis: A new area of research. *Psychotherapy: Theory, Resarch and Practice* 12: 295–301.

Greenberg, J. R., and S. A. Mitchell. 1983. *Object relations in psychoanalytic theory.* Cambridge, MA: Harvard University Press.

Greguire, J. 1990. Therapy with the person who meditates: Diagnosis and treatment strategies. Transactional strategies. *Transactional Analysis Journal* 20, no. 11: 60–76.

Hageman, J. H. 2006. Multicultural religious and spiritual rituals: Meaning and praxis. *Behavioral & Brain Sciences* 29 no. 6: 619–620.

Hageman, J. H. 2007a. The body-mind-spirit profile of Sundo Taoism. In *Proceedings of the First International Sundo Taoist Conference on Health, Peace, and Life Through Sundo,* 46–117). Seoul, South Korea: International Institute for Sundo-Taoist Cultural Research.

Hageman, J. H. 2007b. *Spirituality: A mind-body-spirit cross-cultural perspective on self-healing.* Saarbrüecken, Germany: VDM Verlag Dr. Müller.

Hageman, J. H., S. Krippner, and I. Wickramasekera II. 2006. *Seven advanced meditators in Ramtha's School of Enlightenment.* Paper presented at the Third Psi Meeting: Implications and Applications of Psi Conference, Brazil.

Harte, J. L., G. H. Eifert, and R. Smith. 1995. The effects of running and meditation on beta-endorphin, corticotropin-releasing hormone and cortisol on plasma and on mood. *Biological Psychology* 40, no. 3: 251–265.

Heide, F. J., W. L. Wadlington, and R. M. Lundy. 1980. Hypnotic responsivity as a predictor of outcome in meditation. *International Journal of Clinical and Experimental Hypnosis* 28, no. 4: 358–366.

James, W. 1960. Human immortality: Two supposed objections to the doctrine. In *William James on psychical research*, ed. G. Murphy and R. O. Baliou, 279–308. New York: Viking. (Original work delivered as a lecture, 1898.)

Jevning, R., R. K. Wallace, and M. Beidebach. 1992. The physiology of meditation: A review. Awakeful hypometabolic integrated response. *Neuroscience and Behavioural Reviews* 16: 415–424.

Kirsch, I., and D. Henry. 1979. Self-desensitization and meditation in the reduction of public speaking anxiety. *Journal of Consulting and Clinical Psychology* 47, no. 3: 536–541.

Kokoszka, A. 1990. Axiological aspects of comparing psychotherapy and meditation. *International Journal of Psychosomatics* 37: 78–81.

Kokoszka, A. 1994. A rationale for a multilevel model of relaxation. *International Journal of Psychosomatics* 41: 4–10.

Kutz, I., J. Leserman, C. Dorrington, C. H. Morrison, J. Borysenko, and H. Benson. 1985. Meditation as an adjunct to psychotherapy: An outcome study. *Psychotherapy Psychosomatics* 43: 209–218.

Liu, G. L., C. Rong-Quing, L. Guo-Zhang, and H. Chi-Mang. 1990. Changes in brainstem and cortical auditory potentials during Qi-Gong meditation. *American Journal of Chinese Medicine* 18: 95–103.

Lou, H. C., T. W. Kjaer, L. Friberg, G. Wildschiodtz, S. Holm, and M. Nowak. 1999. A 150-H20 PET study of meditation and the resting state of normal consciousness. *Human Brain Mapping* 7: 98–105.

Morse, D. R. 1984. Who benefits from meditation? *International Journal of Psychosomatics* 31, no. 2: 2.

Newberg, A. B. 2002. Bringing "neuro" and "theology" together again. In *NeuroTheology: Brain, science, spirituality, religious experience,* ed. R. Joseph, 161–162. San Jose, CA: University Press, California.

Newberg, A. B., and Iversen, J. 2002. On the "neuro" in neurotheology. In *NeuroTheology: Brain, science, spirituality, religious experience,* ed. R. Joseph, 247–266. San Jose, CA: University Press, California.

Perez-De-Albeniz, A., and J. Holmes. 2000. *International Journal of Psychotherapy* 5: 49–58.

Peters, R. K., H. Benson, and D. Porter. 1977. Daily relaxation response breaks in a working population: 1. Health, performance and well-being. *American Journal of Public Health* 67: 946–953.

Random House Webster's college dictionary. 1996. New York: Random House.

Scheler, M. F. 1992. Effects of optimism on psychological and physical well being: Theoretical and empirical update. *Cognitive Therapy and Research* 16: 201–228.

Shapiro, D. H. 1982. Overview: Clinical and physiological comparison of meditation with other self-control strategies. *American Journal of Psychiatry* 139: 267–274.

Shapiro, D. H. 1992. Adverse effects of meditation: A preliminary investigation of long-term meditators. *International Journal of Psychosomatics* 39: 62–67.

Shapiro, D. H. 1994. Examining the content and context of meditation: A challenge for psychology in the areas of stress management. *Psychotherapy and Religion Values* 34, no. 4: 101–135.

Smith, J. C. 1978. Personality correlates of continuation and outcome in meditation and erect sitting control treatments. *Journal of Consulting and Clinical Psychology* 46, no. 2: 272–279.

Snaith, P. 1998. Meditation and psychotherapy. *British Journal of Psychiatry* 173: 193–195.

Telles, S., and T. Desraju. 1993. Autonomic changes in Brahmakumaris Raja yoga meditation. *International Journal of Psychophysiology* 15, no. 2: 147–152.

Zuroff, D. C., and J. C. Schwarz. 1978. Effects of transcendental meditation and muscle relaxation on trait anxiety, maladjustment, locus of control and drug use. *Journal of Consulting and Clinical Psychology* 46, no. 2: 264–271.

Marilyn Schlitz and Dean Radin: Prayer and Intention in Distant Healing: Assessing the Evidence

Astin, J. A., E. Harkness, and E. Ernst. 2000. The e cacy of "distant healing": A systematic review of randomized trials. *Annals of Internal Medicine* 132, no. 11: 903–910.

Barnes, P. M., E. Powell-Griner, K. McFann, and R. L. Nahin. 2004. *Complementary and alternative medicine use among adults* (Advance Data Report #343). Bethesda, MD: National Center for Complementary and Alternative Medicine.

Benor, D. J. 1992. *Healing research, Vol. 1.* In (Vol. Chapters 1–2). Deddington, United Kingdom: Helix Editions.

Benor, D. J. 1993. *Healing research: Holistic medicine and spiritual healing.* Munich, Germany: Helix Verlag.

Benson, H., J. A. Dusek, J. B. Sherwood, P. Lam, C. F. Bethea, W. Carpenter et al. 2006. Study of the therapeutic e ects of intercessory prayer (STEP) in cardiac bypass patients: A multicenter randomized trial of uncertainty and certainty of receiving intercessory prayer. *American Heart Journal* 151, no. 4: 934–942.

Braud, W., and M. Schlitz. 1983. Psychokinetic influence on electrodermal activity. *Journal of Parapsychology* 47: 95–119.

Byrd, R. C. 1988. Positive therapeutic e ects of intercessory prayer in a coronary care unit population. *Southern Medical Journal* 81, no. 7: 826–829.

Cassileth, B. R. 1984. Contemporary unorthodox treatment in cancer medicine. *Annals of Internal Medicine* 101: 105–112.

Dossey, L. 1993. *Healing words: The power of prayer and the practice of medicine.* San Francisco: HarperCollins.

Harris, W. S., M. Gowda, J. W. Kolb, C. P. Strachacz, J. L. Vacek, P. G. Jones et al. 1999. A randomized, controlled trial of the e ects of remote intercessory prayer on outcomes in patients admitted to the coronary care unit. *Archives of Internal Medicine* 159, no. 19: 2273–2278.

Johnson, S. C., and B. Spilka. 1991. Coping with breast cancer: The roles of clergy and faith. *Journal of Religion and Health* 30: 21–33.

Kiecolt-Glaser, J., L. McGuire, T. Robles, and R. Glaser. 2002. Psychoneuroimmunology and psychosomatic medicine: Back to the future. *Psychomatic Medicine* 64: 15–28.

Krieger, D. 1979. *The therapeutic touch: How to use your hands to help or heal.*Englewood Cli s, NJ: Prentice-Hall.

Kruco, M., S. Crater, D. Gallup, J. Blankenship, M. Cu e, M. Guarneri et al. 2005. Music, imagery, touch, and prayer as adjuncts to interventional cardiac care: The monitoring and actualisation of noetic trainings (mantra) II randomised study. *Lancet* 366, no. 9481: 211–217.

Kruco, M., S. Crater, and C. Green. 2001. Integrative noetic therapies as adjuncts to percutaneous intervention during unstable coronary syndromes: Monitoring and actualization of noetic training (mantra) feasibility pilot. *American Heart Journal* 142, no. 5: 760–767.

Maxwell, J. 1996. Nursing's new age? *Christianity Today* 40, no. 3: 96–99.

May, E., and L. Vilenskaya. 1994. Some aspects of parapsychological research in the former Soviet Union. *Subtle Energie* 3: 1–24.

Nash, C. B. 1982. ESP of present and future targets. *Journal of the Society for Psychical Research* 51, no. 792: 374–377.

Radin, D. I. 2006. *Entangled minds: Extrasensory experiences in a quantum reality.* New York: Simon & Schuster.

Radin, D. I., J. Stone, E. Levine, S. Eskandarnejad, M. Schlitz, L. Kozak et al. In press. E ects of motivated distant intention on electrodermal activity. *Explore: The Journal of Science and Healing.*

Roberts, L., I. Ahmed, and S. Hall. 2000. Intercessory prayer for the alleviation of ill health. *Cochrane Database Systematic Reviews* 2.

Saudia, T. L., M. R. Kinney, K. C. Brown, and L. Young-Ward. 1991. Health locus of control and helpfulness of prayer. *Heart Lung* 20. no. 1: 60–65.

Schlitz, M., and W. Braud. 1985. Reiki plus natural healing: An ethnographic and experimental study. *Psi Research* 4: 100–123.

Schlitz, M., and W. Braud. 1997a. Distant intentionality and healing: Assessing the evidence. *Alternative Therapies in Health and Medicine* 3, no. 6: 62–73.

Schlitz, M. J., and W. Braud. 1997b. Distant intentionality and healing: Assessing the evidence. *Alternative Therapies* 3, no. 6: 62–73.

Schlitz, M. J., and S. LaBerge. 1997. Covert observation increases skin conductance in subjects unaware of when they are being observed: A replication. *Journal of Parapsychology* 61: 185–196.

Schlitz, M., and N. Lewis. 1996. The healing powers of prayer. *Noetic Sciences Review* 38 (Summer): 29–33.

Schlitz, M., D. Radin, B. F. Malle, S. Schmidt, J. Utts, and G. L. Yount. 2003. Distant healing intention: Definitions and evolving guidelines for laboratory studies. *Alternative Therapies in Health and Medicine* 9. supplement 3: A31–A43.

Schmidt, S., R. Schneider, J. Utts, and H. Walach. 2004. Distant intentionality and the feeling of being stared at. *British Journal of Psychology* 95: 235–247.

Sicher, F., E. Targ, D. Moore, and H. S. Smith. 1998. A randomized double-blind study of the e ect of distant healing in a population with advanced aids: Report of a small scale study. *Western Journal of Medicine* 169, no. 6: 356–363.

Sloan, R., and R. Ramakrishnan. 2005. The mantra II study. *Lancet* 366: 1769–1770.

Snel, F. W. J. J., P. C. van der Sijde, and F. A. C. Wiegant. 1995. Cognitive styles of believers and disbelievers in paranormal phenomena. *Journal of the Society for Psychical Research* 60, no. 839: 251–257.

Solfvin, J. 1984. Mental healing. In *Advances in Parapsychological Research,Vol. 4,* ed. S. Krippner, 31–63. Jefferson, NC: McFarland.

Suarez, M. 1996. Use of folk healing practices by HIV-infected hispanics living in the United States. *AIDS Care* 8, no. 6: 685–690.

Walach, H. 2005. Generalized entanglement: A new theoretical model for understanding the e ects of complementary and alternative medicine. *Journal of Alternative and Complementary Medicine* 11, no. 3: 549–559.

Wallis, C. 1996a. Faith and healing. *Time/CNN poll,* June.

Wallis, C. 1996b. Faith and healing. *Time,* June 24, 58–64.

Whitmont, E. C. 1993. *The alchemy of healing.* Berkeley, CA: North Atlantic.

The authors would like to thank Jenny Mathew, Charlene Farrell, and Cassandra Vieten for their help on the production of this chapter.

Jeanne Achterberg: Evidence for Correlations Between Distant Intentionality and Brain Function in Recipients: A Functional Magnetic Resonance Imaging Analysis

1. M. Schlitz, D. Radin, B. Malle et al., Distant healing intention: Definitions and evolving guidelines for laboratory studies, *Alternative Therapies in Health and Medicine* 9, no. 3 (2004): A31–43.

2. W. B. Jonas and C. C. Crawford, eds., *Healing intention and energy medicine: Science, research methods and clinical implications* (New York: Churchill Livingstone, 2003).

3. E. G. D'Aquili and A. B. Newberg, Mystical states and the experience of God: A model of the neuropsychological substrate, *Zygon* 28 (1993): 177–200.

4. E. G. D'Aquili and A. B. Newberg, The neuropsychology of aesthetic, spiritual, and mystical States, *Zygon* 35, no. 1 (2000): 39–51.

5. S. W. Lazar, G. Bush, R. L. Gollub et al., Functional brain mapping of the relaxation response and meditation, *NeuroReport* 11, no. 7 (2000): 1–5.

6. T. D. Duane and T. Behrendt, Extrasensory electroencephalographic induction between identical twins, *Science* 150 (1965): 367.

7. J. Grinberg-Zylberbaum and J. Ramos, Patterns of interhemispheric correlation during human communication, *International Journal of Neuroscience* 36 (1987): 41–53.

8. J. Grinberg-Zylberbaum, M. Delaflor, M. E. Sanchez-Arellano et al., Human communication: The electrophysiological activity of the brain, *Subtle Energies and Energy Medicine* 3, no. 3 (1993): 25–43.

9. J. Grinberg-Zylberbaum, M. Delaflor, and A. Goswami, The Einstein/Podolsky/Rosen paradox in the brain: The transferred potential, *Physics Essays* 7, no. 4 (1994): 422–428.

10. D. Radin, Event-related electroencephalographic correlations between isolated human subjects, *Journal of Alternative and Complementary Medicine* 10 (2004): 315–323.

11. J. Wackermann, C. Seiter, and H. Keibel et al., Correlations between brain electrical activities of two spatially separated human subjects, *Neuroscience Letters* 336 (2003): 60–64.

12. L. J. Standish, L. C. Johnson, L. Kozak et al., Evidence of correlated functional magnetic resonance imaging signals between distant human brains, *Alternative Therapies in Health and Medicine* 9, no. 1, (2003): 122–125.

13. M. Schlitz and W. Braud, Distant intentionality and healing: Assessing the evidence, *Alternative Therapies in Health and Medicine* 3 (1997): 62–73.

14. N. Tzourio-Mazoyer, B. Landeau, D. Papathanassiou et al., Automated anatomical labeling of activations in SPM using a macroscopic anatomical parcellation of the MNI MRI single subject brain, *Neuroimage* 15 (2002): 273–289.

15. P. Petrovik, E. Kalso, K. M. Petterson et al., Placebo and opioid analgesia: Imaging a shared neuronal network, *Science* 295 (2002): 728–737.

16. T. W. Kjaer, M. Nowak, and H. C. Lou, Reflective self-awareness and conscious states: PET evidence for a common midline parietofrontal core, *Neuroimage* 17, no. 2 (2002): 1080–1086.

17. A. Einstein, B. Podolsky, and N. Rosen, Can quantum-mechanical description of physical reality be considered complete? *Physical Review* 47 (1935): 777–780.

18. R. Pizzi, A. Fantasia, F. Gelain et al., Non-local correlation between human neural networks, in *Quantum information and computation II: Proceedings of SPIE5436*, ed. E. Donkor, A. R. Pirick, and H. E. Brandt (Bellingham, WA: SPIE), 107–117.

Garret Yount: Evaluating Biofield Treatments in the Laboratory

1. K. Hintz, G. Yount, I. Kadar, G. Schwartz, R. Hammerschlag, and S. Lin, Bioenergy definitions and research guidelines, *Alternative Therapies in Health and Medicine* 9, no. 3 (2003): A13–A30.

2. J. Mager, D. Moore, D. Bendl, B. Wong, K. Rachlin, and G. Yount, Evaluating biofield treatments in a cell culture model of oxidative stress, *Explore* (NY) 3, no. 4 (2007): 386–90.

3. J. Walleczek, E. C. Shiu, and G.M. Hahn, Increase in radiation-induced HPRT gene mutation frequency after nonthermal exposure to nonionizing 60 Hz electromagnetic fields, *Radiation Research* 151, no. 4 (1999): 489–97.

4. D. J. Benor, Energy medicine for the internist, *Medical Clinics of North America* 86, no. 1 (2002): 105–25.

5. B. Rubik, The biofield hypothesis: Its biophysical basis and role in medicine, *Journal of Alternative and Complementary Medicine* 8, no. 6 (2002): 703–17.

6. S. W. Porges, Social engagement and attachment: A phylogenetic perspective, *Annals of the New York Academy of Sciences* 1008 (2003): 31–47.

7. J. Engebretson and D. W. Wardell, Energy-based modalities, *Nursing Clinic of North America* 42, no. 2 (2007): 243–59, vi.

8. W. B. Jonas and C. C. Crawford, Science and spiritual healing: A critical review of spiritual healing, "energy" medicine, and intentionality, *Alternative Therapies in Health and Medicine* 9, no. 2 (2003): 56–61.

9. K. W. Chen, An analytic review of studies on measuring effects of external QI in China, *Alternative Therapies in Health and Medicine* 10, no. 4 (2004): 38–50.

10. S. Ohnishi, T. Ohnishi, K. Nishino, Y. Tsurasaki, and M. Yamaguchi, Growth inhibition of cultured human liver carcinoma cells by Ki-energy (life-energy): Scientific evidence for Ki-effects on cancer cells, *Evidence-based Complementary and Alternative Medicine* 2, no. 3, (2005): 387–393.

11. S. Shah, A. Raffo, S. Itescu, and M.C. Oz, A study of the effect of energy healing on in vitro tumor cell proliferation, *Journal of Alternative and Complementary Medicine*, no. 5 (1999): 359–365.

12. R. Zachariae, L. Hojgaard, C. Zachariae, M. Vaeth, B. Bang, and L. Skuo, The effect of spiritual healing on in vitro tumour cell proliferation and viability—An experimental study, *British Journal of Cancer* 93, no. 5 (2005): 538–43.

13. J. G. Kiang, D. Marotta, M. Wirkus, M. Wirkus, and W.B. Jonas, External bioenergy increases intracellular free calcium concentration and reduces cellular response to heat stress, *Journal of Investigative Medicine* 50, no. 1 (2002): 38–45.

14. J. G. Kiang, J.A. Ives, and W.B. Jonas, External bioenergy-induced increases in intracellular free calcium concentrations are nediated by Na+/Ca2+ exchanger and L-type calcium channel, *Molecular and Cellular Biochemistry* 271, no. 1–2 (2005): 51–9.

15. B. Rubik, A. J. Brooks, and G. E. Schwartz, In vitro effect of Reiki treatment on bacterial cultures: Role of experimental context and practitioner well-being, *Journal of Alternative and Complementary Medicine* 12, no. 1 (2006): 7–13.

16. X. Yan, H. Shen, M. Zaharia, J Wang, D. Wolf, F. Li, G. D. Lee, and W. Cao, Involvement of phosphatidylinositol 3-kinase and insulin-like growth factor-I in YXLST-mediated neuroprotection, *Brain Research* 1006 (2004): 198–206.

17. R. G. Cutler, Oxidative stress profiling: Part I; Its potential importance in the optimization of human health, *Annals of the New York Academy of Science* 1055 (2005): 93–135.

18. A. Cellerino, L. Galli-Resta, and L. Colombaioni, The dynamics of neuronal death: A time-lapse study in the retina, *Journal of Neuroscience* 20, no. 16 (2000): RC92.

19. M. Schlitz, D. Radin, B. F. Malle. S. Schmidt, J. Utts, and G. Yount, Distant healing intention: Definitions and evolving guidelines for laboratory studies, *Alternative Therapies in Health and Medicine* 9, no. 3 (2003): A31–43.

20. G. Yount, J. Solfvin, D. Moore, M. Schlitz, M. Reading, K. Aldape, K., and Y. Qian, In vitro test of external Qigong, *BMC Complementary and Alternative Medicine* 15, no. 4 (2004): 5.

21. R. Taft, D. Moore, and G. Yount, Time-lapse snalysis of potential cellular responsiveness to Johrei, a Japanese healing technique, *BMC Complementary and Alternative Medicine* 5, no. 1 (2005): 2.

22. R. Taft, L. Nieto, T. Luu, A. Pennucci, D. Moore, and G. Yount, Cultured human brain tumor cells do not respond to Johrei treatment, *Subtle Energies and Energy Medicine* 14, no. 3 (2005): 253–265.

23. Z. Hall, T. Luu, D. Moore, and G. Yount, Radiation response of cultured human cells is unaffected by Johrei, *Evidence-based Complementary and Alternative Medicine* October 31, 2006, http://ecam.oxfordjournals.org/cgi/content/full/4/2/191.

Stanley Krippner and Ian Wickramasekera: Absorption and Dissociation in Spiritistic Brazilian Mediums

Bastide, R. 1960. *Les religions Africaines au Bresil [The African religions of Brazil]*. Paris: Press Universitaires de France.

Bernstein, E. M., and F. W. Putnam. 1986. Development, reliability, and validity of a dissociation scale. *Journal of Nervous and Mental Disease* 174: 727–735.

Borges, V. da R. 1992. *Manual de parapsicologia [Manual of parapsychology]*. Recife: Edicao Instituto Pernambucano de Pesquisas Psicobiofisicas.

Bourguignon, E. 1976. *Possession*. San Francisco: Chandler & Sharp.

Bourguignon, E., and T. Evascu. 1977. Altered states of consciousness within a general evolutionary perspective: A holocultural analysis. *Behavior Science Research* 12: 199–216.

Brown, D. 1994. *Umbanda: Religion and politics in urban Brazil*. New York: Columbia University Press.

Carlson, E. G., and F. W. Putnam. 1993. An update on the Dissociative Experiences Scale. *Dissociation* 6: 16–27.

Don, N. S., and G. Moura. 2000. Trance surgery in Brazil. *Alternative Therapies* 6, no. 4: 39–48.

Fernandez, L. 2001. The worldview of the Grade V hypnotizable person. *Hypnos* 28: 207–208.

Frederick, C. 2005. Selected topics in ego state therapy. *International Journal of Clinical and Experimental Hypnosis* 53, no. 4: 339–429.

Hageman, J. H. 2002. Assessing the implications of spiritual self-healing paradigms. Unpublished research study. San Francisco, CA: Saybrook Graduate School and Research Center.

Hartmann, E. 1991. *Boundaries of the mind*. New York: Basic Books.

Hastings, A. 1991. *With the tongues of men and angels: A study of channeling*. Fort Worth, TX: Holt, Rinehart and Winston.

Hess, D. J. 1994. *Samba in the night: Spiritism in Brazil*. New York: Columbia University Press.

Hilgard, E. R. 1977/1986. *Divided consciousness*. New York: John Wiley and Sons.

Kirsch, I., and J. R. Council. 1992. Situational and personality correlates of hypnotic responsiveness. In *Contemporary hypnosis research*, ed. E. Fromm and M. R. Nash, 267–291. New York: Guilford.

Klimo, J. 1998. *Channeling: Investigations on receiving information from paranormal sources*. Berkeley, CA: North Atlantic Books.

Krippner, S. 1997. Dissociation in many times and places. In *Broken images, broken selves: Dissociative narratives in clinical practice*, ed. S. Krippner and S. M. Powers, 3–40. Washington, DC: Brunner/Mazel.

Krippner, S. 2005. Trance and the Trickster: Hypnosis as a liminal phenomenon. *International Journal of Clinical and Experimental Hypnosis* 53, no. 2: 97–118.

Krippner, S. 1998/1999. Transcultural and psychotherapeutic aspects of a Candomblé practice in Recife, Brazil. In *Yearbook of cross-cultural medicine and psychotherapy: Mythology, medicine, and healing: Transcultural perspectives,* ed. S. Krippner and H. Kalweit, 67–86. Berlin: Verlag fur Wissenschaft und Bildung.

Krippner, S., I. Wickramasekera, and R. Tartz,. 2000. Scoring thick and scoring thin: The boundaries of psychic claimants. *Subtle Energies & Energy Medicine* 11: 43–63.

Krippner, S., I. Wickramasekera, J. Wickramasekera, and C. W. Winstead III. 1998. The Ramtha phenomenon: Psychological, phenomenological, and geomagnetic data. *Journal of the American Society for Psychical Research* 92: 2–24.

Leacock, S., and R. Leacock. 1972. *Spirits of the deep: A study of an Afro-Brazilian cult*. Garden City, NY: Doubleday Natural History Press.

Lewis-Fernandez, R., and A. Kleinman. 1995. Cultural psychiatry: Theoretical, clinical and research issues. *Psychiatric Clinics of North America* 18: 433–448.

Lex, B. 1979. The neurobiology of ritual trance. In *The spectrum of ritual: A biogenetic structural analysis*, ed. E. G. d'Aquili, C. D. Laughlin Jr., and J. McManus, 117–151. New York: Columbia University Press.

Lima, I. W. R. 1998. Pesquisa de atividade psicopictorafica de Jacques Andrade [Research into the psychic paintings of Jacques Andrade]. *Papels del Tercer Encuentro Psi*, 1998: 121–124. Curitiba, Brazil: Instituto de Psicologia Paranormal.

Lins, R. D. 1999. *Paranormal painting: A new conceptual approach and a case analysis*. Recife: Instituto Pernambucano de Pesquisas Psicobiofisicas.

Lynn, S. J., J. Pintar, and J. W. Rhue. 1997. Fantasy proneness, dissociation, and narrative construction. In *Broken Selves: Dissociative narratives and phenomena*, ed. S. Powers and S. Krippner. New York: Bruner/Mazel.

McIntyre, T. M., J.-M. Klein, and F. Gonçalves. 2001. *Escala de Tellegen* (Portuguese translation of the Tellegen Absorption Scale). Braga, Portugal: University of Minho.

Moreira-Almeida, A., A. A. Silva de Almeida, and F. L. Neto. 2005. History of "spiritist madness" in Brazil. *History of Psychiatry* 16: 5–25.

Murphy, G. 1969. The discovery of gifted sensitives. *Journal of the American Society of Psychical Research* 63: 3–20.

Negro, P. J., Jr., P. Palladino-Negro, and M. R. Louza. 2002. Do religious mediumship dissociative experiences conform to the sociocognitive theory of dissociation? *Journal of Trauma and Dissociation* 3, 51–73.

Oliveira, X. de. 1931. *Espiritismo e loucura [Spiritism and madness]*. Rio de Janeiro: A. Coelho Franco Filho.

Pacheco e Silva, A. C. 1936. *Problemas de higiene mental [Problems of mental hygiene]*. São Paulo: Oficinas Graficas do Juqueri.

Roche, S. M., and K. M. McConkey. 1990. Absorption: Nature, assessment, and correlates. *Journal of Personality & Social Psychology* 59: 91–101.

Rodrigues, N. 1935. *O animismo fetichista dos negros Bahíanas [The animistic fetish of Bahían negros]*. Rio de Janeiro: Civilizacao Brasileira. (Original work published 1896.)

Sarbin, T. R. 1998. Believed in imaginings: A narrative approach. In *Believed-in imaginings: The narrative construction of reality,* ed. J. R. Rivera and T. R. Sarbin. Washington, D.C.: American Psychological Association.

Schumaker, J. F. 1995. Religion: The cultural mask of sanity. In *The corruption of reality: A unified theory of religion, hypnosis, and psychopathology,* ed. J. F. Schumaker, 81–151. Amherst: Prometheus Books.

Spiegel, D. 1990. Hypnosis, dissociation, and trauma: Hidden and overt observers. In *Repression and dissociation: Implications for personality theory, psychopathology, and health* ed. J. Singer, 232–243. Chicago: University of Chicago Press.

Tellegen, A. 1977. *The Multidimensional Personality Questionnaire.* Minneapolis: National Computing Systems.

Tellegen, A., and G. Atkinson. 1974. Openness to absorbing and self-altering experience ("absorption"), a trait related to hypnotic susceptibility. *Journal of Abnormal Psychology* 83: 268–277.

Villoldo, A., and S. Krippner. 1987. *Healing states.* New York: Fireside/Simon & Schuster.

Walker, S. 1972. *Ceremonial spirit possession in Africa and Afro-America.* Leiden: Brill.

Wickramasekera, I. 1986a. Risk factors for parapsychological verbal reports, hypnotizability and somatic complaints. In *Parapsychology and human nature,* ed. B. Shapin and L. Coly, 19–35. New York: Parapsychology Foundation.

Wickramasekera, I. 1986b. A model of people at high risk to develop chronic stress related somatic symptoms: Some predictions. *Professional Psychology: Research and Practice* 17: 437–447.

Wickramasekera, I. 1988. *Clinical behavioral medicine: Some concepts and procedures.* New York: Plenum Press.

Wickramasekera, I. 1989. Is hypnotic ability a risk factor for subjective (verbal report) psi, somatization, and health care costs? In *Psi and clinical practice,* ed. L. Coly and J. D. S. McMahon, 184–191. New York: Parapsychological Foundation.

Wickramasekera, I. 1991. Model of the relationship between hypnotic ability, psi, and sexuality. *Journal of Parapsychology* 55: 159–174.

Wickramasekera, I. 1993. Assessment and treatment of somatization disorders: The high risk model of threat perception. In *Handbook of clinical hypnosis*, ed. J. W. Rhue, S. J. Lynn, and I. Kirsch, 587–621. Washington, DC: American Psychological Association.

Wickramasekera, I. 1995. Somatization: Concepts, data and predictions from the high risk model of threat perception, *Journal of Nervous and Mental Disorders* 183: 15–30.

Wickramasekera, I. 1998. Out of mind is not out of body: Somatization, the high risk model, and psychophysiological psychotherapy. *Biofeedback*, Spring.: 8–11, 32.

Wickramasekera, I., S. Krippner, and I. Wickramasekera II. 1997. Channeling dead spirits and painters in Brazil: Psychophysiological dissociation as "incongruence" between physiological response systems in psychic claimants. Paper presented at the annual meeting of the American Psychological Association, Chicago, IL.

Wickramasekera, I., S. Krippner, and J. Wickramasekera. 2001. Case studies of "psychic sensitives": Testing predictions from a model of threat perception. Unpublished case studies. San Francisco, CA: Saybrook Graduate School and Research Center.

Wickramasekera II, I. E., J. and Szlyk. 2003. Could empathy be a predictor of hypnotic ability? *International Journal of Clinical and Experimental Hypnosis* 51, no. 4: 390–399.

Wilson, S. C., and T. X. Barber. 1978. The Creative Imagination Scale as a measure of hypnotic responsiveness: Applications to experimental and clinical hypnosis. *American Journal of Clinical Hypnosis* 20: 235–249.

Winkelman, M. 1986. Trance states: A theoretical model and cross-cultural analysis. *Ethos* 14: 174–203.

Winkelman, M. 2000. *Shamanism: The neural ecology of consciousness and healing*. Westport, CT: Bergin & Garvey.

Marilyn Mandala Schlitz, Tina Amarok, Cassandra Veiten: The Art and Science of Transformation

Artress, L. 2003. Interview by C. Vieten and T. Amorok. Video recording. February 12. Grace Cathedral, San Francisco.

Eck, D. 2006. *The Pluralism Project at Harvard University*.Pluralism Project, Harvard University. http://www.pluralism.org/research/articles/index.php (accessed July 6, 2007).

Huxley, A. 1945. *The Perennial Philosophy*. Repr., New York: HarperCollins, 2004.

Huxley, A. 1954. *The Doors of Perception and Heaven and Hell*. Repr., New York: HarperCollins, 2004.

Kabat-Zinn, J. 2004. Interview by M. Schlitz. Video recording. February 10. Institute of Noetic Sciences, Petaluma, CA.

Mack, A., and I. Rock. 1998. *Inattentional Blindness*.Cambridge, MA: MIT Press.

Simons, D. J., and C. F. Chabris. 1999. Gorillas in our midst: Sustained inattentional blindness for dynamic events. *Perception* 28, no. 9: 1059–1074.

Miller, W. R., and J. C'de Baca. 2001. *Quantum Change: When Epiphanies and Sudden Insights Transform Ordinary Lives*. New York: Guilford Press.

Steuco, A. 1540. *De Perenni Philosophia Libri X*. Repr., New York: Johnson Reprint Corp., 1972.

Tart, C. 1975. Science, states of consciousness, and spiritual experiences: The need for state-specific sciences. In *Transpersonal Psychologies*, ed. C. T. Tart. New York: Harper & Row.

Grof, S. 2003. Interview by C. Vieten and T. Amorok. Video recording. January 10. Mill Valley, CA.

Vieten, C., A. B. Cohen, and M. Schlitz. 2008. Correlates of transformative experiences and practices: Results of a cross-sectional survey. Manuscript in preparation, Institute of Noetic Sciences, Petaluma, CA.

Credits

"The Science of Emotions and Consciousness" by Candace Pert with Nancy Marriott was reprinted from *Everything You Need to Know to Feel Good*, published by Hay House, 2007.

"Effects of a Fourteen-Day Healthy Longevity Lifestyle Program on Cognition and Brain Function" by Gary Small, adapted version originally appeared in *American Journal of Geriatric Psychiatry* 14:538–545, June 2006.

"Compassion and Healing" by Larry Dossey originally appeared in *Explore: The Journal of Science and Healing* 3(1) (January 2007), pp. 1–5.

"Reflections on the Mindful Brain" from *The Mindful Brain: Reflection and Attunement in the Cultivation of Well-Being* by Daniel J. Siegel. Copyright © 2007 by Mind Your Brain, Inc. Used by permission of W. W. Norton & Company, Inc.

The adapted version of "Doing Optimism, Optimists, Pessimists, and Their Potential for Change" by Suzanne Segerstrom is reprinted from her book, *Breaking Murphy's Law*, published by Guilford Publications, Inc., 2006.

Index

Note: Locators in italics indicate figures, tables, or illustrations.

meditation and, 64, 65, 211–230, 343–348, 377–378

mindfulness meditation and, 64

nature of mind and, 65

neurology and, 269–286

neuroscience and, 343–348

psychology and, 269–286

self and, 378

Tantric Buddhism, 99, 377

Tibetan Buddhist tradition, 170, 229, 336, 393, 406

Zen Buddhism, 6, 211–213, 228–230, 232, 336, 345, 377–378

Byrd, Randolph, 366–367, 395–396

Cade, C. Maxwell, 247

caffeine, 23

California Pacific Medical Center, 52, 397, 413–424

CAM therapies. *See* complementary and alternative medicine (CAM) therapies

cancer, 137, 258, 361, 441–442
biofield treatments and, 417
distant healing and, 393–394
interaction with natural environment and, 150
prayer and, 388–389

Candomblé religion, 425, 426, 427–428, 431

cannabinoids, 24

carcinogens, 361

cardiovascular feedback, 375

Carmelite nuns, 388

Casey, Caroline, 159

Catholicism, 388, 406. *See also* Christianity

CAT scans, 327, 333, 334

Cattell, Raymond B., 381

CD4, 55

CD8, 55

C'de Baca, J., 441

ceiling effect, 381

cells, 188–189, 263. *See also* brain cells

Center for Affective Neuroscience, 329–330

Centers for Disease Control and Prevention National Center for Health Statisitics, 388

central nervous system (CNS), 435–437. *See also* nervous system

cerebral metabolism, 35, 44

cerebrovascular disease, 37

chakras, 92, 297–298, 311

Chan, 211–212. *See also* Zen Buddhism

change, 110–115

channeling, 426, 430, 437, 438

chanting, 374, 377

chaotic meditation, 368

Chaudhuri, Haridas, 447

chemical medicine, 292

chemotaxis, 21

chi, 21

childbirth preparation, 27, 367

childhood, 76, 78, 274

Childre, D., 130–131

children, 76, 78, 281

chimpanzees, 285

Chinese medicine, 21. *See also* Qigong healing

chiropractic medicine, 23

chloride ions, 18

cholesterol, 360, 369

Christ. *See* Jesus

Christianity, 1, 7, 49, 64, 99, 169, 316, 332, 377, 396. *See also* Catholicism; Jesus

Christian nuns, 7

chronic pain, 72, 86, 251, 367

Church, Dawson, 255–257

cingulate cortex, 220, 222, 411, 412

cingulate gyrus, 224, 355, 412

circulatory system, meditation and, 379

cirrhosis, 358

clairvoyance, 324

classical mechanics (CM), 290

climate change, 181

CM. *See* classical mechanics (CM)

CNS. *See* central nervous system (CNS)

COAL (curiosity, openness, acceptance, and love), 70, 74

awareness and, 69–72

cognition, 35, 189, 209, 375

cognitive decline, 36, 37

cognitive dissonance, 218

cognitive mindfulness, 79

cognitive psychology, 146, 314–315

cognitive strategies, 377

coherence, 346

cohesiveness, 375

colchicine, 55

Columbia University College of Physicians and Surgeons, 22

communication, attuned, 77

compassion, x, 47–48, 49, 50, 58, 132, 279. *See also* empathy

caregiving and, 58, 59

compassionate intention, 345

compassionate meditation, 344, 345

compassion-based healing, 55

compassion effect, 50–53

compassion hypothesis, 54

"compassion meters", 54

Einstein and, 179

healing and, 47–60, 401–402

humane care and, 50

meditation and, 379

physiological effects of, 50, 59

positive health outcomes and, 50

secular humanism and, 50

supporting evidence, 53

tears and, 55

compassionate intention, 345

compassionate meditation, 344, 345

compassion-based healing, 55

compassion effect, 50–53

"compassion meters", 54

complementary and alternative medicine (CAM) therapies, 145, 388

comprehension, meditation and, 367

concentration, 279, 281, 375, 376, 377, 378. *See also* focus

concentrative meditation, 375

conceptual processes, 208

Confucius, 49, 333, 337

consciousness, 167, 172, 273, 287, 290, 294, *309*, 311–312

altered states of, 376, 426, 427, 430. *See also* trances

beyond thought, 4–6

biology and, 185–199

the brain and, 201–210, 384, 412

conscious attention, 278–280

conscious experience, 1

conscious mind, 18

Eastern view of, 19

epigenetics and, 185–199

expanded states of, xi

exploring, 3

higher states of, 31

lifestyle and, 19–20

meditation and, 378–379, 384–385

parapsychological approach, 313, 322–325

physiology of, 19

psychological approach, 313–326

science of, 15–33

states of, 212

stream of consciousness, 218, 376

transformations of, 439–457

transpersonal psychological approach, 313, 319–322

water and, 157

consciousness-mediated event, 55

consciousness transformation, 439–457

Consolidated Standards of Reporting Trials (CONSORT criteria), 53

CONSORT criteria. *See* Consolidated Standards of Reporting Trials (CONSORT criteria)

contemplation, 374. *See also* meditation

contemplative neuroscience, 270–286

contemplative practices, 69, 281

fatigue, 251

fats, 37, 264, 360

fear, 23, 223

"feeling felt", 62

feelings. *See* emotions

Fehmi, Les, 231–242

Fenwick, Peter, 347

fibromyalgia, 27, 248, 251
  meditation and, 367

field, 375

"fight or flight" syndrome, 89, 91, 147,
  263–264, 280

Fijian worldview, 139–141

Fisher, Roland, 90, 91, 92

Five Hindrances, 278

Flanagan, Owen, 327–339

flashbacks, 264. *See also* post-
  traumatic stress disorder (PTSD)

flourishing, 338

fMRIs. *See* functional magnetic
  resonance imaging (fMRI)

focus, 343–348, 354–355, 379, 433.
  See also attention; concentration

Fogarty, Linda A., 58

folklore physics, 400–401

forgiveness, 197

Fran and Ray Stark Foundation Fund
  for Alzheimer's Disease Research, 45

Franciscan nuns, 406

Francis of Assisi, St., 168–169

Freud, Sigmund, 214, 383

frontal cortex, 20, 21, 23, 26, 29–31,
  32, 374, 430

frontal lobe, *219*, 354–355

frontal regions, 20, 21, 23, 26, 29–32,
  51, *219*, 354–355, 374, 412, 430

frontal superior areas, 412

frozen shoulder, 260–262

frustration, 269

functional magnetic resonance
  imaging (fMRI), 51, 79, 333, 334,
  354, 405–413. *See also* magnetic
  resonance imaging (MRI)

fusiform gyrus, 220, 222

GABA, 18, 226

GABA receptor, 18

Galileo Galilei, 1

gamma-band activity, 344–345

gamma oscillations, 336

gamma state, 344

gamma-wave activity, 345–346

gamma-wave hyperspace, 345

ganglia, 22

gardens, 144
  healing, 136, 145, 146
  hospices and, 145
  hospitals and, 145
  pain reduction and, 148
  positive changes in mood and, 150
  post-stroke rehabilitation, 150
  restorative, 145
  spirituality and, 144

gas discharge visualization (GDV)
  camera, 162

Gate, the, 226

General Clinical Research Centers
  Program, 45

General Social Survey, 441

generosity, x, 279

genetics, 185–199, 263, 264, 285. *See*
  also deoxyribonucleic acid (DNA);
  epigenetics

genetic control, 186, 187, 197

genetic determinism, 186

genu, 220

German language, 99

Gibbs Thermodynamic Free Energy,
  291–292

global perspective, 404

glucose metabolism, 42

Gnostic text, 169

goals, 116–118

God, 1, 5, 123. *See also* divine, the

medicine. *See also* healing; health care
  chemical medicine, 292
  Chinese medicine, 21. *See also*
    Qigong healing
  chiropractic medicine, 23
  energy medicine, 292
  epigenetic medicine, 255
  future of, 32
  history of, 55
  information medicine, 293
  integrative, 164
  plant spirits and, 142
  preventative medicine, 360
  spirituality and, x
Medicine for the Earth, 157–165
medicine men, 49, 425
meditation, ix, 6, 9–10, 32, 77,
    211–212, *213*, 230, 239, 270, 272,
    281, 293, 343–348, 355, 368,
    378–379. *See also* prayer; spiritual
    practices
  acceptance and, 379
  active meditation, 375–376, 377
  adverse effects of, 380–381, 382,
    384
  affect and, 379
  anxiety and, 367, 380–381
  arthritis and, 367
  attention and, 213, 379
  attrition from, 382
  autonomic nervous system and, 131
  awareness and, 382–383
  beneficial effects of, 379–380,
    382–383, 390
  biofeedback and, xi
  the brain and, x, 3, 343–348, 379,
    407–408
  breathing techniques, 376, 377, 379
  Buddhism and, 65, 377–378
  ceiling effect, 381
  chanting and, 377
  chaotic meditation, 368
  childbirth preparation and, 367
  Christian meditation, 393
  chronic pain and, 367
  circulatory effects of, 379
  cognitive strategies and, 377
  compassion and, 344, 345, 379
  compassionate meditation, 344, 345
  comprehension and, 367
  concentration and, 375, 377, 378

  concentrative, 375
  consciousness and, 378–379,
    384–385
  creativity and, 367
  dance and, 377
  definition of, 374–375
  depression and, 367
  Eastern Orthodox, 377
  effectiveness and, 379
  emotional stability and, 367
  enlightenment and, 377, 378, 383
  experience of, 376
  extroversion and, 381–382
  feelings and, 379
  fibromyalgia and, 367
  focus and, 379
  forms of, 368
  free, 368
  God and, 5
  happiness and, 327–339, 346, 379,
    383
  health and, 349, 367–368, 378–379
  heart function and, 367
  high blood pressure and, 367
  hyperventilation and, 377
  hypnotic response and, 382, 383
  immobile, 368
  immune function and, 346
  inner peace and, 5
  insight and, 378
  integrated, 375, 379
  introversion and, 381–382
  irritability and, 367
  irritable bowel disease and, 367
  Jewish meditation, 377, 393
  joy and, 379
  Kagyupa meditation, 343
  kensho, 211, 212, 228–229
  Kouksundo meditation, 377
  kundalini energy, 377
  Latihan meditation, 368
  learning ability and, 367
  length of practice and, 381–382
  lifestyle and, 383
  logical thought processes and,
    378–379
  lung function and, 367
  mantras and, 377
  medical benefits of, x
meditation techniques, 376–378,
    384–385
memory and, 367, 379

mental illness and, 368, 380–381, 382, 383

metabolic effects of, 379

mindfulness and, 61, 65, 375, 376, 377

mindfulness meditation, 65, 377

misuse of, 384

"monkey mind", 218
nervous system and, 379
neuroscience and, 327–339, 374–375, 376, 384
neuroticism and, 381–383
Nyingmapa meditation, 343
outcomes of, 378–385
passive meditation, 375–376
personality and, 381–382
positive thinking and, 379
postures and, 376, 379
prayer and, 377
problem solving skills and, 379
psoriasis and, 367
psychoanalysis and, 383
psychology and, 378–379, 383
psychopathology and, 368, 380–381, 382, 383
Qigong meditation, 376–377
Rajneesh, 368
reaction time and, 367
receptive, 213
relaxation and, 379, 383
religion and, 383–384
resilience and, 379
sacredness and, 383, 384
satori and, 378
scientific approach to, 378–379, 383–384
seated meditation, 377–378
self-actualization and, 367
self-awareness and, 379
self-confidence and, 379
Siddha Yoga, 368
silence and, 377
spiritual awakening and, 95
spirituality and, 8, 383–384
Sufi tradition, 377
Sundo Taoism, 377
tancheon and, 377
tantras, 377
Tibetan Buddhist tradition, 406
timelessness, 92
tolerance and, 379

Transcendental Meditation (TM), 6, 7
transcendent quality and, 5
types of, 373–385
vigor and, 379
Vipassana meditation, 368
visualization and, 377, 379
well-being and, 383
yoga and, 368, 377
Zazen meditation, 368, 377–378
Zen Buddhism and, 211–213, 377–378

meditative attention, 211

mediumship, 425–438

memory, 133, 189, 218, 273, 344
conscious or unconscious, 22
emotional, 22, 275–281
explicit, 275–276
hippocampus and, 21
implicit, 275–276, 279
lifestyle and, 36
meditation and, 367, 379
memory training, 39–40
molecules of emotion and, 22
receptors and, 22, 29
reduced, 263
stored throughout the body, 22
visual-spatial memory, 272

Memory and Aging Research Center at UCLA, 35, 68

Memory Functioning Questionnaire (MFQ), 39

memory techniques, 40

Mencius, 49, 337

mental activity, 201, 272

mental illness. *See* psychopathology; *specific mental illnesses*

meridians, 259–260, 297–298, 311

meta-awareness, 69

metabolic effects, of meditation, 379

metacognition, 69

methamphetamine, 23

Mezey, Eva, 20

MFQ, 43. *See also* Memory Functioning Questionnaire (MFQ)

Michelson-Morley experiment of 1887, 175

"molecules of emotion", 15, 17, 19, 25, 26

"monkey mind", 218

monkeys, 189, 232

Montague, Chetwynd, 255

Monty Python, 113

mood disorders, 369

moods, 272

Moore, Dan, 413–424

Morgan, Marlo, 139

morphine, 16

mortality, 94–96, 322, 358–359

motivation, 278, 281

motor cortex, 208

motor function, 272

Moura, G., 431

MRI. *See* magnetic resonance imaging (MRI)

MRIcro, 412

MR signal activity, 43

multiple personality disorder (MPD), 25

Mumford, Emily, 59

muscle mass, 263

music, 153, 202–203

musicians, 272

mystical experiences, 320–321, 406

mystical states, 91

mysticism, 94, 441–442

Nag Hammadi Library, 169

National Health Service, 260

National Institute of Mental Health (NIMH), 28

National Institutes of Health, 20, 417–418

Native Americans, 123, 141, 170. *See also specific tribes*
Sioux medicine men, 49
spirituality of, 49
Western science and, 143

natural childbirth training, 27. *See also* childbirth preparation

naturalistic observation, 89

natural laws, 290

natural philosophy, 290

nature, 139
Alzheimer patients and, 150
benefits of interacting with, 136
effects of humans on, 152–154
global cultural patterns and, 139–143
healing and, 136, 137–138, 148
health and, 138, 148
health care and, 144
historical perspective, 143–146
human health and, 137–138
job satisfaction and, 149
mental health and, 135

nature-based recreation, 152
physical health and, 135
primordial forces of, 426
research perspective and, 147
residential satisfaction and, 149
restorative process and, 146, 150
science and, 287–288
sensory experience and, 138
social well-being and, 150
spirituality and, 135–155
spiritual well-being and, 138, 151
stress and, 147, 149
theoretical perspective, 146–147
transcendental writers and, 144
urban public housing and, 151
well-being and, 138, 145, 150, 151
Western perspective on, 143

near death experiences (NDEs), 95, 322

negative emotions, 338

negative experiences, 276–278

negative thinking, 195, 196, 276–278

negativity, 276–278, 338

negentropy, 300

Negro, P. J., 437

nervous system, 188–189, 232, 242, 280, 355–356, 379, 391–392. *See also* autonomic nervous system (ANS); central nervous system

restrosplenial cortex, *219*

reticular nucleus, *222*

retrosplenial coretex, *220, 222*

retrosplenial region, 225

rheumatoid arthritis (RA), 55. *See also* arthritis

Ricard, Mathieu, 280, 329–331, 332, 336

Richards, Todd, 405–413

Robbins, Jim, 231–242, 243–254

Roche, S. M., 433

Rock, Irvin, 450, 451–452

Rockefeller-Samueli Center for Research in Mind-Body Energy, 424

Rodrigues, Nina, 428

Rogers, Carl, 10

Roman pagan religion, 49

RT. *See* relativity theory (RT)

Rumi, 91, 168–169

Russell, Harold, 247

Russell, Peter, 1–13

sacredness, 374, 383, 384. *See also* divine, the

Sai Baba, 159

salience, 222

Salkovskis, Paul, 113

Samueli Institute for Information Biology, 424

Sannella, Lee, 92

satori, 213, 378

Saudia, T. L., 389

Saybrook Graduate Chair for the Study of Consciousness, 438

Schlitz, Marilyn Mandala, 387–404, 439–457

Schmidt, Stefan, 392–393

Schroedinger's wave, 300

Schwarz, Balduin, 129

Schwarz, J. Conrad, 382

Schweitzer, Albert, 121

science, 3, 171, 441–442. *See also* biology; epigenetics; genetics; neuroscience; physics; scientism
  biofield treatments and, 415
  distant healing and, 390–401, 405–413
  materialist, 1
  nature and, 287–288
  reality and, 174
  religion and, 2–4

scientific equations, 287, 289, 291

scientific era, 171

scientific knowledge, 171

scientific method, 3, 167, 290

scientific theories, 172

spirituality and, 1, 2–4, 5, 167–182, 256–257, 267, 269–312, 439–457
  ways of knowing and, 174

scientism, 315, 317–318, 322–323, 326. *See also* science

seat belt use, 360

seated meditation, 377–378

secular humanism, 50

secure attachment, 78
  parent and child and, 76

Sefer Yetzirah, 177

Segerstrom, Suzanne C., 101–119

selective attention, 29–30

self, 214–217, 223–225, 321–322, 456. *See also* egocentrism
  activities of, 282
  Buddhism and, 378
  dissolution of, 9–10
  personality self, 287
  psychic sense of, 216–218
  psychoanalysis and, 378
  psychology and, 378
  sense of, 321–322

self-actualization, meditation and, 367

self-awareness, 375, 379, 448

self-centered processing. *See* egocentrism

self-confidence, 379

self-conscious mind. *See* self-consciousness

spirit domain, 287

spirit incorporation, 426, 429, 430, 436, 437

spirit interaction, 287

spiritism, 425–438

spiritistic mediums, 425–438

spirits, 135, 427

spiritual awakening, 95

spiritual beliefs, ancient, 167

spiritual discoveries, ix

spiritual energies, 162

spiritual experiences, x, 6, 7, 8, 11

spiritual healing, 389, 406. *See also* distant healing

spiritual health, 136, 349–371

spirituality, 35, 315. *See also* prayer; religion; spiritual traditions
benefits of, x
biology and, 31
the brain and, 349–371
deep mind and, 13
emotional trauma and, 262–263
health and, 349–371
neuroscience and, 349–371
pH balance of water and, 157
reality and, 174
science and, 1, 12, 171–173, 174, 256–257, 267, 269–312, 439–457
subjective nature of and difficulty of measuring, 351–354
trauma and, 85–100
ways of knowing and, 174
spiritual practices, 269, 270. *See also* meditation; religion; spiritual traditions
benefits of, ix
brain imaging and, 354–356
neuroscience and, 282–286
scientific evidence of, x

spiritual practioners, psychophysiology of, 425–438

spiritual progress, 255

spiritual science, 287–312

spiritual states, neurophysical changes associated with, 354–357

spiritual technologies, xi, 11–13

spiritual traditions, 99, 158, 172, 174–176. *See also* spiritual practices

spirit world, 140

splenium, 219, 220

SPM. *See* Statistical Parameter Mapping (SPM)

Standish, Lanna J., 405–413

states of mind, 280–281

Statistical Parameter Mapping (SPM), 42

stem cells, 20

Sterman, Barry, 249, 253

Steuco, Agostino, 445

St. John's Wort (*Hypericum perforatum*), 142

Stone, Hal, 25

Stone, Sidra, 25

stream of consciousness, 218, 275, 376

stress, x, 37, 241, 258, 263, 266–267, 280, 356
epigenetic triggers and, 264
nature and, 149
prayer and, 366
stress-reduction techniques, 86–87
tears and, 55

strokes, 37, 145, 251, 259

subconscious mind, 185–199, 223

subjective well-being (SWB), 328

substance abuse, 73, 361–362. *See also* drugs

suffering, 94–96

Sufi tradition, 377

suicide, 359, 363–364

Sundo Taoism, 377

superior colliculus, 222, 223

superior parietal lobes, 216, 222, 355

surgery, 47–48, 50, 56, 359–360, 389, 394, 398

survival responses, 91

Switzerland, 161

sympathetic dominance, 98

About the Authors

JEANNE ACHTERBERG, PH.D. is a scientist who has received international recognition for her pioneering research in medicine and psychology. A faculty member for eleven years at Southwestern Medical School, she is currently a Professor of Psychology at Saybrook Graduate School and Research Center in San Francisco. She has authored over 100 papers and six books, including *Imagery in Healing*, critically acclaimed as a classic in the field of mind/body studies, *Woman as Healer, Rituals of Healing*, and *Lightning at the Gate*. In April of 2001, she was featured in *Time* magazine as one of the six innovators of alternative and complementary medicine for the coming century. Dr. Achterberg is past president of the Association of Transpersonal Psychology. She is a Senior Editor for the *Journal of Alternative and Complementary Medicine*, a peer-reviewed medical journal with an international circulation. Her most recent research on prayer and distant intentionality, using the fMRI technology, was conducted at North Hawaii Community Hospital and sponsored by the Earl and Doris Bakken Foundation.

TINA AMOROK, PSY.D., is a clinical psychologist and research psychologist at the Institute of Noetic Sciences where she coedited the anthology *Consciousness and Healing: Integral Approaches to Mind-Body Medicine* (Churchill Livingston/Elsevier, 2005). With a background in integral health and healing, clinical psychology, and change management, Amorok designs and delivers programs for professional, university, corporate, and lay sectors on personal and social wellness and transformation. Her current research, The Eco-Trauma and Eco-Recovery of Being, examines how to heal and transform the primal wound of human alienation from nature from which destructive ecological behaviors, violence, and unhealthy life styles arise.

JAMES H. AUSTIN, M.D., has spent most of his years as an academic neurologist, first at the University of Oregon Medical School and later at the University of Colorado Health Sciences Center. He is currently Clinical Professor of Neurology at the University of Missouri–Columbia's Health Sciences Center. Included in Dr. Austin's cultural background is his first sabbatical spent in New Delhi, India; and the second spent in Kyoto, Japan, where he began Zen meditation training with an English-speaking Zen master, Kobori-Roshi, in 1974. He maintains a keen interest in the experimental designs and findings of investigators who study meditation, insight, and related states of consciousness. His early research background includes publications in the areas of clinical neurology, neuropathology, neurochemistry, and neuropharmacology. Dr. Austin is the author or co-author of more than 140 professional publications, including three books published by MIT Press: *Zen and the Brain: Toward an*

Understanding of Meditation and Consciousness (1998); *Chase, Chance, and Creativity: The Lucky Art of Novelty* (2003); and *Zen-Brain Reflections: Reviewing Recent Developments in Meditation and States of Consciousness* (2006). His next book from MIT Press, due out in 2008, is entitled, *Zen-Brain and the Meditative Transformations of Consciousness.*

New York Times bestselling author **GREGG BRADEN** is a former Senior Computer Systems Designer for Martin Marietta Aerospace, and internationally renowned as a pioneer in bridging science and spirituality. For more than twenty years Gregg has searched remote monasteries and forgotten texts to uncover their timeless secrets. His work, published in 16 languages in 26 countries, has led to such paradigm-shattering books as *The God Code* and *The Divine Matrix.* (www.greggbraden.com)

DAWSON CHURCH, PH.D., is the author of several books, including *The Genie in Your Genes* (Energy Psychology Press, 2007). Dawson is the Research Director of ACEP, the Association for Comprehensive Energy Psychology, the founder of Soul Medicine Institute (www.SoulMedicineInstitute.org), and former president of two health and spirituality publishing companies, Aslan Publishing and Elite Books. He gives around 100 radio shows and print interviews each year, lectures at psychology and medical conferences, and trains organizations in how to apply the epigenetic insights of Energy Psychology for peak performance. He recently started the Iraq Vets Stress Project (www.StressProject.org) to offer the benefits of these brief therapies to returning veterans.

LARRY DOSSEY, M.D., is a physician of internal medicine and former Chief of Staff of Medical City Dallas Hospital. He received his MD from Southwestern Medical School (Dallas), and trained in internal medicine at the Parkland and VA hospitals in Dallas. He is the author of ten books dealing with consciousness, spirituality, and healing, including the *New York Times* bestseller *Healing Words: The Power of Prayer and the Practice of Medicine* and, most recently, *The Extraordinary Healing Power of Ordinary Things.* Dr. Dossey is the former co-chairman of the Panel on Mind/Body Interventions, National Center for Complementary and Alternative Medicine, National Institutes of Health. He is the executive editor of the peer-reviewed journal *EXPLORE: The Journal of Science and Healing* and lectures around the world. He lives in Santa Fe with his wife Barbara, who is a nurse-consultant and the author of several award-winning books.

ROBERT A. EMMONS, PH.D., is Professor of Psychology at the University of California, Davis. He received his PhD degree in Personality Psychology from the University of Illinois at Urbana-Champaign, and his Bachelor's degree in Psychology from the University of Southern Maine. He is the author of nearly 100 original publications in peer-reviewed journals or chapters and has written or edited four books, including *The Psychology of Ultimate Concerns* (Guilford Press), *The Psychology of Gratitude* (Oxford University Press), and *THANKS! How the New Science of Gratitude Can Make You Happier* (Houghton-Mifflin). A leader in the positive psychology movement, Dr. Emmons is founding editor and editor-in-chief of the *Journal of Positive Psychology.* He is past president of the American Psychological Association's Division 36, The Psychology of Religion. His research focuses on personal goals and purpose, spirituality, the psychology of gratitude and thankfulness, and subjective well-being. Dr. Emmons has received research funding from the National Institute of Mental Health, the John M. Templeton Foundation, and the National Institute for Disability

Research and Rehabilitation. His research has been featured in dozens of popular media outlets including the *New York Times, USA Today, U.S. News and World Report, Newsweek, Time,* NPR, PBS, *The Paul Harvey Show, The Dr. Laura Show, The Osgood Radio Files,* and *Reader's Digest.*

LES FEHMI, PH.D., is Director Emeritus of the Princeton Biofeedback Center in Princeton, New Jersey. Since the late 1960s, he has been one of the pioneers in the field of neurofeedback. In 1968, he chaired the first meeting of biofeedback researchers at the third annual "Winter Brain Research Conference" in Aspen, Colorado. Over nearly four decades, he has been active as a psychologist in private practice, as a conference speaker, as a university lecturer, and as a biofeedback trainer and consultant for numerous corporations and organizations, including Harvard Medical School, Johnson & Johnson, the Veterans Administration, the Dallas Cowboys, and the New Jersey Nets. An active member of numerous scientific societies, his articles and papers have appeared in health, scientific, and psychoanalytic journals throughout his long and distinguished career. Les holds a PhD and MA in Physiological Psychology from UCLA. His wife, Susan Shor Fehmi, a psychoanalyst and social worker, is Executive Director of the Princeton Biofeedback Center.

OWEN FLANAGAN is a James B. Duke Professor of Philosophy at Duke University. He is the author of *The Really Hard Problem, Consciousness Reconsidered* (MIT Press), *The Problem of the Soul: Two Visions of Mind and How to Reconcile Them,* and other books.

DANIEL GOLEMAN is an internationally known psychologist who lectures frequently to professional groups, business audiences, and on college campuses. He is author of the worldwide bestsellers, *Emotional Intelligence, Working With Emotional Intelligence,* and *Destructive Emotions,* and is the co-author of *Primal Leadership.* Nominated twice for the Pulitzer Prize for his journalistic work covering the brain and behavorial sciences published in the *New York Times,* he is currently co-chair of the Consortium for Research on Emotional Intelligence at Rutgers University and a Fellow of the American Association for the Advancement of Science. He is a member of the board of directors of the Mind & Life Institute, which sponsors an ongoing series of dialogues between modern science and the great living contemplative traditions and fosters relevant research. For more information, visit www.danielgoleman.info/blog.

JOAN H. HAGEMAN, PH.D., is the Chair of Research with PSYmore Research Institute, Inc. in Tampa, Florida. In this capacity, she conducts and facilitates cross-cultural research in human consciousness from varied perspectives, such as anthropology, historical, neuroscience, psychology, parapsychology, psychophysiology, and sociology. She is an accomplished international speaker and author on multiple topics regarding consciousness, Kouksundo, spirituality, meditation, hypnosis, dissociation, shamanism, cross-cultural methodology, dreaming, religion, and health, among other subjects related to psychological well-being. Dr. Hageman resides in Tampa, Florida, with her husband.

RICK HANSON, PH.D., is a clinical psychologist, author, and teacher who focuses on the intersection of psychology, neurology, and Buddhism. He has written and taught extensively on personal well-being, relationships, families, and integrating spiritual depth with everyday life. With Rick Mendius, MD, he founded the Heartwood Institute for Neuroscience and Contemplative Wisdom, edits the Wise Brain Bulletin (see www.WiseBrain.org), and teaches the Train Your Brain course (available on-line). He is first author of *Mother Nurture: A Mother's Guide to Health in Body, Mind, and Intimate Relationships* (Penguin, 2002), and first author of a book in progress entitled *Buddha's Brain: The New Neuroscience of Happiness, Love, and Wisdom*. He and his wife have a young adult daughter and son.

SANDRA INGERMAN is the author of *Soul Retrieval: Mending the Fragmented Self, Welcome Home: Following Your Soul's Journey Home, A Fall to Grace, Medicine for the Earth: How to Transform Personal and Environmental Toxins, Shamanic Journeying: A Beginner's Guide,* and *How to Heal Toxic Thoughts: Simple Tools for Personal Transformation*. She is the author of "The Soul Retrieval Journey," "The Beginner's Guide to Shamanic Journeying," and "Miracles for the Earth" lecture programs produced by Sounds True. Sandra teaches workshops internationally on shamanic journeying, healing, and reversing environmental pollution using spiritual methods. She has trained and founded an international alliance of Medicine for the Earth Teachers and shamanic teachers. Sandra is recognized for bridging ancient cross-cultural healing methods into our modern culture, addressing the needs of our times. She is a licensed marriage and family therapist and professional mental health counselor, and is also a board certified expert on traumatic stress, as well as being certified in acute traumatic stress management. Sandra presented her work at the UN on July 27, 2006.

STANLEY KRIPPNER, PH.D., is the Alan Watts Professor of Psychology at the Saybrook Graduate School in San Francisco, California. He was the recipient of the American Psychological Association's Award for Distinguished Contributions to the International Advancement of Psychology, and the Society for Psychological

Hypnosis's Award for Distinguished Contributions to Professional Hypnosis. He received the Parapsychological Association's Lifetime Achievement Award in 1998, and in 2002, Andhra University in Visakhapatnam, India, presented him the J.B. Rhine Award for Outstanding Contributions to Parapsychology. As a result of his book *The Psychological Effects of War Trauma on Civilians: An International Perspective* and his work with civilians in war-torn countries, he received the Ashley Montagu Peace Award in 2003. In 2007, Praeger published his co-authored book *Haunted by Combat: Understanding PTSD in War Veterans Including Women, Reservists, and Those Coming Back from Iraq.*

PETER LEVINE, PH.D., holds doctorates in medical biophysics and in psychology. He was a consultant for NASA on the early space shuttle flights. His internationally bestselling book, *Waking the Tiger, Healing Trauma,* has been published in 20 languages. Dr Levine is the originator of Somatic Experiencing®, the approach to trauma that he has developed over the past 40 years. The dissemination of this work is through the Foundation for Human Enrichment: www.traumahealing.com.

BRUCE H. LIPTON, PH.D., is an internationally recognized authority on bridging science and spirit. He has been a guest speaker on dozens of TV and radio shows, as well as a keynote presenter for national conferences. Dr. Lipton's groundbreaking book *The Biology of Belief: Unleashing the Power of Consciousness, Matter and Miracles* documents the amazing new awareness that is currently rewriting the science of biology and medicine—awareness that the mind's perception of the environment, not genes, controls life at the cellular level. Dr. Lipton describes his own life as "radically transformed" because of his research: "Though I sought science as an alternate to accepting spiritual truths, lessons learned . . . revealed that life was not an issue of science OR spirituality, it was an amalgam of science AND spirituality." (www.brucelipton.com)

LYNNE MCTAGGART is the award-winning author of five books, including the bestsellers *The Intention Experiment* and *The Field,* published in 20 languages and considered one of the seminal works of the New Age. Her book *The Intention Experiment* enlists her readers in ongoing web-based experiments to test whether group thoughts have the power to change the world (www.theintentionexperiment. com). She also runs worldwide Living The Field master classes and groups (www.livingthefield.com), designed to help people adapt the ideas of the new scientific paradigm into their everyday lives. As co-executive director of the newsletter "What Doctors Don't Tell You" (www.wddty.com), she has become an international spokesperson on alternatives to conventional medicine. She lives in London with her husband and business partner Bryan Hubbard and their two children.

ANDREW NEWBERG, M.D., is currently an Associate Professor in the Department of Radiology and Psychiatry at the Hospital of the University of Pennsylvania and is a staff physician in Nuclear Medicine. He has published numerous articles and chapters on brain function, brain imaging, and the study of religious and mystical experiences. He is the author of the new book *Born to Believe: God, Science, and the Origin of Ordinary and Extraordinary Beliefs* (Free Press). He has also co-authored the bestselling book *Why God Won't Go Away: Brain Science and the Biology of Belief* (Ballantine) and *The Mystical Mind: Probing the Biology of Belief* (Fortress Press), both of which explore the relationship between neuroscience and spiritual experience. The latter book received the 2000 award for Outstanding Books in Theology and the Natural Sciences presented by the Center for Theology and the

Natural Sciences. He has presented his work at scientific and religious meetings throughout the world and has appeared on *Good Morning America, Nightline,* and *ABC World News Tonight,* as well as in a number of media articles in such publications as *Newsweek,* the *New Scientist,* the *Los Angeles Times* and *Readers Digest.*

CANDACE PERT, PH.D., is an internationally recognized psychopharmacologist who is a former Research Professor at the Georgetown University School of Medicine and Section Chief at the National Institute of Mental Health. She has published more than 250 scientific articles and has lectured worldwide on pharmacology, neuroanatomy, and her own leading-edge research on emotions and the bodymind connection. Dr. Pert's recent appearance in the film *What the Bleep Do We Know!?,* her most recent book, *Everything You Need to Know to Feel Go(o)d,* and her 1997 bestselling book *Molecules of Emotion: The Science Behind Bodymind Medicine,* have popularized her groundbreaking theories on consciousness, neuropeptides, and reality. You can learn more about her work at www.candacepert.com.

DEAN RADIN, PH.D., holds an adjunct appointment in the Psychology Department at Sonoma State University and is on the Distinguished Consulting Faculty at Saybrook Graduate School. He has worked for AT&T Bell Laboratories and later at GTE Laboratories on advanced telecommunications research and development. He has conducted psi research at Princeton University, University of Edinburgh, University of Nevada, SRI International, and Interval Research Corporation and is currently a Senior Scientist at the Institute of Noetic Sciences. He has been featured in the *New York Times Magazine* among other publications and is author of *Entangled Minds.* For more information, visit www.deanradin.com.

A resident of Montana since 1976, **JIM ROBBINS** is an award-winning journalist and the author of two books. For more than twenty years, he has been a frequent contributor to the *New York Times,* writing for nearly every section of the paper. He also writes for *Smithsonian, Audubon, Vanity Fair, The London Sunday Times, Scientific American, New York Times Magazine, Discover, Psychology Today, Gourmet, Condé Nast Traveler,* and other magazines. Jim has appeared as an analyst on ABC's *Nightline* and National Public Radio's *All Things Considered* and *Morning Edition* numerous times, and as a guest on NBC's *Today Show* to discuss his first book, *Last Refuge: The Environmental Showdown in the American West* (Morrow 1993/HarperCollins 1995). His second book, *A Symphony in the Brain: The Evolution of the New Brain Wave Biofeedback,* was published by Atlantic Monthly Press (2000) and was excerpted in *Newsweek,* the *New York Times,* and *Cerebrum,* a neuroscience journal. He received the first Distinguished Western Journalist Award from the History and Journalism Departments at the University of Colorado at Boulder, and numerous grants from the Fund for Investigative Journalism in Washington, DC.

PETER RUSSELL is the author of ten books and producer of two award-winning videos. His work integrates Eastern and Western understandings of the mind, exploring their relevance to the world today and to humanity's future. He has degrees in theoretical physics, experimental psychology, and computer science from the University of Cambridge, England. In India, he studied meditation and Eastern philosophy, and on his return took up research into the psychophysiology of meditation at the University of Bristol. He was one of the first people to introduce human potential seminars into the corporate field, and for twenty years worked with major corporations on creativity, learning methods, stress management, and personal development. His principal interest is the inner challenges of the times we are passing through. His books include *The Global Brain, Waking Up in Time,* and most recently, *From Science to God.*

MARILYN MANDALA SCHLITZ, PH.D., is a clinical research scientist, medical anthropologist, writer, speaker, thought leader, and change consultant. Her work over the past three decades explores the interface of consciousness, science, and healing. She is vice president for research and education at the Institute of Noetic Sciences and senior scientist at the Research Institute at California Pacific Medical Center. She has published hundreds of articles on consciousness studies and lectured widely on a number of topics, including talks at the United Nations, the Smithsonian Institution, and the Explorers Club. She has taught at Trinity, Stanford, and Harvard Medical Centers, and is the coeditor of *Consciousness and Healing: Integral Approaches to Mind Body Medicine* (Churchill Livingston/Elsevier, 2005).

SUZANNE C. SEGERSTROM, PH.D., is a Professor of Psychology at the University of Kentucky in Lexington and the author of *Breaking Murphy's Law: How Optimists Get What They Want From Life, and Pessimists Can, Too.* Her work on optimism garnered first place in the Templeton Positive Psychology Prize in 2002 and has been supported by the UCLA Norman Cousins Program, the Templeton Foundation, and the National Institute of Mental Health. Her current work focuses on the physical benefits—as well as possible costs—of optimistic expectations.

DAN SIEGEL, M.D., is a graduate of the Harvard Medical School, Director of the Mindsight Institute, and Co-Director of the UCLA Mindful Awareness Research Center. He also serves as the Founding Editor-in-Chief for the Norton Series on

Interpersonal Neurobiology. He has authored *The Developing Mind*, (Guidford, 1999) and *The Mindful Brain: Reflection and Attunement in the Cultivation of Well-Being*, (Norton, 2007). Siegel is a physician, psychiatrist, psychotherapist, and educator, and lectures worldwide.

GARY SMALL, M.D., Professor of Psychiatry and Biobehavioral Sciences, is the Parlow-Solomon Professor on Aging at the David Geffen School of Medicine at UCLA, Director of the UCLA Center on Aging, and a leading expert on memory and aging. Dr. Small has authored over 500 scientific works and received numerous awards and honors, including Senior Investigator Award from the American Association for Geriatric Psychiatry, and the Jack Weinberg Memorial Award for Excellence in Geriatric Psychiatry from the American Psychiatric Association. In 2002, *Scientific American* magazine named him one of the world's top innovators in science and technology. Dr. Small's studies have been featured in the *New York Times*, *Wall Street Journal*, *London Times*, *Washington Post*, *Time*, and *Newsweek*, as well as numerous television programs, including NBC's *Today Show*, ABC's *Good Morning America* and *20/20*, and *Martha Stewart Living*. He is the author of several popular books on healthy aging and memory improvement *(The Memory Bible*, *The Memory Prescription*, *The Longevity Bible)*, which have been translated into two dozen languages.

CHARLES TART, PH.D., Core Faculty at the Institute of Transpersonal Psychology, Professor Emeritus of Psychology at the University of California at Davis, and Senior Research Fellow of the Institute of Noetic Sciences, is internationally known for his research with altered states of consciousness, transpersonal psychology, and parapsychology. His books include two that have been called classics, *Altered States of Consciousness* and

Transpersonal Psychologies, as well as 11 others dealing with states of consciousness, marijuana intoxication, and parapsychology. He is author of *Waking Up: Overcoming the Obstacles to Human Potential* (1986), and *Mind Science: Meditation Training for Practical People* (2000). His primary goals are to build bridges between the scientific and spiritual communities and to help bring about a refinement and integration of Western and Eastern approaches to personal and social growth. Full information is available at www.paradigm-sys.com/cttart/.

WILLIAM TILLER, PH.D., Fellow to the American Academy for the Advancement of Science and Professor Emeritus of Stanford University's Department of Materials Science, spent 34 years in academia after nine years as an advisory physicist with the Westinghouse Research Laboratories. In his conventional science field he has published over 250 scientific papers, three books and several patents. In parallel, for the past 30 years, he has been avocationally pursuing serious experimental and theoretical study of the field of psychoenergetics, which he thinks will become a very important part of "tomorrow's" physics. In this new area, he has published an additional 100 scientific papers and four seminal books: *Science and Human Transformation* (Pavior Publishing, 1997), *Conscious Acts of Creation* (Pavior Publishing, 2001), *Some Science Adventures with Real Magic* (Pavior Publishing, 2005) and *Psychoenergetic Science: A Second Copernican-Scale Revolution* (Pavior Publishing, 2007).

CASSANDRA VIETEN, PH.D., is a licensed clinical psychologist, a research psychologist at the Institute of Noetic Sciences, an associate scientist and codirector of the Mind-Body Medicine Research Group at California Pacific Medical Center Research Institute in San Francisco, and vice president of the Institute for Spirituality and Psychology. Her research over the last twelve years, funded by the National Institutes of Health, the State of California, and several private foundations, has focused on how biology, psychology, and emotion are involved in addiction and recovery; mindfulness-based approaches to cultivating health and well-being; the role of compassionate intent and belief in healing; and factors, experiences, and practices involved in psychospiritual transformation. She has published several academic articles and chapters as well as conducting numerous presentations at international scientific conferences.

IAN WICKRAMASEKERA is a psychologist working in the field of Mind/Body Medicine at the Jesse Brown VA Medical Center in Chicago, IL. He enjoys teaching and conducting research on mind/body phenomena such as hypnosis and meditation and is a member of the faculty of the University of Illinois at Chicago and the Adler School of Professional Psychology. Dr. Wickramasekera has been the president of the American Psychological Association's Society of Psychological Hypnosis (Division 30).

GARRET YOUNT, PH.D., earned a BS in Molecular and Cell Biology from the Pennsylvania State University and a PhD in Neurobiology and Behavior from the State University of New York at Stony Brook. Dr. Yount currently directs a molecular biology laboratory at the California Pacific Medical Center Research Institute in San Francisco where he has established a track record in obtaining research funding from both federal and private agencies, including the National Institutes of Health, the Department of Defense, and the Rockefeller-Samueli Center for Research in Mind-Body Energy. Dr. Yount's interest in evaluating the potential for integrating Traditional Chinese Medicine with Western medicine in the treatment of cancer has led to collaborations with biofield practitioners from China, Japan, Canada, and the United States. Dr. Yount serves as a Scientific Advisor to various federal agencies, including the National Center for Complementary and Alternative Medicine, and as a scientific reviewer for numerous biomedical journals, including *Cancer Research*, *The American Journal of Clinical Hypnosis*, and the *Journal of Consciousness Studies*.